CRIMES AGAINST FEELING

CRIMES AGAINST FEELING

PIRACY, SYMPATHY, AND OCEAN POLITICS IN ANTEBELLUM AMERICAN LEGAL CULTURE

MARK B. KELLEY

University of Massachusetts Press
AMHERST AND BOSTON

Printed in the United States of America

ISBN 978-1-62534-963-7 (paper); 964-4 (hardcover)

Designed by Jen Jackowitz
Set in Minion Pro
Printed and bound by Books International, Inc.

Cover design by adam b. bohannon
Cover art: Illustrated Postal Cover, "Allegorical figure of America" (c. 1861–1865).
Courtesy, American Antiquarian Society.

Library of Congress Cataloging-in-Publication Data

Names: Kelley, Mark Brennan, 1988- author
Title: Crimes against feeling : piracy, sympathy, and ocean politics in
early American legal culture / Mark B. Kelley.
Description: Amherst : University of Massachusetts Press, 2026. |
Includes bibliographical references and index. | Identifiers: LCCN 2026008298 (print) |
LCCN 2026008299 (ebook) | ISBN 9781625349637 paperback | ISBN 9781625349644 hardcover |
ISBN 9781685752842 ebook | ISBN 9781685752859 epub
Subjects: LCSH: Piracy—United States—History—19th century | Piracy—
Law and legislation—United States—History—19th century | Maritime law—United States—
History—19th century | Law and literature—United States—History—19th century
Classification: LCC Kelley, Mark Brennan, 1988- (print) |
LCC Kelley, Mark Brennan, 1988- (ebook)
LC record available at https://lccn.loc.gov/2026008298
LC ebook record available at https://lccn.loc.gov/2026008299

British Library Cataloguing-in-Publication Data
A catalog record for this book is available from the British Library.

Research in chapter 1 previously appeared in "Pirates, Bloodhounds, and White Heirs: Catharine Maria Sedgwick's Fictions of Haiti," *Legacy* 38, nos. 1–2 (2021): 1–25, © 2021 University of Nebraska Press and published by permission of University of Nebraska Press. A version of chapter 4 previously appeared as "'Every India Mail': *The Lamplighter* and the Prospect of U.S. Transoceanic (Postal) Empire, 1847–1854," in *India in the American Imaginary, 1780s–1880s*, ed. Anupama Arora and Rajender Kaur (New York: Palgrave Macmillan, 2017), 141–71, © 2017 Springer Nature and published by permission of the Springer Nature Group.

The authorized representative in the EU for
product safety and compliance is Mare Nostrum Group.
Email: gpsr@mare-nostrum.co.uk
Physical address: Mare Nostrum Group B.V.,
Doelen 72, 4831 GR Breda, The Netherlands

For Nicole

CONTENTS

ILLUSTRATIONS

PREFACE

Piracy has long been a narratively fluid, politically multivalent cultural referent. In global media, swashbuckling mariners remain popular as comedic foils, terroristic villains, and principled freedom fighters. This narrative diversity—and the political debates it textualizes—helps explain the pirate's enduring cultural cachet. A host of competing moral visions may rely on a central pirate trope. *Crimes Against Feeling* concerns such competitions in a less-understood context: the United States of America in the decades leading up to and including the U.S. Civil War. As it shows, antebellum popular writers and political figures defined piracy less as a singular act and more as an emotional antagonism to national families. The feeling state abhorred the unfeeling pirate.

The resulting pirate crew was politically motley. Alleged pirates were monarchs, presidents, enslavers, slaves, abolitionists, secessionists, imperialists, revolutionaries, judges, and anyone whose sea-based politics defied prevailing legal norms. Antebellum piracy law was not marked by ideological consistency. It indexed shifting national investments in legalized enslavement, state-backed white supremacy, and global empire. Most often, the state invoked unfeeling piracy to deny Black, enslaved, or colonized subjects full legal protection. Some writers reclaimed sympathy for alleged pirates and, in the process, attacked the state's moral and legal authority. Sentimental fiction was central to these competitions. Popular writers advanced legal theories about the nation's moral character and political status among a family of nations. Fictional pirates embodied layers of conflicting legal precedent. Ultimately, the Civil War remade but did not resolve the founding sin of legal enslavement that constituted the nation and its pirates.

In sum, *Crimes Against Feeling* reveals piracy as a floating signifier within a deeply conflicted antebellum American culture. This book is at home on both land and water. It parlays with oceanic subjects without leaving the shore. Indeed, pirates landed in these pages almost by accident. To be honest, I don't find pirate stories terribly attractive—too much violence. Instead, I have long enjoyed their seeming opposite: land-based narratives of early American families. Stories of women's emotional depth, rather than pirates' oceanic depths, sparked this book's genesis. Many antebellum women writers—notably, Catharine Maria Sedgwick, Harriet Beecher Stowe, and Maria Susanna Cummins—were members of leading legal families, and they were central to debates on abolition, women's rights, and other legal causes. Their globally popular literary works were also frequently pirated, and thus also guided international copyright law. In short, antebellum women helped build global literary culture. Before I knew this book's specific claim about that culture, I poured over the era's best-selling novels of domestic life. Curious figures floated in the margins. Landed heroines engaged pirates with surprising frequency. These outlaws seemed to be abnormally one-dimensional, often lacking clear motivation beyond their antagonism to model American matriarchs. Yet they were awash with historical referents across a political spectrum. A single pirate had thematic ties to enslavers and slaves, kings and commoners, presidents and revolutionaries. These pirate villains often disappeared from these domestic novels as quickly as they had arrived. Yet their defeat proved to be central to the (mostly white) heroines' ultimate moral development and legal security. Why?

Like any good literary historian, I sought answers in historical archives. Armed with terms such as *piracy*, *family*, and *feeling*, I soon found an inverse phenomenon. I had expected to discover maritime pirates in early American legal records. I was surprised to rediscover paradigmatic American women and sentimental plot points. Trial transcripts, congressional records, popular periodicals, and many other serious documents about piracy seemed to be fixated on domestic families. American presidents, Supreme Court justices, and other (mostly male) political figures consistently appealed to emotions in their legal definitions of piracy. Here, too, alleged pirates seemed to be linked by their supposed antagonism to blameless women and the moral nation that those women embodied. Careful arguments about international law and legal jurisdiction often hinged on an alleged pirate's familial status. Why care if pirates had loving families? I did not yet know. Strict codes of genre, gender, and geography would not provide an answer. Sentimental language about piracy across legal and literary texts would be my guide.

Where I landed is best introduced by this book's title, *Crimes Against Feeling*. Pirates' alleged crimes against feeling helped build an American legal system on land and water. Sympathy, or "fellow feeling," was the era's defining theory of political rights. The idea of America as a family united in sympathy powered both popular fictions and founding documents such as the Declaration of Independence. Pirates, like all potential citizens or subjects, could be defined and punished within a deceptively universal standard of national morality. The U.S. Constitution gave Congress the power to "define and punish piracies" without requiring an actual definition. Defining piracy by action alone unduly limited federal legal power and revealed its ideological inconsistencies. Broadly speaking, piracy may refer to non-state violence at sea against sovereign nations or their subjects. Of course, America's revolution against England arguably met this criterion. Did the Haitian Revolution? Did Confederate secession? All alleged piracies, notwithstanding their political divergences, came to be judged as shared crimes against feeling. The same piracy laws applied to both oceanic enslavers and their mutineering slaves. Fictions of legal coherence obscured piracy's political fluidity. Piracy became a feeling, then, via cultural processes that gave certain political orientations emotional value and legal meaning.

Crimes Against Feeling thus offers a novel docket of pirate law and literature. It officiates a marriage between American sentimental and legal culture. In the process, it testifies to antebellum women writers' enduring purchase in American law, literature, and culture. My work here rides an enduring wave of scholarship. Forerunners such as Jane Tompkins confirmed sentimental fiction's indisputable depth and political power. Nina Baym, Mary Kelley, Nicole Tonkovich, and many others have catalogued a canon of women's fictions that reached every corner of American social, legal, and political life. Contemporaries such as Melissa Gniadek have established that domestic fiction is "terraqueous," consisting of both land and water, in conversation with oceanic studies scholars such as Margaret Cohen, Hester Blum, and Michelle Burnham. I have marshaled the ideas of these thinkers and many more to show how ocean-oriented feeling infused both legal thinking and the law itself. Antebellum sentimental literature's value does not derive from facile moral purity or an insular geography. Instead, it reveals the deeply compromised legal culture that continues to shape American life. Indeed, this book is coming into the world at a painful moment in American constitutional democracy. White supremacist sympathies have been given increased legal force, sometimes via the invocation of the laws and tropes to be discussed. The past is never past when available as legal precedent. This book provides no easy answers to present crimes against feeling. It neither sanctifies nor demonizes piracy as a legal category. It does affirm the power of artistic protest, political activism, and mutual care in the face of legalized oppression. A legacy of feeling otherwise, both within and beyond the law, may prove to be a path forward. Welcome aboard.

ACKNOWLEDGMENTS

This book is the product of my own global wandering. My debt to my students, friends, family, colleagues, and collaborators is vast. I apologize for any omissions in gratitude here, which is surely not this book's only error. Even as I acknowledge this past, I must thank you, my dear reader, for giving this book a future.

A number of funded workshops and residential fellowships built this book's archival foundation and fostered meaningful collaboration. My early-career access to the letters of Maria S. Cummins while a fellow at the Peabody Essex Museum provided necessary background on literary piracy. My month at the Library Company of Philadelphia and the Historical Society of Pennsylvania as an Andrew W. Mellon Foundation Fellow gave me new context for thinking about the region's Haitian diaspora and Civil War–era piracy trials. Laura Miller, Rose Roberto, Michael Verney, Nazera Sadiq Wright, and other co-fellows provided much needed comradery. Thomas Jefferson's role in this book crystalized during my brief but invaluable time at the Harrison Institute at the University of Virginia while a Lillian Gary Taylor Fellow in American Literature. The American Antiquarian Society (AAS) has long been a welcoming academic home for multiple projects. Thanks to Nan Wolverton, John J. Garcia, and the entire AAS staff. Early research on Civil War–era printed envelopes during my month as an American Historical Print Collectors Society Fellow helped guide this work's investment in print culture. I underwent late-stage research at AAS on Supreme Court Justice Joseph Story, following a delightful seminar on "Sex, Gender, and Print" co-captained by Jordan Stein and Greta LaFleur alongside the Program on the History of the Book in American Culture. Numerous funded summer workshops with the Bavarian America Academy (BAA), sponsored by Amerikahaus Munich, have broadened my intellectual world. Heike Paul and Margaretha Schweiger-Wilhelm remain models of transnational mentorship and fellow feeling. I also have the BAA to thank for introducing me to dear colleagues such as Spencer Tricker, who provided valuable feedback on my introduction. My National Endowment for the

Humanities summer seminar on “The American Maritime Commons” at the Munson Institute at Mystic Seaport, led by Glenn Gordinier and Eric Roorda, was the perfect academic summer camp. I learned much and laughed more alongside Matthew Crow, Matthew McKenzie, Christina Bevilacqua, Lincoln Paine, Gabe Loiacono, Anthony Medrano, Chris Pastore, Helen Rozwadowski, and everyone in the cohort.

This book’s intellectual voyage began at Marquette University. Sarah Wadsworth and Amy Blair first cultivated my love of antebellum print culture, maritime literature, and women writers. I am honored that we now share a publisher. Jody Melamed and Rebecca Nowacek taught me vital lessons about radical care and our work’s moral imperative. Sara Mayville never let me forget our work’s political stakes both during her life and after her untimely death. Don, Becky, and Leanne are in my thoughts even when I forget to call. Tyler Monson, Katy Leedy, Camilia Cenek, J. T. Lorino, William Storm, Jesse Wentworth, and the entire department first taught me the joys of academic collegiality. Mo, Mikey, and Garrett kept me company even as I read alone at home. Everyone at the Catharine Maria Sedgwick Society, the first scholarly group I ever joined, has long modeled the kindness and intellectual rigor I hope to emulate.

The University of California—San Diego (UCSD), nestled on the Pacific, gave my work new oceanic meaning. Nicole Tonkovich and Sara E. Johnson shaped this book’s domestic and hemispheric scopes. Sara foregrounded our responsibility to those obscured by available archives, notably the colonized or enslaved, and promoted transdisciplinary practices I can only begin to emulate. Nicole’s dedication to American women writers in their complexity and complicity is a mantle I take on. Daniel Vitkus oriented my work to the early modern Mediterranean while his funding support allowed for an ambitious research program. Michael Davidson taught me the political power of aesthetics. Mark Hanna replaced romanticized notions of the pirate with a far more interesting historical rigor. My colleagues and cohort-mates at UCSD, too numerous to name, remain dear. Clare Rolens, Jimi Damon, Gina di Grazia, Ben Chapin, Holly Bauer, Omar Pimenta, and Marcella Vargas became confidants and friends. The entire Hillcrest squad reminded me that there’s more to life than books. Charles and everyone at Bread and Cie fueled my writing one croissant at a time. Paula at my home panadería has continued this tradition.

My current home department at Florida International University (FIU) remains a safe haven. I was blessed to enter FIU at the same time as Annie Castro, a true friend and source of fierce loyalty, deep insight, and unending kindness. Nathaniel Cadle, Jason Pearl, and Martha Schoolman remain intellectual compatriots in our shared fields. Aza Weir-Soley, Jamie Sutton, Vernon Dickinson, and Michael Gillespie have long taught me our profession's written and unwritten rules. Heather Blatt and Rhona Trauvitch remain vocal champions for my work in the classroom. Thank you to Andy Strycharski and Michael Grafals for reminding me what movies I should probably be watching. My department chairs, Heather Russell, Ana Luszczynska, and, most recently, Shawn Christian, graciously guided many career transitions during a global pandemic. Gretter Machin and the entire office staff have done countless tasks that make my work possible. Thank you all.

My deepest thanks to Brian Halley, Ben Kimball, Sally Nichols, and the entire team at the University of Massachusetts Press for their stewardship of my work. Adam B. Bohannon's brilliant cover design marvelously captured this book's major themes. Thank you to Dawn Potter for her diligent copyediting support and to my anonymous readers for their generous notes. My sincere thanks to the University of Nebraska Press and Springer Publishing for permission to reproduce materials that appeared in their publications.

My family has been steadfast in their support, often from afar. My mother, Michelle, embodies unconditional love and has long nurtured my interests in emotional life. My father, Mark, has always held space for my love of teaching, writing, and justice. My brothers will always be my favorite motley crew: Chris for his lawyer's tenacity, Brendan for his gentle soul, and my twin Michael for his unending curiosity. Martha and Mark Derish continue to open their home and hearts to me. Most of all, my wife, Nicole, is my eternal wellspring of love and partnership. She, alongside our son, Remy, have enriched my life beyond measure. You are my family. I love you all.

CRIMES AGAINST FEELING

INTRODUCTION

CONSTITUTION

Adam Smith, Thomas Jefferson, and the Declaration of Independence (1776)

In an unratified draft of the Declaration of Independence, Thomas Jefferson claimed that King George III "waged cruel war against human nature itself." In other words, the king was akin to *hostis humani generis*, or enemies of the human race. Jefferson ended his list of grievances with George III's "piratical warfare, the opprobrium of infidel powers." Independence was piracy's natural consequence. One can appreciate the claim's rhetorical heft, even before considering Jefferson's specific piracy charge: the king's alleged role in both enslavement and abolition. According to historians Pauline Maier and David Armitage, Jefferson's appeal to "piratical warfare" was the "emotional climax of his case against the king" as well as the "logical climax to the train of abuses." Via the pirate, Jefferson addressed major problems inherent to declaring independence. How did one legally constitute a new nation? What coherent social union existed in fractious colonies? To what degree was revolutionary sovereignty legible to existing global orders? The pirate provided potential answers. To call the British sovereign piratical was to deny his legal right to head the colonies. After all, pirates ostensibly rejected all state-backed mores. As such, Jefferson was not creating a nation. He was merely outlining a supposed fact: nations repelled pirates. The Declaration was not naming a political split but revealing a people already unified in "human nature" against piratical cruelty. By aligning George III with "*infidel* powers," Jefferson was making reference to the North African states in the Ottoman Mediterranean to which England had paid tribute. Jefferson recognized that the region's variably legal maritime raiders had also sailed in the Roman republic that the founding father sought to emulate. In his view, the king had rejected a classical legacy to align himself with past and present pirate scourges. This self-serving genealogy, incomplete in ways to be discussed, allowed Jefferson to distill complex foreign relations into a charge against "the CHRISTIAN king of Great Britain." Blasphemous piracy had justified America's Rome-like turn. Monarchical piracy had begotten American sovereignty. Jeffersons's pirate declaration, if legally ratified, would sail across the globe. Could it float?[1]

Perhaps not. Beginning on June 11, 1776, Jefferson had written his draft over approximately seventeen days in a privately rented room in Philadelphia. The Committee of Five, which included John Adams and Benjamin Franklin, then produced a second document to preserve a fiction of universal consensus. The Second Continental Congress composed the final Declaration. It deemed Jefferson's declared pirates politically perilous and thus legally impracticable.[2] After all, these pirates were laden with the upstart nation's defining legal and moral crisis: African enslavement that had begun at sea and taken root on land. Via the pirate, Jefferson presented both enslavers and abolitionists as piratical threats to the nation. This invective, Armitage notes, "seems doubly anomalous." Jefferson claimed legal rights for people whom he and the nation continued to bind. He himself bound nearly two hundred enslaved persons at Monticello as he drafted the Declaration. The founder's appeal to piracy reveals, for Armitage, the "giant chasm between his words and his deeds." It also confirms the myriad pirates Jefferson impressed to sail through such chasms.[3] The king was akin to corsairs and Barbary pirates in North Africa, sailors in the early modern middle passage, and Black loyalist counter-revolutionaries. Independence would, in practice, leave the new republic vulnerable to varied maritime antagonists across the globe. The capture of American sailors in the Ottoman Mediterranean would continue to power both pro-slavery and abolitionist positions throughout the era.[4] This knotty pirate narrative allowed Jefferson's Declaration to neutralize competing political threats under a shared rubric. He described King George III as a laborer in the piratical transoceanic trade, "captivating and carrying" enslaved persons onto ships and causing their "miserable death" at sea. Here Jefferson appeared to admit that revolutionary abolition, in addition to independence, was piratical enslavement's natural consequence. The enslaving Jefferson was himself not a pirate, it seemed, because he embodied the nation's white supremacist sentiments. Present and future enslavement in the new nation, he hinted, was preferable to white supremacy's overthrow by

Black pirates. The piratical king, Jefferson continued, was "exciting" the same enslaved people to "rise in arms among us" in exchange for freedom. Abolition, Jefferson asserted, was a piratical seduction from without rather than a moral imperative from within. King George had seamlessly shifted from plantation progenitor to slave agitator. Piracy's removal was the nation's global raison d'être even as the question of enslavement remained in legal suspension. Jefferson's own history with Sally Hemmings, the enslaved mother of five of his children and the half-sister of his wife, affirms the deeply intimate and violent denials of Black familial rights that resulted.[5]

The unratified Declaration was America's first domestic pirate fiction. It remains an exemplar of this sentimental legal genre. *Crimes Against Feeling* rides the wave of Jefferson's founding sentiments. At heart, this book concerns law, feeling, and family. It highlights the oceanic pirates invoked by landed authors to delimit domestic culture, define national law, and designate foreign relations. Both antebellum policymakers and popular writers shaped piracy's legal status as a crime against feeling. The book begins with Jefferson because he launched this titular legal and cultural trope. Jefferson deemed piracy an unnatural emotional antipathy toward domestic states rather than a single act at sea. His alleged pirates were not *of a place*—for instance, "pirates of the Caribbean." Instead, they were criminal antagonists *of a feeling*: national sympathy. In short, Jefferson had declared piracy an affect and an act. He railed against oceanic subjects across a political spectrum who had allegedly violated an American family with unfeeling fervor. In the process, he introduced the pirate as a cultural idea against which alleged criminals could be legally judged. Rich layers of legal precedent and literary representation followed his struck-down attempt. Legal parables of piratical crimes against feeling populated antebellum popular periodicals, sentimental narratives, domestic fictions, and material culture such as song sheets, currency, and postal covers. Alleged pirates' crimes against feeling were central to antebellum legal texts such as state papers, international treaties, trial transcripts, and U.S. Supreme Court decisions. Piracy became a floating signifier in this sea of sentimental texts, attacked fore and aft by various political foes who hit one another in the crossfire. For some, a global divorce from unfeeling piracy would be produced via slavery. For others, international union required oceanic abolition, if not full Black citizenship. A select few adjudicated both piracy and feeling anew. They returned sympathy to alleged pirates, often without denying their criminality. After all, feeling against an enslaving state was no crime. For fewer still, piracy was sympathetic precisely *because* of its essential illegality. A state that disenfranchised the enslaved or their descendants should feel just piratical scorn. These debates show why the period's defining domestic pirate fiction—the state's unwavering protection of familial feeling amid political turmoil—failed to hold water time and again. The U.S. Civil War represented a vital rejection of a particularly white supremacist strain of antebellum legal culture. Even so, the internecine war did not resolve how such violence had dominated long before Jefferson's Declaration and would continue long after.

Though this introduction stages piracy's early national history, *Crimes Against Feeling* primarily focuses on 1820—the year Congress declared deep-sea enslavement to be piracy—to 1869—the year the Supreme Court invalidated Confederate legal precedent as piratical. Throughout this period, piracy's supposed antagonism to moral feeling rippled through popular fiction, domestic policy, and international law. Shifting notions of piracy, particularly in relation to global systems of racial bondage, were manifold. Befitting fluctuating political currents, alleged pirates included British monarchs, American presidents, North African corsairs, enslaved mutineers, hemispheric American revolutionaries, global enslavers, imperial filibusters, potential free people, radical abolitionists, Confederate secessionists, Supreme Court justices, and entire nations. These complex political agents were anchored to a common, if unstable, cultural referent. A legal theory of unfeeling piracy persisted among disparate applications. A fiction of domestic union amid political rupture necessitated a singular legal antipode. Indeed, many antebellum figures projected a specious legal theory introduced by Jefferson: racially, sexually, and economically unruly pirates were the sole obstacle to moral union at familial, national, and global levels. In such a view, American state power could perfect moral attachments. Piracy law—and, with it, the state—existed to protect families. In practice, however, what defined antebellum piracy was not a single ideology but shared antagonism to shifting visions of the state. Alleged pirates were antebellum governments' rivals, victims, agents, and uneasy collaborators. Early modern states variably relied on extranational maritime agents to exercise politically contentious power on land and at sea. Antebellum governments violated enslaved, colonized, and subjugated global subjects whose just resistance was often charged as piracy. In fact, pirates were not the unfeeling antipodes of a feeling nation. They were partners in the nation's legal and cultural constitution. In response, *Crimes Against Feeling* organizes an overdue family reunion. Oceanic pirates, their national paternity long denied, must recover their domestic origins. Welcome home.

Legal culture, even more than the related frame of *law and literature* or the stronger response of *law as literature*, captures a constellation of sentimental works around piracy whose generic discreetness matters less than their cumulative powers in antebellum society.[6] In this book, I examine popular sentimental fiction and material culture alongside texts typically under the purview of legal theorists and historians of international law. I afford legal texts and literary fictions nearly equal interpretive space. Each shaped an antebellum sentimental legal culture around piracy, a concept that I often truncate to *antebellum legal culture*. The term *legal culture* is more common in legal anthropology and comparative legal studies, but it also encapsulates the cultural conditions through which varied legal agents constructed piracy as a crime against feeling. First defined by legal historian Lawrence M. Friedman in 1969, legal culture refers to "the network of values and attitudes relating to law, which determines when and why and where people turn to law or government, or turn away." Culture "binds together" working legal systems' other two pillars: "structural" legal institutions defined by courts' material forms or guiding processes and "substantive" legal outputs such as laws.[7] Legal culture's object of study remains a constellation of figures and texts that construct interpretive possibilities on legitimate legal power or sound judicial reasoning. Legal cultures may overlap in space or time. They are not synonymous with written law or legal institutions as such. Current legal scholars such as Rebecca Sanders note that ongoing attention to the "social beliefs and shared practices of law" best reflects the range of figures who make law, interpret its meaning, and shape its application.[8] *Crimes Against Feeling* broadens this interpretative range even further by analyzing the legal theories staged in literature alongside the literary theories presented in law. It recognizes certain antebellum legal texts' generic specificity—for instance, the Supreme Court opinion, the presidential declaration, or the legislative act—apart from the literary text. Even so, legal texts' unique power as speech acts cannot be separated from the legally oriented literary texts and sentimental narrative forms on which jurists often relied. Competing constative utterances in law and literature, or legal interpretations of piracy law, gave way to unique judicial performative utterances that created legal reality in official acts of declaration. "You are guilty of piracy" legally created the pirate only if uttered by a judge in a moment of sentencing. Literary texts did not share this power, but they did fundamentally shape the cultural conditions and linguistic possibilities through which competing constatives became performative.[9] Legal declarations of piracy in particular relied on both sentimental literary tropes and an entire legal system structured by literary sentimentality. Piracy law legalese retained an emotional core.

Antebellum legal culture's status as a culture of print means that formal legal institutions dominated by men shared editors, publishers, marketplaces, and audiences with popular domestic pirate fictions defined by women. This diverse group also built an intersecting culture of letters that included the historical exchange of letters, their representation in literature, and the postal infrastructures on which each relied. In the process, each built a series of nesting and competing legal cultures whose distinct sympathies were not segregated by gender.[10] Thinkers across a political spectrum argued from a shared legal premise: pirates were unable to feel toward the state or its paradigmatic families. This book may be the first to treat popular women writers as equal partners in antebellum legal culture around piracy. It places popular writers such as Catharine Maria Sedgwick, Harriet Beecher Stowe, and Maria Susanna Cummins on equal standing with legal patriarchs such as John Quincy Adams, Justice John Marshall, and Abraham Lincoln. These groups' sentimental pirate narratives collapse a land-water divide. They also destroy equally limiting gender binaries of public-private that pervaded early scholarship, though not antebellum culture.[11] "Part of the cultural work of domesticity," Amy Kaplan affirms of the period, "might be to unite men and women in a national domain." Pirates were central to an increasingly imperialist domestic culture's claims to moral virtue, what Kaplan calls "manifest domesticity."[12] As members of leading legal families, antebellum women dramatized landed women's moral and legal victories over pirates with diverse political analogs. These fictional pirates reflected legal theories about how the national family—and, by extension, a family of nations—should respond to imagined existential threats. The legal theories found in fiction differed from their political counterparts in genre-specific power more than narrative content. Indeed, one finds in state papers appeals to sons separated from their mothers by pirates, daughters seduced by them, or national families under their thrall. Antebellum courts adjudicated whether alleged pirates had family on land. Politicians judged domestic laws with global implications, most notably maritime abolition, on whether they offered familial protection against unfeeling pirates. Sentimental fictions contained multifaceted pirates whose contradictory political allegiances embodied legal tangles presented by Jefferson and others. Pirates of law and literature sailed in a shared cultural pool.

The United States, like any nation, was shaped by oceanic forces it also produced. Alleged pirates were, in practice, products of an antebellum legal culture that engaged the ocean as a practical necessity. The ocean was a source of economic gain, a site of foreign relations, and a space on which to project national or imperial sovereignty. Thousands of historical sailors, smugglers, and revolutionaries populated these waters. Some were called pirates, an appellation a few upheld but most tried to shed. Many were carriers of humans-as-cargo. Some existed only in popular literature or legal fictions. The legal status of all was shaped by ocean politics, or notions of the sea's proper political, social, geographic, and legal organization. Questions of ocean politics were manifold. How did domestic law apply in the deep sea? What was the best means of spreading domestic virtue globally? What law of nations would foster a global family? Such questions powered debates on revolutionary independence, imperial spread, foreign legal jurisdiction, global enslavement, and universal abolition. Each debate contained layered and often contradictory representations of piracy as a crime against feeling. Ultimately, no universal definition of piracy developed in the period. Disagreement persisted on what constituted piracy, who counted as a pirate, or who had jurisdiction over either. Antebellum legal culture's increasing incongruities—piracy law criminalized enslavers, the enslaved, abolitionists, statists, imperialists, and revolutionaries—affirmed the murkiness of these oceanic political waters.

Most notably, piracy's status as a crime against feeling shaped competing legal assessments on enslavement's place in ocean politics. Linked questions of moral feeling and legal reasoning abounded. If the enslaving nation were founded on familial feeling, should enslavement grow with America's geographic body? How did one explain the familial separations inherent to slavery on land and water? Did fellow feeling require abolitionist piracy against the state? Did oceanic enslavement's status as piracy justify reparations for Black families? Distinct yet overlapping legal theories developed in response to enslavement's contested status as a piratical crime against feeling. For a proslavery cohort led by figures such as Senator John C. Calhoun, oceanographer Matthew Fontaine Maury, and Confederate President Jefferson Davis, abolitionist pirates' theft of humans-as-property was anathema and, eventually, validated legal secession. In contrast, many abolitionist thinkers—who included Supreme Court Justice Joseph Story, Harriet Beecher Stowe, and Senator Charles Sumner—contended that only legal abolition could foster social harmony against piratical enslavement. They admitted piracy's fundamental depravity and the state's basis in fellow feeling. In a political appeasement that dominated federal policy, however, American law increasingly deemed both piratical enslavers and radical abolitionists threats to domestic stability. Only the most strident abolitionists—including late-career John Quincy Adams, Caribbean politician and author Michel Maxwell Philip, and journalist William Lloyd Garrison—invoked piracy to undermine the state's monopoly on sympathy. For them, alleged piracies against the state were often due to just resentment toward the familial separation at the heart of legalized enslavement. Abolitionists who returned sympathy to alleged pirates relitigated extralegal violence's moral value in a white supremacist nation. Antebellum legal culture's political boundaries remained porous. Figures such as Maria Susanna Cummins, Abraham Lincoln, and Daniel Webster floated between them. The pirate narratives that resulted affirm that white supremacy legalized from within, rather than unfeeling unruliness expelled from without, remained the nation's founding sentiment.

Attempts to mitigate political unrest around global enslavement led to piracy's intricate layers of legal and literary meaning in antebellum legal culture. A fiction of political stability amid fracture, paired with a common-law tradition of citing precedents, led abolitionist and enslaving pirates to inhabit the same legal narratives. Take, for example, antebellum legal responses to the 1804 Haitian Declaration of Independence in which members of the free Black republic envisioned "a stable Government for the Indigenous of Hayti" that would "forever ensure the empire of liberty" against the "inhumane government" of imperial France.[13] In cases such as *Rose v. Himely* (1808), the U.S. Supreme Court followed federal policy by explicitly denying Haiti's sovereignty and by framing its revolution as piratical. This policy persisted until 1862. Beginning in 1861, courts invoked *Rose* against alleged secessionist pirates to legally counteract the Confederacy's ongoing white supremacist counterrevolution. While secessionists had no fellow feeling for Haitian revolutionaries, federal law linked them as a matter of legal practice and political expedience: both countered sovereign states and were thus pirates. The convoluted pirate villain of the wartime domestic fiction *Haunted Hearts* (1864)—the subject of my final chapter—embodies the political and moral tangles that resulted from this conflation. The novel's villain, Black Bullet, codes as a British naval officer, a multiracial Caribbean revolutionary, a North African corsair, and a Black African all at once. The novel's paradigmatic families, we are assured, are white. The mechanisms for rejecting deviations from antebellum policy—abstracting the specific question of Black freedom and reparations via sentimental appeals to white familial feeling against piracy—powered fictions like *Haunted Hearts* as well as the broader legal culture. Piratical enslavement's shifting legal status complicated antebellum political stability without evicting the state's persistent white supremacy.

The vision of Union displayed on this book's cover thus embodies antebellum legal culture's most self-serving domestic fiction: federalism's endurance as a moral good and a familial inheritance flowing through white womanhood. Derived from a Civil War–era postal cover, it depicts America as a blond-haired woman bathed in light as she girds the national family crest of Union against oceanic threats. God and nature bless federal policy.[14] In foregrounding this trope, I center whiteness as a legal force while rejecting its claimed supremacy. The fact of Black and Brown humanity did not prevent a white supremacist legal culture from taking hold. My book's cover testifies to this fact: in response, my ongoing reference to "white supremacist" in relation to legal culture is a deliberate provocation. Perhaps more any other term, white supremacy cuts through the legalistic and emotionally deceptive racism that defined antebellum law and its modern extensions. White supremacy also has the benefit of accuracy, as do related terms such as white hegemony, in describing whiteness as a constructed supremacist identity, a pervasive set of individual beliefs, and an institutionally backed ideological apparatus. Its use speaks to critical race theory's influence on this book's antiracist politics, even as I fall short of its vast methods as a legal field. Guided by ample evidence, I refuse to perform apolitical posturing or scholarly dispassion in the study of racism embedded in legal institutions.[15]

Attention to critical race studies also confirms this work's methodological shortcomings, derived as it is from predominantly white, landed, and state-aligned authors. As Faith Barter makes clear, the period's Black writers both "documented the violence of law" in legal testimony and "transmute[d] their legal realities and imagine alternative legal worlds" via varied narrative forms. *Crimes Against Feeling* does not do justice to Black, Indigenous, or other diverse legal cultures.[16] Likewise, it rarely calls upon nonwhite laborers, thinkers, and everyday people, freed or enslaved, who shaped the law or its alternatives.[17] It instead centers antebellum subjects who, as Hazel Carby has shown, made possible "the raising of protective barriers, ideological and institutional, around the form of the white mother." Piracy law was once such a barrier. The scenes of white familial supremacy that dominate this book, imagined by some as piracy's moral and legal antidote, may be contrasted with the "convergence of terror and pleasure in the libidinal economy of slavery" that Saidiya Hartman has charted in the slave ship, on the plantation, and in numerous other domestic sites. Legal protections for white women against rapacious pirates developed alongside what Emily Owens terms the "legal doctrine of rape law" that invited sexual violence against enslaved Black women. White mothers legally inherited this progeny of enslaved Black mothers. Such legal histories are relayed indirectly in this book.[18] While largely focused on a white supremacist legal culture, this book also counters the disenfranchisement that resulted then and persists now. I do not confuse legality with morality. Instead, I reconstruct a white supremacist ship of state in rough political seas. All aboard.

PIRACY AND SYMPATHY

In his draft of the Declaration of Independence, Thomas Jefferson asserted that "the last stab to agonizing affection, and manly spirit bids us to renounce for ever these unfeeling brethren!"[19] He thus officiated the colony's legal and emotional self-emancipation from its British family. The founder did not treat feeling as an insular or apolitical concept. He was instead a "sentimental nationalist," as Peter Onuf notes. Jefferson's "organic quasi-familial conception of the nation" was defined by a "thickening weave of family connection, interdependent interest, and affectionate fellow feeling."[20] Thus, according to Elizabeth Barnes, the "idea of the American people as a single unified body" in antebellum culture came to rely on representations of a national "sympathetic chain" as exemplified in Jefferson's Declaration. In this chain, the individual was morally linked to family and the family to nation. Antebellum popular and political writers wove these threads into the fabric of "American sentimental politics," treating citizenship as a familial attachment that required the "conflation of the personal and the political body." Barnes notes in particular how antebellum sentimental politics manifested in seductive incest plots in domestic fictions. Each echoed fears of familial political union among a divergent population.[21] As I will discuss, domestic pirate fictions placed such fears in an oceanic context. Pirates' unique role in sentimental politics primed their centrality in antebellum legal culture. Pirates were not seen as domestic. They were popularly presumed to have abandoned their landed families. Their perceived deviant sexual practices, including queer sex, racial miscegenation, and sexual violence, ran counter to a heteronormative generation of national subjects.[22]

In this way, they did not appear to serve the national collection of families. Denied a landed familial claim, oceanic pirates lacked legal rights derived from statist kinship as an extension of natural moral sense. Feeling flowed with and through a state. This legal frame's political limits remained, as Jefferson's own attempt made clear. In examining this limit, *Crimes Against Feeling* captains a return to a theory of sympathy whose legal force preceded Jefferson's Declaration and persisted long after.

Understanding piracy's contested legal status as a crime against feeling necessitates an equally complex account of sympathy as a moral philosophy and legal theory. Antebellum legal culture around piracy was not defined by genre, geography, or gender. Its agents were linked by sympathy. The word *sympathy* derives from the Greek συμπάθεια, "the state of feeling together," which in turn derives from συν, "fellow," and πάθος, "feeling." Since Plato, philosophers of sympathy have considered how individuals feel or enact a social unity despite embodied separation. Do humans have a shared moral capacity? If so, what powers this universal obligation? Sympathy's early modern philosophical development was most closely associated with Francis Hutcheson (1694–1746), his mentee David Hume (1711–76), and Adam Smith (1723–90), among others. Smith wrote, "As we have no immediate experience of what other men feel, we can form no idea of the manner in which they are affected." In other words, these thinkers considered how distinct subjects were morally and materially attuned. During the antebellum period, literary scholar Caleb Crain notes, "sympathy had the force of a biological fact, as if it were as essential to human nature as sight, hearing, taste, touch, and smell."[23] Pirates' deviation from this essential human trail was a dominant narrative motif across antebellum culture. Sympathy thus shaped piracy as a legal and cultural category. Specifically, it was a historically specific approach to jurisprudence, or the theory of the law's proper meaning and function. "Sentimental jurisprudence" represents a vital thread of legal thought that began with Aristotle and was perfected by Adam Smith, as legal scholar Ian War has shown.[24] As a precursor to modern normative jurisprudence, antebellum sentimental jurisprudence treated deviance from natural moral sense as a crime against feeling itself. In other words, pirates' lack of moral feeling was both a legal plot point and piracy law's structuring ideology. For most antebellum legal thinkers, the state's monopoly on sympathy—the idea that the sovereign nation was fellow feeling's sole guarantor—meant that a familial state naturally repelled immoral pirates. For some legal activists, an immoral state produced unduly orphaned pirates. Illegal acts against the state, including piracy, empowered families who had been legally abandoned by the state.

There's enduring power to a theory of family-based fellow feeling, though it is sometimes maligned as a maudlin relic. This intellectual tradition's power is not due to moral simplicity: sympathy, like piracy, may exist across a political spectrum. Sympathy's global scope and ideological tangles are familiar to antebellum scholars: its status as a politically progressive or conservative philosophy has shaped the past forty years of literary scholarship. If scholarly consensus exists, it sounds something like Marianne Noble's rejoinder: "Sympathy is more complex than the first few pages of *The Theory of Moral Sentiments* and the last few pages of *Uncle Tom's Cabin.*" Trailblazing scholars—including Shirley Samuels, Lora Romero, Karen Sanchez-Eppler, Dana Nelson, and Peter Coviello, among many others—affirm sentimental literature's complex purchase in antebellum constructions of race, class, gender, and empire.[25] More recent work from Xine Yao, Erica Fretwell, and Kyla Schuller follow Saidiya Hartman's defining claim in *Scenes of Subjection* (1997): antebellum narratives of national familial union most often placed readers within a politically bereft "benumbing spectacle" of white privilege, capitalistic cruelty, and scientific racism. My work in this book echoes Lauren Berlant's claim that "the culture of true feeling has no inevitable political ideology," despite its power to denervate political alterity when made to serve "national sentimentality."[26] Piracy elicited complex feelings about the state's legal and moral validity. Sympathy was most often a technology of white supremacy, as will be discussed. Figures who could not feel beyond a white supremacist state revealed their limited political and moral imagination. Nationalist fellow feeling was just one kind of emotional orientation among many, including disgust, shame, complaint, and other "ugly feelings" coded as morally or aesthetically undesirable. Each undermined affective registers that treated positive feeling as a moral good and a political demand.[27] Antebellum piracy's fluid political meaning was the product of the equally dynamic emotional states expressed in the period's legal and literary texts. Drawing a line in the sand about sympathy's essential ideology would unduly limit our understanding of the legal culture that resulted.

Idiosyncratic interpretations of sympathy produced rival definitions of piracy, which in turn powered competitions over the state's legal rights and moral imperatives. Adam Smith's eighteenth-century theories remained antebellum legal culture's beating heart. This work privileges Smith even as I recognize what Duncan Faherty calls a "need to move beyond" the Scottish philosopher in literary studies. Attention to Smith alone fails to capture "the precise political significance of sentimentalism," scholars such as David Luis-Brown note, particularly as wielded by multiracial and decolonial figures across the hemispheric Americas.[28] Smith's was certainly not the basis for all legal thought, but his work lent itself to dominant legal theories of piracy more than that of any other early modern thinker. His contemporary Hume, for example, argued in favor of a disinterested sympathetic desire for social interaction, asserting that natural law produced a "propensity to company and society." The resulting "contagion of manners" caused moral sentiment's organic spread. This mechanism did not easily translate into a theory of the feeling state or the unfeeling pirate.[29] Smith's focus on mediated familial attachments—which could be accessed via narrative, empowered individual action, and led to a defined social collectivity—provided more fertile ground. Via his own domestic fiction, Smith presented moral feeling as produced by self-interest and imagination. In *The Theory of Moral Sentiments*, he staged a thought experiment involving a "brother . . . upon the rack"—that is, one beset by a torture device. In most of the book's pirate narratives, the state or its families are racked. The pirate remains the torturer. Smith saved the question of unfeeling operators for later, as will I. Initially, the viewer shadows the human under torture. In a projection of bodily union, Smith stated, "We place ourselves in his situation, we conceive ourselves enduring all the same torments." Viewers "enter as it were into his body" and reanimate a true approximation of the pained subject's current feeling. Self-interested response to this feeling dictates proper action toward a human object of sympathy. One may become "some measure the same person" as the person on the rack.[30] In Smith's conception, individuals build moral and material attachment via the recognition of their shared embodied capacities and moral compasses. They are inclined to prevent adverse feelings and foster beneficial ones. In this way, they may maintain self-interest and independent embodiment while creating mediated but meaningful social attachments.

Antebellum thinkers who invested in Smith did not share a single political ideology but instead used sentimental jurisprudence to structure competing legal possibilities. For many antebellum figures, pirates lacked feeling because moral sentiments only existed in and through a state. Imagined connection to other individuals necessarily led to a sovereign, national collective. The state could place the pirate on a torture rack without eliciting sympathy. Citizen-subjects did need not to feel for a non-brother on the rack or gallows. The pirate had no family and was thus beyond a natural power of imagination. Indeed, for Smith, familial attachments sustained individuals' moral sense by providing a natural ideal. Ideal familial structures, he claimed, spread fellow feeling and, with it, social cohesion. The viewer of an ideal family felt "peace, cheerfulness, harmony, and contentment" defined by children's "respectful affection" and parents' "kind indulgence." This dynamic created a "reign [of] mutual love and esteem."[31] Within this system, then, individuals subordinated themselves to a dominant filial subject. Vitally, all maintained their individual self-interest or identity because all freely exercised the same self-interest that Smith had outlined. Moral subjects would be motivated to create familial union. People not yet part of this family would be inclined to join out of self-interest. In other words, a personal familial feeling could ripple across social relations. Antebellum legal culture largely presented family as the nation's legal basis and as proof of individual subjects' moral capacity, but Smith's theory also informed alternative moral and legal horizons. For some, pirates themselves might be enslaved on the rack of a white supremacist state or act in feeling for its bound subjects. As Smith admitted, social uniformity was a feature of his natural philosophy. The "wisdom which contrived human affections" dictated that persons "within the sphere both of his abilities and of his understanding" remained most fit for sympathetic identification.[32] That is, the mechanisms of familial feeling bred a preference for like agents. In such cases, a minority subject—one outside a majority political sphere—could be imagined as unfeeling.

Narrations across genres revealed alleged pirates' capacity for moral sentiments. Each had power in antebellum legal culture. Collectively, pirate narratives built a "discursive density around issues of sentiment and their subversive tendencies" that Ann Laura Stoler attributes to the Dutch colonial archive. The pirate was legally produced by an antebellum federal state likewise "troubled by the *distribution* of sentiment, by both its excessive expression and the absence of it."[33] Because piracy was allegedly defined by an excessive expression of feelings against a familial nation-state, antebellum figures often relied on alleged pirates' familial ties to adjudicate their legal status. Each called upon what legal theorists call *narrative empathy*, a term referring to one's fellow feeling toward a legal narrative or a person under legal scrutiny.[34] To feel against alleged pirates was to legally sanction the state as a guarantor of familial feeling. Conversely, proof of familial feeling had legal force to distinguish someone from a pirate. Those defending themselves from charges of piracy—or those seeking to establish legally valid maritime policy—engaged sympathy as a legal necessity. "I am innocent of piracy," they seemed to respond, "because I feel toward the state and its families." Or "my oceanic incursions are legal because they protect familial states from unfeeling pirates." Only a few upended this legal rhetoric. "I am guilty of piracy," they retorted, "because I feel toward those families destroyed by the state." Deciding if this alternative distribution of feeling represented a valid legal argument defined an antebellum legal culture shaped by competing conceptions of legality, sovereignty, and enslavement.

PIRACY, SYMPATHY, AND LEGALITY

Jefferson knew that King George was not breaking English law in his actions as sovereign, piracy charges notwithstanding. Enslavement was legal in the British empire in 1776, as were paternalist policies toward colonies. And contrary to Jefferson's invective against piratical "infidel powers," the early modern Ottoman Mediterranean was a "unified legal space" in which alleged pirates "churned up a sea of paper" in a politically diverse legal culture.[35] Even so, Jefferson strategically invoked piracy's symbolic power and legal murkiness. Once he placed piracy in the Declaration, literary scholar Alexandra Ganser affirms, "the crisis of colonial legitimacy and representation would be performatively resolved."[36] Rather than appeal to clear legal statutes to justify independence, he claimed that the king had broken moral codes with legal force. He made a claim to legality, or the quality of accordance with the law, without appealing to specific legal statutes. Fittingly, the ratified Declaration was itself not a legal text. The document produced no enforceable legal statutes, its pervasive use as precedent notwithstanding.[37] In practice, Jefferson constituted a legal culture shaped by what is known as *popular legality*, a term that refers to competing narrative representations of the law that are based in feeling. According to Greta Olson, popular legality is the product of "people's affective relations to the law," defined as "people's subjective attitudes towards what they feel to be the law." In short, it describes cultural codes that are perceived to have legal force. Jefferson felt that the king's actions were illegal piracy. Therefore, so must the new nation's citizen-subjects. To feel for the Declaration was to feel against the king. Such feelings helped to legalize the nation.[38] Feeling against piracy thus became more than a moral imperative. It was a legal requirement. Of course, antebellum legality was unwieldy. Jefferson's declared nation was just one legalized family. Revolutionary Haiti was another. The Confederate government was another still. In each case, piracy's legal quality as a crime against feeling shaped complex political competitions.

Antebellum appeals to national feeling represented more than legal rhetoric. Feeling was a mechanism for lawmaking itself. Allegations of crimes against feeling not only informed piracy law's practical function but also shaped new legal identities. Foremost among these identities was the pirate. Another was the white citizen-subject. Yet another was the enslaved. The law, we know, is an elastic cultural force rather than an objective ruleset. Imaginative literature impacted antebellum legal thinking on topics such as slavery, capital punishment, and imperial expansion, as scholars have shown. These legal dynamics also produced antebellum constructions of race, gender, and other social categories.[39] Law likewise has a deep relationship to fictionality due to its reliance on narrative as fact, judgment as dispassion, and precedent as proof.[40] Most pressingly, piracy reveals antebellum legal culture's emotional investments—what legal scholar Ravit Reichman calls "law's affective thickets," understood as the notion that "law is built around, through, and in response to a potentially inflammatory, unwieldy core of affect." This core includes emotions, feelings, and bodily interactions. "Affect," Reichman concludes, "lies in the drama and banality of the law" as a lived experience.[41] Antebellum policymakers not only included emotional appeals to make piracy laws. They also put individuals into assumed affective relations. In other words, they determined a legally acceptable set of emotional ties and embodied actions among people. Legal narratives affectively defined piracy and punished it accordingly. People were imprisoned, enslaved, or freed depending on their affective relation to piracy. They were given land, money, or social status. Alleged piracy against historical groups—notably, violence against the enslaved, the colonized, or their heirs—was legally sanctioned once proven to extend popular feelings that were assumed to have legal force. Popular writers modeled these relations, textualizing legal theories and judging their outcomes. These domestic narrations, too, had power on land and water. Notions of piracy law's moral objectivity and stable precedent obscured antebellum legal culture's reliance on a broader sentimental culture.

Piracy's status as a crime against feeling grew from antebellum legal culture's treatment of sympathy as a natural form of jurisprudence. As discussed, jurisprudence refers to a chosen philosophy of law as well as the legal archive structured according to this philosophy. *Natural jurisprudence* was a vital branch of early modern legal thinking in general and sentimental jurisprudence in particular. Each assumed nature's power as the basis for law's creation and interpretation. In *The Theory of Moral Sentiments*, for example, Smith wondered if legal channels could follow natural moral sense. He considered natural jurisprudence "of all sciences by far the most important, but hitherto, perhaps, the least cultivated." In other words, he believed that aligning legal policy with natural feeling should be a culture's highest aim.[42] Piracy's legal status as a crime against feeling likewise resulted from what scholar Stuart Banner calls a "mixed reliance on natural law and positive law." Policymakers and jurists invoked shared feeling against piracy to create legal statutes, or positive law. Domestic law as well as international treaties, trade agreements, and legal statutes produced overlapping forms of positive law around unfeeling piracy. Sentimental language allowed often contradictory statutes to maintain narrative, if not logical, coherence. Even so, legal gaps in positive law on piracy let sympathetic appeals be more than just rhetorical. One could reassess positive law, or alter it outright, by claiming that universal moral precepts should be given explicit legal force. Natural law's legal primacy lasted until the late nineteenth century, Banner concludes, during which time it "provided a reservoir of principles for judges to draw upon." Judges invoked natural law to present themselves as "finders, not makers, of law."[43] For many, piracy was a case study in natural jurisprudence. Oceanic subjects' relative deviation from natural moral sentiment determined their criminality. Piracy was defined as incompatibility with an ostensibly universal but judicially ill-defined natural philosophy. In other words, sympathy was a form of natural law and thus a basis for civil law. Appeals to natural feeling thus provided a mechanism to both establish law and expand legal thinking beyond established bounds. In each case, piracy was less of an act and more of an affront, specifically to nature and its laws. Appeals to national familial feeling could have legal force.

Claims to pirates' crimes against feeling often relied on a relatively narrow view of sympathy as the basis for natural jurisprudence. In *Moral Sentiments*, Smith largely rejected the charge of natural unfeeling that defined the pirate. For him, pirates may be classed among those seemingly unsympathetic subjects who were nonetheless party to human nature. The popularity of their "criminal purposes" was due to their fallen yet powerful moral sentiments: "We are interested even in the exploits of the Buccaneers, and read with some sort of esteem and admiration, the history of the most worthless men." As the product of singular historical struggles, pirates had "endured greater hardships, surmounted greater difficulties, and encountered greater dangers than, perhaps, . . . the ordinary course of history gives us account of."[44] In his view, they were an extreme example of how humans naturally reacted to ongoing state violence. Agents of war could advance or diminish moral feeling. Smith classed pirates among the latter, as persons "without any regard to humanity" and "very worthless characters," a status they large maintained in antebellum legal culture. Notably, however, Smith prefaced his account of the torture rack with a vital caveat: everyone is capable of fellow feeling. He wrote, "The greatest ruffian, the most hardened violator of the laws of society, is not altogether without [sympathetic capacity]."[45] People may habitually act without fellow feeling, but capacity remained. Pirates and other such figures were not beyond human nature. Such universality was necessary in order for Smith to claim a natural philosophy, albeit one with colonialist caveats to be discussed. One might expect antebellum sentimental culture to likewise be predicated on sympathy's universal power, a politics that would give the alleged pirate sympathetic capacity and, by extension, potential membership in the national family. Yet nearly all of the figures I discuss in this book disavowed such universality. In practice, a lack of moral sentiment was pirates' defining characteristic and arguably their only trait. This distinction reflects the political nature of antebellum legal culture. Political competition and the products of state violence made universal feeling impossible. The pirate provided a mechanism for making tortuous violence legally plausible.

To adjudicate pirates' feelings, narratively or otherwise, was to undercut the antebellum state's legal claim to natural jurisprudence. A pirate with a claim to sympathy beyond state power was a dangerous thing. Such pirates revealed social and moral collectivities beyond the nation. They embodied gaps in the narrative of national familial feeling. They felt toward alternative political orders. Smith did not directly advocate for a pirate's claim to sympathy, but he clearly influenced the legal theories that did. Pirates retained natural sentiments for Smith, but not all were positive. Morally aberrant figures like the pirate may embody another natural aspect of human nature: passions. "Passions are very apt to mislead," he wrote, "sometimes to drive him and sometimes to seduce him to violate all the rules which he himself, in all his sober and cool hours, approves of." A pirate, like any subject, may have "perfect knowledge" of virtue. Immoral acts occurred when they followed two sets of passions: "fear and anger" or "love of ease, of pleasure, of applause." A rationale for pirates' passions largely went unexplained in antebellum legal culture. Piracy was merely a hatred of the state and its families. For a few antebellum figures, however, pirates' resentment revealed valid legal grievances. An alleged pirate's antagonism to the state could be the product of liberty denied, particularly due to enslavement. Indeed, for Smith, a person's passionate resentment might be the natural product of "the strongest indignation against the injustice of his persecutors." Abolitionist resentment had legal standing in a world of unjust enslavement, even if it led some to piracy. Those who "suffer in the cause of liberty and justice" could yet receive their peers' fellow feeling, according to Smith. Those denied justice should be met with the "warmest sympathetic gratitude."[46] For some, sympathetic gratitude was a way to prove that alleged pirates were innocent. For others, piracy against an enslaving state retained moral value if not legal sanction.

In antebellum legal culture, national feeling tapped into global legal sentiment to damn the pirate and deify the state. Via the pirate, oceanic projections of domestic law proved national sovereignty. What Barnes terms the "relational model of selfhood" at work in antebellum sentimental politics—the notion that proper individual, familial, and national constitutions were products of emotional relations—shaped legal debates on sovereignty. States of sovereignty, like states of sympathy, exist only in relation to one another. Indeed, both sympathy and sovereignty are, at heart, descriptions of bodies' internal character and external relatedness. Theorists of sympathy and sovereignty ask how and why individual bodies exist independently yet recognize a self-same constitution in like subjects. How does that recognition lead to social unity and the formation of political entities? What does one do with subjects who seemingly reject the ideologies upon which accepted unions are based? Competing notions of piracy's legal meaning and moral application provided some answers. Policies of sympathetic recognition shaped early modern international law. The seventeenth- and eighteen-century British Crown "employed the laws of God, nature, and nations when claiming sovereignty," historian Ken MacMillan concludes. Antebellum writers invoked sympathy to claim sovereignty in this system.[47] Pirates' alleged crimes against a national family—and, with it, a family of nations—allegedly proved American legal standing among oceanic nations. Sovereignty states were legally linked by fellow feeling. Some writers went back to the source—sympathy—to claim alternative forms of sovereignty. They did not define it as membership in a white supremacist family of nations. A family of denied sovereigns, most notably in Haiti, confirmed shifting global investments in enslavement. The pirate was also a vehicle for imagining sovereignty beyond existing state powers. In each case, pirates shaped competitions over sovereignty as a state of sympathy in antebellum legal culture.

PIRACY, SYMPATHY, AND SOVEREIGNTY

In the Declaration, Jefferson slipped away from England. He bound a national body to itself and to other national families. Here and elsewhere, the expatriated pirate allegedly proved American moral sense. Pirates were also vital to legal claims of domestic sovereignty in international waters. That is, Jefferson's claim to revolutionary independence against "piratical warfare" aligned with declarations of sovereignty in early modern legal culture. State sovereignty, or a group's legal and cultural self-determination in a defined political sphere, was becoming less a product of the sovereign head's absolute power and more an assertion of a population's collective will. The notion of Westphalian sovereignty, developed after the global Thirty Years' War (1618–48), ostensibly afforded the involved nations a legal claim to their domestic dominion.[48] Such early modern states were, in terms of international law, more like linked islands than solitary continents. Landed states existed in networked chains of internal coherence and external recognition. In this way, antebellum sovereignty was part of the contested "archipelagic Americas" defined by Brian Russell Roberts and Michelle Stephens as "island-ocean-continent relations which have exceeded US-Americanism."[49] All nations were, in a manner, legal islands in a shared sea. Pirates ostensibly refused to anchor themselves to these states or join a family of nations. What legally bound an early modern ocean of nations—theoretically, if not actually—was shared feeling against piracy. Nested national families populated an international legal order. The pirate provided Jefferson and others with a mechanism to legally tie domestic law to a law of nations. In practice, antebellum legal culture was not an antagonism between opposing political bodies—that is, between the feeling state and the unfeeling pirate. It was an ouroboros. Heads of state consumed a trailing piratical appendage. They perpetrated a never-ending cycle of violence from within under the guise of expulsion from without. Whether piracy could break this statist cycle remained a potent legal and cultural question.

American sovereignty relied on its legal and moral legibility to early modern laws of land and sea. Piracy's established legal status as the state's antipode helped usher America into a family of nations. Early modern legal culture developed a self-serving legal theory of sovereignty during the golden age of Atlantic piracy, which lasted from roughly 1650 to 1726. During each year of this period, an estimated 1,000 to 2,000 pirates were active along Atlantic shores.[50] Like pirates of later eras, these golden-age maritime raiders were the product of varied political currents—in this case, increased metropolitan unemployment, robust illegal markets in colonial outposts, colonial governments' distance from the metropole, and a glut of trained sailors following the War of Spanish Succession (1701–14), among other factors. Though piracy was often presented rhetorically at this time as a universal crime known to all, increased militarization of global maritime space had fostered the legal exclusion of figures who were deemed extranational or piratical. The early modern law of the sea—and, with it, the creation of modern piracy—was deeply influenced by the Dutch jurist Hugo Grotius (1583–1645). In *Mare Librum* (1609), translated into English as *Freedom of the Seas*, he argued that all sovereign nations had equal access to the sea for economic or political purposes. In this system, valid access to the ocean (rather than ownership of it) determined both a nation's legal jurisdiction at sea and its sovereignty on land. Put simply, sovereign nations recognized their shared investment in an allegedly neutral free sea. These shared legal borders could not extend to the deep sea without mutual accords between nations that were often at war. Nonetheless, the legal theories of Grotius and others "expanded the repertoire of rationales from which colliding maritime powers could draw to support self-interested positions," as legal scholar Lauren Benton explains.[51] In other words, all heads of state could agree about piracy's incompatibility with state agendas—in principal. But in practice, piracy was not a total deviation from national legal systems. According to Guy Chet, piracy's legal status developed as a "continuation of conventional practices and understandings of law and jurisdiction."[52] Piracy law was not an exception to early modern legal thinking. It was a legal partner. Even so, state documents and legal texts reinforced the idea of unified lawful states in deep conflict with the lawless pirate. That legal fiction of antagonism had clear benefits. As Jefferson asserted, the revolutionary nation could exist as a global legal entity via its binary opposition with the nationless pirate.

Despite the nation's ongoing entanglements with alleged pirates, many argued that the United States was the purest example of feeling against piracy and was therefore the globe's sovereign advocate. However, the absence of universal moral sentiments meant that piracies, particularly around enslavement, went unpunished. After all, how could the United States claim universal jurisdiction over piracy if the nation itself practiced piratical enslavement? Even so, piracy remained central to competitions over *universal jurisdiction*, or nations' extraterritorial right to prosecute global criminals in domestic courts despite a lack in direct legal ties. "Of the conduct of one independent nation towards another," Smith wrote in *Moral Sentiments*, "neutral nations are the only indifferent and impartial spectators." Smith's call for a natural jurisprudence that could perfect such systems derived from Grotius's *Law of War and Peace* (1625). Natural law required a natural antagonist. Pirates were universal jurisdiction's defining test case due to their global movement and perceived depravity. According to Mark Chadwick, early modern legal thinkers asserted that universal jurisdiction against piracy would "protect the fundamental principle of sovereign equity," by which they meant even shares of domestic state sovereignty.[53] Competing legal norms and ongoing political conflicts proved this ordering to be limited. Lauren Benton and Lisa Ford confirm that "attempts to order oceans in the early to mid-nineteenth century developed in the absence of broad-based legal principles."[54] No one nation claimed total legal control of the ocean. Likewise, piracy's status as "a universal crime justiciable in any municipal court" remained unproven.[55] As Adam Smith knew, political bodies' self-interest did not translate into fellow feeling. "The laws of nations, or for those rules which independent states profess or pretend to think themselves bound to observe" he confirmed, "is often very little more than mere pretence and profession."[56] Modern thinkers have continued this unmaking of statist legal culture. Political theorist Stephen D. Krasner, for example, considers state sovereignty "organized hypocrisy" in which the "logics of consequences dominate the logics of appropriateness." Then and now, state sovereignty is not natural. It is a feature of legal cultures in which overlapping narratives of sovereign recognition *constitute* an international order while claiming merely to *explain* such an order. Appeals to moral sense necessarily occur after state action. In such a system, pirates would not exist without the state. Likewise, the modern state would not exist without pirates.[57]

Piracy's legal definition in America depended on its assumed incompatibility with state-backed moral sense. Some scholars have framed golden-age piracy's fundamentally anti-statist and anti-hierarchical character as a model for more progressive political relations.[58] Indeed, real or imagined pirate collectivities often represented powerful forms of alterity. Nonetheless, pirates and nations were fluid political partners constituted under a guise of fixed and counterposing sympathies. In fact, pirates and statesmen shared a lineage. Take, for example, Jefferson's appeal to Roman law against piracy. Cicero was often credited with the phrase *hostis humani generis*, but the Roman statesman admitted pirates' humanity and their sovereign ties. Instead, the slogan is best attributed to British Admiralty judge Sir Leoline Jenkins in 1668.[59] In practice, alleged pirates' political power was key to both ancient and early modern sovereigns. "Rome, the Mistress of the World, was no more at first than a Refuge for Thieves and Outlaws," affirmed Captain Charles Johnson in his wildly successful and semifictional *A General History of the Pyrates* (1724). Pirates were not wholly divorced from the sovereign nation imagined as a global familial organization. They were, in fact, progenitors of this "Mistress of the World" and her national broods. Roman-era pirates were not powerful enough to declare sovereignty, but "had they all united and settled in some of those islands," wrote Johnson, "they might by this time have been honoured with the name of a commonwealth." In other words, piracy's illegality derived from its status as the state's less-powerful twin.[60] As in the golden age, self-serving antebellum divisions between piracy and the state obscured these deep ties. "The politics of piracy," asserts colonial American historian Douglas R. Burgess, "represents a severely limited state responding to a crisis beyond its control."[61] Like their antebellum counterparts, colonial pirates had competing interests, as did the landed agents that alternately relied on and rebuked them. Far-flung colonies would depend on marginal subjects whose actions could be viewed as piratical. As historian Mark Hanna concludes, the early modern national-imperial project of "transforming pirates' nests into productive and self-sustaining communities" included the social incorporation of some extranational maritime agents as well as the legal exclusion of others.[62] This process of strategic incorporation and rejection carried forward into an antebellum period whose alleged pirates represented a host of competing political interests.

Deeply versed in early modern law, Jefferson's Declaration launched the pirate as a legal antagonist to a feeling state. The U.S. Constitution delimited the legal bounds in which that state and its alleged pirates sailed. In keeping with a need for legal fluidity and statist binaries, the Constitution established piracy as a thing to be continually defined rather than a settled category. Turning the problem of definition into a power of punishment gave federalism durable legal power. The Constitution—written in 1787, ratified in 1788, and operative since 1789—legalized piracy as antagonism to state feeling rather than as a particular action. At the Constitutional Convention of 1787, the Committee of Detail took pains to legally cover a prior founding document's political gap. The 1777 Articles of Confederation did not allow individual states to offer commissions against pirates. Yet it had allowed states "infested with pirates" to make war until the federal government could intervene. In other words, it gave each state independent powers that could spill into global affairs.[63] This legal policy was incompatible with federalism. It was also incongruent with political visions of national fellow feeling. Each state could not be a legal or moral island. In an attempt to join these islands, the committee debated how to create federal piracy law. The question of jurisdiction, or who could legally define and punish piracy, abutted claims by other sovereigns. Should American jurisdiction, like American feeling, be made universal? What kinds of foreign relations best served the domestic nation? A turn to early national constitutional law reveals vital legal precedents and literary powers through which the antebellum state constituted itself. The pirate, like the nation, was heir to the legal culture birthed by the U.S. Constitution.

Piracy's constitutional status as a thing to be continually defined enabled the federal government to legalize a single pirate with fluid political meaning. Constitutional law scholars have probed the document's legal intricacies, including its still-contested clause to "define and punish piracies," more thoroughly than I can do here.[64] Even so, a brief consideration of the Committee of Detail confirms the literary act of enshrining piracy as a crime against feeling. James Madison wrote his contemporaneous record of the Constitutional Convention not for publication but to inform the absent Thomas Jefferson. Even so, Madison tended to "dampen" the "emotional tenor" of often contentious constitutional debate, as historian Mary Sarah Bilder extensively documents. Histories of legal dispassion and objectivity surrounding piracy thus fail to capture the document's formal and historical reliance on feeling. To start, the committee asserted the central government's right to "to declare the law and punishment of piracies committed on the high seas . . . and of offenses against the law of nations." In this straightforward frame, the government set piracy law and its effects. Yet this document did not cite what laws existed to be declared. Nor did it fully protect against external legal definitions taking precedence. Therefore, the convention removed the phrase "declare the law" and replaced "punishment" with "to punish." *Punishment*, as a noun, was weaker than a punishing verb, but this change may have threatened the government's legal position by leaving the power of definition undefined. A motion by James Madison led the insertion of "to define." Narrative authority had to be restored on both land and water.[65] Constitutional power over piracy needed to remain fluid yet unflinching.

The final amendment on piracy enshrined in the ratified Constitution legalized a power of definition that ostensibly covered the globe. It gave the federal government power "to define and punish piracies and felonies committed on the high Seas, and Offences against the Law of Nations."[66] This subtle shift from "declare the law and punishment" to "to define and punish" primed later fictions of stable legal precedent. Government powers of definition may exist in a continual present. A single prior definition need not be cited. The standard would be that the pirate had been government-defined. In this system, no definition for oceanic piracy could exist outside of domestic state control. Moreover, care was taken to make sure the "law of nations" was grammatically subordinate and thus politically captured. The "define and punish" clause was placed before the "law of nations," Madison noted of a motion by New York statesman Gouverneur Morris, "so as to let these [laws of nations] be *definable* as well as punishable, by virtue of the preceding member of the sentence." In this framing, piracy's domestic definition could extend globally. As the convention debated this issue, James Wilson, an associate Supreme Court justice, lamented the "look of arrogance" inherent in a law that "pretend[ed] to define the law of nations which depended on the authority of all the civilized nations of the world." American law, like American feeling, was not universal. The side in favor of America's primary power of definition countered that "the law of nations [was] . . . often too vague and deficient to be a rule."[67] America must have the power to define, lest someone else do so. However, this multiplied power to define, first domestically and then globally, was complicated in practice. The antebellum state did not always claim its global power, particularly when it came to adjudicating oceanic enslavement as piracy. Still, in all cases, the legal power to define was inextricable from the martial power to punish. A power to define ostensibly preceded the power to punish, but punishments could also be retroactively defined. The government's narrative and material power remained a constant. The state must define and punish piracy in equal measure. This constitutional power's practical application would come to rest on real or imagined antagonism to familial feeling.

This government power to define piracy as a crime against feeling—and the punishments it made possible—increased when combined with the legal power to make privateers. Privateers were private volunteers whose maritime action was sanctioned but not wholly determined by a sovereign during times of war. In such cases, states designated violent maritime raiders as extensions of domestic sovereignty and national feeling. The privateer embodied a fiction of martial and narrative control over oceanic space made possible by a culture of letters. That is, privateers were given license by sovereign states via letters of marque. These letters designated proper action toward neutral nations and against belligerents. The Constitution granted the federal government the power "to declare War, grant Letters of Marque and Reprisal, and make Rules concerning Captures on Land and Water."[68] This enumerated power was listed directly after the power "to define and punish piracy." Again, the Constitution did not adequately define how letters of marque would be granted. A pirate and a privateer were often the same person, their only difference being a moment of usefulness to a sovereign. In other words, quasi-piratical violence was legalized via narrative, economic, and emotional ties of unclear validity. Privateering commissions could be provided in bulk and did little to truly regulate the practice.[69] Early national privateering crews, maritime historian Kylie A. Hulbert notes, were more likely to be transnational sailors whose mix of "patriotic fervor and self-interest" reflected their charter's mercenary character. Debates over whether privateers were in fact pirates existed in nearly every instance, with enemies more likely to name them as such. One nation's feeling privateer was another's unfeeling pirate. Attempts to denounce privateering foes often rested on their moral or legal kinship with the pirate. Likewise, the government could denounce a failed privateering expedition as operating outside of its letter of marque. For privateers, the cords of legality would be cut if a claim to national familial attachment were revoked.[70] The same may be said of the enslaved.

PIRACY, SYMPATHY, AND SLAVERY

Despite the many-sided pirate's explicit removal from the Declaration, King George's piratical abolitionism remained in another Jefferson-penned founding document. On May 15, 1776, Jefferson and the revolutionary government of Virginia passed a legal resolution of independence "appealing to the SEARCHER OF HEARTS for the sincerity of former declarations." The delegates presented independence as a just moral response to the king's "piratical and savage war against us, tempting our slaves by every artifice to resort to him, and training and employing them against their masters."[71] This unequivocally abolitionist pirate king lacked the ambivalent duality of his Declaration counterpart. Forced to feel toward the enslaver or the enslaved, Jefferson chose himself. In *Notes on the State of Virginia* (1785), for example, he presented Black men's love for Black women as "more an eager desire, than a tender delicate mixture of sentiment and sensation." He alleged sexual rapacity rather than familial love as a defining sentiment. Likewise, he asserted that Black "griefs are transient" and that "numberless afflictions . . . are less felt, and sooner forgotten in them." Echoing aspects of Smith, Jefferson denied Black bodily pain and sympathetic capacity in what Xine Yao has rightly called the "inaugural text of American race science." The enslaved, like pirates, did not merit state protection.[72] As other antebellum figures like Michel Maxwell Philip would argue, the Black pirate's seeming lack of sympathy reflected antebellum legal culture's white supremacist logic. Just resentment of the white supremacist state bred criminality. Violence against enslavers was an exercise of self-interest and familial protection. In such cases, recovering sympathy for the pirate and the enslaved was a shared project. Whether the enslaved exercised fellow feeling in moments of alleged piratical mutiny against enslavers remained a central debate in antebellum legal culture.

Statist familial feeling, staged as piracy's moral and legal antidote, could not resolve the problem of state-backed enslavement. Claims of national moral union did not prevent political fracture. Jefferson proved as much. The antebellum state's proslavery policies—to say nothing of Jefferson's own status as an enslaver—confirmed the rot at the heart of its legal culture. Pirates troubled the idea that an imperial nation built on bondage could properly adjudicate moral feeling or legal rights. Enslavement's links to piracy preceded the nation's founding. European ships raided the African coast, justified by specious claims to moral superiority, global jurisdiction, and legal sanction over sovereign peoples. In more than one way, the United States was piratical from the outset. Anglo-Dutch marauders first stole enslaved Africans and brought them into the English Atlantic colonies in the early seventeenth century. In 1619, Jamestown colonists purchased dozens of enslaved Africans stolen by pirates from a Portuguese slave ship. The American colonies benefited from what Kevin P. McDonald calls a "pirate-slave trade nexus," in which pirates abetted and protected state-backed enslavement.[73] Statutes such as the 1662 Virginia code established racial slavery as matrilineal. The state named familial ties only to rend them. A family-annihilating pirate nexus was extant throughout the antebellum period despite abolitionism's growing legal prominence.[74]

Abolitionists within antebellum legal culture presented enslavement as a piratical crime against Black feeling. Most, however, gave such feelings, and thus Black civil rights, weaker legal force. Only a few wore charges of abolitionist piracy with antiracist pride. Nearly all demonstrated white supremacist and antiracist interpretations of Smith's thinking. As modern philosopher Jack Russell Weinstein notes, Smith had presented "the impossibility of sympathy in a slaveholding society."[75] In his "Lectures on Jurisprudence," first given at Glasgow University in 1762, he declared, "It is evident that the state of slavery must be very unhappy to the slave himself." This early lecture outlined his "theory of the rules by which civil government ought to be directed." Enslavement's incompatibility with sympathy "need hardly [be] prove[n], though some writers have called it in question." Abolitionist appeals to what Smith called the slave's "miserable life" were a hallmark of antebellum sentimental narratives.[76] Even so, fellow feeling remained a racially exclusionary category that shaped its limits as a form of abolitionist jurisprudence. Smith himself, Yao rightly asserts, forwarded a hierarchy of feelings that "abandon[ed] the guise of universal abstraction" and "reproduce[d] the material relations of colonialism."[77] In *Moral Sentiments*, he compared "civilized nations" capable of fellow feeling to "rude and barbarous nations" across Asia, Africa, and the Americas. He called these groups "equally impenetrable" and espoused their dispassionate "self-denial." Their natural state was "altogether insensible to bodily pain." Sympathy as well as its study was thus predisposed to feel white supremacy as a natural moral sentiment.[78] Enslavement's antebellum proponents certainly did.

Whether enslavement was to be defined and punished as piracy—a decision that often elided enslaved people's claim to human feeling—shifted throughout the antebellum era. Abolitionism was a constant force in antebellum legal culture, but a legal and moral split persisted until the Civil War. As legalized by the Constitution, federal union precluded universal abolition. The state had no legal duty to protect families torn apart by global enslavement. Instead, it served enslaving states' interest in what was known as the *three-fifth's compromise*: the amendment counted the enslaved as "three fifths of all other Persons" for purposes of population, taxation, and political representation.[79] This "mixed character of persons and property," James Madison asserted in *The Federalist Papers*, "is in fact their true character. It is the character bestowed on them by the laws under which they live."[80] Madison published this denial of enslaved people's capacity as "moral persons" anonymously, under the name Publius (Latin for "of the people"), in *The New York Packet* on February 12, 1788. This founder, who had helped to enshrine a constitutional power "to define and punish" piracy, thus appealed to a "true character" deriving from both natural law and public sentiment. Both piracy and Black non-citizenship were, of course, legally bestowed political identities. The power to define and punish both remained linked. The Constitution infamously banned any laws restricting the "migration or importation" of enslaved persons for twenty years.[81] Early national statutes such as the Slave Trade Act of 1794 regulated enslavement without criminalizing it. The act ostensibly made it illegal to "build, fit, equip, load or otherwise prepare any ship or vessel within any port or place of said United States" to be used in international enslavement.[82] As later chapters will show, importation bans that began in 1808 shifted the politics if not the horrors of deep-sea enslavement. The deep-sea trade became piratical in 1820, at least on paper. Antebellum legal institutions, however, largely followed the founding fathers in carrying water for enslavement. As federal court cases show, piracy's status as a feeling rather than an act helped bridge an increasingly untenable tenet in antebellum law: state-backed moral sentiments were divided between land and water. Specifically, limited deep-sea abolition coexisted with widespread landed enslavement. Deep-sea enslavement, though ostensibly piracy, could also be legalized via a foreign state's legal claim or the reenslavement of illegal human cargo under a domestic legal rubric. Enslaving piracy begot legality when a family of nations held the whip.

The pirate's alleged incapacity for fellow feeling was also produced by real or imagined antagonisms to global capitalist systems defined by state-backed enslavement. Legal narratives about domestic victories over pirates relayed more than insular home economics. They provided capitalist political economy's natural law justification. After all, the mechanisms for morality's spread—natural self-interest and that interest's global projection—paralleled capitalism's function as outlined in Smith's later text, *An Inquiry into the Nature and Causes of the Wealth of Nations* (1776). Specifically, Smith's idea of the "collective imagination"—or a group's moral capacity to extend their interest beyond their bodies' borders—advanced a global financial system predicated on state-backed speculation.[83] The state and its families fostered natural capitalist accumulation, including, but not limited to, the accumulated spoils of enslavement. Such accumulation could prevent economic or social collapse. Pirates were, in practice, produced by and active within such systems. Most often, however, their defeat served sentimental heroines whose victories better advanced a "discourse on state finance." As Joseph Fichtelberg notes, white women were imagined to "render more intimate and domestic the abstract forces of economy and polity." Means of preventing economic collapse could be found in their "allegedly unlimited capacity for feeling."[84] Pirates, on the other hand, were allegedly without this economic sympathy. They loved money for its own sake or for reasons contrary to natural accumulation. Many deemed oceanic enslavement's domestic spoils, though lamentable, as preferable to its theft by immoral agents or its loss by economic collapse. Varied figures invoked this frame to label slaveholders, abolitionists, or Black freepersons as piratical threats to capitalist fellow feeling. Others invoked the pirate to consider the morality of wealth redistribution, mutual aid, and Black reparations. In such cases, pirates could be the villainous offspring of corrupted state-backed capitalism or heroic anticapitalist crusaders. In most cases, domestic victories over pirates were temporary salves to an antebellum legal culture that did not have a concrete solution to the problem of enslavement in particular or of capitalism in general.

Narratives of individual familial attachments had real power in antebellum legal culture. Policies that ostensibly ordered global space often hinged on visions of a paradigmatic domestic family. In plots akin to the period's domestic fictions, legal figures contrasted pirates' crimes against feeling with contemporary women's emotional, social, and political growth. These narratives were published in newspapers, magazines, and bound texts alongside other popular outlets. Antebellum pirates' legal status at sea was inseparable from their imagined ties to the landed nation and its families. Therefore, piracy's global legal scale needs to be included in the imaginary geographies we use to study antebellum domestic literature. Like the antebellum period in which they sailed, antebellum domestic fictions were not exclusively oceanic or exclusively landed. To evoke Margaret Cohen, they were terraqueous, "composed of earth and water together."[85] Nineteenth-century American women writers "dr[e]w on the oceanic world . . . from the space of the continental and domestic," as Melissa Gniadek shows in *Oceans at Home*. As I will show, they also drew (that is, shaped the contours of) the oceanic world from domestic spaces. Landed narratives circumscribed the political rights or physical movements of narrated pirates and, with it, the treatment of historical groups in oceanic space. These stories of women's victories over pirates gave cultural cachet to antebellum legal definitions. The pirates that resulted were neither wholly domestic nor strictly foreign. They floated among these categories to reveal antebellum legal culture's continued reliance on foreign relations to legalize domestic policies.[86] Engaging landed narratives with an oceanic imaginary deepens existing pools of scholarship. Transoceanic studies is a material investment in historical sailors; a theoretical engagement with oceanic experiences of time, space, and other phenomena; and a non-nationalistic approach to literary history. Such work has deep crosscurrents with Atlantic history, transpacific and Indian Ocean studies, archipelagic studies, blue humanities, and other sea-based approaches to culture.[87] One may cast domestic fiction deep into this oceanic world. We must parlay with oceanic pirates found in landed texts. Eventually, a land-water binary fails to hold.

PIRACY, SYMPATHY, AND DOMESTIC PIRATE FICTION

As members of legal culture, antebellum American women writers substantiated Margaret Fuller's call in *Woman in the Nineteenth Century* (1845): "Let them be sea-captains, if you will!"[88] Antebellum women's political power extended seaward. They beckoned historical sailors to landed family and away from piracy via maritime charity and sea-based sentimental narrations.[89] Catharine Maria Sedgwick, Maria Susanna Cummins, and Harriet Beecher Stowe also captained the most widely read genre in antebellum legal culture around piracy: sentimental and domestic fiction. The "cultural work" of these related genres—a term popularized by Jane Tompkins in 1985—derives from popular women writers' "attempts to redefine the social order." Writers of domestic pirate fiction redefined a legal order whose own sentimental forms established piracy as a crime against feeling. The literary "burst of women's production and readers' consumption" that followed, literary historian Melissa Homestead adds, also spurred the development of international copyright law. Global piracy cases over popular fiction reinforced foreign relations and defined domestic property rights.[90] A similarly expansive competition often occurred across these landed fictions. Oceanic pirates boarded narratives of domestic interiority. Placing these maritime rovers in American homes, land-based writers staged who should receive the domestic spoils of oceanic cultures and economies. Competing claimants included both enslavers and the enslaved. The legal theory of piracy that resulted from politically diverse narratives—borne from the shared assumption that political status may be justified by appeals to familial fellow feeling—were key to popular domestic writers' global purchase. The pirate's ambivalent presence in many popular and understudied domestic fictions reveals enduring fissures in antebellum law.

Antebellum legal culture's most visible pirates—the corsair, the Black mutineer, the transcolonial revolutionary—remained central to narratives of landed women's social circles. Likewise, the strange plot contrivances, tortured moral logics, and emotional appeals to family life found in antebellum legal writing about piracy found its closest kin in sentimental pirate fictions with a landed focus. In response, I have chosen to privilege what I term *domestic pirate fiction*, or sentimental works whose oceanic pirates exist alongside comprehensive scenes of landed interior life. Domestic pirate fiction performed unique cultural work, its marginality in the vast canon of antebellum pirate literature notwithstanding. Antebellum legal culture was undoubtedly influenced by figures such as the thrilling marauders in *The Pirate's Own Book: Authentic Narratives of the Most Celebrated Sea Robbers* (1837); the gender-bending fictional pirates such as those in *Fanny Campbell, the Female Pirate Captain* (1844); and the popular Barbary captives found in narratives such as Matthew Carey's *A Short*

Account of Algiers (1794), Susanna Rowson's play *Slaves in Algiers, or, A Struggle for Freedom* (1794), and William Ray's *Horrors of Slavery, or, The American Tars in Tripoli* (1808). James Fenimore Cooper's *The Red Rover* (1827) and other semi-abolitionist pirate novels of patriotic fellow feeling responded to perceived crimes against feeling. Oceanic Black mutineers variably called pirates may be found in John Howison's "The Florida Pirate" (1821), Frederick Douglass's *The Heroic Slave* (1852), and Herman Melville's *Benito Cereno* (1855), as I will briefly show. Recent scholarship on these and other pirates is rich.[91] Even so, domestic pirate fictions are less legible to maritime scholars than are more clearly maritime (although less globally popular) antebellum works. As reception studies scholar James L. Machor notes, the current "relative ranking" of Catharine Sedgwick and Herman Melville is "nearly the exact inverse" of their antebellum statures.[92] *Crimes Against Feeling* restores this relative historical standing in order to better recount antebellum legal culture's defining theory of piracy.

Counterintuitively, domestic fiction's limited spatial scope primed the genre's transoceanic purchase. The narrative challenges agitated by pirates engaged legal debates that were also predicated on familial attachments. Other national literary traditions have equally diverse pirate narratives and legal cultures.[93] However, domestic pirate fiction—and, with it, the broader category of sentimental fiction—is a uniquely American node in a global system. After all, the "explosion in transoceanic global commerce in the age of revolutions," recounted by Michelle Burnham, primed antebellum domestic literature's global investments. Like the literary forms that Maria Windell considers in *Transamerican Sentimentalism*, domestic pirate fiction "actively engage[d] anxieties about the nation's permeable boundaries and its expanding imperial presence."[94] Stories of individual homes influenced a legal culture beyond fiction's interior walls. Drawing from Lora Romero, then, we may consider antebellum domestic fictions as part of a "micropolitical framework" within a broader ocean politics. These narratives were the product of "local formations," or the specific historical and social conditions of fictionalized antebellum homes. The worlds that these women (and some men) crafted derived from more than "essential and ineluctable political tendency."[95] Domestic writers recounted interior family lives that were undeniably linked to ocean-based wealth and culture. The pirate's presence reflected authors' attempts to recognize and reconcile their role in a domestic nation defined by deeply contested ocean politics. In conversation with other legal figures with whom they often shared homes, antebellum women writers defined piracy and punished crimes against feeling.

Pirates stand outside our heroine's door. Will she let them in? She will because she must secure a domestic space subsidized by oceanic spoils. Indeed, domestic pirate fictions often had shared plots, which speaks to their repeatability as a cultural and legal precedence. A young woman, almost always coded as white but tied to a racially diverse transcolonial legacy, is alone in the world. She is fundamentally good but has underdeveloped social graces due to tenuous or nonexistent family attachments. Her charming nature attracts a paternal figure, a benefactor, a lover, or some combination of the three. Her growing moral sense is tested but proves to be steadfast. The heroine is rewarded with both familial attachments and social status. Notably, her inheritance often has ties to piracy. The same ocean that built family wealth, often of colonial enslavers, carries alternative claimants. These include liberal-minded northerners with bad gender politics, foreign agents with allegiance to competing sovereigns, enslavement apologists, fervent abolitionists, and disenfranchised people attempting to regain their rights by any means necessary. In sum, such fictions treat the ocean not merely as a threat to domesticity but as a complicated zone for modeling domestic virtue in oceanic space. Who deserves the spoils of an oceanic economy? The abolitionist? The enslaver? The formerly enslaved? No one answer is inherent in the genre. Most often, however, the pirate antagonizes a hoped-for arrangement that privileges white families. These writers widely presented white middle-class women's economic and moral superiority as a model for national virtue. In the process, they also decided whose domestic incorporation would be a threat to family life. In many cases, such threats were forces of global abolition and transoceanic enslavement that were often embodied by the same pirate.[96]

Domestic pirate fiction's political potential was multivalent. Even so, its most common outcome aligned with an antebellum legal culture that privileged imagined domestic stability in the face of global tumult. The pirate of domestic fiction was a response to inescapable oceanic entanglements whom privileged antebellum figures alternately described and disavowed. The domestic heroine's fear of disenfranchisement is understandable, particularly given her vulnerability in patriarchal society. Her control of home, money, and body is tenuous. Heroines' varied methods of success against piracy—typically by marshaling their own oceanic resources and rejecting pirates' seductive promises of even greater oceanic power—are therefore a testament to antebellum women's political maneuvering. At the same time, these successes often rely on the heroines' ability to secure their own legal claims beyond all other considerations.

Universal abolition was one such consideration. Legalized enslavement was another, and reparations were yet another still. Authors of domestic pirate fiction did not shy away from this fact. Heroines' domestic resources typically include ambivalent familial investments in global bondage. This lineage is historically accurate and deeply symbolic. The pirate of any one text may be allied with other global figures that challenge white women's domestic stability. In keeping with domestic fiction's generic convention, only the heroine can create families and establish the domestic nation. For readers, then, to feel for the heroine (or against the pirate) was to enact a proper relation to the state first defined by Thomas Jefferson. In this way, fiction modeled the tenuous stability and tortured morality of an antebellum legal regime that treated enslavement as piratical at sea and sanctioned on land.

Haiti's deep impact on antebellum ocean politics informed pirates' multivalent character in antebellum legal culture. In colonial San Domingue (1697–1803), what began as a large-scale revolt against French rule concluded with the hemisphere's first free Black republic. Haiti's revolution (1789–1804) fundamentally challenged the white supremacist legacy of its American revolutionary counterpart (1775–83). According to Elizabeth Maddock Dillon and Michael Drexler, "compelling similarities" in these revolutions include their basis in rich colonial economies, their separation from "metropolitan seats of power," and their political investment in forms of representative citizenship beyond colonial rule.[97] In turn, antebellum culture confronted the potential disruption of white hegemony at home and across the hemisphere.[98] The fictions I discuss in this book are largely absent from the "transatlantic print culture of the Haitian revolution" recounted by scholars such as Marlene L. Daut.[99] The omission is logical. Popular texts such as Leonora Sansay's epistolary novel *Secret History, or, The Horrors of St. Domingo* (1808) securely located Haitian women in global debates on Black citizenship. Fictions such as the anonymously published historical novel *Zelica, the Creole* (1820) more directly staged fears that Haitian sovereignty's "potentially incendiary revolutionary legacies" might ripple across enslaving nations.[100] Haiti largely remained at a geographic and narrative remove in the fictions I discuss. Yet it loomed large. Its role as an inducement for policies of enslavement and abolition was often embodied in a transcolonial pirate with Haitian ties. Domestic pirate fiction restaged legal and moral inconsistencies towards Haiti in antebellum legal culture. Above all, the pirate embodied an antebellum fear of "transcolonial collaboration" outlined by Sara E. Johnson. Pirates and other oceanic figures with deep ties to the Haitian revolution were perceived as unique threats to existing state orders. These diasporic figures' skill at navigating the British, French, and Spanish Americas allegedly portended white supremacy's political collapse. The multilingual abolitionist could, perhaps, form a new family of nations in Haiti's image. But in practice, as Johnson notes, such transcolonial subjects found that "fostering alliances with slave-trading pirates seemed a more expedient choice than becoming antislavery activists."[101] The pirate's varied representation as both transcolonial enslaver and abolitionist in a post-revolutionary Haiti—often in the same narrative—reflects a historical and legal tangle.

In joining pirate fictions with different levels of visibility, I model how to hunt oceanic pirates who sail undetected in land-based literatures. One may find oceanic flows in landed fictions. Timeworn and new domestic texts merge into a terraqueous whole. The fictions I discuss can be roughly consigned into two ships of domestic pirate fiction. The first includes less heralded works by established domestic fiction writers that expressly centralize pirates. The second includes canonical works that do not fully align with domestic fiction's generic conventions or that contain pirates on the fringes. In each, feelings against piracy are given legal power. Strategic summaries help chart the course ahead and model recoveries yet to be made. In Sedgwick's *Hope Leslie* (1827), a white woman in colonial New England has her British imperial inheritance threatened by pirates who are seeking to establish a transcolonial Haiti. In Sedgwick's *Clarence* (1830), a white woman in 1820s New York almost has her stake in an uncle's Caribbean plantation stolen by a pirate with ties to Haiti, Cuba, and New York. In Stowe's *Uncle Tom's Cabin* (1852), a young white girl in the 1850s American South attempts to save her enslaved friend from a West Indian pirate but only succeeds in sailing a different family to Liberia. In Cummins's *The Lamplighter* (1854), a white woman in late 1840s Boston funds piratical filibustering in Cuba, enslavement in Rio de Janeiro, and potential colonization in Africa via her posted global letters. In Octavia Walton LeVert's *Souvenirs of Travel* (1857), a white southern woman in 1850s Cuba knowingly supports filibustering and enslavement via her own sentimental letters. In Cummins's *Haunted Hearts* (1864), a white woman in 1810s New Jersey is almost seduced by an enslaving White-British-Caribbean-African-Ottoman pirate but recovers with the help of a plantation-owning benefactor in South America. Each text presents a legal theory of piracy that is conversant with those of policymakers, judges, and other legal thinkers. The sentimental family dramas that powered antebellum piracy law are given new life. Most often, these legal and literary dramas present white women's moral virtue as an antidote to piratical unruliness with ties to both enslavement and Black sovereignty. However, two notable domestic pirate fictions reject such appeasements. In Michel Maxwell Philip's *Emmanuel Appadocca* (1854), a mixed-race abolitionist pirate burns his father's plantation to avenge abandoned white women and combat familial separation under enslavement. And in Stowe's *Dred* (1856), a piracy-allied American judge is juxtaposed with a sanctified Black maroon's oceanic power against the enslaving nation. In both works, albeit to different degrees, reclaimed sympathy for the abolitionist, if not the pirate, powers legal theories of full Black citizenship, global abolition, and total reparations.

The sentimental pirate fictions I consider in this book are mirrored in the period's more sensational pirate literature. Future scholars may recount the legal theories of piracy in popular works such as J. H. Ingraham's *Lafitte: The Pirate of the Gulf* (1836) and *The Pirate Chief, or, The Cutter of the Ocean* (1845) or in Harry Hazel's *Harry Tempest, or, The Pirate's Protégé* (1853). Such literature, Shelley Streeby writes, "emphasizes thrills, shock, and horror more than virtuous and socially redemptive feelings."[102] Indeed, the works I discuss do not dwell on pirates' power of sensation but on their absence of sympathy. These pirates neither titillate readers nor violate heroines. Their ravages occur wholly offscreen as the unspoken alternative to a main sentimental plot. This generic distinction undergirds a political one. Sentimental fiction, though widely read, had less representational variety than sensational literature defined by working class, multiracial, and multiethnic protagonists. The assumed, if not real, reader of domestic fiction was a privileged, typically white, non-working-class national subject with threatened but ultimately intact ownership of a stable domestic space. The distinction between sympathy and sensation, however, was not predicated on geographic reach but on narrative form and political ideology. Sentimental and sensational pirate twins embodied the prospect of political tumult throughout the Americas. Sensational pirate fiction provided a mechanism to deconstruct antebellum legal culture's claimed morality by cultivating guilty pleasure around violence by and against pirates. Domestic fiction mostly concealed a pirate's explicitly violent potential to foreground legal stability and state power. In other words, a pirate of sensation's crimes against feeling represented a pirate of sympathy's unspoken potential. Thus, sensational pirate fictions, though unmistakably potent in antebellum legal culture, drift in this book's margins.

Domestic pirate fiction allows one to better appreciate sympathy's power in antebellum legal culture. Literature informed people's affective relations to piracy law, including those who were tasked with writing it. Narratives of familial attachment against piracy compelled readers to feel likewise, thereby reproducing legal logics. Pirates stole. Sympathy robbed. This robbery was often fictional, but it still affected historical subjects. Sentimental fiction, as Michelle Burnham quips, "performs a kind of emotional robbery." The feelings of fictional subjects become our feelings via the act of sentimental reading. The imagined kin on the rack remain a felt-for object under the gaze of a dominant sympathetic subject. Burnham concedes that this act is not strictly robbery because "stolen feelings have no real owner" and "fictional characters have no referential corporeality in the real world."[103] It is a cardinal sin of literary studies to treat fictional characters as real. Even so, the pirate shows how fictional characters without real-world bodies nonetheless informed varied groups' legal status. Fictional pirates had a deferred corporeality whose "robbery" echoed legal mechanisms. Denying someone's natural moral capacity justified the removal of political rights, including one's right to freedom and life. Alleged pirates' legal rights rested on their place in a sentimental thought experiment. Pirates often manned the proverbial torture rack against members of the national family. Even so, narratives that placed the pirate on a state-operated torture rack directly flipped these terms. Readers felt for the pirate, recognized their similar moral passions, and, contrary to law, advocated for the pirate's empowerment. In each case, the antebellum reading subject was presumed to feel toward narrative objects beset by violence. This intimate debate, found in pirate fiction and policy, promoted fellow feeling as a moral sentiment, a narrative apparatus, and a legal requirement.

PIRACY, SYMPATHY, AND ANTEBELLUM LEGAL CULTURE

Jefferson's antebellum reminiscences affirm that national family strife existed well beyond 1776. Writing in 1818, he recalled how he had been forced to remove "offensive expressions" from his original draft of the Declaration. About one-quarter of Jefferson's text had been altered, he noted, including the "severe strictures on the conduct of the British king in negotiating our repeated repeals of the law which permitted the importation of slaves." While the king's "piratical warfare" was present in the first draft, it disappeared from the ratified prose.

The king's oceanic incursions did persist—he "excited domestic Insurrections among us," "plundered our sea," and "constrained our fellow Citizens taken Captive on the high Seas." In keeping with a legal appeal to crimes against feeling, the "excited" king had "plundered" a "domestic" family union "among us." Yet he was no longer declared a piratical abolitionist or an enslaving pirate.[104] "I was not insensible to these mutilations," Jefferson later wrote. In his view, they had been violent cuts to a supposedly perfect political and rhetorical body. This body remained sympathetically bound to Jefferson's own ambivalent politics. He blamed their removal on "Southern gentlemen, whose reflections were not yet matured to the full abhorrence of that traffic." Abolitionist feelings of abhorrence did not have legal force: political appeasement could not prevent ongoing emotional divides about enslavement. Even so, Jefferson called such changes "depredations" to "the instrument," or acts of immoral if not outright piratical plunder against his ideal ship of state.[105] To declare enslavers pirates would, Jefferson believed, precipitate an irrevocable national divorce. One could not call kin a pirate without severing familial tales.

Jefferson made no mention in 1818 of his ongoing status as an enslaving patriarch, a self-serving omission that aligned with the illegal deep-sea trade's looming status as piracy. Still, even as John Adams criticized Jefferson's allegiance to enslavement, his own antebellum memories of the Declaration confirm the tendency toward appeasement that would define the period. In 1822, Adams wrote that he had found Jefferson's charges against the king "too personal" and "too passionate." But he agreed that decrying the king's actions on both land and water was necessary to assert American sovereignty. Piracy retained a rhetorical function. In March 1776, for example, Adams himself had pointed out England's "piratical Act, or plundering Act, or Act of Independency" when lambasting the Prohibitory Act of 1775, which had blockaded colonial ports, removed Crown protection on land and sea, and called for Loyalist sailors to seize goods "being first adjudged as lawful prize."[106] Despite this legal break, he felt in general that challenging the king's personal moral capacity would prevent the development of measured foreign relations. Even so, he celebrated abolitionist feelings that would cause clear familial discord. Writing to Timothy Pickering, his former secretary of state, Adams said, "I was delighted with [the Declaration's] high tone, and the flights of Oratory with which it abounded, especially that concerning Negro Slavery, which though I knew his Southern Bretheren would never suffer to pass in Congress, I certainly never would oppose." The problem, Adams implied with some bitterness, was that we can't choose our family. Jefferson's "Southern Bretheren" would not abide abolition, and thus naming King George a pirate would not align with familial union with either the former king or the new nation.[107] The national union's legal basis in enslavement remained intact, as did domestic fracture. The political appetite for civil war, notes Michael E. Woods, resulted in large part from "powerful feelings of sectional solidarity" that increased throughout the period.[108] Pirates populated sentimental legal dramas that began and ended with civil war.

Each chapter in *Crimes Against Feeling* concerns an antebellum legal culture around piracy that was powered by political policymakers, legal thinkers, and popular writers. Chapter 1 charts an early national jurisprudence of appeasement that culminated in the Piracy Act of 1820, which criminalized deep-sea enslavement as piracy even as it sheltered the landed trade. Chapter 2 concerns moral resentment's legal standing in the decades of appeasement that followed the Piracy Act, as debates persisted on whether piracy laws should follow enslavers' or abolitionists' resentments toward ongoing political compromise. Chapter 3 tracks a culture of the transoceanic post in the late 1840s and early 1850s that shaped ongoing legal debates over piratical enslavement, imperial filibustering, and African colonization. Chapter 4 foregrounds the secessionist legal culture that inaugurated Confederate sovereignty via maritime policy and tested uneasy federal commitments to abolition and Black citizenship. Chapter 5 focuses on wartime and postbellum attempts to preserve benevolent white supremacy and federal union as antidotes to secessionist piracy. Finally, the epilogue introduces Walt Whitman's 1869 ode to the Suez Canal to briefly consider antebellum legal culture's legacy in the present day. Ongoing crimes against feeling confirm that white supremacy's legal appeasement—rather than piratical unruliness—has delayed a more just politics. My hope is that *Crimes Against Feeling* can help us not only recall the convoluted legal culture we have inherited but also reveal an alternative we may yet create. There is still time to feel otherwise. Thomas Jefferson is not our only forebearer. Another world is possible.

CHAPTER ONE

APPEASEMENT

Judge Joseph Story, Catharine Maria Sedgwick, and the Piracy Act (1820)

On May 21, 1824, President James Monroe delivered a "Special Message" to Congress regarding "the ratification of the convention lately concluded with the British Government for the suppression of the slave trade by making it piratical." Abolition's success at sea could invigorate its global spread. Earlier that spring, on March 13, a tentative abolitionist agreement had been reached in London between American and British representatives. At heart, the accord legalized the nations' mutual jurisdiction over "pirates engaged in the African slave trade." The U.S. government had already deemed deep-sea enslavement piracy on May 15, 1820, as Monroe reminded Congress in his message; and as early as February 1823, the House of Representatives had asked the president to undergo global treaty negotiations "for the effectual abolition of the African slave trade and its ultimate denunciation as piracy under the law of nations, by the consent of the civilized world."[1] The pending abolitionist treaty should be ratified, Monroe now instructed the Senate, because it would allow domestic sentiment to extend globally and restore foreign relations weakened by the War of 1812. That year, in an initial declaration of war against England, President James Madison had called upon citizens to "value the precious heritage derived from the virtue and valor of their fathers; as they feel the wrongs which have been forced on them." Postwar foreign relations had been predicated on international fellow feeling and, perhaps, global abolition, in keeping with the 1814 Treaty of Peace and Amity Between the United States and Great Britain. Also known as the Treaty of Ghent, it celebrated "terminating the war which has unhappily subsisted" between the two countries. The treaty encouraged "perfect reciprocity" and "firm and universal peace" between individual subjects, their respective nations, and the nations themselves. As part of this familial union, its signatories asserted a shared dedication to the "entire abolition" of a global system of slavery "irreconcilable with the principles of humanity and Justice."[2]

The 1824 agreement would cement mutual abolition under this moral and legal rubric. Though only Congress could legally ratify the accord, Monroe claimed a president's paternal role in "maintaining the political relations between the United States and other nations."[3] Yet as he noted, "some difficulty exists with the Senate" regarding ratification. The president had first delivered the accord to the Senate on April 30, with no success. The difficulty, it seemed, resulted from hesitancy to declare enslavement piracy or to cede sovereign power at sea. As Monroe admitted, England had made abolitionist treaties with other European powers "without constituting the crime as piracy."[4] This absence had practical and symbolic consequences. A law of nations would establish universal jurisdiction, thereby making U.S. ships liable to search by foreign agents in times of peace. In other words, a shared sentiment against piracy would give foreign nations unique legal powers over American citizens. To allow European vessels to board American ships in time of peace "for an offense not piratical," Monroe stated, would "be repugnant to the feelings of the nation and of dangerous tendency." Moreover, the prospect of U.S. vessels' trial in foreign courts went against constitutional sovereignty and related powers to define and punish piracy. Such political roadblocks would be overcome, Monroe countered, if "nations rest on the same ground." Only a universal rejection of enslavement as piratical—and, with it, shared maritime jurisdiction—would make enforcement mutual. The pirate floated at the center of international relations on both land and water. As Monroe asserted, the question of piracy abutted "sundry other negotiations intimately connected with the welfare and even the peace of our Union." These included territorial disputes, rights of navigation in terrestrial and oceanic waterways, maritime law in times of war, and the international recognition of South American colonial revolutions against Spain. A law of nations on piracy could strengthen the "the political relations between the United States and other nations" in a global familial union. However, the Senate's proslavery contingent and their appeasers were not convinced. On May 22, 1824, one day after Monroe's pleading address, the Senate effectively nullified the treaty's main objectives by ratifying a version without articles on enslavement. Deep-sea enslavement's piratical character, affirmed in the 1820 domestic statute and in various foreign laws, would not be a global sentiment.[5]

Thomas Jefferson invoked piratical crimes against feeling in the Declaration of Independence to make American sovereignty sympathetic to a global legal culture. President Monroe's speech reveals that culture's continued fluidity. To justify universal abolition, he presented a singular enslaving pirate whose removal was key to fellow feeling's global extension. The failure to ratify the British treaty and install universal jurisdiction spoke to more complex political realities. Enslavement remained legal in the United States and throughout the Americas. Likewise, visions of shared seas faced the reality of ongoing maritime competition. Monroe's speech reflected the pirate's variable character in the period. As he knew, alleged pirates could be enslavers who had stolen Africans and brought them to the Americas. Pirates could be those same Africans violently rebelling against their oceanic captors. Pirates could also be any number of transcolonial forces fighting in Haiti and throughout the Americas. Indeed, Monroe's 1824 speech occurred just as piracy had reached its antebellum peak. This peak, like piracy's earlier golden age, was the product of global political shifts. The end of the War of 1812 and the Napoleonic Wars had, like prior early modern world wars, left a glut of unemployed sailors accustomed to privateering in the Americas. Ongoing revolutions in the Americas against Spanish and Portuguese colonial power increased the number of sovereign collectivities willing to provide commissions, or letters of marque, to such sailors. Treaty agreements between the United States and Spain, Great Britain, and other European powers spun complex legal webs around privateering, piracy, smuggling, and other forms of maritime movement. The early national Atlantic remained, as maritime historian Tyson Reeder concludes, a "composite of legal strictures and illicit trade practices."[6] Questions of domestic jurisdiction and global legality were most fraught around the issue of enslavement as piracy. As legal historian Jenny Martinez affirms, "a number of countries had agreed to declare to slave trade as a form of piracy in the hopes of making slave traders, like pirates, *hostis humani generis*, or enemies of mankind, subject to capture and trial in the courts of any nation."[7] A legally enshrined antagonism to enslavement must be universal. Only then would all nations have shared jurisdiction. But universal accord would not be reached in the antebellum era.

Monroe's speech and supplemental materials entered a print culture dense with stated or spectral pirates. The speech was printed under the heading "The

Slave Trade" in a dedicated issue of the widely circulated *Niles Weekly Register*, published in Baltimore as the nation's first weekly news magazine. Its editor, Hezekiah Niles, commented, "We shall, at least, make sufficient sections from the communications before us to afford a complete view of the matter."[8] The "matter" remained whether enslavement's legal status as piracy would spread.

Related domestic court cases, legal texts, and domestic fictions were an inflection point in antebellum legal culture. As the failed 1824 accord confirms, deep-sea abolitionism neither reached domestic shores nor stretched to global waters. Notably, the Piracy Act of 1820 defined enslavement as piracy only if wholly occurring in the deep sea. Federal courts relied on this moral and geographic split to buttress a sentimental jurisprudence of appeasement. Judges appealed to a facile domestic stability predicated on limited abolition amid unfeeling enslavement. The policies that resulted were born from the period's domestic legal cases and its dominant domestic fictions. Such cases addressed questions of maritime jurisdiction, national sovereignty, and oceanic abolition that defined international law. The legal arguments that followed assessed enslaving piracy under both a domestic and a global rubric. Each side presented its opinion as an extension of proper feeling. On the one hand, those who prosecuted alleged pirates presented enslavers' deviation from U.S. piracy law. The defendants' foreign status was deemed a moot point because American courts served a family of nations. On the other hand, those who defended alleged pirates noted the lack of universal sentiment under a law of nations. Others outright defended enslavement as an extension of domestic sovereignty and moral feeling. For some, such legal niceties melted away in a system of universal abolition. Enslavement was a piratical crime against feeling, no matter its location. Landed enslavement sprang from a piratical middle passage from Africa to the Americas. Despite judicial recognition of these facts, courts dismissed global abolition's legal validity. Interest in an imagined political equilibrium led oceanic enslavement to be defined as piracy yet rarely punished as such.

This sentimental jurisprudence of appeasement's literary representations—and its political breaking points—are best introduced via the literary career of Catharine Maria Sedgwick (1789–1867). Born into a family of lawyers, jurists, and politicians, Sedgwick was its most celebrated member. She was one of two women included in the 1834 volume of *The National Portrait Gallery of Distinguished Americans*, alongside Martha Washington. "We know scarcely any writer, certainly not any American writer," the editor noted, "who has read with a quicker and more discerning eye, with a better taste, or with a purer devotion, than Miss Sedgwick." He championed "that power, which speaks from heart to heart" in her published work, defined by "the kindly sympathies they elicit, or the sense of justice which they satisfy." Sedgwick joined Washington Irving, James Fenimore Cooper, and Charles Brockden Brown as one of few fiction writers to appear in the four-volume "appeal to national honor." Other Americans featured in the publication included presidents such as John Quincy Adams and Thomas Jefferson as well as legal leaders like the Supreme Court justices Joseph Story and John Marshall. Each of these figures emphasized the young nation's claim to a national moral and legal sense.[9]

Sedgwick was arguably the collection's most globally popular literary figure. And like the publication's other fiction writers, she was an active legal theorist with parables of piratical crimes against feeling. Her familial narratives around piracy were uniquely American. For example, in "Modern Chivalry" (1826), a story published in seven magazines, newspapers, and collections before 1835, she championed American revolutionary feeling against charges of piracy. In it, a virtuous sailor serving in the American Revolution recovers an English woman who falsely "believe[s] that she ha[s] fallen into the hands of pirates." According to the narrator, American sailors are key to the woman's and the nation's salvation because the revolution has "made the common interest a matter of feeling—a family affair to each individual."[10] Sedgwick continued to judge alleged piratical crimes against feeling against this revolutionary standard.

In keeping with her nationalism, Sedgwick believed that American pirate fiction was morally superior to its foreign counterparts. Yet the foreign versions entertained her: she admitted that she "read the Pirate with delight," calling Sir Walter Scott's new pirate romance "highly poetical" in an 1822 letter. Still, such depictions did not serve American women's political needs. A minor scene in her 1830 pirate novel *Clarence*, for example, mocks the anti-American literary tastes of "a knot of ladies, bold aspirants to the reputation of fine women." The ladies discuss Lord Byron's poem *The Corsair* (1814) as well as an unnamed "latest novel" that, in a metatextual twist, stands in for *Clarence* itself. One responds, "Oh, I doat on it—was there ever such a sweet creature as Conrad?" The Byronic hero and the corsair class had seduced this "sapient young lady." Another woman agrees, stating, "I never read American novels, there's no high life in them."[11] These minor figures embody untoward associations with pirates and mistaken allegiances with British literary models. Rejecting the romantic corsair—and by extension accepting Sedgwick's domestic pirate fictions—will lead American women to virtue. Nonetheless, even as Sedgwick's characters confirm American women's power as agents of proper foreign relations, they reveal her ambivalent appeasement for systems of enslavement.

Monroe's appeal to global feeling notwithstanding, domestic discord and international competition shaped each of the alleged pirates I will consider in this chapter. I begin by analyzing legal debates over national jurisdiction and foreign relations that culminated in the Piracy Act of 1820. I next consider two piracy cases in which Supreme Court justices asserted that foreign relations and a weak law of nations legally overrode piracy's status as an offense against moral feeling. I then turn to Catharine Maria Sedgwick as this legal culture's most complex literary representative. Like the antebellum courts, Sedgwick's legal thinking was defined by an uneasy retreat from abolition. The heirs to enslaving pirates may be legally protected if they served an imagined political stability. An enslaving nation may retain its unjust claim to moral feeling and political union. Abolitionist feeling rose and fell. Enslavement thrived.

"EBBS AND FLOWS": LEGAL CULTURE AND THE PIRACY ACT OF 1820

In the years between Jefferson's Declaration and Monroe's speech, constitutional restrictions had protected the deep-sea trade and, in a grotesque family legacy, fostered the growth of a domestic enslaved population. As intended, later deep-sea abolition did not wash away the rooted institution of slavery. The Act Prohibiting Importation of Slaves (1807) partially ended deep-sea importation, although it by no means ended maritime enslavement.[12] Gradual abolitionists and high-country plantation enslavers, separate yet often intersecting groups, favored such laws. Prohibiting importation "will in some measure stop the increase of this great political and moral evil," wrote Jefferson in *Notes on the State of Virginia* (1785), "while the minds of our citizens may be ripening for a complete emancipation of the human nature." In his view, the ethical "emancipation" of white citizen-subjects, or their recognition of enslavement as contrary to "human nature," needed to precede Black emancipation. A diminished "increase" made possible by gradual deep-sea abolition also aligned with the Virginia planter's motivation to sell an "increase" of his landed human stock to deep-South plantations with higher mortality rates. Jefferson outlined this calculus in a January 1819 private letter to the Kentucky enslaver and politician Joel

Yancy. "It is not their labor," Jefferson wrote of enslaved Black women's value, "but their increase which is the first consideration."[13] Imagined political expedience and economic necessity, not moral resolution, defined his proslavery appeasements: for Jefferson's benefit, women's bound kin could be sold down the coast and worked to death in lowland swamps whose brackish water testified to the domestic trade's dubious legal distinction from deep-sea piracy. The founder was less a cartoonish pirate villain and more a deeply compromised politician, as were nearly all of his contemporaries.

Shaped by this complicated mix of abolition and appeasement, the Piracy Act of 1820 created a new class of pirate: an enslaver "where the sea ebbs and flows." The act was among a series that enhanced the 1807 importation ban. An 1818 act, legal scholar Paul Finkelman notes, had "shifted the burden of proof from prosecution to the defendant" when charged with illegal importation. A more comprehensive 1819 act legalized "armed vessels" to patrol African and American coasts, dictated that captured Africans could not be sold in the United States but must be returned to their country of origin, and created a bounty system for sailors who captured enslaving pirates. The 1820 act added piracy as a specific charge but, like the prior statutes, did nothing to prohibit the domestic landed trade.[14] A divide between land and sea created strange legal bedfellows. To enslave a Black person on land was to engage a domestic state's legal trade. To steal a Black person at sea was illegal piracy against that same state. Specifically, the act stated that a select group that "seize[s] any negro or mulatto, not held to service or labour by the laws of either of the states or territories of the United States, with intent to make such negro or mulatto a slave . . . shall be adjudged a pirate; and, on conviction thereof . . . shall suffer death." This political ebb and flow—abolition at sea, enslavement "by the laws of . . . the United States" on land—relied on the ocean's unique power in legal culture. Enslaving pirates, like all pirates, were defined by their incompatibility with the state or its families. This separation meant they could be killed without remorse. Likewise, enslaving piracy's legal definition aligned domestic jurisdiction with a sailors' relative claim to state attachment.[15] But as I will show, the Piracy Act of 1820 only partially answered pervasive questions of ocean politics. When did piracy laws made on land extend to the ocean? In a law of nations, who defined piracy? And who punished it? When was America the patriarch in a family of nations? Federalist legal thinking did not map onto a clear abolitionist or proslavery binary. Instead, they reflected ongoing attempts to legally contain global abolition and mitigate its imagined ripple effects on domestic and foreign relations. The result was a culture of appeasement under the guise of natural virtue and legal dispassion.

Despite a language of universality, the 1820 statute relied on a land-sea binary. The state's abolitionist feeling at sea did not fully reach land. Whether an act of enslavement was piracy depended on geographic, national, and economic connection to landed states. Enslavement, like other crimes of robbery, was considered piracy only when it occurred in "the high seas, or in any open roadstead, or in any haven, basin, or bay, or in any river where the sea ebbs and flows." The "high seas"—that is, the deep sea without any single sovereign claimant—could be imagined as a morally distinct space from domestic shores. Even so, national legal power could wash over watery spaces with distinct domestic ties. The land-adjacent "roadstead"—a sheltered body of brackish water where ships could easily lie at anchor—retained an oceanic character. An argument could be made that "the sea ebbs and flows" in all domestic rivers. Domestic enslavement likewise flowed from an oceanic source. Even so, the act domesticated some global waters and maritime subjects in favor of others. The practical result was that those enslaved on land gained a perverse sentimental bondage. Their domestic attachment was to their enslavers and to an anti-abolitionist federal policy. An enslaved person at sea, on the other hand, was a protected piece of property whose right to state protection trumped the American citizen-pirate. The oceanic enslaved were allegedly redeemed, as the pirate was damned, via the state's projection of domestic power at sea.[16] The Piracy Act of 1820 thus echoed and extended a fracture within domestic law. The Missouri Compromise of 1820 had recently established the landed geographic line (36°30' latitude) that ostensibly separated enslaving states from abolitionist ones. Missouri, though situated above the line, was admitted as slave state to balance the inclusion of Maine as a free state. These nested contradictions on land and water served a tenuous political truce that damned millions to legalized enslavement.

Enslavement deeply informed the era's various maritime cases, each of which tested the landed state's power over oceanic subjects or sovereigns. The early national Supreme Court's centrality in American declarations of sovereignty, or what legal scholar Kevin Arlyck calls the "saltwater story of the courts' role in American state-building," derived from justices' "growing willingness to assert judicial authority over the sea." As G. Edward White notes, piracy cases were "among the most numerous and controversial" heard by the Supreme Court from 1815 to 1823. In some cases, the pirates in question had plundered merchant vessels containing goods of war. In others, alleged pirates cruised against national governments using legally questionable letters of marque. Increasingly, U.S. federal pirate cases related to oceanic enslavement. Such cases, White affirms, hinged on "the association of the law of nations with the law of nature."[17] Jurists often positioned this association as strong, claiming that a moral law of nature flowed into an international legal pool. In practice, natural law's international power ebbed and flowed depending on state needs. American federal courts continually affirmed the state's legal basis in natural moral sentiments. Yet they often invoked the law of nations to provide legal cover against presumed judicial overreach. In piracy cases leading up to the 1820 statute, American federal courts generally followed a shared sentimental logic with varying political applications. Domestic attachments largely determined the landed court's jurisdiction over piracy. American courts largely claimed jurisdiction if an alleged pirate were an American citizen, if an alleged pirate vessel were American-owned, or if the offense were against American citizens. In other words, domestic law retained oceanic power in alleged piracies connected to a national family on land or water. In the case of alleged piracy committed by those with ties to a foreign sovereign, however, domestic law and moral sentiments were rarely given jurisdiction. Doing so would have imperiled foreign relations and, it seems, the institution of slavery. This logic insulated a legal domestic trade and protected foreign relations with other imperial enslaving nations. The products were vexed legal representations of enslavers as pirates who needed to remain legally protected if not morally sanctioned.

Faced with piracy's many legal meanings beyond enslavement, the High Court temporarily claimed jurisdiction over piracy as an oceanic act and crime against feeling only if tied to American domesticity. As the Court asserted for a period, its power over an alleged pirate depended on the mariner's national protection and the attendant moral sanction. Ocean-based violence may be piratical, but legal power to define and punish flowed through a landed state. The Supreme Court in *United States v. Palmer* (1818), for example, declared that "a robbery committed on the high seas" was piracy "punishable by death," even if "such robbery committed on land" would have held lesser penalties. In other words, oceanic robbery crossed a moral and legal threshold that justified the pirate's annihilation. Notably, this rationale did not apply to "a person who is not a citizen of the United States on the high seas on board of a ship belonging exclusively to subjects of a foreign state." Despite piracy's supposed status as a universal offense, then, the court projected its oceanic reach only to American domestic attachments. An alleged pirate's alternative national tie limited American jurisdiction. The accused was instead an errant maritime subject whose alleged piracy must be adjudicated at home. In an apparent limitation of the "define and punish" clause's global power, the Court alleged that "Congress cannot make that piracy which is not piracy by the law of nations." The Court would ultimately deny this absolute link between domestic and international legal culture. The Constitutional Convention had, with some debate, privileged a domestic power to define and punish. As later cases on oceanic enslavement would show, however, the Court limited its own power to define and punish piratical enslavement.

Judicial discretion concerning jurisdiction over alleged piracy was considered politically expedient in the wake of the Haitian Revolution. The prospect of foreign relations with the first free Black republic tested the balance of American legal culture. Haiti's challenge to legally enshrined white supremacy resulted in its opaque legal status as a quasi-pirate nation rather than a fellow sovereign. In *Rose v. Himely* (1808), for example, the Supreme Court refused to consider "brigands, or rebels of St. Domingo" to be legal trading partners with an American vessel whose Haiti-supplied goods had been taken by French privateers. "All the world considered the blacks of St. Domingo as revolted subjects," the Court asserted. Stopping just short of an outright charge of piracy, it invoked an imagined universal sentiment against Haitian armed bandits. To deny an American ship's economic relations with Haiti would protect foreign relations with France. In such cases, an imagined compatibility with American political aims—though couched in the language of national sovereignty or shared familial attachments—dictated whether a revolutionary sovereign would float in American courts. In practice, Haiti was both legally isolated and politically connected. Sovereign Haiti existed in the gap between a politically useful legal theory of piracy and the reality of antebellum foreign relations. Notably, the Court complicated its own view of Haitian "brigands" in the related case of *Hudson v. Guestier* (1808), which affirmed that a vessel had been "seized within the territorial jurisdiction of the government of St. Domingo" but held a ruling on Haitian sovereignty in legal suspension. As Marlene Daut notes, the legal denial of Haitian sovereignty could not prevent "discursive recognition" by American public figures. Social, political, and commercial links to Haiti remained undeniable. Catharine Maria Sedgwick's own legal theories will show how such vital links may be obscured.[18]

Haiti's successful revolution against France shaped other maritime revolutionaries' legal status in the waning Spanish and Portuguese empires. Each forced the question as to how American courts distinguished a revolutionary sovereign from a pirate. Here, too, a language of family obscured a deferral to existing state power. Spain presented ongoing revolutions throughout the Americas as piratical incursions. Likewise, the glut of American sailors receiving commissions from revolutionary governments tested foreign relations and threatened the prospect of transcolonial organization outside of state control. Secretary of State John Quincy Adams called a set of Baltimore-based privateers "rotten to the heart," claiming they had been assisted domestically by "the whole gang of pirates and their abettors." These privateers had given up their moral allegiance to the American state and thus, for Adams, were no better than pirates. He descried the "judicial logic" of decisions that limited American jurisdiction over privateers as "disingenuous, false, and hollow." American pirate law, like American feeling, should extend as far as its power admitted. No revolutionary sovereign, it seemed, should be abetted by America.[19] The Supreme Court was more circumspect. It concluded in *United States v. Palmer* (1818) that "a civil war between a mother country and its colony" could lead "subjects of such mother country" to issue privateering commissions as part of a "distinct government." Familial separation was possible. An alleged pirate could yet claim a new maternity. In such cases, the Court concluded, legal status followed a new political body's sympathetic recognition by the antebellum state. Those who had "thrown off their allegiance to their mother country but ha[d] never been acknowledged by the United States as a sovereign" could ostensibly only be recognized as pirates. As was the case in the American Revolution, foreign relations differentiated motherless pirates from newly birthed states in a family of nations. In such cases, the antebellum state retained its power to define and punish an entire revolution as piracy. All the while, Haitian sovereignty remained a legal liability and a practical reality.[20]

The political need for an ebbing law of piracy developed in cases in which an alleged pirate's status rippled across foreign relations. Backed by the Constitution, the Supreme Court defined a pirate according to a universal antagonism to the state rather than as a particular political project. "There is a peculiar fitness in giving the power to define as well as to punish," wrote associate justice Joseph Story in *United States v. Smith* (1820). Congress's constitutional power "to define and punish piracy" had made narrative power key to government stability. For Story, such powers had a "peculiar fitness" because they allowed the state to adjudicate maritime figures whose crimes ran counter to overlapping, if not universal, laws. In the process, Story bolstered state power. *Smith* related to a convicted pirate, Thomas Smith, who had mutinied on ships that carried letters of marque from revolutionary governments in Latin America. In an appeal to overturn a Virginia court's judgment, the defense sought to solidify piracy's rhetorical fluidity. Smith had allegedly performed "plunder and robbery," forcibly taking several privateering vessels commissioned by Spanish colonies at war with their mother country. But even if he had committed such offenses "on the high seas," which his American attorney, Daniel Webster, would not admit, failures to define piracy prevented federal powers from punishing him. "Congress should define [piracy], in terms," Webster asserted, "before it proceeded to exercise the power of punishing the offence." In other words, "to define piracy" was less a universal constitutional power than a binding mandate. Instead of providing an "intelligible explanation of the nature of the offence in the act itself," Webster argued, the judiciary had provided its own circular appeal to "the law of nations." He countered: "To refer to the law of nations for a definition of the crime, is not a definition." The pirate was not a tropic character to whom a defendant could be sympathetically attached, Webster implied. Piracy was a legal act that must be tested against clear legal statutes. Thus, legal theories centered on the pirate's lack of sympathy—defined solely by antipathy to domestic states and familial virtues—could be seen as invalid. Webster denied the legal and narrative leeway required to make piracy a crime against feeling. Justice Story affirmed it. In his view, to promote "too narrow a view of the language of the Constitution," as Webster did, was to unduly limit the state's power. If Story promoted anything like a definition of piracy, it was as "an offence against the universal law of society, a pirate being deemed an enemy of the human race." To further align a power of definition to a "universal law of society" was to presume a global correspondence in moral feeling. Defining the pirate was not only a political necessity, Story seemed to say. It was a legally valid solution to the problem of piracy's shifting political meaning.[21] The sovereignty of revolutionary governments in the former Spanish empire would eventually be recognized, only later to be attacked in the 1840s by piratical American filibusters with varying state support (see chapter 3).

Political unease informed failed attempts to further amend the Piracy Act of 1820. As these cases showed, piracy could apply to both acts of enslavement and direct action against the enslaving state. A delicate legal status quo remained. In February 1821, for example, the Senate Committee on the Judiciary debated whether the president may commute convicted pirates' executions. Notably, the committee chair, Senator William Smith of South Carolina, opposed weakening the collected piracy statutes by empowering the president. He did not mention enslavement. As Smith argued, pirates were not a variably sanctioned extension of a slaveholding society; instead, they were an aberrant and unknowable deviation from domestic ideals. The pirate's lack of sympathy, more than any political identity, spoke against a president's power to commute sentencing. After all, Smith noted, pirates incapable of fellow feeling had no right to legal protection: piracy was an offense "supremely distinguished for its enormity over others" because it may "only be committed by those whose hearts have become base by habitual depravity." Pirates had "voluntarily renounced" the nation, so unequivocal death sentences would mean that "no due influence" could add sympathy. Pirates' seductive quality, paired with the public's natural fellow feeling, would incubate false pardons. "Whatever may be the public feeling against a pirate previous to his trial and conviction," Smith claimed, "as soon as that takes place that feeling subsides and becomes enlisted on the part of the criminal." He continued, "There is not a favorable trait in his case but what is brought up and mingled with as many circumstances of pity and compassion as his counsel can condense in a petition, which everybody subscribes to without any knowledge of the facts." In other words, securing mistaken sympathy for pirates was a powerful legal strategy. In reality, Smith countered, pirates boarded a "defenceless ship." They butchered, marooned, or drowned "both male and female" inhabitants, all to "indulge an insatiable thirst for cruelty." Smith did not describe the pirate or family in any detail. As pirates without sympathy, the figures he recounted fostered nothing but crimes against national families. Therefore, he concluded, they must be annihilated without legal recourse.[22]

For proslavery figures such as Senator Smith, an appeal to piracy's universal character could, perhaps counterintuitively, help prevent the Piracy Act from disrupting a delicate political balance. Since, as the biographer Jeffrey R. Young affirms, Smith's "speeches wedding proslavery thought to a state's rights political agenda were enormously influential," his decision to strengthen an abolitionist statute is odd. Likewise, his refusal to address the amendment's ties to abolition seems uncharacteristic.[23] After all, the amendment would also allow a president to commute maritime slave traders' death sentences. Of course, that pardon could equally apply to abolitionists or Africans who took to sea against enslaving states. Or it could embolden revolutionaries in the Americas who were seeking to overthrow enslaving sovereigns. In short, the pirate remained politically multivalent. Increased presidential power would, more than anything, shift the balance away from a Congress whose construction favored proslavery states. The odds of a piratical enslaver being condemned to death and triggering a political storm perhaps seemed slight. The prospect of a federally pardoned pirate abolitionist seemed more dangerous. The amendment failed to move forward. A political status quo remained.[24]

Piracy's political implications clearly influenced legal reasoning. For some people, unapologetic politicking against piracy was preferrable to supposed judicial objectivity. In 1811, for example, John Quincy Adams declined to serve on the Supreme Court despite unanimous confirmation by the Senate. The gap between judicial culture and true feeling, Adams later hinted, had led to his refusal. The expectation of legal restraint against piracy was "so abhorrent to my nature that it gave me an early disgust to the practice of the law, and led me to the unalterable determination never to accept a judicial office." For him, piracy in all of its forms threatened the state's moral purpose and political power. Adams, more so than perhaps any other figure, personally navigated the questions of international relations, domestic law, and moral feeling that shaped piracy. As secretary of state under President Monroe (1817–25), he negotiated the Adams-Onis Treaty with Spain, which limited American-based privateering in Spain's revolting colonies. He was an architect of the Piracy Law of 1820 and the failed 1824 treaty with England. Adams denounced enslavement as a "perverted sentiment" shared by figures such as his own vice president, John C. Calhoun. Enslavement "taints the very sources of moral principle," Adams noted in an 1820 journal entry. It fosters a "false and heartless" doctrine that "makes the first and holiest rights of humanity to depend upon the color of the skin." In other words, the act of enslaving rendered one akin to a pirate whose racism overawed true fellow feeling.[25]

Calhoun, as the scholar Manisha Sinha points out, responded by joining the "Carolinian planter politicians" whose "proslavery, antidemocratic discourse . . . would form the theoretical foundation of southern nationalism." During the nullification crisis (1828–33), he supported the South Carolina legislature's declaration that federal tariff policies on southern states were illegal and unconstitutional due to individual states' legal sovereignty. Though defeated, he would continue to marry proslavery legal theory and natural law in speeches such as "Slavery as a Positive Good" (1837).[26] Faced with hardliners like Calhoun, John Quincy Adams remained party to the period's policies of appeasement. Even so, he rejected the appeals to legal dispassion used to protect enslavers and pirates more generally.

Adams's refusal to join the federal court would ripple across the period's legal culture. Meanwhile, he continued his explicitly political work. As I will show in chapter 2, he would come to denounce his own administration's mistaken sympathy for enslaving piracy in a defense of enslaved Africans who had been charged with piracy. In the process, he would also castigate the legal reasoning of his Supreme Court replacement, Justice Joseph Story.

Notably, Story received the nomination only after his fellow Massachusetts lawyer had declined the seat. A literary man, he served on the Court from 1812 to 1845, where he was "the votary of the muse," according to the editor of *The National Portrait Gallery of Distinguished Americans*. His professional writing revealed "a highly cultivated taste, and a lively sensibility to the beauties of poetry and the richer creations of the imagination." Story used his literary imagination to diverse political effects. As I have shown, he enhanced the state's power to define and punish piracy in cases prior to 1820. In two major cases heard after the Piracy Act of 1820, he curtailed these powers in the case of enslavement. He raised the possibility of principled abolition against piratical enslavement only to defer to judicial restraint that aligned with a political status quo. Regarding his refusal to judge all enslavement as piracy, Story claimed to separate personal feeling from legal reasoning. "You know full well that I have ever been opposed to slavery," he wrote to a fellow judge in 1843. "But I take my standard as a Judge from the Constitution." Such dispassionate reasoning led Adams to spurn the judiciary in favor of naked politics. Story's decisions confirmed that enslavement's ebb-and-flow status as piracy had deep consequences. Couched in a language of natural law and the law of nations, they cemented U.S. federal courts' limited jurisdiction over global enslavement. The result was both a legal protection of the trade and new abolitionist language against unfeeling piracy.[27]

JUDICIAL APPEASEMENT IN *LA JEUNE EUGENIE* (1822) AND *THE ANTELOPE* (1825)

In early 1823, a Boston-based publisher sold a transcript of the case *United States v. The Schooner La Jeune Eugenie* (1822), heard months earlier at the U.S. Circuit Court for the District of Massachusetts. Citing the "interesting nature of the case," the publisher also provided a "brief sketch" of seven other cases cited in the trial. Each decision concerned an enslaving vessel captured at sea whose piratical status or legal ownership had been under dispute. *La Jeune Eugenie*, for example, had been built in the United States by American owners but flew the French flag. It was captured off the coast of Africa on May 17, 1821. Robert F. Stockton, the captain of the American naval schooner USS *Alligator*, had taken the ship as part of his commission against American enslavers, in accordance with the Piracy Act of 1820. He believed that the French flag was a cover for American piracy. *La Jeune Eugenie* had received French papers two years prior, but no bill of sale existed. There were no enslaved Africans on the ship, but its fittings indicated its trade. According to Joseph Story, at that time an associate Supreme Court justice who was presiding over the lower circuit court, the case was "the subject of diplomatic intercourse," testing American piracy law's international power as well as American-French relations. Human lives were also at stake. After the captured ship was delivered to Boston, the French consul petitioned on behalf of its owners to affirm the ship's French status and reject the American court's jurisdiction. Story had to determine if *La Jeune Eugenie* should be considered an American vessel engaged in oceanic enslavement contrary to the 1820 piracy statute. Alternately, he could still claim piracy if he believed the ship had operated contrary to the law of nations. In other words, the case centered on whether or not enslaving was a universal act of piracy and, if not, whether American legal power could overawe that of a foreign sovereign.[28]

Story's opinion—abolitionist in message, pro-enslavement in result—shows how appeasement and its alternatives could narratively cohabitate. His decision reflected what the legal historian Paul Finkelman refers to as a "brief period of antislavery exuberance" in the 1820s. Story's ideas, if not his judgments, made him "the judiciary's most important critic of slavery."[29] Other studies have focused on what legal scholars call Story's "exhaustive and magisterial dissertation on the bases of public international law" as it related to piracy and abolition.[30] His complex legal opinion's narrative force notably rested on sympathy. Story presented natural law, understood as an extension of moral sentiments, as capable of legally shaping and even countermanding positive law. That is, the pirate's clear deviation from moral feeling could have the strength of established law despite gaps in existing statutes. He excoriated the owners of *La Jeune Eugenie* as piratical deviants of abolitionist feeling. At the same time, he refused any power to apply this theory to the pirate case at hand. Story's decision, editors at *Harvard Law Review* note, promoted a "universalist theory accompanied [by] a sovereigntist outcome." He deferred to French foreign relations by refusing American jurisdiction over the case and returned the alleged pirates to France, notwithstanding his unclear legal power to do so. In other words, he named *La Jeune Eugenie* as a pirate against whom the nation had no legal claim.[31] In the process, he abandoned prior claims to American universal jurisdiction over piracy. "Pirates or freebooters," Story had claimed in an 1819 charge to circuit court juries, "are aptly denominated the enemies of the human race, and as such become amenable to the tribunals of all civilized nations for their crimes, and by the laws of all, as I believe, are punished with Death." He would remain skeptical of alleged pirates' claim to domestic protection via foreign attachments, cautioning, "We should take care that our feelings are not wasted upon men, who falsely assume the protection of their flag." Whether Story wasted his feelings upon enslavers remained a contested question.[32]

As an associate Supreme Court justice under Chief Justice John Marshall, Story heard a strikingly similar piracy case less than three years later. *United States v. The Antelope* (1825) revealed the Court's heartless judicial logic. Like *La Jeune Eugenie*, it rested on whether oceanic enslavement ran counter to a "law of nations" defined by a mix of positive law statutes and claims to natural law. In each case, enslavers triumphed. In *The Antelope*, Story and Marshall circumscribed the Court's power to adjudicate piracy or Black sovereignty, deferring instead to foreign relations. According to legal historians, the two justices wrote decisions with "multiple meanings that could satisfy audiences with conflicting interests." Faced with the broad question of enslavement's status as piracy, they "used the specific outcomes of cases to neutralize the political implications of their theories."[33]

Analyzing these trials as literary documents reveals the vexed feelings of appeasement defining an alleged neutrality that, in practice, led to piratical enslavement's legal protection. The trial involving *La Jeune Eugenie* hinged on enslavement's place in positive law and abolitionist feeling's potential legal force as natural law. William Sullivan, who argued for the French claimants, invoked proslavery sentiments that differed in content, if not form, from an abolitionist counterpart. Abolitionists, he hinted, were the true pirates. Specifically, enslavement was an extension of French domestic sovereignty and in keeping with a law of nations. In the process, he denied that oceanic enslavement on *La Jeune Eugenie* or elsewhere was a crime against feeling. To begin, Sullivan plainly asserted that the ship was no longer American due to its French customs papers, French flag, and majority French crew. Myriad texts had divorced one domestic attachment and married another. Even so, he took pains to defend the alleged pirates' emotional orientations. The owners of *La Jeune Eugenie* did not feel against a state. Others might have judged enslavement as immoral, but no such universal feeling for the enslaved yet existed. True, the world's most strident "moralists and jurists" had asserted that "*no man is by nature a slave*." Yet this natural law argument for abolition had yet to be universally accepted. Abolitionist feeling could not legally bind the world. The free sea gave all sovereigns, including those with legal enslavement, "equal right to the uninterrupted use of the ocean." Only the "international relations" found in treaties could define and punish piracies. Sullivan argued that "nations have expressed no opinion, no assent" that would render enslavement piracy. He cautioned that courts must not use sympathy to extend American law across the ocean, valid as those feelings may be. He admitted that perhaps "the welfare and happiness of nations, would be essentially served" if elevated feelings dictated a law of nations. He also affirmed that abolitionist sentiment in Boston was "congenial to universal opinion and feeling." Abolitionist feeling, however, was a purely domestic power without global legal force. To replace the law of nations with Boston's domestic sentiment, Sullivan concluded, would also run contrary to proper jurisprudence. He warned, "There is no place where the use of judicial power, not warranted by law, however humane and amiable the motive, would be more deeply felt, or more sincerely lamented." In other words, proper feeling toward an entire global legal order dictated that *La Jeune Eugenie* was no pirate, no matter the ship's national affiliation.[34]

Daniel Webster, whom some legal scholars consider "the leading attorney of the early nineteenth century," argued for the government's jurisdiction in the case of *La Jeune Eugenie*. Webster had previously attempted to limit the state's power to define and punish piracy in *United States v. Smith* (1820), one of the more than 150 Supreme Court cases he tried in his career. Webster's legal thinking would shift throughout the period. He defended a mutineering privateer in *Smith* to protect foreign relations rather than to undermine abolition. He prosecuted enslavers as pirates in *La Jeune Eugenie*, an approach that was incongruous with the proslavery appeasements that defined his late career (see chapter 2). "By what I learn, there will be no avoiding the main question in the Young Eugenie," he wrote in a December 1821 letter to his colleague Story.[35] Oceanic enslavement's status as piracy—and, by extension, global abolition's legal standing—was on trial.

Story, following Webster's lead, appeared to answer "the main question" unequivocally. In his *La Jeune Eugenie* decision, he presented oceanic enslavers as pirates whose crimes against feeling weakened their legal standing. Such agents' moral failures gave abolitionist feelings legal force. To begin, he presented Sullivan's appeal to international law as technically valid, if not morally suspect. There was some legal justification for "remitting the party to the domestic forum," or treating *La Jeune Eugenie* under French domestic law. Moreover, Story asserted that enslavement "may have a lawful existence" and "form a part of the domestic policy of a nation." Nor did the "unequivocal testimony of the law of nations" prevent the trade. After all, Story agreed, international law "does not rest upon mere theory." It was produced by treaty making and other foreign relations. In this view, unfeeling legal reasoning could distinguish owners of *La Jeune Eugenie* from pirates. Notwithstanding enslavement's variably legal status across the globe, Story took appeals to natural law seriously. He considered enslavement a "violation of some of the first principles, which ought to govern nations." Feeling against enslaving piracy should order a family of nations guided by moral sentiments.[36]

Within this debate on positive and natural law, Story reintroduced a vital claimant that the defense had dismissed: the enslaved themselves. In the process, he roundly condemned the vessel as piratical due to enslavement's base immorality. His "principle justification was natural law," notes historian Andrew Forsyth. A specific theory of moral sentiments gave natural law its narrative form and legal cachet. Story defined natural law as a familial fellow feeling.[37] Questions of the ship's national character, the American court's global jurisdiction, and enslavement's piratical status could all be answered via an appeal to sympathy. In the process, he narrated plots of familial separation and piratical unfeeling akin to those found in sentimental domestic fictions. Piratical enslavement, he asserted,

> breaks down all the ties of parent, and children, and family, and country. It shuts up all sympathy for human suffering and sorrows. It manacles the inoffensive females and the starving infants. It forces the brave to untimely death in defence of their humble homes and firesides, or drives them to despair and self-immolation. It stirs up the worst passions of the human soul darkening the spirit of revenge, sharpening the greediness of avarice, brutalizing the

> selfish, envenoming the cruel, famishing the weak, and crushing to death the broken-hearted.[38]

In his terms, piracy was more than an act. It was familial violence at the individual, national, and global level. Story confirmed enslaved people's denied familial attachments, including the ties of "family" and "country." He cataloged enslaving piracy's deleterious effects on familial feeling. Piratical enslavement choked all moral sentiments. It bound "females and the starving infants" who embodied familial attachment and were thus most deserving of legal protection. In such cases, Black violence was a defense of familial feeling in "humble homes and firesides" rather than a form of piratical unruliness. In other words, violence against agents of the state was not piracy if it was not a crime against feeling. Illegal pirates were, for Story, thus distinguished by a moral failure so strong that legal reasoning must follow. Since piracy "shuts up all sympathy for human suffering and sorrows," then it threatened not only Black families but also an entire moral system. Piratical enslavement "stirs up the worst passions of the human soul," poisoning a global well of moral sentiments. In sum, all enslavement remained a piratical crime against feeling.[39]

Given this forceful argument against enslaving piracy, Story's decision to deny the American court's jurisdiction in the case is perhaps surprising. After all, one might expect the punishment of piracy to fit its definition. Like Jefferson's Declaration draft, however, Story's claims to American moral supremacy against pirates could not withstand political pressure. More than Jefferson, he named abolition's rewards even as he weakly denied its legal standing. Claiming jurisdiction over all piratical enslavers would make global abolition an American legal cause, a doubtful possibility in an enslaving nation. The prospect of civil war or global Black revolution in the spirit of Haiti went unmentioned. Yet it remained unmistakably present. Instead, Story retreated into the ebbs and flows of foreign relations on enslaving piracy. Existing treaties and statutes could yet prove that "the sense of Europe" was unified in abolitionist moral sense. He noted the practical issue: "No nation has ever yet pretended to be the custos morum of the whole world." If piracy was understood as a global offense, there remained no "moral guardian" to define and punish this crime. Instead, "the equality and sovereignty of nations" dictated that no one domestic state could overawe the rest. While Story named why a judge would wish to find the defendant guilty—plainly stating that "the slave trade is a trade prohibited by universal law, and by the law of France"—he refused to extend his claim beyond a domestic shore. American courts, he said, are "not hungry after jurisdiction in foreign causes." He concluded, "I feel myself at perfect liberty, with the express consent of our own government, to decree, that the property be delivered over to the consular agent of the king of France, to be dealt with according to his own sense of duty and right." This personal "perfect liberty" was, like all forms of popular legality, a feeling given wider legal force. Even so, Story undercut his own judicial reasoning. He expressed "great distrust and diffidence of my own judgment respecting its merits." Indeed, he outlined a dissenting opinion's moral and legal basis. To legally remove enslaving pirates was a valuable moral mission, he intimated, if not a politically feasible one.[40] Less than two years later, Congress's refusal to ratify the British-American accord against enslaving piracy proved him to be correct.

Justice Joseph Story, like many figures in antebellum legal culture, believed that the Supreme Court was beholden to political reality. Even so, he later attempted to save face. In an 1843 letter, he presented his decision in *La Jeune Eugenie* as "touching the slave trade being piracy" that was "overruled in the Supreme Court in the case of the *Antelope*." In practice, his mix of abolitionist legal reasoning and practical acquiescence to French enslavers was a political calculation in keeping with the Court's later actions. Story, like the institution he served, operated among a swirl of international relations. The Marshall Court had long since denied abolitionist moral feeling's legal standing in cases of Black legal rights. John Marshall espoused a strict legal interpretation whose ostensible disinterestedness belied proslavery sympathies. "However the feeling of the individual may be interested on the part of a person claiming freedom" he wrote in *Mima Queen v. Hepburn* (1813), "no man could feel safe in any property" that could be taken without full legal support. The case concerned the family members of a woman, Mima Queen, who claimed she had been freed in England prior to her enslavement in the United States. In a departure from lower courts and Maryland law, Marshall determined that their family history was inadmissible hearsay. Both abolitionist feeling and Black familial attachment must not have legal force, he claimed, when they ran counter to an enslaver's feelings of proprietorship. The case would be used to deny later freedom suits. After all, enslavement was in keeping with domestic law.[41]

Although Story heard the case of *La Jeune Eugenie* three years before *United States v. The Antelope*, the events aboard the ship *Antelope* had occurred in 1820. Just as *La Jeune Eugenie* pivoted around a crisis in international relations with France, *The Antelope* centered around a comparable conflict with Spain and

Portugal. The U.S. Court would defer to these international relations in its decision. In June 1820, an American revenue ship had found 280 Africans aboard the *Antelope* off the coast of Spanish Florida. The ship's captain was tried for piracy, and the human cargo was seized. American, Spanish, and Portuguese claimants disputed over who owned the enslaved, and the Africans themselves brought a freedom suit. During the trials that took place over the next seven years, the trafficked people who had been aboard the *Antelope* were "treated as latent property and exploitable laborers," according to historian Sharla M. Fett. Nearly all were put to work for Georgia's leading families, with fifty-one being ordered to work for the state. Almost fifty died. In an 1821 circuit court decision, a judge divided 204 people by lottery into the property of either Spain, Portugal, or the United States. Ultimately, Chief Justice Marshall concluded that immoral oceanic enslavement was to be judged according to alleged pirates' domestic status. A defendant's enslaving could be legally valid if they were tied to a domestic state sympathetic to the trade. In such cases, enslavers were not pirates. Thus, thirty people were legally reenslaved due to their ties to Spain. The government sent 131 Africans aboard the ship *Norfolk* to found "New Georgia" in Liberia. Many had made new families in the United States during the trial, at least three of which were broken up after its conclusion. Certain men had been randomly and capriciously reclaimed for Spanish enslavers. In a perverse form of law, then, illegal enslavement fostered continued familial separation. As Fett concludes, "only 23 percent of the original *Antelope* shipmates remained alive in New Georgia by 1844." Domestic enslavement at home and abroad continued to be protected in a judicially mandated appeasement.[42]

A brief analysis of *The Antelope* decision in light of *La Jeune Eugenie* reveals the judicial sleights of hand invoked to neutralize prior natural law arguments around enslaving piracy. The legal scholar Andrew Forsyth provides a succinct summary: "Whatever the promise of Story's decision in *Jeune Eugenie*, then, *The Antelope* restricted courts' ability to directly appeal to natural law as some form of 'trump' . . . over national laws, foreign or domestic."[43] Like Story, Marshall named both enslavement and piracy as crimes against feeling. Yet he more strongly deferred to a positive law that had yet to follow course. He began, "The African slave trade is contrary to the law of nature, but is not prohibited by the positive law of nations." He briefly admitted oceanic enslavers' incompatibility with natural law but forewent an extended defense of abolitionist sentiments. Like Story, he limited domestic courts' power over a law of nations. As Marshall stated, "The slave trade is not piracy unless made so by the treaties or statutes of the nation to whom the party belongs." Only a clear legal union of sentiments could render the enslaver a pirate. To do otherwise, he implied, was to threaten a global peace. A nation's universal jurisdiction to board suspected enslavers went against a "right of visitation and search" that only existed in war. After all, the 1824 British-American accord had not been ratified. By extension, there could be no extension of judicial feeling across national lines. An enslaved person's individual feelings or domestic attachments did not register in this legal reasoning. Existing international relations dictated one's legal status as free or enslaved. Therefore, Marshall concluded, those enslaved by Spanish forces remained legally bound in the United States. In a true mark of legal dispassion's moral capriciousness, he laid out a careful "apportionment" to be reenslaved according to a proper "ratio." Georgia's acting district attorney had called the Africans in question "persons of color from some Eastern Kingdom of Africa." Marshall dismissed any claim to familial ties or national origins. He described a "residue" of the enslaved to be returned to Spanish claimants. The rest, he coolly asserted, were "to be delivered to the United States, to be disposed of according to law." Those illegally enslaved aboard the *Antelope* could be protected from piracy. Yet their freedom was administered in legal acts of bondage, colonization, and familial separation. This dubious act of abolition defined the period. The decision in *The Antelope*, like the Piracy Act of 1820, unevenly conferred legal rights to people who were equally beset by piratical enslavement.[44]

Marshall and Story both limited the judiciary's power to adjudicate oceanic enslavement. Yet they performed disparate cultural work. Story's decision, though legally limited, entered an abolitionist press seeking proof that natural law supported legal abolition. The public distribution of the transcript of *La Jeune Eugenie* placed the case in a broader legal culture. *The Christian Disciple and Theological Review* saw Story's decision as proof that "the greater part of our fellow beings are sensibly alive to the impulse of *good feelings*," even as it admitted the case favored enslavers. *The United States Law Journal* likewise excerpted Story's account of familial separation and aligned his decision with "a hope . . . that the time is not too far distant, when the courts of all civilized nations will accept the doctrine that the slave trade is repugnant to the law of nations." In 1822, Story's father, perhaps at the justice's direction, sent transcripts of this "very important case" to abolitionists such as John Greenleaf Whittier and Jeremiah Mason. Abolitionists published the bulk of the decision in a pamphlet that derived from a prior grand jury hearing.[45] Story's deferral to a political status quo thus created a split text, abolitionist in character yet proslavery in practice. Marshall further anchored enslavement's federal protection and dismissed abolition's ties to natural law. The abolitionist and the enslaver may be pirates, each seemed to say, depending on their relative tie to the domestic state and its privileged white families.

Story's refusal to define and punish enslavement as piracy caused his reputation to wane in radical abolitionist print. The justice was "earnest and eloquent in his denunciation of the foreign slave trade," stated an article in William Lloyd Garrison's abolitionist paper *The Liberator* in October 1838. Even so, the writer wondered how he was "not instantly suffused with the crimson blushes of shame" when spouting an "idle and false panegyric" of limited deep-sea abolition. Such statutes protected the "slave-breeding States," as the judge well knew. "'Honor!' Glory!' Shame and infamy!" the writer asserted of Story's constitutional thinking. Of his lauded literary imagination, they concluded, "O, Judge S. thou art a bad STORY-teller!" *The Liberator* had told the true story months earlier in the article "Every Slaveholder a Pirate." In it, the writer noted that John Quincy Adams "logically reduces every slaveholder to the level of pirate." Adams had rightly appealed to "Universal Emancipation" as the only path to "justice and mercy." As long as the federal government retained the land-sea split that defined antebellum legal culture, all Americans remained party to piratical enslavement.[46]

As abolitionists such as Garrison knew, both legal maritime trade and illegal enslavement tied America's leading families to piracy. In 1828, for example, the Boston merchant and U.S. consular agent Stephen Cabot was charged with piracy based out of the Caribbean island of Saint Thomas. This charge led to his flight to Haiti, the revelation that he had a secret mixed-race Haitian family, and his Haitian children's emigration to Massachusetts. As I have shown elsewhere, the author Catharine Maria Sedgwick defended her friend in private letters and in her fictions. Each reveal a richer Cabot family history based in Haiti.[47]

Sedgwick's intimate relationship with maritime piracy, part of what scholars call her "hemispheric reality," helps to contextualize her place in antebellum legal culture. Although she lived in either New York or Massachusetts her entire life and did not travel to Europe until 1839, she corresponded with a wide breadth of literary and intellectual figures who had ties to Europe and the Americas.[48] Indeed, Sedgwick's literary career demonstrates piracy's often indirect sources of literary support. Take, for example, her semi-autobiographical travelogue "A Voyage across the Atlantic" (1841). In it, a woman gently mocks a fellow passenger, who upon seeing an "English ship from Barbadoes, . . . thought they were pirates." Legally astute and virtuous women knew the difference between a pirate and a foreign relation. The story's deeper ties to piracy derived from its publication in *The United States Magazine and Democratic Review*, a political and literary magazine founded by John Louis O'Sullivan. In 1812, O'Sullivan's father had served as U.S. consul in the North African "Barbary" States before an American commercial agent in Buenos Aires accused him (falsely, it seems) of being party to piracy. The son, who coined the phrase "manifest destiny," later supported both filibustering operations in Cuba and the secessionist government in the Civil War.[49] In other words, allegedly piratical crimes against feeling infused Sedgwick's historical and social waters.

As a globally famous member of an American founding family, Sedgwick was uniquely positioned to dramatize antebellum legal culture. Her earliest Puritan ancestor was a Cromwell-era commissioner in Jamaica. Sedgwick's connection to antebellum figures such as Joseph Story was more than thematic. Her father, the Federalist politician and lawyer Theodore Sedgwick (1746–1813), worked on John Adams's 1796 presidential campaign. A member of the Massachusetts Supreme Judicial Court from 1802 until his death, the elder Sedgwick collaborated with Story on attempts to increase appellate courts' power and jurisdiction.[50]

Sedgwick shared her father's belief in federal union led by a "virtuous elite" from an early age, as scholar Gretchen Murphy has shown. Most notably, she wrote letters at age eleven lamenting that Thomas Jefferson's 1800 presidential election proved populist democracy's basis in French-allied moral excess and political anarchy. This staunch federalism informed the family's complex relationship to both abolition and white supremacy. Theodore Sedgwick argued on behalf of Elizabeth Freeman's successful 1781 freedom suit, making her the first enslaved person in Massachusetts to achieve freedom through trial. Freeman, or Mum Bet, subsequently became a servant in the Sedgwick household, earning enough to purchase her own home nearby. She remained a mother figure to Sedgwick. "Mumbet—'Mother'—my nurse—my faithful friend," Sedgwick wrote in her diary in November 1829: "She who first received me into her arms—is finishing her career—a life marked by as perfect a performance of duty—perhaps I should say more perfect than I have ever known."[51] Sedgwick's earnest approach to piracy was likewise defined by Black "duty" to serve white families rather than be enslaved by them. Like Story and others, she adjudicated enslavement as a piratical crime against feeling. She invoked a family of nations–led by white, middle-class, American women—but narratively refrained from promoting abolition. She did so by introducing pirates whose multivalent if ill-defined politics were overshadowed by their direct threat to white women's moral virtue. This fact made her less valued by those seeking antebellum champions of abolition. It also made her a singular literary agent in her era's sentimental jurisprudence of appeasement.

"A DARK AND FEARFUL SUBJECT": SEDGWICK'S LITERARY APPEASEMENTS

Antebellum pirates found a robust adversary in Catharine Maria Sedgwick. After all, she had published nine often-pirated popular novels (as well as various sketches and short stories) between 1822 and 1837. Her novel *Redwood* (1824) had been translated into French, German, Swedish, and Italian by 1830.[52] She secured a British copyright for her pirate novel, *Clarence* (1830), to fend off bands of literary pirates. Deeply aware of American domestic fiction's global reach, she was the only antebellum American woman writer to directly petition Congress for international copyright reform. According to Melissa Homestead, Sedgwick's 1838 signature on this petition alongside men with more explicit political rights informed "a particular vision of republican authorship in sync with the logic of existing law rather than in opposition to it."[53]

Sedgwick's strategic empowerment of women in the world of male-dominated copyright law protected her own pirate fictions. The plots of these fictions reveal that Sedgwick's tendency towards conservative legal thinking extended to more explicitly violent piracies. Her white, middle-class heroines often faced pirates with ties to the United States, England, Spain, France, Haiti, and numerous transcolonial orders. Such figures sometimes reflected her "cosmopolitan embrace of the foreign." More directly, however, they represented her crafty legal and literary navigation of foreign relations. Sedgwick's appeal to the "logic of existing law" extended to her definition of maritime piracy as a crime against feeling rather than a single act. Like other legal thinkers of the era, she defined and punished piracy via landed families. Notably, the fictional pirates she launched did not embody coherent legal reasoning or a monolithic political agenda. Some were abolitionist. Some were enslavers. Some were legal merchants. All were racially and nationally diverse. Their ties to northern investments in enslavement belie a claim to moral purity over their southern counterparts.[54] In each case, Sedgwick presented white women as key to domestic union and foreign relations. White women's legal empowerment would prevent piratical crimes against feeling. Ongoing oceanic enslavement was one such piracy. Violent abolition, it seems, was another.

Joseph Story was, for some abolitionists, a bad storyteller whose legal theories displayed mistaken sympathy for pirates. Sedgwick's stories fostered a comparable legal theory. Her personal letters confirm what Karen Woods-Wireman calls "the 'abolitionist problem' in Sedgwick literary history." The problem, for both Sedgwick and later scholars, is that a moral objection to enslavement did not lead her to champion abolition. She saw slavery firsthand during trips to Washington, DC (1831), and Virginia (1833). Even so, as she told the abolitionist Eliza Lee Cabot Follen, "I do indeed *feel* with you—& I would do something more than feel." As Woods-Wireman affirms, Sedgwick's letters reveal a "search for an appropriate role in the antislavery movement." They also indicate a tendency toward appeasement. She wrote to the abolitionist Lydia Marie Child in 1834, "It does not appear to me that immediate abolition is the best for the slaves. God only knows what is best. It is a dark and fearful subject." In other words, Sedgwick presented her non-abolitionist opinion as a sentimental attachment to the enslaved and their divinely ordained needs. Rather than elucidate why enslavement was both morally and politically viable than abolition, she admitted her fundamental fear of political rupture. As Sedgwick knew, her place in an abolitionist literary culture was fraught. She told Child that she would write a piece for Child's abolitionist gift book so long as "I may be one of your contributors without being considered an advocate of the principles of the abolitionists (which I cannot honestly be)." Both the violence of slavery and the prospect of Black citizenship haunted Sedgwick's literary imagination. As Charlene Avallone notes, her "fantasies (and silences) about blacks, revolution, and 'free institutions'" led her to write historical fictions about "white nation-making." In short, her work unevenly distributed legal rights.[55] Tellingly, Sedgwick abandoned her only fiction draft wholly dedicated to the question of enslavement, a piece that concluded with gradual emancipation. Because she could not broach the "fearful subject" directly, her pirate fictions promoted indirect parlays.[56]

Sedgwick's first two novels shaped her place in an antebellum legal culture concerned with the moral and geographic divides epitomized by the Piracy Act of 1820. Her early fiction, writes Christopher C. Apap "[wove] together elements of New England and plantation culture in order to imagine an interconnected nation." In the process, she argued for northern women's power to overcome piratical crimes against feeling. Sedgwick castigated enslavement as misaligned with familial feeling. Even so, she refrained from claiming jurisdiction over universal abolition.[57] In short, she echoed Joseph Story. *A New-England Tale; or, Sketches of New-England Character and Manners* (1822), her bestselling first novel, centers on an orphaned girl's question for moral virtue and familial attachment in a rural village. Its brief seduction subplot foreshadows a future fictional young woman whose moral virtue will overawe a pirate's legal and moral challenge. A relatively toothless villain, readers learn, "sails in the morning for one of the West India islands, where he will no doubt make his debut as a pirate." An immoral domestic figure finds piracy appealing. As the scholar Catherine Q. Forsa argues of *A New-England Tale*, "emotions—and not more traditional means such as wealth—emerge as a major reason for characters' changes in social position." One's social position may be tied to a relative allegiance with pirates: those apt to commit crimes against feeling will find in pirates willing collaborators. Virtuous northern white women will both defeat pirates and enrich the nation. Piracy, like enslavement, remains a legal problem that moral feeling may help solve. At the same time, however, these women's persistently selfish family members continue to foster piratical enslavement and, in turn, increase the prospect of piratical Black revolution.[58]

A comparable legal tension around abolition, including more spectral pirates, operated in *Redwood: A Tale* (1824). Centered on an early national family made wealthy by enslavement, the novel concerns in part how to prevent revolutionary violence in both France and Haiti from extending into the United States. For example, an early chapter recounts the deathbed Christian conversion narrative of an enslaved man, Africk, who "could have poured out the blood of white men, till it should run like the big waters over which they brought us" but who now only sadly prophesizes that enslavers may "see your fair lands drenched with their [wives' and children's] blood." This vision of circumvented Black revenge against American families, what Gretchen Murphy calls "an ocean of blood for the ocean of the middle passage," shows how the enslaved may yet be converted away from piratical violence in response to piratical enslavement. Sedgwick, Murphy notes, thus promotes a "moderate social vision" in which an "ethic of interdependence" and a "morality grounded in liberal Christian zeal" will foster increased social equality, if not racial or class egalitarianism.[59] In the novel's primary plot, a northern orphan named Ellen Bruce is alerted to her legal inheritance of her father's Virginia plantation. Though Ellen refuses this wealth, she receives it anyway once her vain half-sister Caroline "[goes] off to them West Indies, which have proved her death." Caroline's death, Melissa Homestead writes, is a "punishment for her earlier transgressions." The sister, raised in South Carolina, had abetted southern enslavement and had abandoned her family for a British naval officer. In other words, Caroline had advanced improper foreign relations with British sovereigns and piratical enslavers. On the other hand, Ellen's moral attachment to the national family naturally confers economic rewards. A plantation heiress, her domestic virtue will lead the nation. Whether the enslaved have a legal or moral claim to this inheritance remains unclear. Lily, an enslaved woman whose brave actions reveal Ellen's legal claim, marries for love upon successfully escaping from enslavement but remains a minor character. Such an incomplete narrative resolution, Jenifer B. Elmore concludes, befits a novel that is "morally and politically" antislavery yet not strictly "in the genre of *abolitionist* fiction." Sedgwick's resolution favors abolition less than the transfer of wealth from enslaving patriarchs to northern heiresses for the sake of federal union and often at the expense of the presently or formerly enslaved.[60]

The pirate in *Hope Leslie* (1827) represents Sedgwick's first direct engagement with piracy as an index of transcolonial wealth's necessary legal transfer to liberal-minded white northerners rather than either enslavers or the enslaved. It is a major text in antebellum legal culture around piracy, even as its primary debate is Indigenous survivance. After all, Sedgwick's historical fiction is set in seventeenth-century New England dominated by Puritan and Native communities. Treating the historical Pequots as metaphor, she presented Jacksonian-era removal policies as a necessary, if dangerous, gamble, as Paul Pasquaretta argues. While *Hope Leslie* is not strictly a pirate novel, a speculative reading verifies a central tenet of antebellum legal culture: pirate histories, like Indigenous or Puritan ones, undeniably shaped legalized violence and white nation making. Sedgwick's prefatory note on her novel's flexible use of history hints at the speculative trajectory introduced by the pirate: "We are confined not to the actual, but to the possible."[61]

The pirate in *Hope Leslie* is minor yet vital. He is a piratical source with ties to imperial England and colonial Haiti. He threatens the novel's colonial inheritance and primes this wealth's proliferation in New England. Specifically, the novel culminates with the royalist and "corrupt seducer" Sir Philip Gardiner's attempt to kidnap the titular heroine. First, he must find an oceanic agent capable of seizing the orphaned Hope's familial wealth. After all, her "personal connexions were on the royal side—her fortune was still in their hands." If British "royal" attachments are expected to become independent American fortunes, the pirate may alter this birthright's legal and political course. Indeed, Sir Philip solicits Chaddock, a man who "had once been in confederacy with the bucaniers of Tortuga—the self-styled 'brotherhood of the coast.'"[62] Tortuga, named by Christopher Columbus in 1492, was a fitting site for staging a colonial legacy's variable proliferations. As Mark Hanna writes, French, British, and Spanish sovereigns tenuously held the "stubbornly independent" island, but it remained "effectively a pirate colony" during the novel's seventeenth-century setting.[63] It had once been the capital of French colonial Saint Domingue and was part of Haiti during Sedgwick's contemporary moment. In other words, what Sarah Sillin has called the "threat of foreign sympathy" embodied by the European seducer Sir Philip is also a piratical threat with ties to Haiti.[64] The pirates of *Hope Leslie* represent pre-revolutionary Black enslavement as well as post-revolutionary Black sovereignty. Both threaten a domestic culture whose political and moral future must rest, the novel implies, in the hands of virtuous white women.

The novel's kidnapping plot stages this potential divergence: a tale of domestic virtue may yet become a pirate novel. American colonial history could, speculatively, have led to a transcolonial sovereign island with ties to both enslavement and Black sovereignty. Via Hope, a slaveholding pirate outpost may first become a slaveholding colony, then an abolitionist nation. Sir Philip advances this possibility: standing on Chaddock's ship, he promises that all who join him will, "with the remnant of their fortunes, embark with him, and enrol themselves among the adventurers of Tortuga." In other words, he employs both colonial enslavers and transcolonial revolutionaries. Hope, referred to as "the prize," would travel a transatlantic triangle with echoes of the African slave trade. Enslaved in colonial New England, traded for wealth in Britain, and exported (either in body or inheritance) to the West Indies, she would bankroll a new society fathered by these "adventurers of Tortuga." Chaddock's scoffing confirmation that a man who "boarded Spanish galleons" has the power to "capture a single defenceless girl" hints at the pirate's powers of enslavement.[65] Chattel enslavement that began at sea could yet populate a domestic nation, as the United States had shown.

Sir Philip, who may become a pirate by association, introduces the possibility that a pirate could also father a Black sovereign nation built on mistaken sympathy. He assumes that Hope's hand will be "subdued" during this pirate voyage. His ill-defined rationale, it seems, is that the voyage's length and "stern necessity" will make marriage inevitable. Such a union may lead Hope to "go on the account," or join these men of Tortuga on their promised adventures. The prospect, though far-fetched, has some support. After all, Sir Philip has "often deeply interested her with his lively descriptions of countries and manners unknown to her." Caroline in *Redwood* had been seduced by such Anglo-Caribbean forces. Will Hope be similarly moved by a pirate tale? If so, enslaving violence and skillful seduction will lead to a British colonial inheritance's transfer to transcolonial San Domingue. The subsequent Haitian Revolution, one may imagine, would allow this colonial inheritance to be incorporated into the sovereign Haiti that existed in Sedgwick's period. One sees echoes of Supreme Court cases that held Haitian sovereignty in legal suspension. However, Sir Philip's comedically resolved piratical plot shifts focus from Haitian sovereignty's possibility to the domestic state's inevitability. Chaddock's crew mistakenly captures Jennet, the Fletchers' servant. Sir Philip's scorned lover blows up their vessel "to fragments" in an ill-conceived attempt to save Hope. God's grace and human folly make state action against pirates unnecessary. Yet the explosion confirms that a struggle against pirates will be violent, no matter the victors.[66]

The novel's conclusion echoes legal cases that privilege domestic stability among the nation's paradigmatic white families. An unscathed Hope marries Everell Fletcher. Their colonial inheritance, the novel implies, will reach its rightful beneficiaries: the white families of Sedgwick's antebellum America. Past or present Haitians recede from Sedgwick's vision of the future, even more so than the novel's Indigenous community. In fact, these removals are linked. Sedgwick's novel and others like it "enfold the Indian American presence into the Anglo-American freedom story," as Laura Anne Doyle has argued. The pirate agitates this freedom story. Sir Philip's pirate plot presents Haitian sovereignty as an impossible future for Hope's familial wealth. Haitians' removal from a colonial order and a national present seem to need no explanation. After all, cases such as *Rose v. Himley* had denied their legal claims to sovereignty. The pirates' attempt to enslave a white heroine renders their crimes against feeling self-evident. In the process, *Hope Leslie* advances the "forms of nativism fed by a disavowed or distorted African Atlantic subjectivity" that Doyle associates with other "Anglo-Atlantic" authors such as William Hill Brown and Susanna Rowson. In this case, an African Atlantic is represented by racially ambiguous pirates with familial allegiance to Tortuga. The pirate's later invisibility, both at the novel's close and in subsequent scholarship, confirms Sedgwick's skillful removal of legal and historical alterity. Though threatened by the prospect of a pirate novel, the New England historical romance retains its desired course.[67]

In *Hope Leslie*, Sedgwick invoked piracy to contrast white supremacy with an unconscionable transcolonial future. In *Clarence: or, A Tale of Our Own Times* (1830), she presented piracy as embedded in an unmistakably transcolonial present and, in its defeat, integral to a benevolently white supremacist future. Sedgwick's most fully realized pirate fiction, *Clarence* stages an 1820s-era New York City deeply shaped by illicit and legalized enslavement in the wake of the Piracy Act of 1820.[68] The novel's main events concern Gertrude Clarence's use of her newfound inheritance to fight piracy. Gertrude, like the nation, is a plantation heiress resolute about her moral supremacy. As her grandfather, Edmund Clarence, relays in the novel's late eighteenth-century prehistory, the British family's "lucrative business in the West Indies" prospers even as drowning, infidelity, fratricide, and suicide—acts she attributes to French, Spanish, and Caribbean foreign relations—destroy its members. Most notable is Marceline Clarence, Edmund's once-enslaved prodigal son, who shares his mother's "tinge" of "African blood." Goaded by a Spaniard, Marceline commits suicide in shame over gambling debts, demonstrating that prospective Black sovereignty fails due to moral lack rather than legal hindrance. In other words, Sedgwick mobilized the gambling trope's generic function in nineteenth-century sentimental fiction. Gambling, Lori Merish notes, was considered "an unsurpassed form of selfishness" that proved one's incapacity for "sustained proprietorship" of "familial wealth."[69] Gertrude could not prevent her progenitors' deeply dysfunctional domestic and foreign relations. She can only protect herself against the pirates that such relations have produced. Specifically, she must protect a national family against the dual gambles of Black sovereignty and global enslavement. In the novel's main plot, Gertrude uses her wealth to disentangle her New York social circle's ties with piracy. Like Story, Sedgwick chose to exercise a limited jurisdiction over such pirates in *Clarence*. She presented enslavement as a lamentable product of political antecedents and imperfect foreign relations. There is no consideration of whether or not Gertrude can give up her enslavers' inheritance to Black heirs or advocate for a larger program of abolition. Despite the heroine's clear investments in white supremacy, Gertrude and other white women's economic and moral power defined Sedgwick's political vision.

Clarence's pirate villain, Henrique Pedrillo, embodies the seemingly contradictory crimes against feeling—enslavement and abolition—that Jefferson first described in his Declaration. Pedrillo is a Spanish-passing, Connecticut-born polyglot with legal ties to New York, France, England, Spain, and Caribbean islands such as Cuba and Haiti. He embodies antebellum legal culture's host of foreign relations across a spectrum of legal trade and illegal piracy. Pedrillo owns a "fair mercantile house in Cuba," whose "honorable commercial relations," the narrator notes with scorn, is a favorite of New York's "first merchants." Figures such as Mr. Layton, the father of Gertrude's best friend, build northern wealth in a Caribbean slaveholding economy. As Pedrillo notes, "Layton is a name well known in the West Indies—a proud *unsullied* name."[70] Though buoyed by Layton, Pedrillo's piracy is defined by his lack of familial ties. He "does not look at all Spanish" and, the narrator first surmises, "probably descended from on the Irish Catholic families that emigrated to Spain." To deny his Spanishness—and, by extension, disallow the trope of racial passing—reintroduces the thorny question of domestic allegiance that defined the period's piracy trials. This "Spaniard," we learn, had left his Connecticut family farm due to a "dark crime." Pedrillo's true motivation is called "one of those aberrations in the moral history of a man." The pirate has an "aberrant" and unknowable motivation because deviations from proper domesticity are self-evidently uncanny.[71]

Above all, Pedrillo commits crimes against feeling whose basis in enslavement remains indirect. This pirate controls the waves and, it seems, overawes domestic animals that include both the doggedly enslaved and the slavecatching bloodhound. Indeed, Pedrillo is "master" to a "little spaniel" named Triton and enslaves a "docile" Greek god of the sea. His eventual murder of this loyal companion—he "separate[s] the carotid artery" in the novel's sole scene of explicit violence—proves the pirate's crimes against feeling.[72] It also places Sedgwick's ambivalent legal theory of white nation making in proper context. In her children's story "Dogs" (1828), published in *The Juvenile Miscellany*, a bimonthly children's magazine founded by Child, she had presented humans' treatment of dogs as a test of inherited moral sense across human races and animal species. She denied inheritability by "inferior animals" based on their inability to follow the dictum that "one race of boys educated, teaches the rest." The mother character's brief note that dogfighting and bullbaiting are spectacles "only fit for Hottentots" further raises the specter of racialized animals and animalized races. "Dogs" climaxes with a graphic scene of French colonial violence against revolutionary Haitian families. The novel's matriarch distinguishes between "murderers and robbers" who deserve "no mercy" and the immoral use of bloodhounds by the "French of St. Domingo." She continues: "Their slaves rebelled, and, determined to be free, carried on a war against their masters by which they finally obtained their liberty." This clear acceptance of Haitian sovereignty, as I argue elsewhere, complicates the denial of spectral Haitians in *Hope Leslie* and Sedgwick's explicit rejection of Haiti's revolutionary promise in *Clarence*.[73]

The pirate Henrique Pedrillo is certainly not an abolitionist. Nor is he a Haitian revolutionary. Like the pirates of *Hope Leslie*, he represents transcolonial threats that may be overcome by benevolent white nation making. His transcolonial credentials are evident in his multilingualism: he "spoke English, French, and Spanish equally well . . . so well as to leave his hearer in doubt which was his vernacular." Many during the antebellum era feared that linguistically and culturally fluid pirates in the Haitian diaspora had the skills required to fund transcolonial revolution using colonial resources. Indeed, in the novel, Pedrillo first attempts to seduce the shallow youngest daughter of a "seigneur of St. Domingo"—in other words, an enslaver in colonial Haiti. That immigrant Frenchman was "happy to escape, during the troubles, with his life, his family, and a few jewels," as well as, he admits, the extortionate sovereign debt paid by Haiti to its former enslavers.[74] The novel's all-American hero, Gerald Roscoe, rebukes the pirate and refuses a reward of money or marriage. The Haitian plantation heiress, it seems, is not the nation's moral or economic model. Even so, the family's eldest daughter receives a dowry at the "bequest of a ci-devant slave" to fund her marriage to a "poor Yankee." "Ci-devant" denotes a slave "from before," but the term also disparagingly refers to those French nobles who refused to accept a new revolutionary order.[75] Haitian sovereignty, if not piratical, may be voluntarily ceded to protect former enslavers' American domesticity.

The gambling trope's return indicates that northerners invested in piracy were, like the novel's paradigmatic Black heir, committing crimes against feeling. While Sedgwick censured piratical enslavers, such rebukes did not lead legal storytellers such as Story or herself to favor global abolition or Black reparations. Instead, each offered appeasement in the name of political stability. In the novel, rebuffed by Roscoe, Pedrillo attempts to forcibly marry Emilie Layton as payment for a $60,000 gambling debt. The novel's greatest horror is white slavery. Emilie's father, Mr. Layton, cowers from Pedrillo "as a newly captured slave would dart from the presence of his master." Gertrude, who believes "an unwilling marriage is the worst slavery," pays a ransom that is "within the compass of our fortune." Her gift to Emilie is an exercise of "authority," Susan K. Harris argues, that makes her one of Sedgwick's "models for Republican Womanhood." But the moral and economic compass of Gertrude's fortune as a plantation heiress reveals a more complicated politics. Mr. Layton gambles away "the largest portion of that money" and is blackmailed, regardless of payment.[76] This failed gamble of familial wealth does not tarnish Gertrude, as it had her uncle. Instead, it agitates a moral laundering. An enslavers' inheritance is made morally pure and racially white. Gertrude must triumph over the pirate and any other legal claimants, including her spectral uncle, to prevent white slavery.

In a testament to Sedgwick's theory of appeasement as a moral good, the novel concludes with a scene of northern domestic bliss among plantation heiresses and their benefactors. As in later fiction, Sedgwick "generate[d] a new sphere of sympathy" by economically joining nonrelated families via gifting. Gertrude's wealth "gives the privilege of selection," the narrator notes, allegedly based on the "character of our guests" but clearly in alignment with white nation making and limited transcolonial foreign relations. Gertrude gives Emilie Layton $20,000, making the daughter of pirate-allied enslavers akin to "the youngest daughters in fairy tales."[77] Notably, the novel's Haitian plantation heiress's own wealth had been compared to "the gifts of a fairy tale" purchased by denied Haitian sovereignty. Gertrude hosts these relations in her husband's newly repurchased "fine old family mansion," thereby restoring a depressed American lineage with the spoils of enslavement. She stocks her transcolonial library with "classics in English, French, German, Italian, and Spanish, and all of the best editions," a testament to her ongoing foreign relations across legal and literary culture. Benevolent patronage in a narrow domestic circle, rather than global agitation over abolition, defines the novel's political vision. *Clarence*, like antebellum legal decisions, thus concludes with narratively complex yet morally hollow appeasements.[78]

Sedgwick's next novel, *The Linwoods* (1835), reveals an ongoing investment in appeasement as a moral and legal strategy. This historical fiction of the American Revolution, Avallone concludes, "relegates freed African Americans to the status of permanent menials" in favor of white nation making. This process remains oceanic. The figures "shackled and sentinelled by a foreign power" are not enslaved Africans but, as the narrator notes, white revolutionaries. American sovereignty is set against an "ocean covered with rebel privateers."[79] The British are not pirates because postwar foreign relations had been secured by 1835. Even so, a hope for American national glory persists in the novel. "How long before we may look out upon this avenue to the ocean as the entrance to our independent homes," the heroic Eliot Lee asks, "and open or shut it, as it pleases us, to the commerce and friendship of the world!" The novel promises a union of domestic interiority and foreign relations that had yet to come to fruition in real life. Even so, the "prediction of the future and recreation of the past" that Michelle Sizemore reads in the affective enchantments of *The Linwoods* may be tied to American global supremacy at sea.[80] Sedgwick, like the antebellum courts, refrained from claiming jurisdiction over global abolition as part of this political project.

In keeping with her legal culture's ongoing appeasements, Sedgwick continued to reject domestic enslavement and universal abolition in her vision of national family. In 1830, she sent a copy of *Clarence* to Child, though we do not know how Child reacted to its circumspect treatment of abolition. When *Clarence* was reissued in 1849, antebellum legal culture still relied on the Piracy Act of 1820 to circumscribe abolition. Alleged pirates continued to populate the era's political waters (see chapters 2 and 3). Advocates for enslavement turned to South America and Latin America as new domestic sites to be gained by privately mounted military campaigners. The reissued *Clarence* could thus be read as "a kind of historical fiction," according to Homestead, in which Pedrillo operated alongside imperial filibusters.[81] Even so, Sedgwick's edits to the novel demonstrate an even greater fear of abolitionist futures. Her largest change is a deepened lament over Black revolutionary sovereignty as embodied by Haiti. What the 1830 edition calls "the troubles" become "the disastrous period of '92" in the 1849 version. In the world outside of the novel, direct action against enslavement continued, and the limits of legal appeasement remained hard to deny. Like many of her contemporaries, however, Sedgwick often favored limited victories over crimes against feeling. She retained a focus on domestic virtue, national union, and a moralizing yet conciliatory stance toward enslavement. In "Slavery in New England" (1853), published in *Bentley's Miscellany*, she recounted the formerly enslaved Elizabeth Freeman's charitable acts following her legal emancipation. This seemingly abolitionist tract nonetheless distinguishes between southern enslavement and the "parental kindness" found in a northern bondage system whose "hard masters and cruel mistresses" were as infrequent as "cruel fathers and exacting mothers."[82] Such apologetics lacked the abolitionist vigor required to call enslavement a piratical crime against feeling.

Rather than retreat from legal culture, Sedgwick continued to adjudicate the national family's moral responsibility in her late career. She published didactic fiction, children's stories, and two more novels in the 1840s and 1850s. She remained a champion of prison reform and women's political rights. Above all, she championed white women's unique moral virtue and necessary political rights. Her final novel, *Married or Single?* (1857), presents white women's legal choice over their marital status as the national family's best political recourse. Black women's legal rights remain visible in the brief incursion of "hounds . . . hunting down their fellow-sufferin' creatures," an enslaved women and her child in the North. In the novel, domestic enslavement's increasing legal protections sever individual families and threaten the national one. Yet Sedgwick's brief appeal lacks the resentment that would increasingly influence writers such as Harriet Beecher Stowe. Such comparisons appear to have fed Sedgwick's personal doubts in her late life. "Is it not rather a folly (is it worse?) at my time of life to perpetrate a novel without any purpose or hope to slay giants, slavery, or the like," she wrote in an 1857 letter to the Unitarian minister Orville Dewey, "but only to supply mediocre readers with small moral hints on various subjects that come up in daily life?" Sedgwick's potential "folly," she admitted with painful self-deprecation, was to engage individual readers' common feelings without placing daily domestic life in its full political context.[83] Her late career, Deborah Gussman affirms, revealed the tension between the "nuances of moderate politics" that she espoused and scholarly models of "progressive social change." As Gussman notes, respecting Sedgwick's and other women writers' complexity represents the "next stage of the recovery movement" that has previously aligned women's literary value with their political progressivism. As part of a more nuanced next stage, scholars such as Jordan L. Von Cannon have astutely engaged Sedgwick's "idle activism," or her ambivalence around issues such as enslavement, as a political stance that "underscores the energy of sheer contradiction." Sedgwick's contradicting energies toward enslavement led her to legal theories of piracy. Her appeasements aligned with federal laws that were also energized by sheer contradiction or, to some, sheer nonsense.[84]

"LAW—NONSENSE": ABOLITION IN THE WAKE OF 1820

Debates over enslavement's status as piracy persisted in the decades following the Piracy Act of 1820. New York City and New Orleans remained hubs for human trafficking. A dubious legal binary and delicate political balance endured. Deep-sea enslavement's piratical status weakened the trade, and naval squadrons tasked with capturing enslaving pirates increased. This policy also legally sheltered and positively incubated the trade. Tellingly, the West African squadron caught and tried only one enslaver in African waters between 1822 and 1844.[85] The West Indies squadron and related forces in the Caribbean were more successful. Notably, the 1822 removal of Jean Lafitte, a New Orleans–based pirate (and a privateer during the War of 1812), considered by historian Ernest Obadele-Starks to be "the most ruthless of all Gulf Coast slave smugglers," marked the illegal trade's decline. As Lafitte's career had made clear, however, illegal deep-sea enslavement could lead to legal enslavement on land. In the years before his capture, customs officials had legally sold enslaved Africans on his behalf. Lafitte had allegedly stolen this human cargo from piratical smugglers and was thus legally entitled to compensation. In reality, Sara E. Johnson notes, Lafitte had worked with planters, smugglers, and government officials to sell prearranged human lots. In other words, Lafitte oversaw a laundering process with echoes of both the *Antelope* decision and Sedgwick's *Clarence*. Illegal, or dirty, human cargo could be washed clean by abolitionist statutes that forced government sales of contraband. Policymakers considered the alternative—captured Africans' domestic freedom in the United States—a threat to necessary political stability that was grounded in white supremacy.[86]

Both legal abolition and extralegal emancipation persisted in the decades after the Piracy Act. To strengthen America's foreign relations with abolitionist England, Daniel Webster brokered the Webster-Ashburton Treaty (1842), which not only settled early national border disputes but revived the spirit of abolitionist and antipiracy treaties by calling for "the final Suppression of the African Slave Trade." Its signatories promised to "deliver up to justice" all of those who committed "murder, or Piracy, or arson, or robbery, or Forgery." The treaty did not address the question of maritime search or establish universal jurisdiction over piracy. It designated an exchange of sentiments more than an actionable policy against slave markets in Africa and elsewhere. The nations would "unite" to "urge upon all such Powers the propriety and duty of closing such markets effectually at once and forever."[87] In other words, they would attempt to give abolitionist feeling legal force via the power of sympathy. Enslavers bristled at this real and symbolic threat but remained protected by judgments such as *The Antelope*. They imported nearly 2 million enslaved persons throughout the Americas between 1820 and 1850. American plantation owners benefited from chattel enslavement's legal power as a family inheritance. During this same period, the domestic population of enslaved persons more than doubled to 3.2 million.[88] In other words, appeals to domestic interiority and oceanic security did not prevent enslaving piracy. Nor did they prevent Black revolutions on either land and water. Examples include Denmark Vesey's

Rebellion (1822), Nat Turner's Rebellion (1831), the Baptist War (1831), the Black Seminole Slave Rebellion (1835–38), the *Amistad* Rebellion (1839), the *Creole* Mutiny (1841), and innumerable other forms of active and passive resistance.[89]

During this period of appeasement and rebellion, an article titled "Pirates" in an October 1846 issue of *The Liberator* sought to combat the pervasive domestic fiction of a moral nation fighting immoral pirates. The author imagined the antebellum nation as a family born onto a pirate ship: "I have called this a nation of Robbers and Pirates, and there is a great outcry among those that are deepest in guilt." The latter included not only political policymakers but also white American families. Shared investments in enslavement made piracy "a question that concerns every man, woman and child in the Union." "Generation after generation has arisen under the system of wickedness established by their fathers," establishing piracy as a national inheritance. "Children [are] thus trained to piracy," their individual moral characters notwithstanding. Heiresses such as Sedgwick's Gertrude Clarence were, perhaps, pirates who refused to recognize their role in enslavement. Both Sedgwick and figures such as Justice Joseph Story variably proved *The Liberator* author's lament that, when it came to the nation's piratical status, many "will not even listen to the question, and much less are they willing to give it a candid answer." In truth, Sedgwick and Story, unlike many of their peers, did listen to the question. Even so, they refrained from a legal or familial reckoning. The writer concluded that one must "renounce a government of Pirates and Robbers, as the United States' government most truly is." One must refuse to appease a piratical ship of state, even if that means "destroy[ing] the boat." After all, the boat is a slave ship "whose walls are built with human carcasses cemented with tears and blood." In the eyes of this author, the slave ship, rather than the white parlor, remained the nation's defining domestic space. In such a vision, violent abolition was not piracy. It struck against state-backed family annihilators and their domestic appeasers.[90]

As *The Liberator* writer knew, antebellum legal institutions positioned both enslavement and abolition as piracy. This culture's moral failures were best staged by a fiction that juxtaposed abolitionist Black piracy with proslavery legal reasoning. "Law—nonsense—tortures, death, eternal curses!": so declares the enslaver Mr. Sexton in "The Florida Pirate" (1821), a short story first published by John Howison in *Blackwood's Edinburgh Magazine*. The popular narrative was reprinted at least seven times between 1821 and 1834. In the story, Sexton is struck by the enslaved Manuel after the death of Sabrina, a fellow slave and Manuel's beloved. "Does God Almighty really permit this?—A slave! A black! A Negro!—Strike me—a noble Carolinian! Is there a law to punish this?" Manuel's literal strike against enslavement's power pushes Sexton to seek legal recourse, and his outburst is rich in meaning. The possibility that white supremacy does not have legal protection represents, for him, an "eternal curse" contrary to natural law. His reaction also reveals the law itself to be nonsense in its sanctioning of "tortures, death, and eternal curses" for the enslaved. White supremacist legal nonsense grew from the fear of Black resistance as epitomized by revolutionary Haiti. Enslavement received a partial check in the Piracy Act of 1820. In response, Howison's "exploitation of the 1820 legislation," Gretchen J. Woertendyke notes, led him to present Black piracy as a direct product of piratical enslavers and their legally sanctioned brethren. The tragic story's main plot treats Manuel's piracy as an act of necessity rather than of moral unfeeling. Manuel loses his hand in punishment for striking Sexton. He then burns down his enslaver's plantation and becomes captain of the pirate ship *La Esperanza*, now crewed by the formerly enslaved. Though certainly not hopeful, the pirate captain "took refuge upon the sea" that allows him to temporarily "escape the blood-hounds of the Southern States of America." Condemned to die after his eventual capture, he accepts the law's martial, if not moral, power. "Oh perhaps not," Manuel states in reference to his moral innocence "but, law—law—law, you know." We know. As in Sedgwick's fiction, removed Black heirs purchase white domestic bliss in "The Florida Pirate." The narrative concludes with the "mutual happiness" of a white narrator and his betrothed after they receive Manuel's fortune. In a parable of legal critique and political confirmation, Howison restages antebellum legal culture's guiding logic: a nation predicated on white familial supremacy criminalizes direct action against enslavers as piratical crimes against feeling.[91]

Some abolitionists continued to hope that judicial fellow feeling would prevent political violence. Despite Justice Story's appeasements, many valued his sentimental opinions against enslaving piracy. Primary among them was Senator Charles Sumner of Massachusetts, Story's former student at Harvard Law School and a frequent collaborator. On October 6, 1851, Sumner wrote a letter to Story's son William following the judge's death. Surveying his friend's storied legal career, Sumner lamented that Story could no longer extend his work in maritime law to "one grander still, on the Law of Nations." Aware of his compromises, the abolitionist Sumner nonetheless presented Story as capable of bringing together a family of nations. This generous interpretation was a fitting condolence for Story's family. William Story included the letter in his father's edited works as proof that the judge had "looked forward to new and vast juridical and literary plans for the future, which were cut short by death." William considered his father to be "the creator of Admiralty law, in America." This somewhat accurate yet self-serving family story paralleled a persistent hope in national union. Years later, Sumner would appeal to Story's "remarkable judgement" in *La Jeune Eugenie* to decry piratical enslavement as a "violation of International Law." Story had, in practice, appeased enslavers while supporting abolitionists' legal theories. The question of how to solve a question such as piratical enslavement remained active. Sumner, considered by the poet Henry Wadsworth Longfellow to be "a colossus holding his burning heart in his hand to light up the sea of life," represented a bridge between Story's restrained legal thinking and more open abolitionist politicking. Continued appeasement for enslavers would, for Sumner and others, lead to resentment's legal and moral potential.[92] Whether an abolitionist pirate's resentment of the state could or should justify violence against a white supremacist legal regime remained an open question.

CHAPTER TWO

RESENTMENT

John Quincy Adams, Harriet Beecher Stowe, and United States v. Schooner Amistad *(1841)*

"The great majority, South as well as North, have human sympathies," asserted Abraham Lincoln on October 16, 1854, "of which they can no more divest themselves than they can of their sensibility to physical pain." In this speech, delivered in Peoria, Illinois, Lincoln appealed to the theory of moral sentiments that defined antebellum legal culture. As he told the crowd, abolitionist fellow feeling legalized by the Piracy Act of 1820 might yet cut knots of political difference. Unfeeling piratical figures lurked outside the national "great majority," he admitted. But the "sympathies in the bosoms of the Southern people" had been proven by their acquiescence in "declaring the African slave trade piracy." Yet Lincoln's familiar narrative—that of federal union against piratical unfeeling—belied ongoing national support for enslavement. Imagining universal southern support for the act, he asked the crowd, "Why did you do this? If you did not feel that it was wrong, why did you join in providing that men should be hung for it?" The Piracy Act of 1820, we know, resulted from hard-fought political compromises rather than universal sentiments. For Lincoln, however, feeling against piracy would spur even more expansive abolitionist laws. He continued, "It is your sense of justice, and human sympathy, continually telling you, that the poor Negro has some natural right to himself." Natural law, he suggested, must dictate positive law, despite prior denials. Lincoln's assertion that enslavers who denied Black sympathy and "ma[d]e mere merchandise of him, deserve kickings, contempt and death" was perhaps his most forceful abolitionist statement to date.[1] Enslaving pirates could be met with just violence.

Lincoln's Peoria speech was, like many recounted in this book, a domestic pirate fiction that obscured more complex political undercurrents. Indeed, Lincoln recounted the anxieties of "heart" and "conscience" that had powered its delivery in a copy of the speech that he sent to a legal colleague in December 1854. "We shall have a terrible struggle with our adversaries," he wrote of proslavery politicians that he had aligned with pirates. "They are desperate, and bent on desperate deeds."[2] Lincoln's own political desperation, though suppressed in his public address, is palpable in the note. Recent political shifts had roused him from private legal practice. In 1849, he had left the U.S. House of Representatives after serving a two-year term. Political appeasement for enslavement by northerners and southerners alike, more so than southern desperation, defined the years that followed. The 1850 Fugitive Slave Act further empowered enslavers by forcing the return of runaways in free states. The act was part of the Compromise of 1850, a set of five bills that attempted to create domestic stability by balancing enslavement's legality: enslavement would be illegal in the new state of California while Washington, DC, would ban the slave trade but not enslavement itself. Lincoln's Peoria speech was a direct response to the 1854 Kansas-Nebraska Act, which act allowed enslavement in these new territories and negated landed enslavement's northernmost limit as defined by the 1820 Missouri Compromise. The act enshrined "popular sovereignty," the notion that communal sentiment should determine enslavement's legality. As historian John Burt writes, Kansas and Nebraska became "theatres of proxy war over slavery" across the landed nation. The act also represented a vital shift in antebellum legal culture around piracy. Enslavers' share of land amid the land-sea divide grew stronger. The prospect of oceanic enslavement's legalization loomed large.[3]

Though Lincoln appealed to hoped-for abolitionist fellow feeling, his 1854 speech also appeased enslavers in the name of national union. He espoused abolition but denied Black equality. He aligned established law with white supremacist fellow feeling. In other words, like Justice Story, Lincoln mixed sentimental form and cold legal reasoning. He considered the repeal of the Missouri Compromise of 1820 an offense against national feeling and called for a return to the divisions set in the Piracy Act of 1820. The restoration of prior compromise, Burt writes, afforded him a "concrete but limited, specific action." Lincoln could morally dismiss enslavement without giving abolition universal jurisdiction.[4] Like Story, he presented moral feeling against piracy as a strategic path forward but refused to adjudicate where that path should lead in relation to global enslavement. "If all earthy power were given to me," he admitted, "I should not know what to do, as to the existing institution." Ongoing enslavement was a moral injury, he knew. Emancipation followed by colonization in Liberia seemed impractical, he thought, since there was "not surplus shipping and surplus money enough." Emancipation follow by Black equality was incompatible with the white supremacist feelings to which he gave legal force. Lincoln's "own feelings [would] not admit" Black equality, nor would "the great mass of white people." Of this seeming moral failure, he noted: "Whether this feeling accords with justice and sound judgment, is not the sole question, if indeed, it is any part of it." Political pragmatism might trump feelings of justice, he concluded, even in the context of natural law: "A universal feeling, whether well or ill-founded, cannot be safely disregarded. We cannot, then, make them equals." Black Americans' feelings did not have the same legal force as the white supremacy that Lincoln framed as natural, if not moral. His politics would shift after the secession that followed his eventual victory over Stephen Douglass, the author of the Kansas-Nebraska Act, in the 1860 presidential election (see chapter 4).[5] For Lincoln, political reality would continue to shape piracy's definition and punishment.

Lincoln had strategically omitted persistent political fracture in his sentimental appeal to the Piracy Act of 1820. He remained a centrist on the spectrum of legal culture around piracy. Ongoing debates on the act's legacy hinged on whether deep-sea enslavement's status as piracy represented a legal model or a moral injury to be reversed. In keeping with piracy's legal power across a political spectrum, an alleged pirate could be a radical abolitionist, an immoral enslaver, or a just revolutionary. During an 1848 congressional debate, John C. Calhoun, a former vice president who was then serving as a senator for South Carolina, railed against abolitionist lawmakers and activists who committed "these atrocities—these piratical attempts" when they protected a group of fugitive slaves who had escaped to the sea.[6] As Calhoun argued in the widely published March 1850 congressional speech that proved to be his last, the proposed Fugitive Slave Act restored "nearly a perfect equilibrium" of legal enslavement as enshrined in the Constitution. Policies such as the Piracy Act of 1820 had swung the balance toward abolitionist pirates. In an appeal to sentiments, Calhoun asserted that if the abolitionist North had "half the love of the Union which she professes to have," it would "do justice" and "cease the agitation of the slave question." The moral alternative to abolitionist piracy, in his view, was domestic enslavement's legal sanction.

Senator Daniel Webster of Massachusetts addressed the Senate on March 7, 1850, with "a solicitous and anxious heart," speaking in favor of such appeasements "for the preservation of union."[7] In what became known as his "Seventh of March Speech," he clearly demonstrated that his politics had shifted since his arguments against enslaving piracy in *La Jeune Eugenie* (1822). In a speech given directly after the passage of the Piracy Act of 1820, Webster had unapologetically asserted that "the African slaver trader is a pirate and a felon" who retained illegal sanction from citizens "in whose hearts dwell no sentiments of humanity or of justice." Transcripts of such early speeches, republished in the 1850s, led Webster into public arguments against his prior self.[8] Universal abolition would not defeat unfeeling pirates, he now argued in 1850, but would only "exasperate the feelings, and subdue the sense of fraternal affection, patriotic love, and mutual regard." Such appeasement, he concluded, would allow for a "golden chain" powered by the Constitution and the "affections of the whole people" to further envelop a nation that now spanned the "two great seas of the world."[9] Legal enslavement remained key to familial union and imperial supremacy, a platform that was central to his support for the 1850 Compromise, his return as U.S. secretary of state in July 1851, and his failed 1852 presidential campaign.

For abolitionists such as Ralph Waldo Emerson, "Mr. Webster's treachery" increased the imbalance between antebellum law and natural moral sentiments. As Emerson argued in May 1851, the Piracy Act of 1820 was not supposed to be a hard limit. Rather, it was supposed to spur an abolitionist wave in keeping with natural law. In his "Address to the Citizens of Concord on the Fugitive Slave Law," Emerson outlined how immoral laws were "contravened by the written laws themselves, because the sentiments, of course, write the statutes." For him, both the Piracy Act and the Fugitive Slave Law were rare moral deviations from natural law through which positive law derived. He contrasted enslavement's legal status as piracy at sea—"Off soundings, it is piracy and murder to enslave him"—with the Fugitive Slave Act's forced piracy—"On soundings, it is fine and prison not to re-enslave." Emerson wondered resentfully, "What kind of legislation is this? What kind of Constitution which covers it?" He ended his speech not with absolutely fealty to the law but with an appeal to civil disobedience and moral feeling. He argued that breaking a fugitive slave law "contravened by all the sentiments" corresponded with both legal reasoning and moral virtue. Emerson concluded, "An immoral law makes it a man's duty to break it, even at hazard." Only direct, possibly illegal, action could recall the world to proper sentiments.[10]

As these various men made clear, resentment was a force in antebellum legal culture around piracy in the 1840s and 1850s. Legal figures treated both positive fellow feeling and sentimental resentment as models for aligning federal policy with natural law. Resentment could help index existing piracy law's moral shortcomings. It could also be a tool for enacting new law. Some resented abolition as piracy; others resented enslavement; still others resented an entire antebellum legal culture that wanted it both ways. This jurisprudence of resentment remained powerful because it, like the legal theory of piracy, was predicated on feeling rather than action. It could thus be wielded by figures across a political spectrum. The state's claim to feeling—and, with it, the pirate's claim to resentment—needed to be adjudicated. Figures like Emerson showed how positive fellow feeling, known as beneficence, may exist alongside violent resentment of existing law. As a product of sympathy, beneficence was understood as a self-interested correspondence with another subject's pain. Emerson's and Lincoln's calls for beneficence toward the enslaved were key to their rejection of enslavement as piracy. Each resented enslavement, although only Emerson called for civil disobedience. John C. Calhoun, however, applied beneficence only to enslavers or those who resented legal challenges to white supremacy. Such diversity of feeling befits a moral philosophy predicated on self-interested projections. Who represented one's brother and who operated the rack in violent clashes over enslavement were political calculations. As Joseph Story had made clear in *La Jeune Eugenie* (1822) and related rulings, the state of positive law and its protections for enslavement limited beneficence's legal power. Natural feelings against enslavement had not been given universal legal sanction.

Though in political conflict, each of the figures I have mentioned relied on resentment's legal and moral power as outlined in Adam Smith's *The Theory of Moral Sentiments*. Although feeling against the state typically rendered one a pirate, just resentment was a mechanism for valid legal challenge. Smith remained statist in philosophy but also considered it natural for individuals to feel beyond institutional directives. As Michael L. Frazer concludes, Smith "developed an individualist, rights based, and recognizably liberal conception of justice."[11] For Smith, fellow feeling was not determined by governments, nor was it pacifistic. After all, it was natural to resent those with "no regard to the sufferings of his bretheren."[12] Moral antagonists operated a rack against one's family, often with legal impunity. In such moments, beneficence alone was not sufficient for justice. Resentment was a natural response to the rack's operator.

Resentment derived from the feeling that the "violator of the laws of justice ought to be made to feel himself the evil which he has done to another." Such "resentment," Smith noted, "seems to have been given us by nature for defence, and for defence only." While Webster discredited abolitionist resentment as offensive both morally and politically, others argued that just defense naturally required recalling immoral agents to rational self-interest. Those who failed to imagine the pain of their brother on the rack, Smith wrote, "ought to be overawed by the fear of his own." Moreover, he confirmed that sympathy's political power was actually stronger when tied to resentment. In his view, the response to a person in pain was an "indolent and passive fellow feeling" whereas one's attachment to a person who righteously inflicts pain was a "more vigorous and active sentiment." To sympathize with a resentful abolitionist, many argued, was to actively counter the source of his pain: state violence.[13] In such cases, an alleged pirate's feeling against the state might help diagnose the state's legal failures. Abolitionist piracy was, in this view, less a legal hazard and more a just natural sentiment. The beneficence one felt for the enslaved powered natural action against enslavers and their sovereign protectors.[14] In this case, the pirate's limited beneficence did not preclude a claim to moral sympathy and legal standing. Competing theories of justice variably applied. "The end of justice," Smith asserted, "is to secure from injury." He presented three forms of injury in his "Lectures on Jurisprudence": one may be injured "as a man, . . . as a member of a family, . . . [or] as a member of a state." All may be mapped onto domestic pirate fictions with competing ideologies and comparable plot points.[15]

Legal and literary challenges to ongoing global enslavement revealed ongoing fractures in antebellum legal culture around piracy. The status of a national family and the state's power to protect it remained in question. In this chapter, I will begin by studying the legal theories of resentment on display in the Supreme Court case *United States v. Schooner Amistad* (1841) and in later criminal cases against alleged enslaving pirates who escaped punishment. I will next outline varied appeals to resentment in domestic pirate fictions by Harriet Beecher Stowe and Michel Maxwell Philip in light of ongoing legal appeasement. Then, after a short analysis of Herman Melville's refusals of sympathy in *Benito Cereno* (1855), I will briefly consider debates on John Brown's 1859 raid on Harpers Ferry as an act of piracy. Taken together, all represent a sentimental jurisprudence of resentment that variably deemed abolitionist violence a natural reaction to unnatural, piratical laws.

"SYMPATHY WAS WRONG BEFORE": RESENTMENT IN *AMISTAD* AND LATER PIRACY CASES

On February 29, 1841, John Quincy Adams took the stand in *United States v. Schooner Amistad.* The case concerned thirty-eight enslaved Africans whom had been arrested as pirates after mutinying aboard the Spanish slaver *La Amistad* in July 1839. Adams, a former president, was then seventy-three years old. He had not argued a case before the Supreme Court in decades. A year earlier, Adams had aided the captives' successful defense in district court. Now he stood in defense of those whose emancipation had been deemed piratical. Justice Joseph Story, the man who had adjudicated both *La Jeune Eugenie* (1822) and *Antelope* (1825), sat in judgment as a member of the High Court, as did Chief Justice John Marshall, who had penned the *Antelope* decision. These judicial reunions—and, with them, a tendency toward congratulatory self-reference and political stratagem under the guise of legal dispassion—were the prerogative of an insulated legal institution that bestowed lifelong terms to white male jurists to hear cases of Black freedom.

Adams pierced the Court's veil of apolitical neutrality in his *Amistad* arguments, a stance that befitted his prior refusal to be confirmed as a justice. Via a rousing sentimental narration (which I will discuss shortly), Adams bemoaned the Court's enduring allegiance to unfeeling pirates. He distilled his opinion by admonishing the Court's prior rulings, declaring that "sympathy was wrong before." The justices had protected oceanic enslavers in prior piracy cases. Antebellum jurists across the country had continually failed to prosecute or punish enslaving pirates. Officials now leveled accusations of piracy against Africans that had been illegally enslaved aboard *La Amistad.* This lineage, in Adams's view, reflected a tortuous tangle of legal and moral compromises. The Court's mistaken sympathy, he argued, could be traced to decades of federal policy. As a member of the House of Representatives, Adams had fought stridently against a gag rule prohibiting open debates regarding abolition, a resolution that had first passed in 1836 and had been renewed yearly until its repeal in 1844. Speaking now to the Court, he revealed his unmistakable resentment against congressional and judicial appeasement. He recounted how abolitionist feeling aligned with legal precedence. Universal abolition was not yet on the court's docket, he admitted. Nor was the court's legal power under scrutiny. Adams did not consider whether piracy represented a productive legal and moral alternative to such power, though others would.[16]

Though it energized abolitionist activism, *Amistad* further established a jurisprudence of appeasement in the name of foreign relations and domestic stability. As in prior cases, the alleged pirates on trial had stolen property. Befitting the law's rejection of Black humanity, the stolen property was themselves. In 1839, forty-nine West African men and four children, members of the Mende people, had been enslaved in West Africa and transported to Cuba under the guise of the Spanish domestic trade. After forcibly taking the ship, the Mendeans were recaptured by a U.S. Navy ship in New York. The case, which took years to adjudicate, "united abolitionists across factional lines," as historian Manisha Sinha notes. *Amistad* was a flashpoint in antebellum legal culture. William Lloyd Garrison published interviews with the revolt's leaders, Cinque and his lieutenant, Grabeau, who discussed the ordeal and Mendean culture. A group calling itself the Amistad Committee raised money for the captives and provided a legal defense that could serve as a model for other abolitionists tried as pirates. This legal team included Catharine Maria Sedgwick's nephew, Theodore Sedgwick, as well as Roger Sherman Baldwin, who would become governor of Connecticut.[17]

As in earlier cases, the federal government attempted to limit its jurisdiction over a political ally. Spain, citing prior treaties, sought to retain the enslaved and considered the Mendeans to be pirates. The United States, seeking to protect its foreign relations and appease domestic proslavery forces, advocated for the alleged pirates' return to Spain. Once again, the Court adjudicated the state's jurisdiction and legal feeling. It reversed a prior course, to a degree: Spain's claim would be denied and the Mendeans freed. By removing the piracy charge against the Mendeans, the Court confirmed that violent rejection of state power was not the domain of pirates alone. Yet it also affirmed that appeasement remained federal policy. The government continued to uphold the claim that American piracy statutes around oceanic enslavement could not overawe a morally circumscribed law of nations.

The federal response to *Amistad* before and after the trial revealed the U.S. government's continued advocacy that revolutionary Black sovereignty was piratical. Oceanic enslavement's legal status as a piratical crime against feeling had not precluded its domestic or global protection in cases such as *Antelope* (1825). In its arguments in *Amistad*, the United States presented foreign enslavers and the Spanish government as legally aligned. Appealing to the law of nations, international treaties, and moral feeling, it claimed that the enslaved aboard *La Amistad* were pirates. "That the acts committed by the negroes amount to piracy and robbery," stated Attorney General Henry Dilworth Gilpin, "seems too clear to be questioned." He pointed out that, as pirates, they had violently overthrown national subjects and had stolen property. Although the property and the pirate were the same entity, Gilpin argued against "any difference between property in slaves and other property." The Mende people's humanity or feelings did not give them legal claim to a family or to the state's protection. They were pirates and thus did not deserve sympathy. Their political motivations were overshadowed by their antagonism to a sovereign.

The United States was not strictly the aggrieved party in this case, but existing treaties with Spain created a legal sympathetic tie. A December 1839 letter from Secretary of State John Forsyth to the Spanish government defined these relations. Forsyth presented the arrest of the Mendeans as pirates to be an act of national feeling backed by law. He described "officers of the United States, who [were] moved towards [*La Amistad*'s Spanish owners] by sympathetic feeling which subsequently became as it were national." Legal action against pirates reflected individual, national, and international familial feeling. This feeling was supported, Forsyth claimed, by Pickney's Treaty of 1795 and the Adams-Onis Treaty of 1819. The fact that the latter treaty's architect, John Quincy Adams, opposed this interpretation shows how foreign relations strayed beyond their initial wedded pairs. Without respect for Spanish-American treaties, Gilpin concluded, "there could be no peace or comity among nations; all harmony, all mutual respect would be destroyed." As in the *Antelope* trial, foreign relations trumped domestic law, particularly the 1820 piracy statute. Citing *Antelope*, Gilpin claimed that arresting the enslaved aboard *La Amistad* as pirates represented "the course required by the laws of nations." Positive law, he concluded, precluded an abolitionist appeal to natural law in this case. To punish piracies and join national sympathies necessitated the captives' reenslavement.[18]

In his defense of the Mendeans, the abolitionist lawyer Roger Sherman Baldwin presented an alternative reading of the same precedents. He considered whether the formerly enslaved on *La Amistad* were pirates whom the state should punish and rejected the *Antelope* decision as a valid precedent in positive or natural law: "Neither the law of nature nor the law of nations authorizes the slave-trade; although it was holden in the case of the *Antelope*."[19] Much had changed in the decades between the cases, including Spanish treaties with both the United States and England that further restricted oceanic enslavement. Baldwin accepted that "it is lawful for, and the duty of, all nations to capture and to punish [piracy]." Yet he argued that if the state had no feeling toward the pirate, it must feel for those aboard *La Amistad*. After all, their moral feeling belied their charge as pirates. He asserted that the Mendeans "were not pirates, nor in any sense *hostes humani generis*." Unlike pirates, they served a "single object" based in moral sentiment. Specifically, Baldwin claimed, "That object was—not piracy or robbery—but the deliverance of himself and his companions in suffering." Violence against enslavers was not piracy if based on the capacity to feel pain and prevent pain in others. Beneficence, not piratical unfeeling or extranational resentment, distinguished the Mendeans from pirates.[20]

Notably, Baldwin's testimony did not rely on resentment toward the state. He carefully aligned the Mendeans with statist feeling. He did not espouse global abolition based in natural law. In an appeal to positive law, he admitted that international law would not permit an American cruiser to overtake a Spanish enslaving vessel in Cuba. American law did not have universal global reach. Nevertheless, the Mendeans could claim domestic attachment at the moment they sailed themselves onto American shores. Existing treaties with Spain "authorized us to treat them with hospitality, as freemen"—that is, as familial subjects with corresponding rights. To do otherwise would deny American sovereignty by "giving extra-territorial force to a foreign slave law." For Baldwin, American legal jurisdiction corresponded with its moral sentiment: "Such a duty would not only be repugnant to the feelings of a large portion of the citizens of the United States, but it would be wholly inconsistent with the fundamental principles of our government." Citizens' antislavery feelings were again presumed to have legal force. Baldwin admitted that alternative feelings existed, saying, "It may comport with the interest or feelings of a slave state to surrender a fugitive slave to a foreigner." Yet he argued that such mistaken sympathies did not have legal force. Pirates or their allies were meager claimants compared to the enslaved. Legal reasoning and moral sense abhorred the "fraud" of holding these people as pirates. "And yet strange as it may seem, during all this time," Baldwin concluded, "not only the sympathies of the Spanish minister, but the powerful aid of our own Government have been enlisted in their behalf!" While Baldwin stopped short of calling the government piratical, one thing was clear: in his view, the federal government, not the Mendeans, had committed crimes against feeling.[21]

Though Adams's testimony was less cited than Baldwin's in the Court's decision, it powerfully extended his colleague's pervading theme: the government's culpability in piratical enslavement. Like Baldwin, Adams displayed a keen knowledge of both case law and its reliance on sympathy. He did not deny the government's moral or legal right to punish piracy. He accepted that the state joined feeling subjects and defined piracy as a crime against feeling. Adams did, however, present the government's deference to Spain in *Amistad* as worthy of resentment. The federal government and its courts were "bound" to be just, he argued. Yet "instead of justice . . . they have substituted *Sympathy*! . . . Sympathy with the white and antipathy to the black." Adams quoted Secretary of State Forsyth's letter about national "sympathetic feeling" with Spain as proof of the mutineers' piracy. In *Amistad*, Adams declared, "The national sympathy with the slave traders of the baracoons is officially declared to have been the prime motive of the government." Even though abolitionist feeling was not universal, federal policy had mistakenly valued immoral enslaving sympathies.[22] Adams provided a succinct breakdown of the ruptures within antebellum legal culture. "It is but too true," he said of Forsyth's letter, "that the same spirit of sympathy and antipathy has nearly pervaded the whole nation." Proslavery feelings persisted, he admitted, but antipathy to abolition did not correspond with legal reason or a natural law. He wondered "by what right, all this *sympathy*" could be given to Spanish perpetrators of "lawless violence" instead of to the enslaved Africans who "had restored themselves to freedom." For Adams, the enslaved were under the protection of American national feeling once they entered national waters. Though the Mendeans unmistakably engaged in violence, they were "in peace with the United States" and therefore "were not pirates." Once ashore, the formerly enslaved were fit for domestic protection against pirates.[23]

Adams, more than Baldwin, directly challenged prior Supreme Court decisions as unjust crimes against feeling. Those decisions, in his view, threatened the nation's legal and moral standing. Even so, he understood that one could reapply legal precedence to repair prior mistaken sympathies. He stated of *Amistad's* case history, "the decisions of JUSTICE were not in accordance with the impulses of sympathy, and that consequently the sympathy was wrong before. And consequently it now appears that everything which has flowed from this mistaken or misapplied sympathy, was wrong from the beginning." In short, a legal precedence had been established in *Antelope* and related cases that applied sympathy to piratical enslavers rather than the illegally enslaved. These decisions materially altered legal statuses—rendering the enslaved unfit for national feeling and piratical enslavers fit for protection—and set a precedent for future forms of mistaken sympathy. Oceanic enslavement's status as piracy, Adams stated, "embrace[s] both the cases of the *Antelope* and of the *Amistad*." The "sympathy with Spanish slave-traders" shown by the federal government in 1841 mistakenly reinforced the 1825 *Antelope* decision. In it, Chief Justice Marshall had appealed to the positive law of nations to protect an admittedly "odious" form of piracy.[24]

Adams also believed that Marshall had misapplied a "*legal standard of morality*" that unduly ignored both natural law and national feeling. He noted that Marshall had cited the British judge Sir William Scott's definition of criminality based on "that [moral] standard found in the law of nations" rather than an individual judge's moral feeling. In other words, this perspective assumed that a law that felt right (or wrong) must be judged against the feelings of global bodies. Adams did not wholly deny this approach to jurisprudence. He focused instead on popular legality's misapplication. For him, piratical enslavement was contrary to the Declaration of Independence as a legal and moral repudiation of piracy. In that document, Adams claimed, Jefferson had announced that "all obligatory human laws" were extensions of "Laws of Nature." In other words, the Court had to defer to a theory of abolition that began at the nation's inception. This claim necessitated a selective reading of the Declaration. Jefferson's removed pirate represented both abolitionist and pro-enslavement politics. For Adams, the enslaving pirate removed from Jefferson's initial draft had never truly left. The abolitionist pirate had never truly existed. Instead, only abolition could fulfill the founding document's legal and moral promise.[25]

Although the Supreme Court ruled in favor of the *Amistad* captives, it did not fundamentally reject the appeasement at the heart of the *Antelope* decision. That is, it did not remake the period's separation between domestic enslavement and incomplete global abolition. Justice Story did not champion abolition as a form of natural law as he had in his prior decision. Instead, as legal scholar Peter Charles Hoffer notes, he "wrote a narrow opinion based on international law rather than the Constitution." For Story, the government's capacity to punish pirates and pirates' absence of moral feeling were never in doubt. Nor was global enslavement's legality when protected by domestic and international law. Instead, the Court ruled that existing positive law, or the clear abolition of deep-sea trade on the African coast, made questions of natural law or international relations moot. As Paul Finkelman writes, the decision "did not threaten the institution of slavery of even challenge the legitimacy of slavery." It was "almost entirely about a treaty and a specific set of facts." The *Amistad* captives had never been legally enslaved because they retained African sovereignty. Justly freeing themselves, they had committed no robbery. Specifically, they "[could not] be deemed pirates or robbers in the sense of the law of nations, or the treaty with Spain, or the laws of Spain itself." The Court, in keeping with prior precedent, presented piracy as incompatible with domestic attachment to an existing sovereign. Unlike pirates, the violent revolutionaries aboard *La Amistad* had domestic ties. They remained African, a right that had been stripped from millions of others in the middle passage. Spain had no claim to these captives, though it did to other colonized or enslaved subjects. The Mendeans were not unfeeling pirates, but neither were myriad enslavers in both Spain and the United States. A moral and legal chasm remained.[26]

Enslavers tried for piracy in later cases continued to sail through this chasm. Mistaken sympathy remained powerful in a legal culture beset by national appeasement and regional fracture. In November 1854, for example, Captain James Smith of the *Julia Moulton*, which had been purchased in Boston, was the first person convicted of enslaving piracy in U.S. federal court. According to the indictment, he had "piratically and feloniously forcibly confine[d] and detain[ed] five hundred negroes" in violation of the Piracy Act of 1820. On the trial's first day, the prosecutor read the pertinent section of the act to the jury and, by extension, to readers of *The New York Times* and other papers that covered the trial. While the act embodied antebellum legal culture's moral and geographic split over enslavement, he argued that the charge was "one which civilized nations have all stamped as piracy." He also admitted that "the City of New York has been disgraced by this traffic." Captain Smith, as Jeannine Marie DeLombard notes, implicated an entire network of northern merchant families whose "slaver narratives" often rested on selectively disavowing national citizenship to evade legal challenge.[27] His defense rested on his alleged status as German rather than American. Following his conviction, he presented himself as an unrepentant, if reluctant, pirate who was interested in domestic family attachments. "I tried to get another captain to take charge of my ship," he told *The New York Evangelist* in an interview from jail. "I wanted to stay home and get married." Many former pirates, and perhaps the nation itself, had purchased domestic stability via the spoils of oceanic bondage. Northern domesticity's moral and economic tangles with pirates, as reflected in Catharine Maria Sedgwick's fiction, persisted (see chapter 1). Smith's interview, republished in *Frederick Douglass' Paper* and elsewhere, shows how a shared legal fiction of enslaving piracy as a southern institution insulated northern families. *The Anti-Slavery Reporter*, a London-based journal, decried New York merchants at the illicit trade's center who were "wallowing in wealth" when they should have met "the same fate that awaits Captain Smith." There is a clear parallel here with the "first merchants" of Sedgwick's domestic pirate fiction as well as in later works by Maria Susanna Cummins (see chapter 3). Smith's eventual fate further demonstrated an ongoing culture of appeasement. A mistrial was declared following his initial conviction. Smith subsequently pleaded guilty to lesser charges and served thirty-two months of a two-year sentence. He received a $1,000 fine that was later rescinded.[28]

In southern courts, proslavery politicians and newspaper editors redoubled efforts to reopen the oceanic trade via the Piracy Act's repeal. Enslavers charged as pirates in federal court "sailed directly into the sights of slave trade revivalists," writes historian Sharla M. Fett, and became case studies for the piracy statute's unconstitutionality. These "revivalists" had success in at least five cases. For instance, in April 1859, the crew of the *Echo*, captured in 1858 off the coast of Cuba with a cargo of more than three hundred enslaved humans, was acquitted of piracy by an all-white jury in Charleston, South Carolina. Defense lawyers appealed to enslavement's alignment with white supremacist natural law, state sovereignty, and an appeasing law of nations. Above all, they argued that the crew's act of oceanic enslavement, nearly impossible to refute, was not piracy because it aligned with southern familial feeling. After all, the defense claimed, law-abiding southern families had been unduly framed as pirates due to abolitionist policies "repulsive to the feelings of the South." The Piracy Act of 1820 had unduly affirmed "that our fathers were sea-robbers and pirates; for if the slave trade is now piracy and theft, so it was always." According to this argument, the law's moral and logical gap, its split between land and sea, needed to be closed in favor of enslavement. To do otherwise would render entire southern lineages as piratical. "If the law is true, then are we the descendants of pirates," the lawyers asked, "and our slaves entitled to their freedom, for their parents were stolen and there is no shadow of title by which we can hold them?" Abolitionists writing in *The Liberator* and elsewhere also made this exact appeal to familial ties. They argued that mistaken sympathy made some families both *akin* to pirates and *kin* to pirates. In a proslavery jurisprudence, however, generations of chattel slavery prevented unnatural Black sovereignty. Defense lawyers in *Echo* asked the jury to "put aside the law" and consider enslavement's "moral aspect." "Look to Hayti, sovereign, imperial Hayti," they demanded with resentment. Legal freedom for those with "instincts and passions of the animal" threatened an entire global order. In short, they framed enslavement as sustaining white families while preventing abolitionist piracy and unnatural Black sovereignty. This successful argument, weak on its merits, gave credence to abolitionists who sought to operate outside of the law.[29]

These courtroom debates of the 1840s and 1850s found their counterparts in popular literature. For many abolitionists, rejecting legal appeasement meant affirming alleged pirates' claim to national attachment. Literary responses to *Amistad* and related cases, Lenora Warren notes, demonstrated how "the pirate label could be almost immediately unraveled and replaced by revolutionary heroism." Narratives such as Frederick Douglass's *The Heroic Slave* (1841) and Martin Delaney's *Blake: The Huts of Africa* (1859), in addition to commentaries in the *Liberator* and elsewhere, distinguished Black mutineers from pirates by aligning their quest for liberty with the American Revolution. Focused on the "legality of the act," these texts relied on "the rhetoric of natural rights" to justify armed abolitionist insurrection at sea despite persistent white fears of Black violence.[30] Ongoing piratical enslavement affirmed the pressing need for legal and moral reform beyond strict pacifism. In this view, an enslaved mutineer's legal rights were as irreproachable as the feelings that had guided American revolutionaries. In *The Heroic Slave*, for example, Douglass dramatized the real-life successful 1841 revolution aboard the *Creole*, which was engaged in the coastwise slave trade. Upon the ship's landing in Nassau, a British admiralty court deemed the mutineers' violence to be in keeping with British acts of abolition. In short, the enslaved were defined as free people and not punished as pirates. U.S. Secretary of State Daniel Webster objected to the decision, in keeping with his complicated legal legacy. Webster appealed to southern property rights, England's alleged lack of jurisdiction, and the coastwise trade's legality in American law. His subsequent negotiation of the Webster-Ashburton Treaty (1842), which affirmed mutual, if limited, enforcement of deep-sea abolition, demonstrated his ongoing attempt to reach something like political balance.[31]

Douglass's narrative, like contemporaneous legal debates, centered on American proslavery law, its global jurisdiction, and abolition's place in foreign relations. *The Heroic Slave* was first published in a March 1853 issue of the author's antislavery newspaper, *North Star*. Douglass presented the leader of the mutineers, who was evocatively named Madison Washington, as a recovered founding father who could recall the state to its true feelings. The main failure of antebellum policy, Douglass explained in an echo of Emerson, remained the moral gap between land and sea. Indeed, the narrator of *The Heroic Slave* rebukes the "strange and perverse . . . moral sentiment" that brands the African coastal trade "as piracy and as deserving of death" while failing to be moved by an American coastal trade "carried on with the same motives and purposes, and characterized by even *more* odious peculiarities." In other words, the land-sea binaries in the Piracy Act of 1820 and related decisions flouted natural law, for feelings that land on African shores must logically extend to the waters off the so-called "MODEL REPUBLIC." Proximity to domesticity should render an ongoing sea trade "*more* odious." Otherwise, Douglass argued, one may reasonably doubt the validity of the theory of moral sentiments or "the doctrine of the innate moral sense of mankind." Piratical enslavement transformed fellow feeling into a suspect natural and legal philosophy, and "odious" feelings toward enslavement introduced resentment as a natural response. After all, how could a legal order built on beneficence survive flagrant state-backed acts of unfeeling? Douglass briefly introduced resentment and maritime violence, if not piracy, as legally valid. Even so, he appealed to national fellow feeling. His abolitionist literary and legal treatises on piracy were echoed by Harriet Beecher Stowe, the writer who received top billing in a giftbook that also included *The Heroic Slave*.[32]

"A TREATISE ON PIRACY": *UNCLE TOM'S CABIN* AND *DRED*

On November 15, 1852, H. J. Conway opened a theatrical rendition of Harriet Beecher Stowe's novel *Uncle Tom's Cabin* at the Boston Museum, a show that subsequently ran for more than a hundred performances. In New York City, the showman P. T. Barnum also produced an alternative extended run of the staged novel. Like all adaptors of Stowe's abolitionist text, Conway was tasked with translating the story's abolitionist pathos and sentimental plot. Myriad proslavery responses had begun to twist the author's politics. They presented enslavement as a paternal institution that protected southern families and the infantilized enslaved. In this view, abolition represented piratical robbery and familial discord. Though Conway's attempt was largely sympathetic, as scholar John W. Frick writes, the narrative was "stripped of an unequivocal abolitionist voice" due to his deletion or misrepresentation of the novel's Black figures. Nonetheless, posters and playbills for the show affirmed an abiding fealty to a major theme: amid the list of characters and players appeared "Simon Legree, A Negro Trader Formerly A Pirate." Legree is the novel's most unredeemable villain, so labeling him as a villainous pirate (a familiar trope in antebellum theater) was useful shorthand for indicating that he was a character without sympathy. Staging Legree as "formerly a pirate" was a way to accurately reproduce his history, but it also served as a major shortcut for adapting Stowe's text. The theatrical pirate Legree is a "warped soul" whose evil "is strictly personal," Frick affirms, rather than the embodiment of an entire national disease. This Legree, unlike his novel counterpart, dies unceremoniously at the play's conclusion. Conway was not the only adaptor to emphasize victory over pirates: as Sarah Meer notes, a contemporary stage adaptation in England also "had Legree arrested as a pirate." Legree's failure in each play shows the political value of piracy's theatrical removal. Enslavement must be punished in order for fellow feeling to return.[33]

Notably, however, Stowe herself did not kill off Legree in *Uncle Tom's Cabin*. She eschewed the enslaving pirate's removal because his character embodied antebellum appeasement toward enslavers. To kill him would have misconstrued piracy's legal protection. Ocean pirates had penetrated the domestic body so were legally part of the national family. Stowe narratively positioned 1820 as a flashpoint for this mistaken incorporation. What Martha Schoolman calls the novel's land-based "intranational plot" takes place solely in states that had been incorporated up to the Missouri Compromise of 1820. Schoolman maps the plot's terrestrial scale to reveal the novel's "unexpectedly limited geographic proportions," which were also the product of the Piracy Act of 1820.[34] As in Sedgwick's *Hope Leslie*, *Uncle Tom's Cabin* includes both a pirate prehistory and a pirate side plot. In Sedgwick's novel, the pirate Chaddock represents an alternative national family powered by white enslavement and Black sovereignty. He, like her later pirate in *Clarence*, may be removed to model a national family embodied by the moral white heirs to global enslavement. In Stowe's novel, however, the white pirate Legree is less a piratical possibility and more a political reality. In the antebellum United States, piratical enslavement remained federal policy. For Stowe, this policy's moral failures were most evident in the separation of enslaved families and the moral impoverishment of enslaving ones. Thus, the pirates in her texts embody a powerful stream of resentment, one that is dammed up in *Uncle Tom's Cabin* (1852) but momentarily left to flow in *Dred* (1856). In *Uncle Tom's Cabin*, she made her famous turn to beneficence, though by the time she published *Dred* she seemed more willing to consider that there was a rot that beneficence could not touch. Rather than locate that rot in the nation as a whole or in whiteness itself, Stowe made an appeal akin to John Quincy Adams's *Amistad* trial plea. Sympathy had been wrong before. Judges had appeased pirates. Just resentment against increasingly obtuse piracy law was opening for Stowe, ever so slightly, the possibility of direct action against the state. To highlight the piracy in *Uncle Tom's Cabin* and its spectral return in *Dred* is to give context to her shifting role within a sentimental jurisprudence of resentment.

The global political import of Stowe's political message has long been established. *Uncle Tom's Cabin* was first serialized in the abolitionist periodical *The National Era* over forty weeks from June 1851 to April 1852. Published in two volumes the following May, it sold over 300,000 copies in the United States and more 1 million copies globally in its first year. In this context, Stowe's case against literary pirates has been more visible than the maritime pirates in her novels but no less instructive. In the case *Stowe v. Thomas* (1854), for example, she tried to protect her copyright against alleged piracy by a Philadelphia publisher who had printed a German-language edition of the novel. She lost the case, which, as Melissa Homestead shows, was decided by a "prominent enforcer of the Fugitive Slave Law" who sought to "undermine Stowe's authority and the abolitionist message in the novel." Her legal defeat echoed the protection of enslavement under a specious form of property rights.[35]

Typically, discussions of resentment refer less to Stowe herself and more to the various political figures who viewed sympathy with suspicion or disdain. A tale of familial separation under enslavement, the novel has become a stand-in for the limits of white antebellum sympathy itself. It does not call for civil disobedience in the name of natural law in the way that Emerson or Douglass had proposed. It also lacks the dripping resentment of her brother Charles Beecher's abolitionist legal tract *The Duty of Disobedience to Wicked Laws* (1851). For him, the Piracy Act of 1820 reflected the "deep instinct of every heart." It affirmed the "intuitive sense of right our fathers felt" that they nonetheless ignored in acts of legal appeasement. Abolitionists who "resist unto blood, striving against sin," Beecher concluded, must break national law in order to protect natural law. Harriet Beecher Stowe likewise recalled the law's moral limits.[36] But her response in *Uncle Tom's Cabin* squarely places the enslaved on the rack operated by piratical enslavers and calls upon her readers to watch. In his essay "Everybody's Protest Novel," James Baldwin famously called Stowe's narrative "a catalogue of violence." For him, she traded political honesty about Black bondage for "the ostentatious parading of excessive and spurious emotion" found in white sentimentality. He and others saw such sentimental turns as "the signal of secret and violent inhumanity, the mask of cruelty."[37] Even so, Stowe's novel was integral to Baldwin's own "sentimental-political aesthetic," as Lauren Berlant terms it, defined by Black revolutionary intimacy and political rejections of the "normatively real." Stowe revealed an "affectively complex" other world even as she staged white liberalism's imaginative limits. In the novel, white feeling trumps Black lives. Tom dies. The Harris family departs for Liberia, an African colony populated in part by the descendants of the pirate ship *Antelope*.[38] Meanwhile, the pirates who sail in *Uncle Tom's Cabin* and its wake reveal the competing legal theories of appeasement and resentment that Stowe continued to platform.

In *Uncle Tom's Cabin*, Stowe famously staged all enslavement as fit for legal sanction and moral resentment. The source of resentment—and the call for beneficence—was sympathy for the Black and white families destroyed by piracy. Her parable of enslavers' crimes against feeling defines what Cynthia Alicia Smith has called Stowe's "maritime sentimentalism." In the novel, Uncle Tom is forcibly separated from his family due to the debts incurred by his former enslaver. For Stowe, Tom embodies how piratical enslavement prevent familial rights: "One of the bitterest apportionments of a lot of slavery," the narrator notes at the moment of Tom's sale, "[is] that the negro, sympathetic and assimilative, after acquiring, in a refined family, the tastes and feelings which form the atmosphere of such a place, is not the less liable to become the bond-slave of the coarsest and most brutal." Tom's familial attachment and capacity for broader sympathetic assimilation prove his value in a national family in which white supremacy remains the standard. Strategic invocations of his maritime labors shape his status as a "sentimental sailor," Smith notes, whose oceanic capacity confirms his legal rights on both land and water. Simon Legree, on the other hand, embodies what the narrator calls the "coarsest and most brutal" antebellum figure: the pirate. Little is known of his history other than that he was born a northerner and "learned his trade well, among the pirates in the West Indies." In other words, northern domesticity may be corrupted by piratical crimes against feeling.[39]

Like Adams and Douglass, Stowe rejected the appeasement that defined antebellum piracy law. As the narrator points out, despite a "legal enactment" that allows Legree to own humans as he would any other commodity, the law "cannot blot out [the enslaved's] soul, with its own private little world of memories, hopes, loves, fears, and desires." Federal policy distinguished between the river and ocean, treating the latter as beyond the nation's jurisdiction or feeling. Even so, before Stowe published *Uncle Tom's Cabin*, no one had been hung for enslaving piracy. In its account of Tom's enslavement, the novel reveals the facile geographic and moral binaries established by the Piracy Act of 1820, particularly its pretended abolition "in any river where the sea ebbs and flows."[40] In the chapter titled "The Middle Passage," Legree brings Tom and other bound persons onto "the good steamer Pirate," which is docked on the Red River. A "red, muddy, turbid current," the river evokes similar oceanic passages that at that historical moment were legally piratical. Its "abrupt tortuous windings" speak to both geological complexity and the sudden, extended torture of its bound sailors.[41] Enslavement's oceanic source undermines the facile distinctions between land and sea made in antebellum law. For Stowe, then, the state's refusal to apply oceanic abolition domestically reflected a pirate sympathy. "The slave-trade is now, by American law, considered as piracy," she wrote in the novel's conclusion. The state had properly marked the slave trade as piratical unruliness, at least in oceanic space. She continued, "But a slave-trade, as systematic as every was carried on the coast of Africa, is an inevitable attendant and result of American slavery." In short, she joined the chorus of Emerson, Douglass, and many other abolitionists.[42]

In the conclusion of *Uncle Tom's Cabin*, Stowe presented beneficence as an antidote to pirates. Yet resentment toward enslavers and their appeasers remains latent in the novel. She was more direct in *A Key to Uncle Tom's Cabin* (1853), a supplement that aimed to prove the novel's historical accuracy in the face of political challenge. In it, she again called federal policy piratical, referring to slavery as "that awful system of legalized piracy and oppression by which hundreds and thousands are yearly torn from home and friends, and that all heart holds dear, and carried to be sold like beasts in the markets of the South." Positive law flouted a natural law of human familial attachments. Stowe wrote, "To the pirate Legree the law gives power" that belongs only God: the power to control the souls of humanity. In her view, those who used biblical quotes "to justify all manner of oppression" had confused the holy document with "a treatise on piracy."[43] Legree embodies enslavers who, though given moral cover in legal culture, "may have been a pirate on the high seas" in prior days. "A man may have made all his property by piracy upon the high seas, as we have represented in the case of Legree," Stowe asserted, "and there is no law whatever to prevent his investing that property in acquiring this absolute control over the souls and bodies of his fellow beings." A literal pirate's inheritance had purchased a privileged domestic position. Positive law had failed. Natural law was flouted. Existing policy had failed to protect national families from piracy. It had also empowered piratical enslavers in the name of national sovereignty. Enslavement, Stowe replied, remained piratical at heart.[44]

As an advocate of abolitionist jurisprudence that spurned violence, Stowe presented moral victory over the pirate as key to a national familial reunion. She introduced abolitionist resentment in *Uncle Tom's Cabin*, but her final appeal was to beneficence. Like Lincoln in his 1854 speech, she appealed to her audience's ostensibly universal fellow feeling. For Stowe, enslaving pirates were fit for annihilation but only when guided by natural law. God's impending wrath was surer than "the eternal law by which the millstone sinks in the ocean." Natural law would undergird proper abolitionist action. However, she believed that acting on resentment was in God's power alone. Famously, her final charge to readers was to "*feel right.*" Justice would derive from the "atmosphere of sympathetic influence" fostered by the subject "who *feels* strongly, healthily and justly."[45] Stowe's assertions of beneficence alone, or her rejection of retributive violence in just feeling, derived from a limited application of Adam Smith's moral theory. In a section of *Moral Sentiments* entitled "Justice and Beneficence," he affirmed positive fellow feeling but noted its limits as a just virtue. Justice was powered by the social spread of natural resentments. Beneficent actions "proceed from proper motives," he wrote, and led persons to recognize their shared humanity. For Smith, beneficence spread positive virtue, yet positive sentiments were a weak force against fundamental lapses in fellow feeling. He affirmed, "Beneficence . . . is less essential to the existence of society than justice. Society may subsist, though not in the most comfortable state, without beneficence; but the prevalence of injustice must utterly destroy it."[46] Smith's skepticism about the "comfortable state" of beneficence aligns with criticisms of Stowe's appeal to positive feeling as a weak counter to unfeeling enslavement.

In Smith's view, justice could also derive from resentments that had moral and legal force. Operating from its own sympathetic base, resentment was the desire to personally inflict equal harm on those who had injured you or another sympathetic subject. In other words, it was a means of extending your pained feelings to a subject who had refused to exercise sympathy. He wrote, "In the same manner, as we sympathize with the sorrow of our fellow creature when we see his distress, so likewise we enter into his abhorrence and aversion for whatever has given occasion to it." Smith did not claim that all resentful passions led to justice. Instead, the social legibility of one's resentments—and, by extension, the justice to which they led—derived from outsiders' ability to share in the resenting subject's feelings. When just, shared resentment was an act of fellow feeling based on the "safeguard of justice and the security of innocence." According to Smith, the "natural gratification" of resentment necessarily structured the "political ends of punishment"—namely, the "correction of the criminal." In this system, justifications for state violence against pirates could be an exercise in natural sentiments and a valuable deterrent. On viewing this correction, "others, through fear of like punishment may be terrified from being guilty of the like offense."[47] For some, this process of forcibly recalling unsympathetic subjects to proper feeling made abolitionist piracy a moral, if illegal, act. Stowe did not deny abolitionist resentment's existence in *Uncle Tom's Cabin* but displayed it toward both piratical enslavers and an antebellum legal regime. Even so, pirates such as Legree tested her dedication to beneficence as a moral virtue and a legal theory.

Stowe's next novel, *Dred: A Tale of the Great Dismal Swamp (1856)*, is an attempt to come to terms with ongoing domestic violence and proslavery legal obtuseness. As Maria Windell notes, the author faced ongoing calls for "a revolution-ready sentimentalism" in response to ongoing violence.[48] In *Dred*, however, she did not merely restage the pacifistic beneficence of *Uncle Tom's Cabin*. Nor did she align illegal violence against the state with piracy. Instead, she partially validated revolutionary Black subjects' resentment against legal but piratical enslavement. Like Adams, Stowe outlined a legal precedence of mistaken sympathies. *Dred* is the story of revolutionary Black violence, inspired by Denmark Vesey's 1822 revolt and Nat Turner 1831 rebellion. Stowe imagined Dred as the son of Vesey, a man who, in the novel, reads the "embodied sentiments of the most insurrectionary character" in newspapers' declarations of independence and rightly applies them to the enslaved.[49] For Stowe, familial separation under enslavement indexed the necessary recovery of familial attachments. The triumph over piracy was key to this recovery, as was the unmaking of antebellum laws that treated abolition as piratical. Indeed, courtroom dramas dominate the novel's main plot. These "legal appropriations," Laura H. Korobkin writes, include the explicit inclusion of proslavery court decisions as well as a subtle appeal to abolitionist legal texts such as Theodore Weld's *American Slavery as It Is* (1839). The question of piracy, both the enslaver's and the Black revolutionary's, is also a vital aspect of the legal thinking in *Dred*. In her preface, Stowe offered her "sympathizing heart" to those "called to struggle for all that is noble in our laws and institutions." In other words, she appealed to beneficence toward those judges who could strike against enslavement's legal appeasement. Amid failures to heed natural law, however, she also offered beneficence to the enslaved people who might act illegally. For Stowe, federal judges had married the state to unfeeling piracy, so Black revolutionaries' moral claim to resentment distinguished them from pirates. [50] Specifically, she contrasted judicial failures of beneficence—that is, antebellum legal protections for enslavement—with natural, if not politically laudable, resentment toward the antebellum state. Dred's direct action, though potentially piratical, must be contrasted with enslavers' legalized piracy.

The primary trial in *Dred* shows that legalized piratical enslavement destroys families and breeds resentment. In the process, Stowe "offers a revealing critique of the trial trope that structured abolitionist discourse," as Jeannine Marie DeLombard notes. Like *Uncle Tom's Cabin*, *Dred* platforms both antebellum piracy law and legal theory, showing that neither the Piracy Act of 1820 nor appeasement's dramatic rejection can protect the enslaved in court.[51] In the novel's primary plot, vain attempts to restore southern familial union remain choked by this moral miasma. Nina Gordon, the heiress to an increasingly worthless southern plantation, is set to marry Edward Clayton, a liberal-minded southern lawyer and the heir to a "now almost decayed, family of Virginia." Legalized piracy has weakened even white familial bonds. In the novel's major trial, Edward sues the enslaver who beat a slave, Milly, when she was out on loan from Nina's plantation. He wins the initial case, only to lose on an appellate court decision written by his own father, Judge Clayton. Proslavery judges, the novel suggests, do not even value their own families. Stowe modeled these decisions on *State v. Mann* (1829), a case heard by Justice Thomas Ruffin of North Carolina's Supreme Court. Yet they also evoke the legacy of Justice Joseph Story and an entire legal regime that selectively invoked familial feeling to appease enslavers. In the novel, Judge Clayton admits struggling "between the feelings of the man and the duty of the magistrate." Nonetheless, violence that would be considered criminal in "other domestic relations" remains legal when performed by enslavers toward the enslaved. In this historical moment, positive law and white supremacist familial logic favored enslavement. White familial bonds, ostensibly the model for beneficent national union, could not overcome injustice.[52]

Beyond invoking an individual case, Stowe rejected an entire antebellum legal regime as piratical. In *Dred*, a brief conversation between Edward Clayton and Reverend Titmarsh takes place immediately after the decision. Their debate further reveals that legal appeals to positive and natural law are weak cover for piracy. Edward Clayton laments his prior "illusion" about the law's justice and says he will resign from his legal practice since it would be immoral to "remain in the practice of law in a slave state." Though Edward may not become a pirate, he certainly rejects a legal regime that Stowe has aligned with piracy. However, the deeply unsentimental Reverend Titmarsh is not "disposed to sympathize with him in the feelings he expressed." Titmarsh considers Edward's resentment too strong. Moreover, he argues that "Divine Providence" has allowed for the establishment of enslavement. Titmarsh's mistake, it seems, is his conflation of common law with natural law. He, like many antebellum jurists, is willing to treat policies that protect enslavement as akin to universal statutes. Indeed, he does not deny that he sympathizes with the "institution of piracy" as proven by natural law. Piracy "becomes right by that fact" of "Divine Providence," which itself is evidenced by piracy's ongoing legal practice. This circular reasoning retains shades of Supreme Court logic in its cases on piratical enslavement. Titmarsh later laments that abolitionists will call figures such as himself "a cut-throat, pirate, sheep-stealer, and all the rest of their elegant little list of embellishments." His incapacity to recognize piracy is clear shorthand for his failure in moral and legal thinking. His abolitionist interlocutor's retort—"*things were divinely ordered because they were right*"—presents natural law not as a mere extension of positive law but as having separate legal force. This judicial reasoning is necessary to overturn enslaving piracy's positive law protections. In keeping with antebellum sentimental culture, however, familial fractures index a political split. Edward's beloved Nina dies of cholera. A legal culture that has not protected Black families will cause the death of white ones.[53]

As in *Uncle Tom's Cabin*, a gap between federal policy and divine law must be bridged by abolitionist sympathies. In *Dred*, however, the titular character embodies just resentment rather than universal beneficence. Like the novel's white abolitionist lawyer, Dred is just. Indeed, Stowe thematically twinned their moral outlooks. After the trial, Edward naturally fills a void of beneficence by "struggle[ing] with this great system of injustice." He advocates for judicial solutions to injustice but also wants to spark inured fellow feelings through direct action. "People have got to be shocked," he says, "in order to wake them up out of old absurd routine. Use paralyzes us to almost every injustice; when people are shocked, they begin to think and to inquire."[54] Here, Stowe eschewed beneficence to platform something like Adam Smith's theory of just resentment. As the leader of the marooned freepersons who inhabit the Great Dismal Swamp, Dred offers an equally just, if unmistakably more violent, sentimental shock. Though he feels against the antebellum state, he is not a pirate. Nor does he lack sympathy. Instead, the novel presents his "moral constitution" as a natural form of resentment shared "in some degree in us all." Echoing Smith, the narrator notes that human nature "leads us to feel pain at the sight of injustice, and to desire retribution for cruelty and crime." They conclude, "This sentiment is justice, this agony in view of cruelty and crime, is in men a strong attribute of their highest natures." Beneficence still exists "in nature and in the human heart [as] a pleasing, interceding element," but it softens resentment rather than removes it.[55] Dred's resentment is a deep feeling in "sympathy and communion with nature." He is among those who, "looking on the great volume of nature, sees there a reflection of its own internal passions, and seizes on that in it which sympathizes with itself." Indeed, Dred finds support for his violence in "the roar of torrents, the thunder of avalanches, and the whirl of ocean-storms." His resentment has a basis in natural law, for he has been moved by "the wrathful denunciations of ancient prophets against oppression and injustice." In this way, the novel begins to develop a sentimental jurisprudence of resentment in response to piratical enslavement.[56]

Dred's death at the hands of enslavers confirms that natural resentment has yet to overawe state-protected enslavement. In *Dred*, Kevin Pelletier argues, Stowe "insists on the necessary pairing of love and fear to form the novel's sentimental core." Dred's violence is sanctified by God and natural moral feeling.[57] His moral sanction is inseparable from Stowe's growing adherence to a legal theory of sympathy that included just resentment against enslavers. His final call to God, "that inarticulate moaning which goes before the earthquake," indicates that his natural resentment remains potent. Beneficence, too, has a place for those who are willing to see the morality of his cause. In a call for readers' sympathy, Stowe aligned Dred's resentment with sanctified familial feeling. "If we would estimate the force of almighty justice," says the narrator, appealing to an audience that seeks to understand his final exaltation, "let us ask ourselves what a mother might feel for the abuse of her helpless child, and multiply that by infinity." Dred, like God and a mother, has proven that his resentment is in the service of familial attachment. The prospect of divine retribution introduced in *Uncle Tom's Cabin* has been given a human agent in *Dred*. Even so, Dred's death affirms that justice is elusive.[58] Likewise, the novel's final scenes of potential yet unperformed revolution, one stopped by shaken but still powerful white liberal politics, maintain a certain status quo. Stowe "leaves the law behind" in the resolution to *Dred*, Carrie Hyde has shown, in favor of "theological models of resistance and critique" that tout "heavenly citizenship" as a moral replacement for legal rights. The novel concludes by showing a group of people escaping northward from the swamps rather than staying to fight in the South. For Stowe, white liberal sympathy neither sanctions Dred's resentments nor offers them legal protection.[59]

Pirates largely disappear from Stowe's later works, but these texts nonetheless continue to present piracy as a uniquely powerful corruptor of moral sense. Melissa Gniadek has tracked Stowe's "coastal gothic" in *The Minister's Wooing* (1859) and *The Pearl of Orr's Island* (1862), in which "maritime plots and coastal settings" drive moral tensions and "hint at the absorption of imperial violence, dispossession, and alterity into the domestic scene." The spectral pirates in these works suggest a dynamic that Stowe had warned about in her earlier fictions: little by little, piracy corrupts moral sense and political stability on both land and water. In *The Minister's Wooing*, for example, the fictionalized Aaron Burr's political fall from grace is complete once he is "heart-stricken in his domestic relation, his only daughter taken by pirates, and dying in untold horrors." A founding father who fails to protect his family from piracy cannot lead the nation. The youth also have a duty to guard against piracy. In *The Pearl of Orr's Island*, a young sailor named Moses laments that "he had propositions of piracy and robbery made to him, and he had not dared to knock down the man that made them." Youths avow "the power of bad, unprincipled, heartless men" if they do not immediately strike directly against piracy. Otherwise, they will "feel the terrible logic of evil which constrains them to pass from the less to greater crime." Moses's situation is not so dire—the pirates he overcomes are more symbolic than real—but the point is clear: a single moment of appeasement conceals pirates and corrupts virtues. In antebellum society, such corruptions had reached their highest level in the sentimental jurisprudence of appeasement that followed the Piracy Act of 1820, as Stowe had made clear in her more overtly political novels. Propositions in regard to enslaving robbery and piracy had been accepted before the events of *Uncle Tom's Cabin* took place. The nation had not dared to knock down pirates.[60]

Dred, more than any Stowe work, outlines a natural law justification for abolitionist violence against entrenched piracy. Notably, Stowe finished writing it as she was sailing across the Atlantic in advance of her application for British copyright. Perhaps crossing an ocean of piratical enslavement had an effect. The novel's publication history reveals her awareness that she was "writing for a global—not a national—market," and its content reflects a growing, if limited, acceptance of resentment by global authors of domestic pirate fiction.[61]

"BEINGS WHO POSSESS FEELINGS": JUST RESENTMENT IN *EMMANUEL APPADOCCA*

Michael Maxwell Philip's *Emmanuel Appadocca, or, Blighted Life: A Tale of the Boucaneers* (1854) is less a direct parlay with *Uncle Tom's Cabin* and more an independent sail in shared political waters. A lawyer, Philip was a member of what Christine Levecq describes as an "emergent brown [Caribbean] middle class whose members were familiar with the devices of the . . . American sentimental novel."[62] He was among the Black abolitionists who considered how the "world might be moved to care more broadly."[63] The Caribbean scholar William Cain speculates that Philip likely read Stowe's novel and aimed to "articulate an alternative to it—his vision of vengeance and retribution." As Cain notes, *Uncle Tom's Cabin* sold a million and a half copies in the United Kingdom in the year that Philip lived there. Stowe herself visited London in 1853 to much fanfare.[64] However, the pirates she portrayed were not Philip's models. Unlike nearly all of his contemporaries, he championed a pirate's just violence against the state and its privileged white families. Thus, to read *Emmanuel Appadocca* is to ponder Xine Yao's own skepticism about fellow feeling as the nation's beating heart: "What does it mean to withdraw from that totalizing embrace, to be heartless?"[65] For Yao, a disaffected stance is a useful "disruptive negation" of nineteenth-century sympathy. In this frame, rejections of antebellum white supremacy reveal "unfeeling not as oppression from above but as a tactic from below."[66] The character Emmanuel Appadocca's supposed heartlessness, later echoed in Herman Melville's portrayal of Babo in *Benito Cereno*, presents just resentment as a legal and moral challenge to state-backed white supremacy.

Set in the late eighteenth century, *Emmanuel Appadocca* is a striking inversion of Catharine Maria Sedgwick's *Clarence*. Like the character Marceline Clarence, Appadocca is the abandoned son of a white plantation-owning father and a free mixed-race mother. Unlike this prior fallen heir, however, Appadocca reclaims both his inheritance and a sentimental jurisprudence of resentment. In a climactic scene, the pirate stands among white children, his half-siblings, whose plantation he has just destroyed. Abandoned by his father, James Wilmington, and descended from an enslaved mother whom Wilmington has also abandoned, he has now captured the father he shares with these children. He has freed their human property. Unmistakably a pirate, he surveys the destruction of white familial attachment that cements his legal status. Appadocca presents himself as kin to those "who are branded and repudiated by society." He is doubly branded, as both abolitionist pirates and the global enslaved have both been falsely accused of crimes against feeling. While this scene retains the generic conventions (if not the political ideology) that produced the antebellum pirate, it does include a twist: Appadocca presents antebellum legal culture's defining feature—a pirate's lack of attachment to the state and its privileged white families—as a just exercise of fellow feeling. The destruction of the family plantation, he asserts, is proof that both the pirate and the enslaved "are beings who possess feelings, and who claim the same measure of justice as is meted out to all." The pirate's feeling toward the enslaved leads him to place the enslaver on the proverbial rack while his friends and families watch. The result is sympathy's moral and legal just reordering. Michel Maxwell Philip's biographer, Selwyn Cudjoe, argues that "the pirates [in his novel have] robbed the slave-owning class of their illusions about their system."[67] One such illusion is that violence toward enslavers is a crime against feeling. For Appadocca, illegal piracy forwards justice, and his aim is practical: if "the wretch . . . [is] made to suffer the one-hundredth part of that misery which he has caused, his mates in vile wickedness, appalled by the example, will shrink in trembling fear from the perpetration of like crimes." The natural self-interest of immoral agents, he concludes in a seeming appeal to Smith's philosophy, will recall them to proper action, if not proper feeling. White enslavers and their heirs should not be protected from a just pirate who, unlike the state, has no sympathy for enslavement. "The sins of the fathers," Appadocca tells his half-siblings, "are visited on their children."[68] Only piratical violence against a global plantation order can undo state-backed familial separation and, perhaps, recall the world to justice.

According to Cudjoe, Michel Maxwell Philip was "one of the most important Caribbean intellectual-activists of the nineteenth century."[69] His privileged place in that post-revolutionary era informed both his legal theory of piracy and his relative investments in colorism, if not white supremacy. As Philip wrote in the preface to *Emmanuel Appadocca*, the protagonist's piracy is justified by the "feelings . . . roused up" by the "cruel manner in which the slave holders of America deal with their slave-children," as embodied in this abandoned son who "found himself picking cotton under the encouragement of 'Jimboes' or 'Quimboes' on his own father's plantation." Philip sought to retain the supremacy of a Caribbean generation caught between colonial slavery and partial abolition. Britain's Slavery Abolition Act of 1833 applied to most of the empire, although it did not free many enslaved children in the Caribbean until 1838.[70] Philip had been born in Trinidad in 1829, and his birthright was revolutionary violence and plantation slavery. His foremost ancestor was a free Black matriarch who had inherited a nearly five hundred–acre Grenadian estate, which included enslaved persons, following her French husband's death sometime before 1775. Philip was named after a former slave who had fought in the Fédon Rebellion and now managed the family's large (and, for a period, slave-holding) sugar plantation in Trinidad.[71] Philip's father was a white "owner." His mother was either an enslaved woman on the Philip estate, a free person, or part of the Philip family.[72] Although the father failed to support his child, his well-established family supported Philip's literary and legal labors in Europe: he received a classical education in Scotland and studied law in London while working as a correspondent for *The Trinidad Free Press*. During this time, Philip, now age twenty-four, published his only novel, *Emmanuel Appadocca*, which, as Belinda Edmondson writes, became "a Trinidadian best seller of sorts" and seemingly earned him enough money to pay for his legal studies.[73] In 1855, Philip returned to Trinidad and became Port of Spain's first nonwhite mayor. He later served as Trinidad's solicitor general, holding that position until his death in 1888.

The parable of abolitionist jurisprudence that defined Philip's literary career—one that privileged brown transcolonial families such as his own—is embodied by his titular pirate. At the heart of *Emmanuel Appadocca* is the claim that piracy against familial separation's source (enslaving or errant transcolonial fathers) can sympathetically counter an unnatural legal regime. Philip scholar William Cain first outlined the author's investment in *lex talionis*, or the "law of equivalent retribution," in light of his legal study of Aristotle, Francis Bacon, and Georg Hege. Adam Smith, one must add, was a cornerstone of Philip's classical education.[74] The novel positions Appadocca's turn to piracy not as a crime against feeling but as a restoration of natural law. In an embedded domestic pirate fiction told from the other side, Appadocca recalls how two abandoned women sparked his turn to piracy. The first was his mother, who was guided by "the loftiest attributes of human nature—the sentiments." The second was antebellum legal culture's most cherished subject: the white mother. While pondering natural law, he had come across a fallen woman who was holding a baby "as pale as the moon." As he saved the woman from suicide, he noted her "pale emaciated face" and the "whiteness of her forehead." Piracy, Appadocca soon concludes, is a just counter to legal systems out of natural balance. The abolitionist pirate is sympathetic *because* of his illegal violence.[75] He makes reference to Smith's moral philosophy while explicitly crediting an African intellectual tradition: "Every animal carries in itself a law and undergoes a pain of retribution whenever it violates that law." [76] In legal culture, however, appeasing states prevent "retribution." Nature remains misaligned. Those persons who "forget their instinct"—notably, parents who abandon or enslave children—are not dashed by a natural force. Appadocca decides that he will no longer allow the law to "blunt the double edge sword of retribution." He becomes a pirate to prevent crimes against feeling.[77]

For resentment to become justice, spectators who have not shared Appadocca's embodied experience must access his feelings. That is, white and middle-class readers must feel with the transcolonial pirate and the enslaved. An obtrusive narrator instructs, "Reader, have you ever felt the absorbing love that sank and merged your existence into that of a cherished object, and have you ever felt the gall of sneering ridicule from her? If you have, then you know the feeling that possessed the pirate captain." The pirate, not the domestic heroine, is fit for a reader's fellow feeling. The pirate ship, rather than the upper-class white home, is sympathy's locus. In other words, Philip reimagined the pirate's status in domestic fiction.[78] When Appadocca casts his father adrift on a small raft, he feels no remorse. Instead, "every fibre of feeling is burnt into hard callousness." Again, the narrator treats Appadocca's refusal of beneficence as a moral sentiment.[79] According to Adam Smith, a spectator is not moved by pain felt by the unjust: "When an inhuman murdered is brought to the scaffold, though we have some compassion for his misery, we can have no sort of fellow feeling with his resentment." In Philip's novel, Appadocca's desire for justice against his father has the force of natural law.[80]

Yet to feel for the pirate—supposedly the natural opposite of the moral nation-state—is to doom oneself as unsympathetic. Therefore, rather than undo this bind, the novel stages Appadocca's tragic death as a final act of resentment. Like many other antebellum sentimental fictions, this one concludes with the pirate's removal. The destruction of Appadocca's vessel by the hurricane that also kills his father leads the pirate to conclude that justice will not come, and he commits suicide. His first mate, Lorenzo, marries a plantation heiress named Agnes. Lorenzo's real identity is St. James Carmonte, heir to a noble French family. This marriage appears to reproduce the white supremacist domesticity found in texts such as *Clarence*. The prospect (or threat) of racialized lineages has given way to white heirs. White families inherit oceanic spoils over legal Black heirs. Even the most powerful pirate cannot undo global enslavement.

If one judges *Emmanuel Appadocca* by the standards of domestic fiction, the novel's final marriage undermines Philip's legal theory. For justice to materialize, the pirate should have reclaimed his inheritance rather than resented it.[81] Yet Philip killed Appadocca for the same reason that Stowe spared Legree. As she knew, the enslaving pirate embodied the antebellum state's unjust laws. Legree lived to enslave again. The just pirate, Philip contended, was doomed to die by those same enslaving nations. As scholar Ralph Dalloe affirms, limited abolition makes Appadocca the "only kind of hero possible in such infamous times."[82]

The ending of Philip's novel is highly sentimental because it undercuts its own success and, in the process, promotes future legal and martial action. If a righteous pursuer of justice dies without success, Smith had argued, "we feel the resentment that we imagine he . . . would feel if in his cold and lifeless body there remained any consciousness of what passes on earth. His blood, we think, calls aloud for vengeance." In other words, the deceased body's insensibility does not preclude one from extending beneficence toward the slain and resentment toward their slayer. For Smith, unjust death produces a "natural sympathy with the imaginary resentment of the slain."[83] Resentment remains powerful after death because only a sympathetic subject is required. Readers who feel for Appadocca as a subject, by extension, take up his just action against enslavement. Abolition, like enslavement, can yet become the basis for domestic life. Appadocca tells a skeptical friend, "Systems and notions which are now as familiar as household terms, were, once upon a time, quite as new, strange, and extraordinary."[84] Ways of knowing have been domesticated, but they can and should be defamiliarized. Because domestic fictions make social ideologies appear natural, a politics of beneficence alone, according to Philip, will not lead to new systems. Only direct, systematic, and, if necessary, allegedly piratical, action against a system of legal enslavement will restore justice.

While works such as *Emmanuel Appadocca* attempt to square abolitionist violence with antebellum legal culture, Herman Melville's novella *Benito Cereno* (1855) highlights deathly struggles that needed no legal or moral justification. The "spectral mutinies" that were evident throughout Melville's literary career, affirms Lenora Warren, allowed him to "examine both the possibility and impossibility of radical change through violence." *Benito Cereno*, serialized in three issues of *Putnam's Monthly* in 1855 and published in the short story collection *The Piazza Tales* in 1856, is a story of unspoken yet unmistakable resentment against enslavers' legal cover.[85] It is also, perhaps, Melville's wry commentary on sympathy's limits as a legal theory of piracy across a political spectrum. Set in 1799, the novella unfolds via the limited point of view of an American sea captain named Amasa Delano. Delano comes upon the ship *San Dominick* (whose name alludes to colonial Haiti, then known as Saint-Domingue), ostensibly captained by a Spaniard, Don Benito Cereno. In fact, the ship is controlled by enslaved mutineers led by the seemingly officious attendant Babo. As scholar Andy Doolen notes, Melville's narrative deliberately "blur[s] the lines between privateer and pirate." Delano's inability to recognize piratical mutiny and his willingness to take over the ship because of the gold it carries represents a "failure of sovereign authority" over piracy, argues Hester Blum.[86] Indeed, the vessel's "comfortable family of a crew" appears to signal domestic union rather than piratical crimes against feeling. Delano is confounded by not only the prospect of a Black family but also by enslaved people's willingness to violently self-emancipate. Notably, the American captain mistakenly applies the "sympathetic experience" of familial loss to explain Benito Cereno's apparent grief over the death of Babo's enslaver, Alexandro Aranda. Delano also does not internalize "the feeling of resentment" that he vaguely perceives from Cereno after a "playful allusion to the Spaniard's singularly evidenced lordship over the black."[87] Delano cannot imagine the possibility of successful Black emancipation and, by extension, recognize furtive abolition's distinction from conspicuous piracy. Black resentment remains likewise overshadowed by the specter of whiteness that serves, as Xine Yao writes, "as the standard measure of humanity and feeling" in antebellum culture. In practice, material necessity and just resentment mark Babo's potential moral distinction from enslaving pirates. Even so, he commits acts of violence. As readers will learn, Babo has attached Aranda's skeleton to the ship's figurehead alongside the phrase "FOLLOW YOUR LEADER."[88]

The captured Babo refuses to give sentimental meaning to an allegedly piratical slave ship mutiny. Faced with a ready closing argument against mistaken sympathy, one provided by John Quincy Adams and others, Melville seems to reply, "I would prefer not to." Embodying what Yao calls Melville's "explorations of refusal" in the story, Babo's actions deny both beneficence and resentment in a white supremacist legal culture. Babo does not speak when the truth is shown, as it will not help. After all, Black-led abolition will always be piracy. When caught, he fights back. Delano's appeal to temporal collapse following Babo's attack—"past, present, and future seemed one"—may be given sense via piracy laws that used a temporal trick of past precedent as present and future criminality. Once he discerns the truth, Delano declares, "This plotting pirate means murder!" Babo, now labeled a pirate by the colonial power, makes a final defense in "an apparent verification of the words." His apparent piracy is the product of enslavers' narrative power to treat self-emancipation as a "ferocious piratical revolt."[89] The lengthy and staid legal deposition embedded in the narrative fixes Babo's status and misreads his unspoken sentiments. "His aspect seemed to say," the narrator concludes, "since I cannot do deeds, I will not speak words." Neither the narrator nor Melville invite us to imagine the slain as an object of just resentment, as Michel Maxwell Philip had done. Instead, Babo's embodied defiance—his severed head "met, unabashed, the gaze of the whites" at port—signals that direct embodied action against global enslavement will remain a constant while the trade remains legal. Cereno, like the reader, is forced to sit with Babo's resentment forever. "But the past is passed; why moralize upon it?" Delano asks his friend. Delano refuses to internalize legal and moral precedents, a reaction that befits his status as a poor judge of piracy. Cereno cannot shake the fact that "human-like healing" of friendship, or perhaps the white supremacy embedded in antebellum legal culture, provides no succor. The inscription "follow your leader" remained painted on his ship's hull. Whether the law's subsequent "leader" will be the dead enslaver or the enslaved mutineer is unclear. In either case, the future will hold more violence.[90]

In response to the pressures of abolition in any form, the Supreme Court continued its violent appeasement of enslavers. The court's rightwing political bent increased after Roger B. Taney replaced John Marshall as Chief Justice. According to historian William M. Wiecek, Taney, who served on the Court from 1836 until 1864, "blended concern for the security of slavery, a racist worldview, and a dedication to state sovereignty."[91] Notably, he wrote the majority decision in *Dred Scott v. Sandford* (1857), a case brought by Dred Scott and his wife, Harriet Robinson Scott, after their enslavers carried them from Missouri to the free states of Illinois and Wisconsin. Though not directly related to piracy, *Dred Scott* shifted the proslavery legal balance on land. It also foretold a potential shift at sea. Specifically, the Court denied Black Americans legal standing to sue because they "cannot be and were never intended to be citizens under the U.S. Constitution." The Court rejected abolitionist feeling's legal force or constitutional precedence. In an appeal to constitutionally enshrined proslavery sentiment, Taney wrote, "The change in public opinion and feeling in relation to the African race, which has taken place since the adoption of the Constitution, cannot change its construction and meaning, and it must be construct and administered now according to its true meaning and intention when it was formed and adopted." Only white supremacy had legal force. The legal arguments made in *Dred Scott* were thus "an expression of the southern mood—fearful, angry, defiant," as historian and federal judge A. Leon Higginbotham confirms.[92] Abolitionist jurisprudence was losing judicial ground to proslavery resentment. The decision also rendered the 1820 Missouri Compromise unconstitutional. The idea that Congress "cannot ban slavery in the territories" gave proslavery forces hope that that Piracy Act of 1820 could likewise be struck down. The *Dred Scott* decision led abolitionists such as Garrison to reconsider arguments against "moral suasion," or legal abolition by pacifistic moral example, and take more seriously those in favor of political violence against the enslaving state.[93]

Abolitionist resentment would find its champion in John Brown. Brown, Kevin Pelletier notes, "exemplified nineteenth-century sentimental sympathy, so much so that this sympathy moved him to fight, kill, and die on behalf of America's slaves." On October 16th, 1859, Brown led twenty-two men in an attack on the federal armory at Harper's Ferry, Virginia. He hoped to spur a revolution across the region's plantations. An avalanche of literary responses followed his capture and death, as myriad scholars have demonstrated. John Brown "signaled the decline of apocalyptic sentimentalism," Pelletier argues, because sympathetic fear of God's wrath could no longer overawe national division and pending war. Thought another way, neither natural law arguments nor the vision of a nation united against piracy could sustain. Brown represented a direct moral and martial challenge from an extrajudicial yet just force. As the final section will show, Brown tested antebellum legal culture's ongoing sentimental jurisprudence of appeasement. Just resentment against enslavement, including beneficence towards the enslaved, validated direct and perhaps piratical action against the state. Brown's contested status as a dangerous pirate or a paradigmatic familial subject echoed fractures in antebellum legal culture.[94]

"JUDGES FEAR COLLISION": FEELING JOHN BROWN

During a meeting "in relief of the family of John Brown" on November 18, 1859, Ralph Waldo Emerson lamented the "sympathy and sorrow" that followed the abolitionist's conviction. In his appeals to justice, Emerson did not deny Brown's criminality in the attack on the arsenal at Harpers Ferry. He rejected the state's monopoly on fellow feeling. According to Emerson, "nothing can resist the sympathy which all elevated minds must feel with Brown." For him, Brown's alleged crimes against feeling confirmed the nation's misalignment with natural law. Emerson compared the "malignity of public sentiment in Slave States" and the moral "common feeling" in abolitionist ones. A false allegiance to positive law and political appeasement had given the former undue power. "How deceptive the forms are," he stated of American jurisprudence. "Judges rely on the forms, and do not, like John Brown, use their eyes to see the facts behind the forms." In this case, the "fact behind the forms" was federal policy's abandonment of the enslaved. Emerson said, "Substantial injustice" is done when "judges fear collision between their two allegiances," abolitionist natural law and legal enslavement. Contrary to those who championed appeasement in the name of political stability, he presented enslavement as an evil "worse . . . than collision." Like Michel Maxwell Philip, Emerson believed violence that may be deemed piratical could exercise justice. He called on a judge "who has the Declaration of Independence in his heart" to pardon Brown. In other words, he asked the state to recall itself to moral feeling via judicial reinvestments in sympathy. Brown, unlike alleged pirates, had a claim to familial attachments that could reconfigure an entire national order.[95]

The abolitionist orator Wendell Phillips used even stronger terms when he advocated for a sentimental jurisprudence of resentment in response to Brown's violence. He treated Brown as a sanctified privateer against state-allied piracy, one who had received celestial letters of marque whose basis in natural law gave them legal force. In a fiery speech first given in 1859, Phillips promoted a theory of retribution akin to Adam Smith's and Emmanuel Appadocca's. "Disunion leaves God's natural laws to work their good results," he argued, because "God gives every animal means of self-protection. Under God's law, insurrection is the tyrant's check." Only extralegal violence could restore moral order. If that same violence were to further disunion, then divorce was preferable.[96] Even so, to directly call John Brown a pirate would undercut the nationalist fellow feeling that Phillips was calling for. Citizenship remained a moral and willing "submission" to a state that responded by "rendering equal justice between man and man." Brown was an extralegal, though not a piratical, agent of feeling. After all, Phillips concluded, Virginia itself was a Barbary pirate:

> Everything that calls itself a government, and refuses that duty, or has not that assent, is no government. It is only a pirate ship. Virginia, the Commonwealth of Virginia! She is only a chronic insurrection. I mean exactly what I say. I am weighing my words now. She is a pirate ship, and John Brown sails the sea a Lord High admiral of the Almighty, with his commission to sink every pirate he meets

> on God's ocean of the nineteenth-century. (Cheers and applause.) I mean literally and exactly what I say.[97]

Virginia was a "pirate ship" because it was guided by insurrectionary, slaveholding feeling. "[The state] is another Algiers, . . . a larger and blacker Algiers," Phillips asserted, due to its "barbarous" treatment of the enslaved.[98] Federal policy had yet to recognize this slavery as piratical and then act against as it had against the Barbary States. Therefore, Brown must receive his "commission" from a higher source. Phillips was one among a number of abolitionists whose support of Brown relied on the "Barbary crises as setting a precedent for (white) militant opposition to slavery." Reverend George B. Cheever, for example, compared Brown's "breaking up the system of Slavery" to those "seeking to break up the piracy of the Algerines."[99] Senator Charles Sumner argued that the "Barbary States of America" could be overcome via both law and fellow feeling (see chapter 3). Phillips concluded his speech with "John Brown has conquered the pirate. (Applause.) Hope! There is hope every where." In a fundamentally abolitionist jurisprudence, the enslaving pirate's removal was the first step toward justice.[100]

Of course, John Brown's violent abolitionism was a crime against the state. Therefore, he was piratical in the eyes of proslavery forces, appeasers, and those in favor of gradual abolition. Antebellum newspapers, essays, and political speeches presented Brown as a piratical filibuster, as Daniel J. Burge has shown. "His manner is courteous and affable, and he appears to make a favorable impression," wrote a special reporter for *The New York Herald* on October 21, 1859. The paper's notice of Brown's personal character two days after his revolt contrasted with its conclusion that he was "the commander of the abolition filibuster army"—that is, a privately mounted military campaigner who fomented political revolution in a foreign territory. The filibuster's stated aim was to install government. Filibustering campaigns of the late 1840s and early 1850s saw figures sympathetic to enslavement attempt to foster proxy states that could be annexed to the United States. For instance, William Walker in Nicaragua and Narciso Lopez in Cuba claimed to be sympathetic extensions of domestic imperialism. While the abolitionist Brown had opposite aims from proslavery filibusters, detractors presented his turn to extranational violence and Black sovereignty as equally piratical. The treatment of an abolitionist as a filibuster, even by antislavery Republicans, Burge concludes, befitted a political class more interested in "stabilizing" national union rather than "revolutionizing" federal policy. As before, both enslaving and abolitionist pirates could be positioned against a feeling state in the name of supposed political balance.[101]

The legal defense of a Brown accomplice, John E. Cook, in his November 1859 trial embodied strategic attempts to present Brown as a pirate apart from the national family. Cook's lawyer was Daniel W. Voorhees, an Indiana politician who favored appeasement of enslavers over civil war even after the war began. Here, Vorhees presented enslavement as enshrined by both positive law and natural law, or "not merely of legislatures and law-makers, but by the law of his being." Brown's pending death proved that abolitionist "sympathy is repudiated." Therefore, he continued, the defendant Cook's death would not represent "a sacrifice to heal the wrongs of your state." The defense admitted Cook's actions at Harpers Ferry but responded with an appeal to fellow feeling: "But does this fact debar him from human sympathy?" Voorhees responded that this "erring brother" represented the prospect of continued union against seductive piracy. The case revolved around "hearts and feelings woven in the destiny of the prisoner." In this destiny, Brown's perverse power of sympathy could be refuted. Excluding "others whose sympathies he has enlisted," Brown was a "pirate and robber of civil warfare." He had pirated from an entire civil domestic order. Cook, on the other hand, was a son whose national, familial attachment remained. Looking at Cook revealed that his face, unlike Brown's, was one "for a mother to love, and a sister to idolize." A cord of familial attachment could never be cut. Instead, the defense argued, "the natural goodness of his heart pleads trumpet-tongued against the deep damnation that estranged him from home and its principles." Cook's actions had revealed a temporary resentment fostered by a pirate's crimes against feeling. His present state confirmed his commitment to a national family. In the end, Cook was found guilty of murder but not of treason. Even so, he was hung. An alliance with abolitionist piracy could not be legalized.[102]

John Brown's trial was a flashpoint in antebellum legal culture. His raid fed into the resentment among both enslavers and abolitionists that would lead to peak antebellum violence in 1859 and 1860. "I have little hope of the freedom of the slave by peaceful means," wrote Frederick Douglass in a June 1860 letter to the abolitionist James Redpath, in response to a celebration of Brown's raid announced in *The Liberator*. After decades of enjoying legalized mastery, enslavers "have neither ears nor hearts for the appeals of justice and humanity." Douglass concluded, "The only penetrable point of a tyrant is fear of death." The "spotless integrity" of Brown's bellicosity, though in tension with Douglass's prior principles, had been "vindicated."[103] In short, direct abolitionist action had legal and moral sanction in a sentimental jurisprudence of resentment.

Disunion had long preceded the events at Harpers Ferry, as had political violence. Sumner's own resentment had met its resentful match on May 22, 1856, when he was almost caned to death in the halls of Congress by proslavery Representative Preston Brooks of South Carolina. Only days before, Sumner had repeated an abolitionist rallying cry against enslavement. For him, the 1854 Kansas-Nebraska Act and related statutes had empowered the "Barbary States of America." He accused southern pirates of flouting natural law and national feeling, as my next chapter will discuss. Brooks's response confirms that enslavers' real, if not just, resentment also carried political force. The beating was extensively covered in the popular press and led to further political breakdown.[104] There might seem to be a certain narrative elegance in seeing these events as inevitable steps toward the war to come. But that linear narrative would be a mistake. The 1850s, though often discussed as part of the teleological march toward civil war, were defined by ongoing attempts to gain political advantage on land and at sea. Universal abolition, oceanic enslavement, African colonization, global empire, or regional secession each remained imagined legal alternatives to alleged piracies that cut across a political spectrum. Though pirates never disappeared from antebellum legal culture, they could be temporarily vacated to serve tenuous visions of American imperial supremacy.

CHAPTER THREE

SUPREMACY

Charles Sumner, Maria Susanna Cummins, and the Ocean Postage Bill (1858)

In November 1852, Senator Charles Sumner delivered a speech to Congress about a policy that had no clear ties to piracy. The Massachusetts statesman was eager to increase government subsidies for U.S.-based transoceanic mail routes. Read in the context of the era's competing political resentments, however, Sumner was describing an imagined alternative to piracy: a perfection of feeling on land and water made possible by American imperial supremacy across the globe. These postal circuits, like the families invoked to support them, were terraqueous. Domestic mail was sent abroad via landed routes that floated seamlessly into the ocean. Cheaper global mail would thus "promot[e] the intercourse of family and friends, now separated by the ocean," and, in so doing, "add to the sum of human happiness." This "intercourse" was both economic and social: for instance, it took place between lovers separated by the ocean but whose correspondence generated positive feeling and eventually procreative attachments. High postal rates were inimical to such domestic and global fellow feeling, whereas cheap ocean postage would "be a new bond of peace among nations, and . . . extend good will among men." Amid this global expansion of feeling and peace, U.S. sovereignty would reign supreme. The subsidized sentimental letter would materially expand state power. As Sumner argued, transoceanic postal routes "vindicate for us a peaceful supremacy of the seas, and help to weave a golden tissue between the two hemispheres." This supremacy would supposedly result from mutual feeling rather than martial force. State-backed infrastructure would perfect a political "golden tissue." In his speech, Sumner did not consider whether the mail could bridge competing politics of enslavement or abolition. He did not address Daniel Webster's similar claim in March 1850 that appeasement for enslavers would lead to a transoceanic "golden chain" of national glory (see chapter 2). Instead, Sumner extended sympathy to a universal end, claiming that "with every faculty of correspondence, there is naturally a new expansion of human intercourse."[1] Familial feeling would reach as far as its postal infrastructure. The promise of antebellum legal culture—the removal of piratical unruliness and the perfection of feeling on both land and water—would be complete. A world of perfectly posted sympathy would stamp out all piratical crimes against feeling.

Sumner's speech was part of robust political debate about transoceanic mail and, by extension, the domestic state's legal jurisdiction in oceanic space. Central to this debate was whether abolition would extend globally. Thus, Sumner became a central figure in both antebellum legal culture around piracy and an overlapping legal culture of the transoceanic post. Each was dominated by competitions over enslavement's status as piratical or as an extension of valid proslavery familial feelings. Sumner's speech and related postal policies were republished in national newspapers as well as trade magazines such as *The Merchants' Magazine and Commercial Review*. Tellingly, the *Merchants'* editor, Freeman Hunt, explicitly advanced a sentimental vision akin to Sumner's. For Hunt, the true merchant "learns to look upon all nations as knit together by the ties of mutual dependence, to regard all men as kindred. . . . To teach that lesson HAS BEEN, and SHALL BE, one of the great purposes of *The Merchants' Magazine*."[2] The editor's call for global "ties of mutual dependence" and familial feeling among "kindred" mirrored Sumner's appeals for international union and oceanic conquest. With Sumner at the helm, this vision grew: he produced dozens of mail-related petitions on behalf of maritime communities. And he appears to have been successful. In 1854, the federal government paid $2 million in postal subsidies and secured less than $250,000 in postage revenue, just one-eighth of the cost of handling the nation's oceanic mail.[3] At the same time, the number of letters exchanged between the United States and Europe grew from 1.5 million in 1844 to 6 million in 1860.[4] A subsidized "golden tissue" was growing at home and abroad. Even so, domestic or global union was not so simple. Enslavement loomed large, as Sumner's own speeches against piracy confirmed. Postal ships were, for some, central to piracy law's martial enforcement, abolition's international spread, and ongoing African colonization's practical enactment. In practice, postal vessels were plying the watery graves of millions. They were landing in ports whose enslaved populations had been literally and figurately stamped.

Despite Sumner's sentimental appeal to universal union, debates over ocean mail subsidies were closely tied to piratical enslavement and the prospect of a legalized global trade. *The Merchants' Magazine* platformed Sumner's vision of postal union without conflict, but outlets such as *De Bow's Review: Agricultural, Commercial, Industrial Progress and Resources* countered with a southern, proslavery response. In its 1846 inaugural issue, the magazine's founder, James Dunwoody Brownson De Bow, wrote that his publication's purpose was to "advance[e] individual fortune, . . . [and connect] section with section . . . by ties of reciprocal interest and fraternal affection."[5] Considered "the antebellum South's most influential editor," De Bow shared Sumner's familial language of "interest" and "fraternal affection."[6] Yet the social and economic connections he advocated demonstrated ongoing fractures. The magazine's first complete article, for example, highlighted a "Convention of Southern and Western States" that demonstrated "the elevated tone of feeling and sentiment—the fraternal courtesies and regards—the ardent patriotism." As De Bow noted pointedly, such nationalistic fellow feeling "as by one consent" had not been seen "since the adoption of the Federal Constitution."[7] A distinctly southern legal culture was evolving. Perhaps the nation would follow. But if enslavement continued to be deemed piratical, a new legal order might be required. Like Sumner and *The Merchants' Magazine*, *De Bow's Review* and its political allies aligned a domestic, potentially secessionist union with the global mail. Each staged the mail as central to the slave trade's future legalization and advocated for postal companies that funded filibustering. In other words, they used letters' legal and symbolic power to turn an alleged pirate into a state agent.

Contests over piracy's definition and the state's legal and territorial bounds informed political debates about transoceanic postal systems. Invoking national feeling and victory against largely unnamed piracies, policymakers proposed the installation of competing global postal circuits among the United States, Europe, Asia, and the Americas. In this chapter I analyze those debates alongside Maria Susanna Cummins's domestic fiction *The Lamplighter* (1854), a singular artifact of transoceanic postal culture deeply informed by legal debates over piracy. Tellingly, the postal exchanges in the novel would not have been realistic at any period before its 1853 composition. The novel's events take place over the course of slightly more than five years, corresponding nearly exactly with the first comprehensive transoceanic American postal policies. Its plot tests competing postal visions. Specifically, *The Lamplighter* revolves around letter exchanges (or nonexchanges) between Gertrude Flint, a teenage orphan in Boston, and the eventual inhabitants of her ideal domestic space. They include Willie Sullivan, her love interest, who is a shipping clerk for a U.S. trading house in Calcutta; Emily Graham, Gertrude's saintly mentor, the daughter of a Boston shipping magnate with ties to Cuba; and Phillip Amory, Gertrude's father (and Emily's one-time lover), who was presumed dead in Rio de Janeiro but had in fact been wandering in the Ottoman Mediterranean. Postal ties among these locations mark Gertrude's moral development. Notably, Willie's constant letters from India allow her to care for his family and reject an ill-conceived trip to Cuba. Letters from Cuba carry both bad news and a rake thematically aligned with piratical crimes against feeling. The narrative's global mail is unbelievably reliable—the trope of the lost letter nowhere to be found. Competing circuits are judged according to the quality of their sentiments. The novel's primary crisis occurs only when Willie stops sending letters from India. Gertrude eventually reunites with him as well as with her father after a letter from Rio declaring Philip dead proves to be false. Willie, our sentimental hero, had in fact saved her father from enslavers with thematic ties to Barbary corsairs. The novel concludes with marriages whose success Cummins explicitly ascribes to Gertrude's powers of sympathy rather than the transoceanic mail. Even so, the political vision advocated by Sumner and others turns out to be true: a well-subsidized post is required to maintain national feeling across both land and water. Southern-based postal circuits threaten domestic stability and empower those with real or symbolic ties to piracy.

The Lamplighter contains an avalanche of letters but only spectral pirates. Even so, it shows how violent global incursions may become state policy rather than illegal piracy. It also offers competing visions of a world in which pirates would be obsolete. Thus, Cummins helped to show that antebellum legal culture was neither an ideological monolith (its advocates could advance conflicting policies related to enslavement, for example) nor a single, unbroken, literary-historical current. Depending on one's politics, filibusters, corsairs, and other pirates may be allies to or antagonists of proposed postal routes. Most often, policymakers subsumed debates on enslaving piracy into competitions over the landed letter.

At first blush, the postal stamp seems like a paltry weapon for attacking a pirate. Why bring a postage stamp to a gun fight? First, postal circuits dictated flows of information, as prior abolition mail campaigns had made clear. In 1835, for example, waves of abolitionist tracts from the north flooded Charleston, South Carolina, and surrounding states, leading to fierce political outrage and attempts to stop the mail.[8] Even beyond their content, stamped letters had particular power within antebellum legal culture around piracy. The difference between a privateer and a pirate was that the former carried a letter of marque proving legal attachment to a sovereign and its families. The privateer's letter of marque demonstrated a capacity for state-directed action that was ostensibly unavailable to the pirate. The sentimental letter likewise proved a postal circuit's moral and legal claim. Neither Cummins nor policymakers denied the state power's oceanic extension. Instead, they debated how it would be spread and for whose benefit. A latent appeasement for enslavement remained in postal policies that did not challenge abolition's land-water divide. Debates over enslavement in postal policy were, as in Cummins's novel, found in the margins. In response, this chapter pairs political debates over northern and southern circuits with Cummins's fictionalized judgment of these policies. As it shows, both policymakers and Cummins cast doubt on whether the global mail could perfect familial attachments or prevent piratical incursions given growing political fracture.

PIRACY AND THE CULTURE OF THE TRANSOCEANIC POST

Delivering fictional mail in its historical context reveals the oceanic contours of domestic culture, foreign relations, and imperial power that produced the pirate. As Peter Shulman succinctly states in *Coal and Empire*, international mail steamers were "embedded in complex networks of private capital, international markets, government regulation, naval strategy, diplomatic relations, and . . . material constraints."[9] The real or imagined letters such ships carried were likewise embedded in a legal culture around piracy. The letter reflected and projected domestic feeling's global spread. In other words, the pirate's legal and moral threat to state power could be overawed by a unique culture of the transoceanic post. As David Henkin's *The Postal Age* and related works have shown, the "culture of the post" is a fitting lens for discussing nineteenth-century American "interconnections and interdependencies."[10] Scholars now use government documents, personal letters, and other postal ephemera to trace the post's material history and its connections to nineteenth-century culture. The transoceanic post requires its own complete history, Henkin affirms, because it "required special thinking" on how postal ties would manifest.[11] Receiving a land-based letter was "an event rather than a feature of ordinary experience" that was normalized after the "revolutionary era" of domestic postal policy (1845–51). Receiving transoceanic mail, however, was an event long after this period.[12] By 1851, the U.S. government had established a three-cent charge for any domestic letter but did not standardize the international mail until the 1874 General Postal Union. Between 1847 and 1874, the government made treaties to define transoceanic mail service and set rates: an average transoceanic letter cost twenty-four cents or more, but its price depended on standing treaties. In these postal accords, as in related treaties over piracy, competing nations built global circuits of economic and sympathetic exchange. They used individual domestic sentiments to subsidize imperial competitions over both land and water.[13]

Debates on piracy provide a vital narrative framework for understanding a legal culture of the transoceanic post. While the British imperial post was the primary rival to the U.S. circuit that Sumner and others championed, proposals for an alternative U.S. southern circuit soon developed. *The Lamplighter* made these competitions central to the world of the novel, and its letters required a host of familiar and unstated imperial infrastructures. Befitting complex foreign relations, letter writers' material and emotional connections resulted from uneasy imperial cooperation. Britain's abolitionist policies had threatened American enslavement and introduced the prospect of their jurisdiction over American vessels under suspicion of piracy. Both Britain and the United States treated the international mail ships as political tools in such ocean politics. As the postal historian Wayne Fuller notes, the British government began subsidizing mail steamships in the early 1840s to "wrest control of the Atlantic carrying trade from the Americans" and provide a ready navy.[14] Throughout the decade, members of the Congressional Naval Committee recognized that England's routes posed a commercial and military threat.[15] In reference to an 1845 act authorizing government subsidies for steamship companies, the postmaster general stated, "The object of Congress . . . *seems to have been to build a naval steam marine which might temporarily be employed for commercial purposes*."[16] Though this "naval steam marine" was based on a commercial subsidy, the distinction is slight when one considers why the subsidy would be effective. Mail boats could become war boats. Domestic letters could become letters of marque. In other words, sentimental investments distinguished the subsidized steamship from the extranational pirate ship. Only the former has a claim to fellow feeling on both land and water.

In keeping with antebellum statecraft, the federal government's first transoceanic postal treaty was not with England but with the Prussian state of Bremen, which had promised to provide its own subsidy in addition to other economic incentives.[17] The 1847 treaty was consummated as U.S. armies were preparing to overrun Mexico City during the Mexican-American War. It was concurrent with natural scientists' "imperial archeology" via mapmaking in South and Latin America.[18] Thus, the postal treaty was tied to foreign relations and imperial contests among the United States, Britain, and various national and extranational groups. Those entrusted with building transoceanic mail systems overflowed with sentimental visions. Quoted in an 1847 issue of *The Merchants' Magazine*, the postmaster general justified the Bremen treaty by noting that "the whole continent of Europe was intimately connected with us in commercial and social relations." Because American familial feeling knew no bounds, he said, American shipping should not be "entirely at [Britain's] mercy in time of peace, and . . . be cut off in case of war."[19] In other words, even though intimate connections based in sympathy dictated which treaties should be made, strained sentiment between the U.S. and British governments was a political liability. Likewise, "commercial and social relations" during peacetime were inextricably bound to competitions of empire and the wars those competitions might include. The boat that carried letters could also enforce commercial and martial power.[20]

Despite America's ongoing economic proxy war with England, however, a truly transoceanic U.S. postal system required ties with the island power. Such foreign relations would bolster both empires' claims to moral supremacy. In December 1848, the writers of the Anglo-American Postal Treaty narrated a voluntary sympathetic exchange between individuals and nations. The agreement reflected an uneasy alliance that joined Britain's strained imperial infrastructure and America's burgeoning empire.[21] In the treaty's opening, George Bancroft, the U.S. minister to Britain and a former secretary of the navy, and Lord Palmerston, the British secretary of state, presented themselves as "desirous to promote the friendly relations existing between their respective citizens and subjects." Fellow feeling between individual national subjects allegedly necessitated a treaty between the nations themselves. All citizens and subjects had equal right to exchange sentiment, further conflating moral feeling with capitalist exchange. This shift toward equal exchange created a more standardized system for the sake of both British and American commercial interests. But despite the appeal to "friendly relations" as the treaty's universal result, the mail did not have the same effect on citizens as it did on subjects. For the former, the treaty made transnational exchanges of sentiment more economical; for the latter, it created imperial infrastructure that could be mobilized to bind or otherwise limit legal rights in times of peace and war. The treaty's second article presented stipulations, "in case of war between the two nations," that explained which routes would be maintained.[22] Mail ships would remain privateers rather than pirates due to the power of state-backed letters.

The 1848 postal treaty did not address the failed 1824 British-American accord to mutually enforce legal abolition versus enslaving pirates. Nor did it invoke the Piracy Act of 1820. Even so, American politicians recognized the postal accord's impact on abolition's oceanic enforcement and, perhaps, on the landed abolition that could follow. According to an 1850 House Naval Committee report, transoceanic mail ships that carried domestic sentiments could also help divest the nation of both piratical enslavers and the unwanted Black victims of such bondage. Subsidized mail steamships to London via the western coast of Africa, it concluded, were "chiefly for the great and beneficent objects of removing the free persons of color from this country to the coast of Africa, and of suppressing the slave trade." As in prior legal decisions and domestic fictions, rejections of Black enslavement as piratical did not lead to advocacy of Black citizenship. Instead, African colonization remained a form of beneficence focused on the feelings of politically conflicted white Americans. To sail the formerly enslaved via government-backed mail ships "beyond the limits of our country" to Liberia and elsewhere would remove "one cause of dangerous irritation" between states. In other words, the post could solve both the practical problem of colonization and the political problem of disunion. The report, which did not lead to legislation, included detailed accounts of the number of ships needed. It also included a letter of support from the American Colonization Society.[23] As each affirmed, oceanic postal sentiments could remove piracy while also installing white nation making's material infrastructure.

Unlike the divisive 1824 piracy accord, the political power of Congress's approved postal treaty derived in part from its seeming banality. Its architect, George Bancroft, officially framed the agreement as mutually beneficial even as he privately affirmed a U.S. martial victory. On December 15, 1848, he sent an official dispatch from London to U.S. Secretary of State James Buchanan, averring, "I have aimed at a just and fair reciprocity." As in British-American piracy treaties, each side claimed that the nations' political sentiments were united. Bancroft's optimism about the treaty may be traced to a simple fact: it installed an imperial infrastructure whose growth appeared to be all but assured. Still, earlier, on December 8, he had expressed more nationalist feeling in a private letter to Postmaster General Cave Johnson: "You charged me to whip John Bull into a good Postal Treaty. The defects in Con[gress] somewhat hurt the snapper to my whip: but I think I have done what was necessary for all that. [The Earl of] Clanricarde complains of the treaty: and thinks we have had everything our way. And so we have."[24] Public expressions of multinational feeling may be belied in private letters. Bancroft's appeal to his whip confirms the layers of violence under legal appeals to sympathy. He had to contend not only with external forces but also with political party whips who maintained legislative discipline among their members. Debates on enslavers' whips, often held by those same men, were never far behind.

In practice, postal infrastructure shaped the nation's imperial power on both land and water. The India mail, for example, anchored an existing as well as a hoped-for imperial circuit. Namely, it would facilitate a circuit joining Calcutta, New York, and San Francisco via a transcontinental railroad or a South American canal. The November 1853 issue of *The Merchants' Magazine* included a congressional report suggesting that mail be carried overland via a transcontinental railroad and to Asia by steamer, an idea that the editor believed was "worthy of consideration . . . for all who are interested in the welfare of our country." In other words, energies of empire and national familial feeling moved in concert.[25] The report supported authorizing new mail lines "in our provisions for rapid travel and safe and easy means of communication with the great commercial emporiums of the several nations of the earth."[26] The policy relied on the construction of a transcontinental railroad, a technology that would require further appropriation of Native lands and immense foreign labor. This assumption, countered by Indigenous survivance then and now, confirms Chickasaw scholar Jodi Byrd's lament that "indigenous peoples, especially in lands now occupied by the United States, continue to serve as signposts and grave markers along the roads of empire."[27] As recounted in *The Merchants' Magazine*, such violent expansion was allegedly necessary so that "from Calcutta to New York the [delivery] time would be twenty-seven days, . . . being a saving of twenty-three days."[28] An efficient yet violent imperial circuit was a moral good because it fed the sympathetic "golden tissue." Violence was not piratical if it advanced national moral sentiments.

These political appeals were in line with a broader sentimental culture of letters. Sumner was correct about domestic letters' political import. According to Konstantin Dierks, education for men and women in early America treated "personal disclosure and mutual sympathy . . . as the critical purposes of letter writing." Skilled letter writing allowed an increasingly socially and geographically mobile white American middle class to "to carve out more economic, social, and cultural space for itself, all without the appearance of competition or conflict."[29] In other words, letters of class- and race-based fellow feeling increased the political clout of their writers, in part because politicians such as Sumner invoked individual letter writers' freely made attachments in their policies. In this way, postal policy assumed even more gender-inclusive systems of political engagement than could be found in other aspects of antebellum legal culture. According to an 1856 *Merchants' Magazine* editorial, for example, cheap postage was "a question that concerns the female sex as well as the lords of creation" because women were the primary writers and recipients of letters.[30] Women's imagined, if not actual, supremacy in a sentimental culture of letters aligned with their right to engage legal debates about ocean postage and, by extension, global piracy.

"EVERY INDIA MAIL": TRANSOCEANIC POSTAL CULTURE IN *THE LAMPLIGHTER*

Like the other women writers discussed in this book, Maria Susanna Cummins was a privileged member of American legal culture. Her novel *The Lamplighter* (1854) reflects that privilege while also serving as the emblematic work of transoceanic postal culture. Cummins was born in 1827 to a relatively wealthy family in Salem, Massachusetts. Her mother, Mehitable Cave Cummins, was the third wife of David Cummins. Maria was the oldest of their four children. David was a successful lawyer who in time became judge of the court of common pleas in Norfolk Country. The patriarch was respected in his legal world, but his daughter performed more visible cultural work. *The Lamplighter*, her first novel, reportedly sold 40,000 copies in its first month of publication and 73,000 copies in its first year, figures matched only by Susan Warner's *The Wide Wide World* (1850) and Harriet Beecher Stowe's *Uncle Tom's Cabin* (1852).[31] Cummins was famously the main subject of Nathaniel Hawthorne's invective against the "d——d mob of scribbling women" whose fiction outsold his own. He estimated the combined value of his real estate in Concord and of the copyrights of his books published since 1837 at $5,000. Cummins, in contrast, had earned at least $7,000 from sales of *The Lamplighter* by the end of 1854.[32] As reception scholar

Susan Williams notes, the novel's multiple British and American editions, in addition to its French, German, Danish, Italian, Dutch, and Czech translations, allowed it to "perform and extend its cultural work" across age, class, gender, and national lines. Publishers also produced card game and picture-book spinoffs.[33] Between 1853 and 1876, *The Lamplighter* spawned sixteen separate licensed and unlicensed stage iterations in Britain and the United States, with thirteen written prior to 1860. An 1855 production in New York City shared a bill with a staged version of *Uncle Tom's Cabin*, and the actor Cordelia Howard played both Little Eva and Gertrude.[34] Gertrude did not face the same enslaving pirates as her fellow white heroine, but she would navigate their implied threat.

In *The Lamplighter*, the legal theory of the post—and, by indirect extension, piracy—is embedded in a series of letter exchanges between the white American hero and heroine, Willie Sullivan and Gertrude Flint. Introducing her scholarly edition of the novel, Nina Baym argues that the text was Cummins's attempt to "write about women's experience in a particularly contemporary setting." Other scholars have added legal, economic, and formalist readings, among others, but none have focused on the oceanic mail.[35] This omission is surprising because the heart of the novel's "contemporary setting" is Cummins's fictionalization of transoceanic postal circuits. In the main plot, Gertrude, an orphan who lives with her friend Emily Graham, navigates the social world of Boston after her lover, Willie, joins a class of American "financiers" in India who "abetted the accumulation of wealth and financial capital in the hands on the wealthiest Americans."[36] Before leaving, he tells her, "I shall be always hearing from you, and we can talk about it by letters, and arrange everything."[37] The post's practical power is matched by its power of sympathy, just as Sumner had promised. The mails may "arrange everything," including feelings, to fund American domestic life via global empire.

Indeed, the first section of *The Lamplighter* finds Gertrude "one Sabbath afternoon . . . with an open letter in her hand, the numerous postmarks upon the outside of which proclaimed from whence it came." Though the scene is otherwise unremarkable, it represents a major narrative thread in Cummins's sentimental fiction. As the narrator has already revealed, "every India mail brought news from William Sullivan." Now, by mentioning these "numerous postmarks" and the material history they "proclaim," the narrator signals that the letter has traveled the postal empire and is now a domestic commodity. Notably, the stamps are proof of Willie's sympathy. Likewise, in the novel's second section, a friend brings Gertrude an "evidently foreign document, the envelope literally covered with various colored post-office stamps," and tells her, "See here, Gerty, genuine Calcutta; no mistake!"[38] The domestic incorporation of this "evidently foreign document" materializes Willie's ability to make "genuine Calcutta" part of domestic Boston. In short, Sumner's promised link appears to hold.

Nonetheless, a close reading of scenes that describe global letter exchanges does not fully capture the post's or the novel's power in antebellum legal culture. Questions remain. How did a particular letter get to Boston? Who handled it? How much did it cost to send? And, perhaps most crucially, why track a fictional letter? Answers to all of these questions reveal the shared cultures of piracy and the post. As Joseph Roach skillfully shows in *Cities of the Dead*, tracking objects uncovers their social history. Roach follows a South American feather from an indigenous body to the London stage. He concludes that, "as a material object, [it] marks an act of violence: what it cost to produce was the original wearer's life, and what it served to dramatize was the prediction of overarching symbol systems on the material basis of waste."[39] Willie Sullivan's letter, though originating from a dominant (fictional) subject, also names historic acts of violence. What it cost to produce was letter writers' complicity with acts of empire building, and what it served to naturalize was the prediction of overarching transoceanic postal systems on the material basis of sympathy. Failing to track the letter therefore obscures sympathy's material impacts and trivializes the letter's connection to imperial circuits. For while Willie's fictional letter did not travel in real time, Cummins presupposed that new imperial postal routes would maintain the power of sympathy that Sumner and his allies had promised.

By all appearances, Gertrude and Willie successfully maintain the "friendly relations" promised in the British and American treaty. Their letters' travels in the post and in print culture reveal the vast imperial energies this exchange required. Willie's letters from India, if real, would have cost forty-eight cents each (comparable to a modern consumer good priced between $15 and $20).[40] This fee would have gone to British and American governments as well as to subsidized private companies. To reach Gertrude, each letter would have passed through no fewer than six foreign ports over the span of sixty-two days: possibly Calcutta, India; Madras, India; Point de Galle, Sri Lanka; Aden, Yemen; Suez, Egypt; Valletta, Malta; Southampton, England; New York City; and Boston. This voyage would have included an overland camel route across Egypt rather than sea passage around the Cape of Good Hope, as the Suez Canal was not completed until 1869.[41] The ship's initial travel would have been announced in *Allen's India Mail*, a trade magazine and "Register of Intelligence for British and Foreign India, China, & All Parts of the East." It might also have been tracked in *The New York Times*, as in a September 5, 1853, letter to the editor headlined "The Mails from India," which noted, "The steamer *Hermann* arrived in New York [from India] Wednesday night, and her mails should have reached [Boston] on Thursday evening."[42]

Thus, the movement of letters, real or fictional, was part of global print and postal culture. In the novel, the letter that Gertrude receives, an "evidently foreign document, the envelope literally covered with various colored post-office stamps," signals the landed home as a vital node in this circuit. Such a letter would have carried at least five front and two back postage markings in various colors, each signaling the letter's travel and cost. Gertrude's might have featured one red and one black circular date stamp on the front, two black circular date stamps on the back, two red straight-line postmarks on the front, a black debit number mark showing amount due to the British for services, and a black number indicating total postage due. Specific markings would depend on the ports of entry and the kinds of payments applied.[43] Taken together, however, they textualized the foreign relations that were allegedly predicated on international fellow feeling against piracy.

Bolstered by the alignment of imperial travel with true feeling, Willie's correspondence validates the Boston-to-Calcutta imperial circuit and introduces alternative visions based in Cuba. After he leaves for Calcutta, Gertrude tends to his mother and grandfather while also spending time with Emily Graham and her father, a wealthy shipping merchant. The Grahams have much in common with the Laytons in Catharine Maria Sedgwick's *Clarence*. Each family is beholden to a piratical slave economy, although the Grahams are not beset by literal pirates. Yet even though Gertrude is happy to be living with the generous Grahams, she rejects their invitation to join them on a "journey to the south" and an extended stay in Havana.[44] Her decision displeases Mr. Graham; and according to Baym, becomes "by far the most important test" of the heroine's initial moral development.[45] The India mail is Gertrude's justification. She tells Mr. Graham that duty requires her to stay with Willie's family. Chiding her, he responds, "Just because you used to live in the same house with them, and that boy out in Calcutta has sent you home a camel's-hair scarf, and a cage full of miserable little birds, and written you a great package of letters, you think you must forfeit your own interests to take care of his sick relations! I can't say that I see how their claim compares with mine."[46] According to this merchant's sentimental calculus, domestic ties are competing claims determined by economic interests and forfeits. Mr. Graham does not see the ongoing viability of Willie's claim because the young man no longer exists in domestic space. In turn, he bases his own claim to Gertrude on the money he has spent on her education. Ultimately, his "prejudiced and narrow sentiments" model an utterly incorrect view of sympathy's economic value or the transoceanic post's sentimental power.[47]

Indeed, Mr. Graham's claim is self-evidently false due to his rejection of the India mail's value. The political implication is central. He overlooks the material and sympathetic cost of "a great package of letters" and other posted gifts, a view that is anathema to Sumner's postal vision, domestic fiction, and middle-class consumer culture. As Lori Merish confirms, "spatial distance is surmounted by the power of sympathy; familial bonds are marked and sustained through the exchange of letters and, especially, gifts."[48] In this case, "familial bonds" are based on prior sympathetic attachments and are neither limited to domestic boundaries nor invalidated by transoceanic separation. Letters from "every India mail" justify Gertrude's decision and affirm Willie's feeling. This link is bound to their economic access as imperial agents. Only those with ready capital can consistently pay for letters that cost forty-eight cents each. Gertrude is active in these exchanges. Postage policy at the time did not allow for total prepayment, so one must imagine that she pays either half or the entire fee for each letter she receives from Willie. It would be fitting if the would-be lovers could mirror their exchange of perfect sympathy by splitting the cost of postage. But whatever the case, their transoceanic exchange invalidates Mr. Graham's claim to Gertrude.

Cummins introduced shipped goods beyond the common mail to further endorse Willie's sympathetic attachment and the sentimental power of postal circuits. In addition to valuable letters from him, Gertrude treasures a "camel's hair scarf" and "cage full of miserable birds." Such possessions were instrumental during the period for "imparting and conveying personal feelings and sentimental commitments."[49] And as the reference to "camel's hair" confirms, the foreign gifts' travel across the sea and along a camel route increases their value. Readers are not told how the scarf and the birds are transported across the ocean. We know they do not travel as official mail: the 1848 treaty covered letters, newspapers, and periodicals but made no provisions for other goods.[50] Yet anything traveling from Calcutta to Boston would have followed an imperial route because companies carried official mail, passengers, and cargo through an individual contract or agreement. The scarf that Willie sends is a greater and more explicit act of sympathetic power than a letter is because it requires a personal network of exchange. In addition to paying what can only be an exorbitant price, he must convince someone to foster his sympathy at sea and feed the birds that stand as the symbolic and material mark of his connection to Gertrude's domestic space. Neither Mr. Graham nor Cuba have an equal legal claim to Gertrude or, it seems, to the national family she embodies.

"A PIRATE SYMPATHY": SOUTHERN POSTAL SUPREMACY

Gertrude's other postal attachments in *The Lamplighter* reveal the alleged piracies that derived from hoped-for southern postal supremacy during this period. The enslaving pirates on the margins of antebellum postal debates made an appearance in a series of speeches given by the transoceanic post's biggest champion, Senator Charles Sumner. Beginning in 1847 and then continuing throughout the Civil War, Sumner decried the "*Barbary States of America*" as party to immoral piracy. "Virginia, Carolina, Mississippi, and Texas," he claimed, were "the American compliment to Morocco, Algiers, Tripoli, and Tunis." Enslaving southern states were akin to the North African states that had bound—or, in his view, enslaved—early American sailors. The prodigal pirates of Jefferson's Declaration had returned, this time in the service of abolition. As Sumner admitted, enslaving piracy was rooted in that document. British colonial powers had protected "wretched piracy," he opined, and the "mother country" had "prostituted [herself] to the same base ends in her American colonies." Like Jefferson, Sumner aligned African enslavement with British maternal unfeeling, a frame that allowed him to present domestic union, embodied by white American families but now including Black ones, as legally and morally unbroken. The prospect of future union, marked by the "peace and prosperity" of new territories, was challenged by "the black flag of the land pirates." Lawmakers who sought to legalize enslavement in new states were "a pirate crew" in whose "laws you hear the pirate-yell and see the flash of the pirate-knife." Continuing federal acquiescence to enslavement, Sumner concluded, "testifies a pirate sympathy."[51] In a similar speech that year, he had proposed a marshaling of feeling against enslaving pirates. After all, as victory over corsairs in the Ottoman Mediterranean had shown, "endeavors for freedom are animating," leading to an action-causing "throb of sympathy."

Americans' "fraternal feeling," which had resulted from early national bondage, should, after "confessing in [their] heart," be applied to their "wretched colored brother in bonds." This rationale for these equal hearts, according to Sumner, was familial attachment across racial lines. After all, the enslaved were "beings whose complexion and blood claim kindred with my own." Victory over piracy, he concluded, would perfect multiracial familial feeling and confer new legal rights on the formerly enslaved.[52]

Sumner treated the oceanic mail as key to perfecting domestic fellow feeling and, perhaps, to rejecting enslaving piracy. Others treated the transoceanic post as a necessary outlet for proslavery sentiments. According to Paul Quigley in his study of southern nationalism, "challenges to affective national community" defined domestic politics in the 1850s. He refers here to "southern anxieties about the disintegration of the affective bonds of sympathy that were seen as a crucial adhesive of national community."[53] The southern novelist and commentator William Gilmore Simms, for example, lamented sentimental political breakdown in an 1851 letter to a fellow southern novelist, John Pendleton Kennedy. Despite what Simms called the "genial and natural" character of "Southern life generally among the old & wealthy families," abolitionists failed to recognize these families as viable national models. In the process, he concluded, abolitionists had "utterly subverted the only bond (that of sympathy) by which the people of our separate sections were every truly held together. Common cause, common necessities, and the belief in a common feeling—these were the true articles of confederation."[54] The question of southern nationalism that developed was, as Quigley argues, a matter of "shifting grounds." Unionist- and secessionist-minded southerners debated the relative possibility of familial feeling.[55] For abolitionists, mail ships could hunt pirates in accordance with the Piracy Act of 1820 and perhaps export the landed enslaved. For proslavery politicians, mail ships could help legalize former pirates following the Piracy Act of 1820's nullification. After all, mail vessels could just as likely import state-backed slaves as export them. Or perhaps the mail could offer the breakaway South a sympathetic and concrete infrastructure.

The culture of transoceanic post, like the broader legal culture, was not planning an inevitable march toward internecine war. Instead, it became a site for competing regional policies with various political outcomes. During the Civil War, Confederate politicians would invoke the mail to assert secessionist sovereignty at sea. But from the vantage of the 1850s, postal policy cut across the nation's political spectrum. "Political support for [oceanic] mail steam lines did not fall into simple partisan or sectional categories," Peter Shulman accurately concludes.[56] The American South was a secondary but vital part of the global circuit championed by Sumner in 1853. The route was strongest in New York City to the north and San Francisco to the west. Along the so-called Ocean Route, however, ships made intermediate stops in Charleston, Savannah, Key West, New Orleans, and Havana prior to their arrival in Chagres, Panama, for an overland crossing and a Pacific trip.[57] The Ocean Route rendered the American post truly transoceanic and, as postal historian Carl H. Scheele writes, was the "most significant east-west mail service between 1849 and 1858."[58] The capital gained from this service was centralized in northern companies and interests. According to postal historian Wayne Fuller, "Southerners . . . had tried as hard as Northerners to get what [mail steamship routes] they could, and they had, in fact, obtained much. But they had not received the prize."[59] Though southern ports were active in the larger transoceanic circuit, the prize was subsidized routes based in New Orleans and other southern cities, including Havana. From 1849 to 1852, seven ships served Cuba twice per month, and two more ships were added in 1854.[60] Before that year, only $50,000 had been docketed for carrying mail from Charleston to Havana. This subsidy, a minor figure within the $2 million in subsidies approved for the year, indicated that southern infrastructure was deemed less necessary to the postal empire.[61]

Advocacy for southern-based postal infrastructures was far from monolithic, nor was it insular. As in the case of piracy law, postal policymakers offered competing applications of natural law as the basis for positive law. As Matthew Pratt Guterl writes, popular narrations presented annexed Cuba as part of the "supposedly predestined advance of Southern slavery into the global South."[62] Many Cuban exiles publishing in the antebellum popular press applied "sentido común," or the unity of sentiments as described in Thomas Paine's *Common Sense*, to the annexation of Cuba.[63] The Gulf of Mexico region was the "original engine" of U.S. expansionism, as Kirsten Gruesz has shown, one that fostered antebellum "visions of the 'natural' shape of the national body." Even as the British-backed postal empire was the model for eventual U.S. supremacy, southern agents envisioned a "near in-empire, analogous to the British in India," in which control over the gulf coast would facilitate an American-controlled link between the Atlantic and Pacific.[64] Because they believed an "in-empire" would be built on transoceanic postal infrastructure, supporters of various southern subsidies tried to reproduce northern infrastructures' material and symbolic precedents.[65] Debates regarding which states were supported by postal subsidies and which empires those subsidies should serve took the shape of competing domestic fictions whose pirates remained spectral but unmistakable.

The most strident advocate of a southern postal circuit was Matthew Fontaine Maury, a celebrated oceanographer who later became an officer in the Confederate navy. In Maury's proslavery theory of natural law, the mail would concretize the correspondence between natural sea currents and slaveholding sentiments. It would also deter pirates. As he had claimed in 1842, England and its antislavery ships, "under the *black* flag, preache[d] a crusade against the rights of neutrality and American principles." Thus, the spread of American enslaving "principles" might overawe British crimes against feeling. Historians such as Matthew Karp align Maury with southern attempts at "a proslavery naval empire of their own," but the mail's primacy in this vision was also vital.[66] As the scholar Walter Johnson notes, Maury's call was part of a broader "expansionist program of the 1850s" in which the Mississippi steamboat could become part of a global "Cotton Kingdom."[67] Maury was attempting to leverage an existing transoceanic postal culture and its assumed power of sympathy. In an 1851 speech at the Virginia Mercantile Convention, for example, he called for southern postal circuits to reach the Amazon River and Atlantic Europe. According to an editor at *The Southern Literary Messenger*, the plan "commend[ed] itself to the attention of every man who ha[d] at heart the commercial independence of the South." Maury presented this unity of sentiments as predestined by nature. Drawing on his oceanographic work, he stated that the southern cities near the gulf and the gulf stream were "destined by Nature to be the greatest commercial receptacles in the world." Southern fellow feeling, as an alternative "golden tissue," could be perfected if mail were given the chance to travel along oceanic currents. Maury pointed out that New York City interests had created mail routes to which "the federal government [had] committed . . . many millions for her steam ship enterprise." His hoped-for southern empire would follow that legal path: "The contract for carrying the mails would protect those who may be first to embark in this field, from competition for a few years, which, while the company is getting a foothold, is no small consideration." The mail would create the necessary conditions for building economic and social ties based on southern supremacy. After this circuit was set, "the whole of Europe must pass by our very doors on the great highway to the markets both of the East and the West Indies."[68] The Indian mail sent by men such as Cummins's Willie Sullivan would secure southern power across the globe.

Maury assumed that federal ocean mail could obliquely entrench global enslavement even amid policies that treated oceanic trade itself as piratical. The subsidized movement of mail might not necessarily presage oceanic enslavement's expansion, but it could provide a mechanism for escape. Maury noted of the mail routes, "It is well to have the ability to go or to send [ourselves and our slaves further south], in case it may become expedient to do so."[69] If secession did not occur, a postal empire would still be a valuable entity. Versions of Maury's postal plan reappeared in other venues, and he repeated them himself in *De Bow's*.[70] Politicians treated his suggestions as a serious matter. In an 1854 gathering of northern congressmen, the Whig senator Solomon Foot and others who were aligned with the antislavery free-soil movement expressed worries that Maury's plan would allow Cuba, the Dominican Republic, and Haiti to be annexed to the United States.[71] Though this southern empire failed to gain traction, the idea represented southern commercial groups' attempts to legalize something like piracy. Southern ports had become domestic nodes in a global system. They could have been incorporated into a legal regime whose distinction between piratical enslavement at sea and legal bondage on land was at ongoing risk of annulment.

Despite a relative lack of support for a proslavery postal network, advocates for the subsidy system accepted that existing southern postal circuits facilitated violence in the Caribbean, Europe, and Asia. The debate was not whether empire was violent but for whose gain the violence would be enacted. By extension, sympathy could be satirized to reject one vision, if not the program as a whole. For example, *The Merchants' Magazine* published an 1853 government report on the prospect of further postal connections among New York City, Calcutta, and San Francisco that stated, "To the Christian and philanthropist this enterprise appeals with irresistible force. The influence which such a regular and extensive communication must have with the spiritual conditions of the Asiatic races is incalculable."[72] Benevolent feeling sanctified the imperial "philanthropist," whose "communication" could be both commercial and moral. The editor of *Merchants'*, however, mocked this cross-racial beneficence, if not its imperial outcome. He advocated the shipment of "two or three hundred million baby-jumpers" to China on subsidized mail ships to "mitigate the sufferings, and straighten the bow legs, of the children now slung on their anxious mothers' backs."[73] The sarcastic language affirms the incongruity between this philanthropic impulse, a narration of disinterested sympathy, and the creation of new consumer markets and cheap labor. Postal subsidies were not domestic charity to foreign families, the editor noted, but would "improve the breed" of Chinese laborers sent to Cuba.[74] Chinese and Cuban circuits were connected, as in *The Lamplighter*. Imagined transoceanic postal supremacy would be distinct from the African slavery that marked the southern empire but would forward its own forms of white supremacist violence.

Pirates persisted in these competing visions of postal empire. A potent question remained: could extranational maritime agents be made part of the national family via real or imagined letters? Debates over the mail were deeply tied to the period's filibustering campaigns. For example, agents of a New York City–based postal empire funded filibustering operations, as demonstrated by the 1852 alliance between Senator Stephen Douglass and the businessman George Law. Both attempted to influence government attitudes toward Cuban annexation. Law's firm, the U.S. Mail Steamship Company, had an Ocean Route subsidy, a highly lucrative contract that connected the American South to Cuba, Panama, and the Pacific. [75] This meant that Law was positioned to control future circuits, which fed his support of pirate-adjacent filibusters. He advocated for Narcisco Lopez's failed 1850 and 1851 Cuban filibusters, offered 5,000 rifles to John Quitman for a planned 1854 Cuba expedition, and provided rifles to William Walker successful campaign in Nicaragua in 1856. Existing postal circuits and the laws that supported them could be leveraged for alternative ends, and such campaigns had tacit and direct support from members of the government. [76] Like the other pirates discussed in this book, such piratical figures represented varied political visions on both land and water. Their extranational collectivities were ostensibly outside government policy yet had clear state ties. Their filibustering nations were not easily distinguished from sovereign states once they were given political and martial power. Therefore, thwarting hoped-for southern supremacy required a narrative and material dismantling of its postal infrastructure.

"THAT INHOSPITABLE SOUTHERN DISEASE": REJECTING SOUTHERN SUPREMACY IN *THE LAMPLIGHTER*

Political and legal competitions over piratical filibustering are the backdrop of *The Lamplighter*'s representations of southern postal circuits. As Gertrude's engagement with the India mail affirms, Cummins did not treat all postal cultures equally. Specifically, Mr. Graham's planned voyage to Havana and Willie's status as a "boy in Calcutta" create a distinction between Cuba and India, one that parallels contemporaneous policy debates on enslavement. In the novel, a friend supports Gertrude's decision to turn down the trip to Cuba by citing Mr. Graham's "dictatorial way of acting, as if he were the Grand Mogul of Cochin China."[77] This offhand phrase aligns Cuba with China at a period when some officials were presenting the bondage of laborers from China and the Indian subcontinent as a solution to the problem of abolition. Throughout *The Lamplighter*, Cummins disavows southern plantation slavery while affirming imperial circuits in India and elsewhere. The novel's primary events occur alongside extranational campaigns in Cuba and elsewhere. Though Cummins did not directly dramatize piratical filibustering, the form and content of the novel's southern-based posted letters represent a rejection of the legal argument that American interests needed to overtake failed sovereigns throughout the Americas. The novel's Cuba-based letters are wholly unlike those that appear in Octavia Walton Le Vert's travelogue *Souvenirs of Travel* (1857). According to Robert E. May, Le Vert and other women who aided filibustering campaigns "asserted themselves as planners, propagandists, participants, and populizers—achieving a degree of agency by involvement in the movements, and occasionally exerting leverage at its upper echelons."[78] Cummins, in contrast, rejected southern postal agents by treating them as familial annihilators and spectral pirates in *The Lamplighter*. In other words, she represented piracy's postal contours.

Notably, Mr. Graham's letters from Cuba reflect the antebellum South's unique place in transoceanic postal culture. His unfeeling, China-aligned mockery of Willie as a "boy in Calcutta" establishes the India mail's compatibility with familial feeling. Cummins's fictionalization of the mail between Cuba and Boston, including its material travel, must be read alongside visions of a southern postal empire. Any letter from Cuba would have traveled from Havana to Boston via the Ocean Route on a subsidized private steam vessel such as the real-life *Black Warrior*. Tellingly, this ship played a part in American attempts to seize, control, and otherwise influence the economic, political, and social character of the island. For example, in February 1854, the Spanish government seized the *Black Warrior*, reportedly due to the owner's failure to properly follow port regulations. According to *The New York Times*, the ship was taken for "having some cotton on board not included in the manifest," but the seizure was odd because "no attempt ha[d] ever before been made by authorities of Havana to inspect cargo in American steamers calling at the port."[79] Scholars have often overlooked the fact that *Black Warrior* was one of two new ships on the Cuba route that regularly carried mail. So if this privately owned mail ship were also a contracted military force, one financed by filibusters or their allies, then Spain's seizure makes more sense. In any case, President Franklin Pierce's administration tried to use the seizure as a pretext for military action that would lead to U.S. control over the Cuba trade or the island itself. After the ship's return to the United States, Pierce began a series of attempts to buy Cuba for as much as $130 million.[80] Though he failed, the possibility of success deeply informs the world of *The Lamplighter*, a novel invested in the prospect of southern expansion via the subsidized mail.

Cummins obliquely addressed southern postal supremacy by rendering its letters and ports incompatible with domestic fellow feeling. In the novel, this claim begins in Boston with Phillip Amory, Gertrude's estranged father. The young Amory accidentally blinds his lover, Emily Graham, and then randomly boards a ship that he discovers is bound for Rio de Janeiro. In telling the story of her lost love, Emily states she sent "a letter of love, and an entreaty for his return." Can a southern circuit reestablish domestic attachment? It does not. She is told he has died of malaria, "that inhospitable southern disease, which takes the stranger for its victim."[81] The fact that such a letter can be sent signals an ongoing connection with a southern postal empire, but the novel presents this empire as incompatible with moral sense. Though Maury had offered sentimental arguments about the nation's "natural" connection to Brazil, the narrator of *The Lamplighter* emphasizes that "infection prevail[s] in the low and unhealthy region" of the country's interior.[82] Amory's business in Brazil inevitably entwines with the country's enslaving economy, further indicating its dangerous character as a locus of sympathy. While Emily believes that her lover is dead, Amory has not only survived but has married someone else, the daughter of a dead ship captain. She gives birth to Gertrude and then dies of malaria while her husband is away. Gertrude is sent back to Boston, where she given over to the care of the mother of a sailor who had once traveled with Amory.

Gertrude inheritance is not plantation wealth, as it had been for Catharine Maria Sedgwick's heroines. Her status as an orphan at the novel's opening is the product of familial isolation endemic to unnatural southern climates. Amy Kaplan frames Gertrude's birth in Rio as the start of a "civilizing narrative wherein she must purge herself of her origins in a dark, diseased, uncivilized terrain." Yet the "hostile foreign environment" of Rio must also be read as part of a more nuanced critique that differentiates between northern and southern (postal) supremacy.[83] In the novel, mail-based threats to Gertrude's happiness are based in Rio, Havana, and New Orleans—the three cities most closely associated with a southern postal circuit. When Gertrude chooses to remain in Boston while the Grahams travel south, Emily, like Willie, promises they will remain attached via letter. These distinct postal circuits allow Gertrude to test competing imperial sentiments simultaneously. Willie's success and Emily's failure are not due to Emily's lack of sympathy. Instead, the post itself delivers proof of the southern circuit's incompatibility with feeling.

Antebellum accounts of the Cuban post vary, as an examination of Le Vert's contemporaneous letters from Cuba demonstrate. Those that appear in *Souvenirs of Travel* forward Cuba's natural and inevitable attachment to the United States.[84] According to Guterl, Le Vert's attitudes were "a reflection of the near future of the American South"—that is, "the South *in process*, as it reached out to the Americas."[85] Though there is no indication that Le Vert read or responded to *The Lamplighter*, her account of Cuba contains striking similarities to aspects of the novel. In 1855, Le Vert "embarked in the noble 'Black Warrior,'" the mail ship I mentioned in my discussion of the Pierce Administration's pretexts for Cuban annexation.[86] Though *The Lamplighter* does not name the *Black Warrior*, the Grahams travel on the ship's exact route, stopping in New York City, Charleston, New Orleans, and Cuba.[87] Therefore, Le Vert and the Grahams represent alternative visions of a domesticated Cuba made possible by subsidized postal circuits. Pirates inhabit these circuits' historical analogues but remain unseen in the narratives or their letters.

Like Le Vert, Cummins invoked sympathy in her judgment of Cuba as a potential global extension of enslavement, but the domestic space of Havana in the novel lacks familial feeling. Both writers focused on attempted transportations of antebellum domesticity into American-owned Havana hotels, a common phenomenon in the period. "Southerners—alongside some New England families," Guterl notes, "owned plantations in colonial Cuba, ran hotels and operated businesses in Havana."[88] For Le Vert, the southern trip was not a deviation from familial feeling but materially compatible with it. Her letters describe the "excellent rooms" at the Hotel Cubano, kept by Mrs. Brewers, a "lady-like, agreeable woman," who forwarded "many courtesies and pleasant attentions," including "a delicious breakfast." The space is pleasant; its "windows are immense, with heavy wooden shutters" that allow for peaceful sleeping.[89] In sum, Le Vert's narrative presents Cuba as a domestic space in both a personal and a national sense. *The Lamplighter* stages Cuba's incompatibility with posted moral sentiment. Gertrude receives only one letter from the Grahams while they are in Cuba, and it "contain[s] little that [is] satisfactory." The letter, written in a Havana boarding house "kept by an American lady, and crowded with visitors from Boston, New York, and other northern cities," describes a domestic space that is devoid of proper sympathy and capable of breeding false sentiment. The novel calls out northerners as dominant figures in this ostensibly southern space, thereby affirming Cuba's centrality as a node in various visions of American global empire. Emily does not complain in the letter but says that she "feels kind of strange here" because it is a "dreadful uncomfortable sort of place." A lack of domestic comfort codes as moral failing: in addition to lacking carpets and fireplaces, the "windows have no glass about them but are grated just like a prison." [90] This prison house evinces, perhaps spectrally, the plantation houses that bind Cuba's enslaved. Any person, northerner or southerner, who attempts to incorporate Cuba into their domestic space is destined to be disappointed.

Cummins's novel counteracts arguments for Havana's compatibility with national feeling, thereby subsuming debates on piratical enslavement with accounts of the oceanic mail. Yet like Sedgwick, the author did not deny her northern social circle's investments in slave economies. Readers are not told why Mr. Graham decides to go to Cuba, though we know he leaves his family and travels to unstated locations. One might speculate that this successful Boston warehouse owner, like other businessmen from "American companies along the Atlantic seaboard," was part of what Guterl describes as an attempt to "modernize Cuban sugar production" during the 1850s."[91] Le Vert commented on the sugar industry in *Souvenirs of Travel*, making a dubious stab at aligning Havana with proper sympathy due to its slave system: "There certainly must be five negroes to one white person, . . . [but] the slaves are certainly the happiest and most independent looking people imaginable."[92] As she dubiously implied, abolitionist laws that treated enslavement as piracy committed their own crimes against the happy Black subjects of natural white supremacy.

In an imagined southern empire, Cuba was envisioned as a major port. But in the more circumspect politics of Cummins's novel, naming slavery would have stolen attention from Gertrude's ascendent white, middle-class domesticity. Still, Cummins signaled that northerners should be wary of Cuba because its inhabitants lack sympathetic capacity. Of note is a "flaunting kind of woman" who marries the equally sentiment-deprived Mr. Graham.[93] Gertrude learns from Emily, "She followed Mr. Graham up pretty well at Havana, but I guess he thought better of it, and didn't really mean to have her. When we got to New Orleans, however, she was there; and the long and short of it is, she carried her point, and married him."[94] That this ill-conceived attachment begins in Cuba and is confirmed in New Orleans signals the power of false sentiment when exported to the domestic nation. New Orleans and Havana represent a circuit of mistaken sympathy in a southern empire whose spread would be disastrous.

The novel juxtaposes the India letters' power to elicit sympathetic and sexual feelings with the sexual violence of Mr. Bruce, a rake associated with New Orleans, the port city whose brackish water marked the Piracy Act of 1820's legal limits. Bruce is not a pirate, but he represents a comparable threat: he is a maritime agent based in the enslaving South who commits crimes against feeling. Bruce sails the Mississippi River during the same period as Stowe's pirate Legree. Bruce meets the Grahams in New Orleans, becomes a favorite of Emily's vapid stepsisters, and after their return to Boston joins them at a dinner party in their home. Though he was not born a southerner, he is aligned with the South, where "amid the gayety and dissipation of southern cities [he] contrive[s] to waste his time with tolerable satisfaction." This tendency toward "gayety and dissipation" is code for sexual indiscretion and indicates the sexual threat facing those northerners who abide southern sentiments. Bruce is also sexually imperialistic and violent. When Gertrude receives a letter from Willie during a dinner party, Bruce keeps "his eyes upon her, and half expect[s] to see her change color and look disconcerted, on the letter being handed to her in the presence of so many witnesses." His expectations signal the intimate sexual power of letters, which require writers and recipients to exchange fluid, break seals, wield pens, fondle paper, and open what was previously closed. Posted letters are ostensibly private but can be made promiscuous or perhaps violent. Gertrude attempts to enact this ritual in its appropriate setting, her private bedroom, but Bruce "notice[s] the movement" and forces himself between her and the stairs "in time to arrest her steps."[95] A hoped-for private exchange of sentiment now exists alongside a public act of sexual and psychic violence. Just as the Cuban letter from Emily indicates that mistaken sympathy prevails in a southern circuit, Bruce's rakishness signals that such sympathy's spread north is a sexual and political threat. He is the narrative's closest thing to an unfeeling pirate.

The imagined southern conquest of northern virtue reveals itself as a danger, albeit one that can be overcome. Gertrude appears to enact her desire when she escapes from Bruce and reads Willie's "fervent and earnest expression of gratitude." His letter is a response to his mother's death and reasserts the transoceanic post's sympathetic power to maintain domestic attachment. Gertrude spends a fulfilling hour "lost in meditation" over thoughts of Willie.

However, the southern threat does not abate. She hears Bruce beneath her window and recalls the "professions of admiration he had contrived to whisper in her ear." Remembrance of that violation overcomes her exchange with Willie, and she is "wounded by the confident and assured manner in which Mr. Bruce made his advances."[96] Though she rejects the rake, Willie's protective authority has proven to be limited. In the end, Gertrude relies on her own virtue and distances herself from this unwanted suitor. She avoids Bruce and waits patiently for Willie's future letters and eventual return. The question of whether his letters—or any postal infrastructure—can maintain domestic fellow feeling across the globe remains an open question in both the narrative and its contemporary setting.

"THE GLORY HAS DEPARTED": DISUNION AND THE 1858 OCEAN POSTAGE BILL

Postal debates reflected antebellum political investments in a world without pirates. Even so, the imagined absence of domestic discord or oceanic unruliness was not enough to instill global circuits of perfect fellow feeling. Despite Sumner's appeal that sympathy would guarantee any subsidy's success, regional conflict and rising costs made an unfettered supremacy difficult to justify. After the 1848 treaty, Congress came to more agreements and increased subsidies. For example, an 1853 provision stated that U.S. mail to the western coast of South America would be exchanged at Panama with British steamers; private U.S. companies could not yet pay for such regular service, and no subsidy existed that would cement a regular economic and military presence. Any future presence, and the subsidy it would require, would likely be validated by claims of current and future sentiments. Even so, companies invariably carried less mail than they were subsidized for carrying. For example, the company that secured the route between New York City and Liverpool was paid $858,000 for twenty-six trips, no matter the number of letters carried that year.[97] The use of private companies and mail subsidies established global circuits that domestic sympathy materially and discursively subsidized. The letter that paid for empire also justified it. Though the unequal cost of land and sea postage was understandable, given differing economies, Sumner argued that ocean postage was more valuable than any financial consideration. To recover the economic gap, fellow feeling must be considered more valuable than its cost. But those accounts were not always accepted. Politicians sought to protect domestic fellow feeling and spread it globally, but the state's role remained under debate. Cummins's novel presents middle-class women's global investments as the key to perfecting a domestic virtue that was more expansive than even the ocean mail.

Even for those in favor of postal supremacy, the subsidy system unfairly burdened national fellow feeling that was seen as independently valuable. The letter may have traveled along empire's infrastructure, but the best system would have allowed a sentimental letter to pay for itself and nothing else. Policymakers such as Representative R. E. Fenton of New York extolled the "interchange of sentiment" facilitated by the subsidized post but bristled against such sentiments' subsidy of rapidly expanding circuits. "Parental, filial, and fraternal sentiments are fostered and kept fresh in the hearts of separated friends," he admitted, but growing costs dictated that "this species of enterprise . . . must receive a check." In short, the oceanic subsidy should not outpace the domestic sentiments it carried.[98] Similarly, a *Merchants'* writer asserted that private letter writers' subsidy of martial power violated the state's role in fostering fellow feeling, imperial supremacy's value notwithstanding: "A naval steam marine may be all very well, but why, in the name of humanity, should it be saddled as a tax upon letter postage?" The subsidy, though narrated as an extension of sentiment, unfairly paid for martial infrastructure using "the business and affections of the great universal public." The Departments of State, Navy, War, and Judiciary relied on the post, which forced the transoceanic post to "carry, in addition to its own proper burdens, those [costs] of all the other departments."[99] National families could not be burdened by a subsidy whose costs outpaced their posted sentiments.

The end of the subsidy system in 1858 represented a move away from Sumner's political vision. According to *The New York Times*, the 1858 Ocean Postage Bill installed a "plan of compensation based entirely upon the *receipts of sea and inland postage*." In other words, real letters rather than imagined sentiments would determine the federal government's contribution to private companies. Domestic recipients of oceanic mail would need to weigh the cost of their sentiments against higher rates. Additional terms included a two-year limit on private firms' postal contracts with the government and preferential treatment for American companies. Not surprisingly, steamship companies were not in favor. At any rate, the increase in ocean postage came after a decade of building the transoceanic network with complex ties to domestic culture and global bondage.[100]

Ongoing domestic political fracture likely limited appetites for such a global federal project. The cost of the subsidies, confirms postal historian Wayne Fuller, "convinced many members of Congress in the early 1850s that the subsidization program had been a mistake."[101] Representative Joshua Giddings of Ohio said, "The whole truth is . . . this extravagant expenditure has been made for the purpose of national glory. . . . Well sir, the glory has departed." He did not state why appeals to national fellow feeling or glory had lessened, but the strident abolitionist's speeches rejecting "American Piracy" provides a clue. Giddings had reserved special scorn for northern politicians in an 1843 speech, later republished in 1853 by Ticknor and Fields, the publisher of both *The Lamplighter* and *Uncle Tom's Cabin*: "If [northern] gentlemen really feel that our people are bound to maintain this slave-trade, [and believe they] are under constitutional obligations . . . that these pirates may pursue their vocation, let them say it." National glory at sea "departed" so long as enslavement persisted and feelings of appeasement retained legal force.[102] Senator Robert Toombs of Georgia, an enslaver and eventually the Confederacy's secretary of state, likewise noted that he "had heard enough talk about the mastery of the seas. . . . That was the pretext under which millions of public money was squandered a few years ago. . . . That is all over now." Toombs, as modern biographer Mark Scroggins notes, favored proslavery expansionism across the Americas and vocally opposed all abolitionist statutes related to enslavement, including the Piracy Act of 1820 and the 1842 Webster-Ashburton Treaty. The Georgia senator went so far as to call British antislavery patrols pirates who deserved death by hanging. Though unabashedly pro-South, Toombs rejected all forms of national postal supremacy. No golden thread would unite a nation mired in sectarian conflict.[103]

If Cummins's novel had been set in 1859, Willie's letters would have been much more expensive. Despite her rejection of Cuba, she did signal letters' limits across *any* imperial circuit, thereby distinguishing between perfect domestic sentiments and mediated political ones. The basis for antebellum legal culture around piracy—that familial attachments glorified the state and would ensure its success—was far from guaranteed. Even as the narrator announces, "Every India mail brought news from William Sullivan," she indicates that the sympathy maintained across postal empires may strain domestic relations. The passage continues by celebrating Willie, "who, prosperous in business, and rendered happy, even in his exile, by the belief that the friends he loved best were in the enjoyment of the fruits of his exertions, wrote always in his accustomed strain of cheerfulness."[104] The contrast between "the belief" and "his exile" indicates that imperial agents perhaps overemphasized subsidized letters' sentimental power. The family welcomes the money that Willie gains in the global merchant trade—the "fruits of his exertions"—but the novel suggests that the material benefits of trade may not outweigh the familial costs. For example, at his mother's request, Gertrude does not tell Willie about the death of his grandfather. Of course, he is not to be blamed for his optimism, given that Gertrude's letter had "mentioned [nothing] which would be likely to alarm him on [her] account."[105] Nonetheless, letters are synonymous with both true sympathetic connection and the inherent threat to sympathy across global imperial circuits.

The novel's resolution relies on imperial agents' ability to navigate postal empires. It presumes the success of American imperial efforts against pirates and their allies. If the southern-based post breaks familial bonds and promises sickness and death, its broken circuit of sympathy must be rebuilt on a new circuit based in New York and extending to India. Though a false letter had claimed that he was dead, Amory survives Rio and travels across the American West to Asia and the Middle East. In other words, his prior failure in the southern circuit leads to increased economic and sympathetic power in a northern-backed one. Amazingly, the hero Willie, Gertrude's "boy in Calcutta," saves Amory during a fight with an "Arab traitor . . . and his rascally army of Bedouin rogues," a reference to Middle Eastern and North African nomadic peoples whose rich history and traditions (dating to at least 6000 BCE in what is now Syria) have often been minimized in favor of facile orientalism.[106] Like corsairs, Bedouin raiders threatened a transoceanic circuit of trade connected via Egypt's overland camel route. Indeed, states in the early modern Ottoman Mediterranean had ordered ships on the Suez "to protect grain ships from pirates and Bedouin raids."[107] They were, in a manner, piratical antagonists. In the novel, these unfeeling mobile figures serve as foils for sympathetic connections made on the India mail route over land and water. Willie's so-called heroism parallels the installment of imperial infrastructures in the hopes of vacating transcolonial collaboration. While his act of selflessness establishes his capacity for sympathy, it also reasserts his status as an imperial agent against pirates or their allies. In addition, the meeting leads to the novel's final domestic arrangement: Willie marries Gertrude, and Amory marries Emily. The model family has been formed. Pirates lurk in the waters that surround them but do not surface.

Like Sedgwick's fictions, *The Lamplighter* was Cummins's attempt to place domestic culture into its global context. The novel's conclusion "weds capitalist and religious values": Gertrude's moral feeling is rewarded with the ability to buy a home and its related commodities.[108] But even though Willie's return may secure insular domesticity, global relations remain. Her father's prior wealth, though meager, is in part the product of the Rio trade and the enslaving economy. His wife Emily, Gertrude's main benefactor, is the daughter of a Cuba-aligned merchant. Readers are not told if Gertrude keeps Willie's letters in their married home, but certainly she had kept them during his absence. In any case, she has no reason to dispose of the scarf or the birds. To purge these commodities would weaken the couple's attachment and, perhaps indirectly, deny that prior postal attachments are compatible with domestic life. Neither Gertrude nor Willie considers larger policy debates, questions which empires their letters fund, or names Willie's complicity in imperial violence. The oceanic post has become just another part of domestic life. By extension, Gertrude's comfortable Boston home is the locus of "peaceful supremacy" promised by Charles Sumner. Yet the nation and its homes were still vulnerable to pirates who claimed proslavery supremacy, as the events of 1861 would make clear.

"TWO NATIONS IN FEELING": REASSESSING 1848 AND ENTERING 1861

Postal policies are one means to track, in the words of Ann Stoler, the "familiar, strange, and unarticulated ways in which empire has appeared and disappeared from the intimate and public spaces of United States." Like the pirate, the post reveals an imagined "distribution of sentiments" between imperial states and their subjects.[109] Early American letter writers, as Konstantin Dierks notes, shaped imperial formations produced by the "discrete and cumulative energies of innumerable people anonymous to history."[110] Likewise, global letter writing may be added to Amy Kaplan's list of "the multiple ways [in which] empire becomes a way of life" for persons who benefit, resist, and are subjected to domestic cultures built through intranational relations.[111] Transoceanic mail, both real and historical, posted competing forms of familial attachment that also shaped debates on foreign relations and piratical enslavement. In *The Lamplighter*, as I have shown, Cummins gave antebellum energies further cultural meaning by fictionalizing contrasting accounts of the transoceanic post's sentimental power.

Guided by the 1848 Anglo-American Postal Treaty, the novel posits a future of perfected imperial foreign relations amid various oceanic threats. In this way, Cummins and a culture of the transoceanic post reaffirmed 1848 as a historical flashpoint for U.S. imperialism. The historian Walter Johnson highlights the year as the "geographic limit of the frontier of accumulation" that led southerners to push even further south in a quest to expand their "Cotton Kingdom."[112] The postal treaty became a practical and symbolic anchor for similarly expansive visions of postal empire. The sensational fictions of 1848, according to Shelley Streeby, require the "re-examination of a longer history of empire in the Americas" based on "global and internal dynamics of empire building" prior to the 1898 Spanish-American War.[113] Streeby focuses on the conflict between the United States and Mexico that year as well the European revolutions also taking place. Yet the "boost to U.S. power in world systems" was also materially enacted in the postal treaty and related narrations. Postal debates were primary among the "battles for influence in and control of the Americas."[114] The post was vital for imagining and enacting empires that came (or did not come) from subsidized circuits on both land and water. The circuit promised by transoceanic mail included the use of immigrant labor to build transcontinental rail, further encroachment into Native American lands, and a default on land grants under the 1848 Treaty of Guadalupe Hidalgo. For example, a postal agent began to establish offices in the land taken in that treaty. The first mail steamship left New York City for Panama and San Francisco by year's end, ushering in a dramatic increase in colonizers. Even as the India mail brought news from Willie Sullivan, it also traveled a world remade by transoceanic postal empires.

As in much domestic pirate fiction, the white middle-class figures in *The Lamplighter* retain the spoils of enslavement against unnamed Black claimants and their heirs. Ultimately, Cummins created an ideological parallel between the figures I discuss in chapter 1 and a historical parallel with the more clearly violent events I describe in chapter 2. Much like Sedgwick in the 1820s and 1830s, she remained allied to a jurisprudence of appeasement in keeping with their shared social standing.[115] Sedgwick's various pirates do not map onto a simple ideological binary of enslaver or abolitionist. Even so, pirates' removal from her fictions allowed her to narratively refrain from adjudicating enslavement or promoting abolition. No such pirates threaten the paradigmatic white heroine of *The Lamplighter*, notwithstanding the novel's spectral filibusters and corsairs. Even so, the reality of enslavement and the prospect of its spread remain weakly but undeniably embedded in postal exchanges derived from southern circuits but also connected to northern agents. In other words, Cummins staged the competing policies of white imperial supremacy invoked by antebellum policymakers.

Cummins struggled to retain the optimistic vision of *The Lamplighter* following John Brown's raid and related violence, as she indicated in a December 1860 letter to her British publisher, Sampson Low. She had recently returned home from visiting Low in London to secure British copyright for her latest book (an act which foreshadowed piracies to come). Her colorfully stamped passport, like Gertrude Flint's India mail, affirmed her navigation of various foreign relations such as Germany, France, and Switzerland.[116] Now home, Cummins reported that she was "sufficiently convinced of the advisability of laying the scene of a future story on my nation[al] soil" despite the "distractions which at present agitate us." The distraction, of course, was growing sectarian conflict. "No person with the slightest love of country can be unmoved by our present alarming condition," she continued. In a statement of universal national feeling that spoke to her personal state, she asserted, "Many are already suffering from the effects of it & the depression of spirit is universal." The five-year delay between this letter and *Haunted Hearts* (1864), her subsequent wartime pirate novel, indicates the imaginative and emotional challenges inherent to telling "the story of what they are doing in the United States." The story, she would conclude, is a "depression of the spirit" at the hands of secessionist pirates.[117]

As Cummins sailed the Atlantic to defeat literary pirates, antagonists over postal policy entered a growing sectarian fray. In 1860, southern jurists and lawmakers had again attempted to nullify federal law by rejecting the Piracy Act of 1820 and related statutes. "The African slave trade is not piracy," declared Judge Andrew G. Magrath in response to federal prosecution of sailors aboard two deep-sea enslaving vessels, the *Echo* and the *Wander*. Attempts to prevent such prosecutions and reopen the trade, as Manisha Sinha notes, resulted in legal failures and ideological victories. Even southern lawmakers against nullification "refused to endorse a moral condemnation."[118] "We shall become two nations in feeling," wrote De Bow in 1860, "which must soon render us two nations in fact." He was, in fact, quoting the "wonderfully prophetic" words of a *Princeton Review* article from twenty years earlier. De Bow's missive, *The Interest in Slavery of the Southern Non-Slave-Holder: The Right of Peaceful Secession*, promoted economic as well as biblical natural law justifications across a southern "family." Some northern outlets accepted this moral and legal split. "We believe the Southern people are pretty well united in the belief that the

African slave-trade is not 'piracy,'" declared a March 1859 editorial in *The Times* of Columbus, Ohio, "and that the act that so declares it, should be repealed."[119] Sumner, on the other hand, continued to argue that one could not stamp out oceanic unruliness without removing enslavement's land-sea legal divide. His ultimate warning in 1860—that "Slavery must breed Barbarians, while it develops everywhere, alike in the individual and in the society to which he belongs"—represented piratical enslavement as a poisoned lineage. Without a domestic check, pirates would "breed" a fundamentally immoral familial and national order that threatened the entire world. Notably, Sumner would repeat this speech during the war itself, with an added touch in a published 1863 edition: "Was I not right?" He also admitted, "There are old nations already in the family still tolerating Slavery." Yet while secessionists had received tacit and active international support amid declarations of neutrality, Sumner refused to support a secessionist force that "flaunts in piracy and blood before the civilized world."[120] As before, the pirate's removal would allegedly lead to union.

Befitting letters' centrality in these conflicts, a printed postal envelope, or cover, summarized the state of antebellum legal culture in 1861 (fig. 1). Produced in the war's opening years by the prominent New York City printer Charles Magnus, the image on the cover borrows its perspective from *A General Map of the World, or Terraqueous Globe* (1794). The globe, sliced into two hemispheres, retains its oceanic focal points. Named watery bodies receive equal standing with landed ones. Indeed, the cover's particular connection to a domestic conflict is evident only in its title: "THE WHOLE WORLD IN COMMOTION ABOUT THE WAR IN AMERICA." Civil War legal culture, like its antebellum counterpart, would develop on both land and water. "An internal struggle . . . took on international ramifications almost immediately," asserts the legal scholar Mark Weitz, and a domestic conflagration spread across a watery globe. The resulting conflict, as the naval historian Warren F. Spencer confirms, was "a total war with worldwide economic and maritime implications," one that included competitions over secession's legal status as piracy.[121] Alongside competing legal claims, thousands of printed postal covers quickly flooded the wartime North and South. They most often cost one or two cents each and were sometimes sold in packs of ten. Approximately three hundred printers in the North and at least thirty in the South produced more than 15,000 different kinds of covers with wartime iconography. Many depicted pirates, typically secessionist, as they committed crimes against feeling.[122] The covers were part of a broader material visual culture that included photographs, *cartes de*

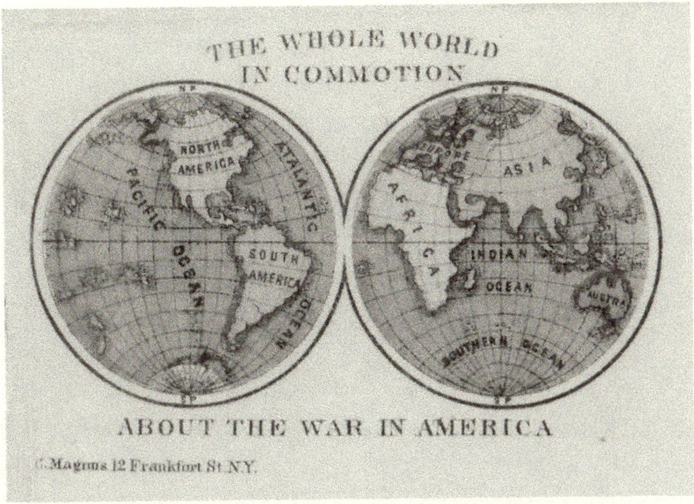

FIGURE 1. Illustrated postal cover, "THE WHOLE WORLD IN COMMOTION ABOUT THE WAR IN AMERICA" (1861). Courtesy of the American Antiquarian Society.

visite, posters, songbooks, paintings, and advertising manuals.[123] They circulated alongside wartime fictions, secessionist founding documents, transcripts of wartime piracy cases, and other forms of legal culture around piracy. In each, competing appeals to crimes against feeling helped adjudicate secession's legal status on both land and sea.

CHAPTER FOUR

SECESSION

Abraham Lincoln, Jefferson Davis, and the Confederate Constitution (1861)

On March 4, 1861, standing at the East Portico of the U.S. Capitol, President Abraham Lincoln delivered his first inaugural address. Following his election in November 1860, seven states had seceded from the Union. By the following February, they had formally initiated a secessionist government. Despite these undeniable ruptures, Lincoln applauded national sympathy. He upheld antebellum legal culture's defining premise: the national family's perpetual perfection and enslavement's compatibility with this union. The handwritten edits and additions on Lincoln's printed copy of the speech reveal his attempt to present unionist feeling's legal force up to the moment of delivery. The president, for example, added a section on "the restoration of fraternal sympathies and affection." He edited an appeal to "national union," a politically charged legal phrase, to the more sentimentally inflected "national fabric, with all its benefits, its memories, and its hopes." Unionism, he implied, was a feeling before it was a law.

Amid this appeal to national feelings, Lincoln noted the "apprehension" of the southern states, or worries that "their property and their peace and personal security are to be endangered." He responded unequivocally, "I have no purpose, directly or indirectly, to interfere with the institution of slavery in the States where it exists. I believe I have no lawful right to do so, and I have no inclination to do so." As in his 1854 Peoria speech, Lincoln confirmed that the enslaved and the disenfranchised remained legally unprotected. He instead focused on a "perpetual" union enshrined by the Constitution and "the fundamental law of all national governments." He challenged the notion that "disunion sentiments" in enslaving states could lead to a sustained government. He asked, "Is there such perfect identity of interests among the States to compose a new union as to produce harmony only and prevent renewed secession?" In other words, he wondered if secessionist states lacked the familial feeling required for sustained national sovereignty. Moreover, he believed that secessionists mistook global sympathies. Lincoln stated, "Our intercourse with foreign nations has been attended with profound solicitude, chiefly turning upon our own domestic affairs." Such global "intercourse" was marked, he implied, by solicitous foreign relations. Unionist sympathy retained legal power on both land and water. Lincoln was clear, however, that the "issue of civil war" remained in the hands of every countryman. Democracy required sympathy to flow freely, at least in theory. "Though passion may have strained it must not break our bonds of affection," he pleaded in a handwritten addition. Familial bonds would remain once the "mystic chords of memory" reinvigorated shared national pain for "every living heart and hearthstone all over this broad land."[1] All were on the torture rack against past and present pirates, he implied. The Union would hold. Antebellum legal culture had made its final stand.

Despite Lincoln's appeal to the nation's enduring union, secessionist legal culture had already ascended. A headline in *The Charleston Mercury's* December 20, 1860, extra edition declared, "The Union is Dissolved!"[2] Secessionists championed the Union's rupture as an act of southern sympathy in keeping with the nation's founding. Thomas Jefferson had invoked feelings against piracy to claim revolutionary sovereignty. Abraham Lincoln appealed to Jefferson and this regime in his inauguration. Like both of those statesmen, Confederate President Jefferson Davis was adept at navigating legal culture. He knew charges of piracy could sink secessionist claims to sovereignty. He needed to mount a legal offensive in addition to a martial one. Most notably, on April 17, 1861, two days after the attack on Fort Sumter, Davis expressed his intention to offer letters of marque to would-be Confederate privateers. In other words, he was mobilizing Confederate feeling at sea. As the scholar Jennifer Rae Greeson writes, secessionist politicians "appropriated the mantle of the Revolutionary break with the British empire to characterize their bid for independence."[3] In the process, they carefully positioned themselves as Jefferson had done against King George. Namely, secessionist sailors embodied southern fellow feeling against northern piracy in particular and piratical unfeeling in general. Letters of marque secured this claim to sympathy and sovereignty. Letters allegedly rife with feeling joined secessionist oceanic movements to a Confederate domestic state. In short, secessionists floated sovereignty using antebellum legal and cultural precedents.

More than perhaps any other document, an 1861 Confederate ten-cent postage stamp captures the deep history of secessionists' legal claim to independence in the name of white supremacy (fig. 2). On it, the portrait of a young Thomas Jefferson is framed by the words "Confederate States of America," creating both visual balance and ideological cohesion between distinct declarations. Designed and printed in Richmond, Virginia, alongside Confederate currency as well as other political documents and cultural artifacts, such stamps served practical and symbolic functions. With the word "Postage" hanging above him, Jefferson seems to stamp his approval of secessionist letters and letters of marque. The founder has been adopted by, or perhaps reunited with, his enslaving national kin. He marks all of their letters, no matter their content. Other Confederate stamps similarly depicted George Washington and Andrew Jackson in addition to Jefferson Davis and the fervent anti-abolitionist John C. Calhoun.[4] Would Jefferson, if alive, have rejected this association with his southern brethren? Would he have considered secession a piratical crime

FIGURE 2. Confederate ten-cent postage stamp, featuring a portrait of Thomas Jefferson (1861). Courtesy of the Boston Athenaeum.

against feeling? One cannot know. But looking at the stamp with this question in mind evokes another image: a pirate's wanted poster. If Confederates were pirates, was Jefferson as well? Neither unionists nor secessionists had incentive to provide an answer. Both relied on Jefferson's legal and symbolic Declaration of Independence from piracy, even as they differed over which of his alleged pirates to focus on. So armed, each side claimed a familial inheritance.

Piracy debates in the war's opening years reveal that the nation's long-strained antebellum legal culture had finally dissolved. Secessionist sentimental jurisprudence had taken hold. Though later defeated in battle and declared to be piracy in court, its rise provides vital insight into the war's ocean politics. Piracy's definition was central to questions of secession's validity, foreign relations' stability, reunion's possibility, and Black citizenship's desirability. Confederate sailors' relative status as pirates shaped the Civil War's competing popular and political narrations on these questions. For Union figures such as Lincoln and Sumner, secessionist mariners embodied the crimes against feeling inherent to the Confederate slaveholding regime. Their antecedents were prior pirates, including Mediterranean corsairs and, paradoxically, abolitionist radicals with ties to the Haitian Revolution. These layered connections reflect Union attempts to craft a coherent national mythos despite enslavement's shifting legality. The treatment of secessionists as pirates indicated that *all* forms of enslavement, including the landed trade unchallenged in the Piracy Act of 1820, would no longer be appeased. Even so, neither universal abolition nor Black citizenship was Lincoln's primary focus. For him and many others, an acceptance of full Black citizenship could prohibit future reunion with a defeated South. Likewise, to treat secessionist sovereignty as piratical could also rupture any idea of perpetual union by rupturing southerners' federal ties. Pirates could not be recovered to a national family. The clashing outcomes of two October 1861 jury trials held in the North against the Confederate crews of the *Jefferson Davis* (guilty of piracy) and the *Savannah* (hung jury) signaled piracy's contested legal status. Confederate legal challenges would ostensibly be removed by the war's close. Even so, its initial years reveal a dedication to appeasement in the service of white supremacy that had begun in 1776 and would continue well past the war's end.

The prewar transoceanic post had been a vehicle for competing imperial visions. The wartime postal system confirmed that legal culture had been reordered. Lincoln had promised in his inaugural address that the mail would continue "unless repelled" so that "people everywhere shall have that sense of perfect security." National fellow feeling would continue to be posted. In practice, regular postal service continued for the war's first seven weeks, after which point secessionist powers broke domestic circuits and built new ones. Jefferson Davis established a Confederate post in one of his first acts as president. Mail was smuggled by Union and Confederate vessels as well as private companies during the war.[5] As before, popular letters representing piracy proved to be vital in varied political visions. Secessionist policy relied on letters of marque that transformed private sailors from would-be pirates into extensions of Confederate domestic sovereignty. These letters' legality rested on the sympathetic chain between their signatories, the Confederate government, and a secessionist family. Popular fictions depicting northern pirates were central to substantiating Confederate legal claims. Pro-secessionist domestic objects such as printed postal covers helped build the forms of bond promised by Davis. One northern newspaper writer asserted in response, "We believe that Secessia invented the idea of burthening Uncle Sam's mails with letters which bore upon their envelopes, pictures of seven starred flags, and portraits of arch rebels."[6] Cultures of piracy and the post remained linked.

In this chapter on wartime legal culture, I examine competing government policies and popular accounts of piracy. I begin by tracking Confederate legal claims to secessionist feeling on both land and water before outlining Unionist debates on how best to define piracy and punish secession. I then turn to the aforementioned highly visible 1861 piracy trials that placed secessionist maritime agents—and the Confederacy itself—at the center of a wartime legal culture. The final section tracks the white supremacy that undergirded northern rejections of southern legal claims. Despite legal abolition, abiding appeasements to enslaving piracy were central to the contested legal culture that shaped the global Civil War and its aftermath.

"FORMS OF BOND": SECESSIONIST LEGAL CULTURE

On April 11, 1861, one day before the firing on Fort Sumter, the editors of *The Charleston Mercury* announced that southerners' "compromising, sentimental generosity," which had once allowed the "encroachment of the North," would soon end. The South was ready for war. No more familial feeling existed between North and South: as the editors asserted, "There is now no common interest, sympathy, or hope."[7] On April 20, editors at *The Richmond Enquirer* echoed this sentimental language. Virginia, they said, had joined the cause among her "Southern Sisters, to whom she was closely united by the bonds of sympathy, interest and danger." Sentimental generosity would not prevent the reclamation of southern familial attachment. According to scholar Elizabeth Duquette, these and other secessionist texts demonstrated "sympathy's treasonous dimensions" and led Unionists to affirm the "virtue of loyalty, defined against a caricatured version of sympathy as arbitrary, contingent, and uncontrolled."[8] Unionist sympathy no longer had legal force. Ongoing battles over secession, enslavement, and abolition proved as much. For many Unionists, familial reunion remained viable, at least for a time. Figures such as Sumner argued that mistaken sympathy for piracy, rather than sympathy itself, had caused the fracture. In other words, he updated John Quincy Adams's abolitionist invective in *United States v. Amistad*—that federal "sympathy was wrong before" in its protection of enslavers—to assert that sympathy was wrong *now*. Secessionist sympathy and the legal culture it made possible, as Sumner and others knew, had been built at sea for the sake of global sovereignty.[9]

Before turning to federal rejections of secessionist legal culture, however, one must reconstruct the Confederate ship of state. Doing so reveals narrative and legal investment in antebellum precedents. Floating secessionist sovereignty required an explicit repudiation of piracy in favor of familial feeling on both land and water. Secessionist maritime policy ostensibly forced a related binary decision: to accept a Jeffersonian declaration of independence or reject secessionist sovereignty as piratical. In keeping with the flexibility of the law of nations, foreign countries neither legally affirmed nor condemned secessionist sovereignty. On May 13, the British government proclaimed itself to be "happily at peace with all sovereigns, powers, and states" and "command[ed] all our loving subjects to maintain a strict neutrality in and during the aforesaid hostilities."[10] The "loving subjects" of a Britain "happily at peace" had no cause to feel against alleged pirates. Lord John Russell, the British foreign secretary, reportedly responded, "We are not as yet involved in any way in this matter, and for God's sake let us keep out of it."[11] France, Spain, and other governments also declared neutrality in the war's opening months.[12] From this vantage, the internecine conflict was not taking place between a singular feeling sovereign against external pirates. Instead, it was a martial and legal battle between two political forces.

In 1861, Lincoln made it clear that the Union's perpetual triumph was the only possible outcome. By 1863, however, the relative success of secessionist privateering policy left Union statesmen such as Sumner scrambling. As chair of the Senate Foreign Relations Committee, he remained committed to an imagined global antipathy toward piracy. While Sumner's 1852 congressional speech on oceanic mail had touted a "golden tissue between the two hemispheres," his wartime speeches evinced fractures in foreign relations. Sumner's frustrations dominated a public speech he gave in New York City on September 10, 1863, as the war entered its twenty-ninth month. He named the conflict's terraqueous terms, paralleling "current events at home" with a "distant current abroad," thereby joining land and sea.[13] Likewise, he referred to the family of nations, or "foreign relations," as necessarily tied to the national family, or "domestic relations." An assumed unity of familial feeling had been disrupted. For Union subjects waiting to hear of secession's diplomatic success, "a packet from Europe has been like a messenger from a seat of war." While Sumner had previously presented the transoceanic post as a "golden thread" that would join the world in feeling, wartime postal "packets" exemplified a world in commotion. This commotion, he noted, was grounded in maritime policy that "may not have the attraction of waving standards or victorious marches, but, more than any conflict of arms . . . concerns the Civilization of the age."[14] Martial spectacles might have been dominating attention, but legal rip currents were pulling the issue of union to sea.

Specifically, Sumner's speech against secessionist sovereignty focused on mistaken sympathy for "Oceanic Belligerency," a reference to secessionist sailors who bolstered the Confederacy's alternative claim to sovereignty.[15] In keeping with antebellum models, Confederate founding figures were staging their independence at sea. Sumner believed that to treat secessionist maritime agents as other than pirates was to confirm the state that backed them. A terraqueous Confederacy was therefore a singular threat to the Union. Though upstart nations' relative access to this space had recently been limited, European powers had found it politically expedient to apply a prior order. The 1854 Treaty of Paris had made privateering illegal, but signatory nations had ignored these terms in the case of the nonsignatory United States.[16] Now Union officials attempted to retroactively sign the agreement to prohibit Confederate claims of sovereignty. In a government dispatch from April 24, 1861, subsequently published on the front page of *The New York Times*, Secretary of State William Seward claimed that the government had "merely suspended the negotiation" and now accepted the ban.[17] European signatories rejected this plot. According to Sumner, Confederate sailors "without a home and without a legal character" had thus received support from foreign nations who affirmed these sailors' belligerent status. He deplored the "mistaken sympathy which Foreign Powers now bestow upon Slavery . . . under the plausible name of 'neutrality.'"[18] A public turn to "home," "character," and "mistaken sympathy" aligned legal status with proper feeling. For him, "every argument of fact and reason—every whisper of conscience and humanity—every indignant outburst of an honest man . . . is equally strong against any concession of Ocean Belligerency." Legal "fact and reason" shared power with moral feelings of "conscience and humanity." In his view, this neutrality made "[Confederate] cruisers lawful instead of piratical."[19] The response to Sumner's hours-long address confirmed secessionist legal culture's real gravity. The speech allegedly drew 3,000 spectators and was printed in its entirety in the following day's edition of *The New York Times*, covering four pages. The transcript was also subsequently bound and sold.[20] Like many texts of the era, Sumner's speech was at heart a pirate narrative.

Civil War diplomacy has received much scholarly focus. Sympathy is at the forefront of such histories.[21] Sumner lamented the relative success of secessionist foreign relations that had also staked their claim to global fellow feeling. On September 23, 1861, Robert Hunter, the Confederacy's secretary of state, had instructed James Mason, its ambassador to Britain, to characterize the breakaway states as other than "rebellious subjects seeking to overthrow the authority of a common sovereign." Instead, the break was due to a "Union whose very bonds prevented them from defending themselves" and against threats to "destroy their social system." What Lincoln called the perpetual and sympathetic "bonds" of Union were instead, in Hunter's terms, a form of bondage. The protection of a shared "social system," a careful euphemism for plantation slavery, necessitated a new legal order. Mason was therefore instructed to assert that "eleven sovereign states, bound together by the tie of a common social system and the sympathies of identical interests[,] have instituted a new confederacy and a new government." Like America's revolutionary colonies, each state freely bound itself to a new government due to "sympathies of identical interests." This sphere of secessionist fellow feeling would increase, said Hunter, given that Maryland, Missouri, and Kentucky had "interests and sympathies [that] must bind them to the south."[22] According to this legal logic, the Confederacy had committed no crimes against feeling. Enslaved noncitizens' legal bondage defined secessionist bonds. Making that sentimental claim to sovereignty legible to a global legal culture was a political and military objective.

Secessionist privateers embodied the federal government's fundamental problem at the war's outset: assertions of unbroken union floundered in the face of secessionists' shrewd invocations of antebellum precedent. Assertions of national familial feeling needed to be backed by access to oceanic space. In keeping with these terms, the March 1861 Constitution of the Confederate States of America gave the secessionist government the power to "declare war, grant letters of marque and reprisal, and make rules concerning captures on land and water." Like the U.S. Constitution, this founding document legalized the power of definition. The secessionist government had the right "to define and punish piracies and felonies committed on the high seas, and offenses against the law of nations." [23] Defining piracy or its alternatives was a founding government principle. The pairing of war-making power with privateering infrastructure signaled the secessionist government's legal and emotional discernment. A privateer was hard to distinguish from a pirate at sea, but the difference could be proven by his economic and social bond to land. In antebellum legal culture, this bond had to be one of fellow feeling.

Confederate policymakers passed another founding document, "An Act Recognizing the Existence of War," in May 1861. Each of its fifteen sections proved Confederate sovereignty via the establishment of privateering policy. Because piracy was understood as unchecked aggression against nations, the act's first section declared that neutral vessels "shall not be subject to seizure."[24] Davis hinted at this charge's moral and sexual politics, instructing his maritime agents "particularly to avoid even the appearance of force or seduction" in relation to nonmilitary personnel.[25] In other words, such entrapment would allow Union forces to call secessionists seductive pirates. Conversely, he directed the men to maintain the "justice and humanity which characterizes this government and its citizens."[26] The implication was that secessionist sailors, as the maritime extension of Confederal legal culture, did not perform piracies that were detached from either the nation or its families. Instead, they aided domestic infrastructures. The formation of a Confederate "prize court," in which sailors would deposit their spoils to be judged and distributed by the state, cemented this familial connection. Ingeniously, the act's final section allocated 5 percent of the prize money for a fund for "widows and orphans" and "wounded and disabled [privateers]."[27] The first comparable U.S. privateering act, passed during the War of 1812, had made no such provision. A later example had allocated a fund of less than 5 percent.[28] In antebellum legal culture, the government's ability to rebuild familial bonds and individual bodies was legal proof of nationhood. For Confederates, the privateer underwrote secessionist sovereignty. Confederate familial ties between land and sea proved its independent historical, moral, and legal standing relative to its federal counterpart.

The privateers' contracts, distributed by the Confederate government, symbolically marked and materially enacted this secessionist family. To receive a letter of marque, a ship captain was ostensibly required to complete and sign the "Form of Bond" attached to the act of war, which would legalize the emotional bonds among individuals, their families, and the nation. The document promoted a legally binding economic attachment: its signatories were "bound to the CONFEDERATE STATES OF AMERICA." Moreover, they agreed to adhere to state policy and bring all prizes to landed courts. As a "Form of Bond," it was also a new kind of legally bound fellow feeling. Specifically, the document called its signatories to "bind ourselves, our heirs, executors, and administrators" to the Confederacy. In other words, it established a legal attachment that linked secession's familial and national bodies. This bond could be "revoked by the President of the Confederate States." The nation's sovereign head, as opposed to individual and unruly pirates, dictated maritime action. The form required witnesses to validate this communal process of signing, sealing, and delivering Confederate claims to sympathy and sovereignty.[29]

The issuance of paper currency that began in April 1861 bolstered a secessionist legal culture whose monetary policies—which included privateering bonds and other financial instruments—advanced secessionist legal claims to government authority and familial feeling. A $5 note, issued more than 1 million times in Richmond between April and September 1862, epitomized the ocean-facing domestic fictions that resulted. The note was *tender legal tender*. It depicted a neatly dressed sailor sitting at the center of the bill, braced on bales of cotton and looking skyward. Secessionist ships in the distance place the sailor and his goods in a global context. Confederate Treasury Secretary C. G. Memminger flanks the sailor on the left. Lady Justice and Ceres, the goddess of motherhood, flank him on the right. No collectivity supported by law, justice, government, and familial attachment could be said to commit piratical crimes against feeling.[30] Other notes depicted sailors overlooking the laboring enslaved, all proudly affirming the bondage at the heart of secessionist policy. Each countered the vision of Union promoted on this book's cover (see introduction). The hope was that bearers would exchange secessionist goods and proclaim the good of secessionist sentiments. Instead, Confederate currency was beset by rapid inflation, widespread counterfeit, and an increased delay in the notes' maturity: the first series in 1861 bore interest payable after twelve months while the seventh set in 1864 was payable two years after the war's conclusion via treaty.[31] The weakening promissory notes came to reflect the waning promise of a secessionist global economy.

Privateering was a practical means to support the secessionist government legally, martially, and symbolically. A secessionist press celebrated the privateers' launch as a victory for secessionist legal culture: northern crimes against feeling required secessionist antipiracy measures. Compared to Confederate naval ships, however, privateering vessels had a relatively minor role in the war. Of the fifty-two given commissions, only twenty recorded service as privateers.[32] Sumner and other Unionists referred to both privateers and dedicated Confederate naval vessels as pirates, but privateers' status dominated the war's initial debates.

In May 1861, the *Savannah* became the first of fifty-two Confederate ships to receive letters of marque. Fittingly, its heaviest artillery was a converted eighteen-pound gun from the War of 1812. Via such weaponry, the Confederacy had refashioned the prior revolution's material and symbolic power.[33] The ship quickly claimed the *Joseph*, a sugar-laden merchant vessel, which it sent to a Confederate prize court. Shortly thereafter, on June 3, the USS *Perry* captured the *Savannah*. Meanwhile, the Confederacy's most successful early privateer, the *Jefferson Davis*, captured nine ships following its June 1861 launch. Two of its prizes were successfully auctioned in the South, affirming the ship's domestic connection; but in August, the ship ran aground off the coast of Florida. The remaining Confederate prize ships met similar fates. Nonetheless, they had performed their task: secessionist state power had wielded its claims to land and sea. Secessionist privateering's legality was "more obvious than under the old Union," concluded J. D. B. De Bow in a December 1861 issue of *De Bow's Magazine*. Federal foes who "profess[ed] no allegiance to the laws of morality" had been met by privateers who embodied "the law of humanity implanted in every human bosom." Not everyone was so sanguine. For instance, a writer for *The Charleston Mercury* noted in November 1862 that European powers were showing signs of "having all their sympathies with the United States," given that they were "refus[ing] to allow the Confederate States to carry their prizes, taken on the high seas, into their ports."[34] Yet Robert Howison's "History of the War," published between 1862 and 1864 in twenty-four installments in *The Southern Literary Messenger*, narrated Confederate sovereignty as a historical fact. According to Howison, "France and Great Britain both recognized the fact that the United States, as they formerly existed, were no longer one sovereignty."[35] He highlighted a Confederate "revolution of sea warfare" only days before Sumner delivered his 1863 speech, thus emphasizing that secession's foreign recognition was a means of influencing ongoing debates.[36]

Unlike its northern counterpart, the secessionist literary press was hampered by a lack of resources. Even so, it successfully projected Confederate legal culture globally. As Coleman Hutchinson has shown, secessionist literature was both an "essential vehicle for Confederate nationalism" and "internationally minded."[37] Confederate broadsides in particular contained "resolutely occasional poetry." Poems against Lincoln or emancipation were a "weapon in the Confederate ideological arsenal." These cultural weapons also turned seaward.[38] For example, Nicholas Greenberry Ridgely published dozens of broadsides and song sheets with titles such as "Our Hope" and "Southern Sentiments." The former included anchors and other nautical imagery to declare "Outraged tho' be our laws, / God be our trust!," while the latter mocked Harriet Beecher Stowe and other abolitionists' legal protection of "*Nigger brides*."[39] Secessionist sovereignty followed natural law, each claimed, in the service of domestic white supremacy. Another such sheet, "Song of the Privateer," dated "Baltimore, Oct. 10, 1861," staged the fulfillment of secessionist maritime policy via southern fellow feeling. In the lyrics, each "jolly tar" announces his sentimental attachment to the South and its cause. The song begins:

> Away o'er the boundless sea,
> With steady hearts and free,
> We man the Sumter we;
> Who for the South and liberty,
> Are ready all to die.[40]

The men in the song are not pirates without feeling since they share southern forms of bond. As Sumner feared, their secessionist quest begins with access to the "boundless" sea but remains tied to land. Hearty and full-hearted, they are "Ever mindful of our home, / Which they to destroy come." Each verse recounts acts done in the service of this familial attachment, including overtaking "Abe's cruisers." The song's chorus, sung from the perspective of those on land, completes this form of bond:

> Then let each jolly tar,
> Huzza! For the noble war,
> Give three time three for the Sumter now,
> Whose flag shall ne'er to the tyrant bow![41]

In other words, the "noble war" fought against northern tyranny will be resolved on land and at sea. Another broadside poem, "Hail! To the South," confirms the ultimate goal of such declarations, announcing "Another star arisen, another flag unfurled, / Another name inscribed among the nations of the world." The secessionist privateer could hasten the Confederacy's legal entry into a family of nations, just as their American revolutionary ancestors had done: as it affirms, "The spirits of the fathers in the children liveth yet."[42]

Entry into this family would also require the ongoing legal and moral defense of enslavement. In the sentimental novel *Old Toney and His Master, or, The Abolitionist and the Land-Pirate* (1861), one southern sympathizer writing under the name Desmos presented his own domestic pirate fiction. He contrasted legal enslavement with "piratical" abolition. Written immediately before the engagement at Fort Sumter, the novel reflected prewar attempts to nullify federal laws that linked the deep-sea slave trade to piracy. Desmos hoped that the proslavery tale would "touch the heart of the reader," who would recognize it as the product of a "humble heart, but a hopeful spirit."[43] Set in the 1820s, the decade of the Piracy Act, the novel concerns Colonel Shelton, a "lordly Southern planter," who embodies southern claims to national slaveholding feeling. Shelton's home life demonstrates the "feelings and . . . endearing ties which bind together the master and his slave." The "benevolent-hearted" planter also aids all of his guests, "even if [they] had crossed the broad Atlantic in quest of pecuniary aid."[44] In short, he advances moral foreign relations. The novel contrasts this plantation form of bond with northern aggression. Abolition, rather than slavery, is the pirate's true calling. According to literary scholar Joy Jordan-Lake, the authors of *Old Toney* and other anti–Uncle Tom novels relied on "portraying abolitionists as unfeeling." [45] The novel's villain, "notorious as a land-pirate," also hints at that trope's direct ties to legal culture.[46] By removing the pirate from the ocean, as other writers of domestic pirate fictions had done, Desmos was able to make a broader claim about southern property rights on both land and water.

In keeping with secessionist legal claims, Desmos's path to global fellow feeling included the reassertion of slaveholding order against piracy. Ultimately, the abolitionist pirate "suffer[s] upon the gallows for the double crimes of murder and negro stealing."[47] In the prewar climate, theft of southern state-backed property, unchecked by official governments, could force the kind of extrajudicial action that would soon underwrite secession. In the novel, the pirate's death is not due to the "verdict of a regularly constituted judge and jury." It is the work of "calm, collected, dignified men, who felt pained and grieved at the step which they felt . . . [was] a stern and unavoidable necessity."[48] Southern deviations from established law, which made secession piratical in the eyes of unionists, were, according to this perspective, the product of "calm" rationality. Northern piracy's removal was the only moral option for those southerners who "felt pained and grieved." In the novel, the abolitionist's death is necessary for the model marriage of the slaveholding hero and heroine to take place. Contemporaneous readers who "unite[d] Christian hearts" with this pair endorsed the claim to familial feeling at the heart of Confederate legal claims.[49] Ultimately, then, *Old Toney* is a paradigmatic example of Confederate legal culture: the abolitionist pirate's removal perfects southern familial feeling.

In the war's opening year, printed postal covers such as the "WHOLE WORLD IN COMMOTION" (fig. 1) had already begun to display the global stakes of these competing legal cultures. Secession had ruptured the vision of national union as embodied by the antebellum post. Postal covers printed during wartime reimagined competing sovereign bodies. Fittingly, the peak popularity of covers adorned with pro-Union or -Confederate imagery—what editors in the August 1861 issue of *Littell's Living Age* called the "envelope mania"—coincided with the most heated period of debate regarding Confederate letters of marque. The writer for *Littell's* stated, "It is astonishing to see how many of these patriotic emblems have been called into existence within the past three months." Though the northern states were "slightly ridiculous in this mania for envelopes," the writer aligned such eagerness with "love of country" and the urge to find "outlets enough for the exuberance of our new love."[50] These covers, as Alice Fahs confirms, "provided individuals with a means of displaying—and sending—their patriotism."[51] Those that displayed the Confederate flag or government officials represented the "informal emergence of Confederate nationalism," writes Steven Boyd, and also bolstered Confederate legal culture.[52] Namely, they allowed southerners to align legal *letters of marque* with private *letters that marked*. Antebellum governments had relied on posted letters as a material and symbolic subsidies for state policies. The wartime subsidy was less formal than its 1850s counterpart but remained powerful nonetheless. Even when kept as souvenirs, as they most often were, postal covers gave imagined intimate exchanges a distinctly national character. In the South, printed covers were the twin of secessionist policy. Southern letters marked Confederate letters of marque as valid by confirming their grounding claim. Publicly stamped covers sealed secessionist forms of bond. These covers bore the Confederate flag and named its leaders. In such cases, the entire cover marked secessionist feeling.

Of course, northern narrators debated secessionist letters' legal power using similar iconography. In Unionist song sheets such as "Pirates Chorus. From the Enchantress," sailors aboard the Jefferson Davis–commanded privateer sing their crimes against feeling, and each declares himself "Pride of the Pirate's Heart."[53] One magazine writer wed artistic and political critique: "The secession envelopes, in all cases. . . there was not a single evidence of inventive ability. . . [, as] nearly all were blazoned with the second-rate bank note vignette portraits."[54] Wartime postal covers reflected Union responses to these secessionist legal maneuvers. For example, rather than presenting the Confederate president as a statesman who binds sailors to a feeling nation via letters of marque, the cover "Jeff Davis's Letters of Marks" shadows him with the word "Pirate" (fig. 3). For Unionists, this piratical shadow marked all secessionist sailors. Real or imagined exchanges of such covers marked a unionist circuit that rejected piratical unruliness. No matter what the letter's content might be, senders and recipients of anti-pirate covers affirmed their defiance of secessionist letters of marque. In practice, however, this iconography oversimplified delicate attempts to assert an unbroken union. At least one postal cover, titled "The Savannah," promoted a straightforward union maritime victory with no pirate iconography. Below a color portrait of the defeated secessionist ship, the cover reads, "Confederate

FIGURE 3. Illustrated postal cover, "Jeff Davis's Letters of Mark" (c. 1861–1865). Courtesy of the American Antiquarian Society.

Privateer Savannah, letter of Marque No. 1 Captured off Charleston." The ship flies both federal and secessionist flags. [55] Did such northern postal letters reinforce secessionist policy, perhaps unintentionally, by also posting a southern letter of marque? Or did accepting secessionists as privateers rather than pirates make space for the possibility of future union? These questions defined northern debates on secessionist legal culture.

"ARE SOUTHERN PRIVATEERSMEN PIRATES?": ADJUDICATING SECESSIONIST LEGAL CULTURE

An 1861 article in *The New York Times* titled "Are Southern Privateersmen Pirates?" perfectly distilled the rhetorical tangle at the heart of the federal response. It was undeniable that "southern privateersmen" had received letters of marque. Yet could one admit the existence of such letters—and, with it, a claim to secessionist national attachment—while claiming that the sailors were pirates? Partially shedding his inaugural sentiments of perpetual union, President Lincoln presented the letters as isolated yet undeniably piratical threats in the war's early days. He announced his "Proclamation of Blockade Against Southern Ports" on April 19, 1861, one day after Jefferson Davis announced he would produce secessionist letters of marque. The blockade was perhaps the early war's most decisive military strategy, one that went well beyond the actions of southern privateering policy. Nonetheless, Lincoln made the question of piracy central to the blockade's legal and moral justification, describing "an insurrection" that included "pretended letters of marque" secured by "a combination of such persons engaged in such insurrection." These maritime agents both frustrated the blockade and challenged its very legal standing: only a blockade that effectively controlled oceanic space could be considered legally viable.[56] Though Lincoln's legal support was unclear, as later piracy cases would show, the president relied on fellow feeling's legal power. He concluded that all who took up this "pretended authority" at sea "[would] be amenable to the laws of the United States for the prevention and punishment of piracy."[57] The legal punishment, all knew, was death.

For some, secessionist actions against northern commerce were piratical crimes to feelings that had begun in the early national era. According to an April 23, 1861, editorial in *The New York Times*, for example, "the Slave Confederation could not have possibly taken a more direct road to cut themselves off from the sympathy of mankind, than by their crusade against private property on the seas." The author's assumed equation of the "sympathy of mankind" with "private property on the seas" corresponded with antebellum sympathy's status as a form of commodity exchange.[58] Economic antagonism against union in particular and mankind in general would render secessionists pirates across the globe. For others, the legal and narrative precedents for anti-secessionist action could be found in the Ottoman Mediterranean. According to another *New York Times* editorial, this one published on February 9, 1863, to admit Confederate sovereignty was to deny America's prior rejections of early national "pirates of the Mediterranean." The U.S. Constitution had saved the nation from a "position of intolerable degradation" and had legalized global feeling against piracy. The editorial continued, "The world believed as we believed, that it indissolubly united us in peace or war, in weal or woe, and gave the Government an indisputable and irresistible claim." Faced with a new piratical threat, compromise with secession would undo this legal and moral inheritance. Citizens would soon "learn depths of sorrow and suffering and humiliation." Foreign powers would no longer respect federal union. In short, compromise meant a return to an era in which any national or piratical force, foreign or domestic, could undermine American sovereignty.[59]

Would treating secessionists as pirates doom domestic relations? This was an urgent question in the United States and abroad. "If that threat [of hanging pirates] be earnest, and not the mere expression of a legal fact," wrote a British commentator in an editorial reprinted domestically, "the Federal Government has thrown over the dream of a purely defensive policy, and is resolved not simply to resist, but to subdue, the South."[60] Lincoln's appeal to "legal fact" notwithstanding, his approach to oceanic space would decide the conflict's moral character. Claims to unbroken union relied on "the dream of a purely defensive policy" in which a small band of unruly pirates must be dismissed. In other words, the removal of a few pirates did not prevent the union of North and South. Yet treating the entire south as piratical—and therefore unfit for domestic reincorporation—represented a seismic shift in policy. Union would not be the product of fellow feeling toward the state and its families. It would instead require the violent subduing of an external force. The act of hanging secessionist sailors—former members of the national body—would seemingly disprove indissoluble union. In either case, secessionist claims to domestic sovereignty at sea fundamentally disrupted union. Antebellum legal models could no longer hold.

Faced with a binary choice between secession's legal sovereignty and piracy, foreign governments chose a third path. They affirmed piracy law's practical fluidity. Ostensibly neutral state merchants aided the Confederacy by providing ports of call in England as well as supplies. In addition, blockade runners often first imported goods into Mexico or the West Indies or via specially equipped vessels. Charles Hodge's slim volume *England and America*, published in multiple editions in 1862, outlined a program by which familial feeling between empires would restore American domestic order. It began, "No two nations are bound together by so many bonds of sympathy and interest as England and America. England is our mother." Again, maternal sympathy was a form of "interest" that was both moral and economic. The postal treaties of the 1850s appeared to support this familial precedence. Of course, such treaties were the product of imperial competitions. Despite claims of an "intimate relationship" with the United States and a "family bond [that] remains unbroken," Britain and other nations had tacitly accepted Confederate legal rights.[61] U.S. domestic enslavement was central to nominally abolitionist nations' economic growth and, as a result, placed stress on political will for union. A British columnist writing at the war's outset hoped that "so long as the slaves are uninterested, an additional supply from India, and the few smaller markets may keep the [British] mills at work." But he conceded that the "probability of disturbances in the [British] interior increases with the protraction of the [American] struggle."[62] England's own reliance on enslaved labor shaped its domestic response to the global conflict.

An illustrated postal cover, "John Bull on the Fence," confirmed Britain's fence-sitting neutrality (fig. 4). On it, John Bull, the national personification of Britain, straddles a fence that holds a scale. A bale of cotton rests on one side of the scale; on the other is a slave and a Confederate soldier waving a pirate flag. According to the illustration, a political calculus had been made. Secessionism's enslaving piracy could be balanced by southern cotton's economic weight.[63]

Another postal cover captures the piratical violence that shaped the secessionist form of bond, at least according to Unionists. Published by the New York City printer D. B. Murphy, it displays a "Secession Web" with a piratical spider at its center (fig. 5). The cover includes a misquoted line from an 1828 poem by Mary Howitt—"'Walk into my parlor,' says the Spider to the Fly"—warning children against false flattery by predators.[64] The pirate spider, one presumes, represents Jefferson Davis, who had warned his sailors about seduction

FIGURE 4. Illustrated postal cover, "John Bull on the Fence" (c. 1861–1865). Courtesy of the American Antiquarian Society.

when he offered his letters of marque. The cover suggests that secession had involved a prior seduction and that the Confederate states were like so many flies, unified by duress and blood. Secessionist unity was not the result of fellow feeling but a web of bondage spun by a piratical leader. Visually, this web grows from the nation itself, which on the envelope is represented by the Stars and Stripes. This tenuous connection, held together by only one visible thread, may represent the Confederacy's basis in an earlier national order. Would threads of union be cut? Could such threads be recovered? Befitting an unclear future, the question of union remains unanswered in this representation.

In such perspectives, Confederates' alleged status as piratical made them fit for death. It also created a unique sympathetic attachment between them and individual Union sailors, for the latter would directly feel the pain of the former. In a letter to Lincoln, written on July 6, 1861, Davis asserted that the hanging of Confederate sailors from the *Savannah* would lead to an equal number of northern prisoners' deaths. Brothers would share a rack. Davis offered this threat as a means to maintain moral order amid northern piratical brutality. He stated, "Retaliation will be extended so far as shall be requisite to secure the abandonment of a practice unknown to the warfare of civilized man, and so barbarous, as to disgrace the nation which shall be guilty of inaugurating it." In

FIGURE 5. Illustrated postal cover, "Secession Web" (c. 1861–1865). Courtesy of the American Antiquarian Society.

sum, he presented proper national feeling rather than secessionist sympathies as the primary questions at hand. This letter, published in *The New York Times* and elsewhere, entered the popular debate.[65] Some, however, felt no need to deliberate. A *Chicago Tribune* editorial framed the *Savannah* crew's prospects as grim, for "no Judge who is loyal to his country can fail to define their crime as piracy, punishable by death."[66] A *New York Times* article published on August 2 likewise argued in favor of "no leniency, no recognition of letters of marque, no attention to the threats of retaliation. Let the Government be firm, and swift in its punishment of treason and piracy, and peace will sooner return to our borders." To punish crimes against feeling, many related articles argued, would create domestic harmony against piracy.[67]

Those who wanted to accept secessionist legal claims nonetheless took pains to defend their allegiance to a Unionist legal culture. The author of an August 1861 letter to the editor in *The New York Times* wanted to "avoid any misunderstanding" regarding his objection to secessionists' murder as pirates. Staunchly pro-Union, he had "no sympathy with the insurgents," nor was he "guided by . . . false sentimentality."[68] The author of a July 21 *New York Times* editorial affirmed the *Savannah*'s piracy yet also wondered, "Is it not a poor exchange, to give up good men to be murdered, in return for the satisfaction of hanging a few characterless pirates?" This "poor exchange" was based on a dark sympathetic calculus: if the dead body of one equaled the dead body of another, then the "satisfaction" of a dead Confederate did not equal one's fellow feeling for northern captives. If these bodies were unequal, however, then altering the calculus could render exchanges of pain conceivable. The editorial concluded that "fifty rebel prisoners shall answer with their lives for every liege citizen of the United States so murdered."[69] Such calculus could be applied on the Confederate side as well. On May 2 a writer for *The Charleston Mercury* noted, "Old ABE might suppose his Proclamation frightened our boys. Let them hang one privateer, and so sure will fifty of his hirelings pay the forfeit."[70] Both sides asserted that such deaths were necessary to guarantee legal and moral order. Northern juries, it appeared, would have the final say.

"OUT OF THE UNION": SECESSION ON TRIAL

The 1861 capture and trial of two secessionist privateering vessels, although a relatively minor feature of the war's martial action, placed competing legal cultures on trial. Taking place only six months after the war began, the trials linked to the *Jefferson Davis* and the *Savannah* staged miniature versions of broader policy debates about Confederate piracy. The juries' most immediate concern was whether the holders of Confederate letters of marque were pirates. Yet this question could not be answered without judging Confederate claims to sovereignty. In both cases, the prosecution and the defense each had three attorneys, all of whom were northerners. Judges Samuel Nelson and William Shipman presided over the *Savannah* case; Judge John Cadawalader and Justice Robert Grier sat for the *Jefferson Davis case*. The two trials occurred nearly concurrently: the *Jefferson Davis* trial began on October 22 in Philadelphia and concluded on October 29, while the *Savannah* case ran in New York City from October 23 to October 31. Both prosecutions and defenses discussed the issue's extensive case law, which I will address here but not exhaust. [71] Appeals to feeling shaped each side's form and content. A defense attorney in *Jefferson Davis* admitted that "the reality of law" dictated that he must rely on the jury's objective "judicial mind." He also proclaimed his right to "persuade their judgments, that the law is as I have argued it." His closing statement, itself a recapitulation of his overall defense, was framed by his "feeling [the] interest and importance" of the case. He extended this feeling to the jury.[72] A lawyer's sympathetic attachment to the jury guaranteed both parties' attachment to the defendant. The prosecution, on the other hand, aimed to prevent such sympathy.

The trials, though ostensibly directed at juries, were widely covered in the popular press. *The New York Times* provided daily coverage of both. *The New York Herald* published the *Savannah* proceedings, often mixing the appellations "pirate" and "privateer" in headlines.[73] The papers also recounted simultaneous scenes of battle, thereby textualizing the narrative and material connections among events in court, on land, and at sea. For example, the *Savannah* trial's October 24 arguments appeared on the *Times's* October 25 back page alongside the war's other maritime news.[74] Unlike other sea battles, however, these trials were open to the public. The *Savannah* venue was "densely crowded" on its first day.[75] Its third was "densely thronged long before the hour appointed for resuming the proceedings."[76] By day 5, as *The New York Herald* noted, "the rush for seats was immense," and officers barely "prevented the doors from being burst open by the masses who were anxious to hear . . . this important and exciting case."[77] One article counted "a number of ladies also present" among the throng and speculated that "countless more were reading at home."[78]

Taken as a whole, the daily coverage became a serialized domestic drama. Lawyers were the primary characters. One *Jefferson Davis* defense attorney went so far as to "beg my friends the reporters here, who appear to be taking notes of what I am saying, not to misunderstand me, or misquote me." He continued, "At a time like this, it is as much as a man's liberty, or even his life is worth, to be correctly quoted." The defense distinguished between its legal argument and the mistaken sympathies that such an argument could include. The attorney explained, "Admitting secession to be all wrong; and admitting that the Southern Confederacy has no right whatsoever to revolutionize, still it has revolutionized—it ha[s] not only gone out of the Union, but it has taken eleven of the states out with it, and it has left, at least, two more upon the fence top."[79] He had reason to be cautious: a member of the *Savannah* legal defense, a northerner named Algernon S. Sullivan, had been arrested due to his interactions with the Confederate government. The New York City police took this action under the advisement of U.S. Secretary of State William Seward.[80] The distinction between legal and martial loyalty was slight, given the trials' implications for ongoing battles on land, at sea, and in the courts.

As part of these competing narrations, each side's legal argument revolved around the alleged pirates' domestic attachments. Each defense declared that pirates, unlike these sailors, were bereft of fellow feeling and without domestic attachment. Confederate sailors had acted according to the exigencies of a domestic arrangement based on Confederate sympathy and southern geography. Likewise, attorneys claimed that secessionist privateering, though not validated by the U.S. government, was tied to prior revolutionary sovereignties and existing laws among the "family of nations" and that national families would be shattered by the sailors' death by hanging. In both cases, the defense also critiqued the distinct treatment given to landed versus sea-bound Confederate agents. Neither side in either case directly addressed the legality of the Confederacy as a government. Even so, all acknowledged that the sailors embodied a secessionist legal culture. Not surprisingly, the prosecutions undermined the defense appeals by denying historical justifications for Confederate action and framing piracy as indicative of secessionist crimes against feeling.

Both defenses claimed that Confederate sailors, unlike pirates, had acted upon a true, if misguided, domestic allegiance. According to this argument, even if secessionist legal culture's ideology was unsupportable, its moral conditions were real. Sympathetic connections existed between the Confederacy and its privateers because the sailors and their families earnestly felt those connections. According to the defense in *Jefferson Davis*, the Confederacy "had so far acquired the mastery or control of the particular territory within its limits" to "demand and exact allegiance."[81] Southern land was domesticated space, so its maritime agents were privateers rather than pirates. In contrast, the defense in *Savannah* explicitly refused to validate the sailors' Confederate allegiance but did admit the "sympathy that existed between Mr. [John C.] Calhoun and his constituents." The sailors had been "indoctrinated" with the idea of "States' Rights, Nullification, and Secession" and had been "actuated by these principles."[82] Therefore, they "were acting in good faith," according to their letters of marque. Though the prosecution rightly disputed Jefferson Davis's capacity to issue letters and the Confederacy's ability to seal them, the defense responded with claims of Confederate sympathy. A letter of marque, though "nominally" under Davis's aegis, was "virtually and actually a commission issuing from eight millions of people, who recognize[d] and sanction[ed] it under the hand of their president and the seal of their government." By treating the letter as an artifact of popular sovereignty, the defense argued that secessionist families had validated the Confederate government's legal power.[83]

In keeping with antebellum legal culture's guiding logic, sailors' familial attachments shaped their status as pirates. The *Jefferson Davis* defense not only relied on claims of southern domestic attachment to prove the sailors' innocence but also named connections to northern families. According to the attorneys, the trial was "a grave case, because the happiness of a Northern wife, a little boy at a Northern college, and . . . an aged ancestor living in the South, hang upon your verdict."[84] The prosecution, however, rejected the legal force of this domestic appeal: "While the counsel for the government do not wish you to forget that the prisoner has a home, a wife, a child, and an aged grandmother, they are unable to see what those facts, so important to him, have to do with the case."[85] Questions of domestic attachment were only important in relation to families who had been disrupted by secessionist actions.

For each side, a person's status among a "family of nations" dictated their domestic legal status. The prosecution in *Savannah* noted that the "political authority of the [U.S.] nation . . . has never recognized the so-called Confederate States as one of the family of nations." Only the United States had entered that family, and therefore only it could define sovereignty. Moreover, the geographical and emotional closeness of the Union was based on "the superior fortune which attended our introduction into the family of nations."[86] Likewise, the prosecution in *Jefferson Davis* claimed that letters of marque "can only be granted by a member of the family of nations—by a State whose national existence is recognized, and which has, or may have, diplomatic relations."[87] For both prosecutions, the federal government's power to define and punish piracy derived from a "family of nations" produced by sympathy. However, the defense in *Savannah* argued that international law as well as the "moral obligation upon us to occupy our position in the great family of nations" supported the defendants' privateering status.[88] The defense in *Jefferson Davis* did not deny that laws against piracy were based on "the United States of America, claiming to be one of the great family of the civilized nations of the earth." While the attorney asserted that the nation should protect the "great highway of all nations," he believed that, in practice, the U.S. government was neither the arbiter of global sovereignty nor the sole judge of secessionist sympathy. Indeed, Joseph Story had made a similar argument to deny the federal government's jurisdiction over enslavers in the 1822 piracy case *United States v. The Schooner La Jeune Eugenie* (see chapter 1).[89]

Both defenses also aligned Confederate privateers with earlier revolutionary agents. False charges of piracy were common before a revolution's success, and the federal government had shown itself to be sympathetic to alleged pirates. According to the defense in *Jefferson Davis*, "if this man [the defendant William Smith] is a pirate, upon what principle, or by what authority, did the Congress of the United States dare to appropriate one cent to the real or personal representatives of John Paul Jones?"[90] Britain, the former sovereign, certainly had not recognized the Revolutionary-era privateer as anything other than a pirate. Yet the economic support that the United States had recently given to the Jones family affirmed his domestic attachment to the revolutionary nation. In this way, current secessionist sovereigns have the right to legalize a revolutionary tie between their agents on both land and water. Moreover, as the defenses argued, the accepted stance toward sovereignty that had fed national expansion justified Confederate legal rights. According to the defense in *Savannah*, it was foolish to assume "once a sovereign, always a sovereign until independence shall be acknowledged." The idea that an initial sovereign could prevent a legal break had been rejected after Texas declared its independence from Mexico, even though Mexico, like the Union, did not recognize a valid revolutionary claim. Given that Mexico's "odious sentiments" had been rejected, why was the same false sentiment being applied to the Confederacy?[91] Such mistaken sympathy would have long-lasting effects because future revolutions would seek "a word of sympathy" from the United States. The defense asked the jury to "listen therefore to the better voices whispering to each heart" rather than act according to their justified prejudice against the Confederate cause.[92]

Prosecutors, however, rejected claims that the American Revolution had given secession either moral or legal precedent. The prosecution in *Jefferson Davis* admitted "no analogy" between a revolutionary government united in feeling and the minority sentiments that secessionists espoused. Unlike the Confederates, who disregarded law and decency, the American revolutionaries "were not in the minority; we were the people of the country." As extensions of national feeling, they "had a cause that invoked the sympathy, prayers, and aid of all good men." Of course, Confederate agents argued for their nation's sympathy in their public and private relations. Yet the Confederacy should elicit no such fellow feeling because "who sympathizes with the ambitious and unprincipled demagogues . . . drenching the country in blood?" The prosecution thereby relied on the correlation between the Confederate government's lack of sympathy and its maritime agents' unchecked unruliness. The sailors remained “unprincipled demagogues” who must be legally removed to restore the early national revolution’s promise.[93] Unfeeling pirates were the same, no matter their location.

The defense in *Savannah* invoked the period’s fictional pirates to prove that, unlike such unfeeling monsters, the secessionist sailors had familial attachments. Though many northerners had expected to see “‘monsters of the deep’ as they were manacled through the streets,” observers saw instead “gentlemen of character, intelligence, refinement, and education.” The men’s familial and social positions, the defense argued, made them utterly incompatible with pirates. A pirate was “an enemy of the human race,” incapable of familial feeling or human connection; his lack of a “fixed place of residence” rendered him nondomestic. A pirate’s economic and political position depended on “pillage and depredation” that were linked to “no sovereign, no law.”[94] Via the figure of the pirate, the defense affirmed something like Confederate sympathy. Its closing appeal for “a due sympathy for the accused” resulted, according to the *New York Herald*, in “manifestations of applause in court.”[95] Such a reaction in a northern courtroom is perhaps surprising, given the ongoing war. It speaks to sympathy’s enduring legal power and the deep, if fractured, national ties that remained.

Both defenses distinguished their clients from pirates by asserting sympathy’s universal form. In the process, their closing arguments challenged the very idea of crimes against feeling. One defense attorney in *Savannah* admitted that the jury might be guided by “popular prejudice, or feeling, or fury” against the defendants. Yet he trusted that “the sympathy that arises properly in every well-constituted heart and mind, in favor of the accused, their relatives and friends, would overcome such wrong impulse.”[96] In other words, natural sympathy should reject popular prejudice and render secessionists fit for fellow feeling. As the defense in *Jefferson Davis* affirmed, the jury’s legal power had to be wielded alongside its sympathetic one. Attorneys argued in their closing statement that a guilty verdict would threaten the core of moral feeling and familial attachments:

> The meanest wretch that crawls upon the face of the earth has still a claim upon the sympathy of some one. You cannot separate him; you cannot alienate him; you cannot tear him from that sympathy. You cannot touch a chord in his bosom which does not vibrate, by a thousand feelings, and with a thousand sympathies and emotions,

> through the hearts of others. Place him where you may, dishonor and degrade him, as you choose; in all the time of his tribulation; in all time of his distress, . . . in weal or in woe, he is still the centre of a circle, which he calls his own, and to which kindred, and home, and friends and family, and a thousand interesting and endearing associations have indissolubly and forever bound him.[97]

This expansive sentimental appeal was inseparable from the larger legal claim being made. If, as the defense argued, the wretch were "still the centre of a circle" from which his bosom "vibrate[d] . . . with a thousand sympathies and emotions, through the hearts of others," then he had a claim to family that was seemingly unavailable to pirates. Sympathy's universal power undermined piracy's legal character. Even a "degraded" pirate had a "claim upon the sympathy of some one."[98] Moreover, the reference to a "thousand interesting and endearing associations" indicated a communal, potentially national, circle of sympathy. Abstracting sympathy from its historical context skirted questions of Confederate sovereignty. Nonetheless, the sailors' status extended to the secessionist cause and its claims of Confederate domesticity. Both defenses ultimately forwarded visions of "indissoluble" attachment that were more expansive than those typically found in antebellum legal culture.

Whereas one defense lawyer in *Jefferson Davis* argued for the positive existence of shared sympathy and full hearts, the *Savannah* defense asserted that a guilty verdict would lead to haunted hearts and sympathetic violence. Namely, the sailors' death as pirates would bind them to the fate of Union sailors. Therefore, the jury's fellow feeling for Union sailors should move them to acquit. According to the defense, even if the jury had "no other feeling which can influence your judgment" or "no sympathy in common" with the accused, there was "a sympathy you should have." Carefully shifting to a guarded threat couched in a language of fellow feeling, the defense named the jury's "sympathy for those brave and valiant spirits . . . who are now prisoners of war." Given Davis's threats, the defense argued, "it would be expecting too much clemency from the hands of the enemy to suppose that they would allow the sacrifice of these [Confederate] men to go unavenged." A violent sympathetic calculus bound the jury to the accused. One "sacrifice" would beget another. The defense's final words, "Do unto others as you would that they should do unto you," asserted that a guilty verdict would affirm the jury's lack of sympathy and forward further domestic disruption.[99]

Though these cases were nearly identical, the *Jefferson Davis* trial resulted in a guilty verdict while the *Savannah* case led to a dismissal via a hung jury. The *Jefferson Davis* jury deliberated for only forty-five minutes before rendering its guilty verdict. The *Savannah* jury, who had been informed of that decision, remained undecided after a day of deliberation. In a careful study of these two cases, legal scholar Mark Weitz concludes that the *Jefferson Davis* conviction "reflected the rigidity of [Justice Robert Grier's] jury charge." Grier had precluded the possibility of secession's legality and had directly rebutted the defense in his closing statement.[100] He had compelled the jury to treat piracy as an act alone. In his final instructions to the jury, he had stated, "This court sitting here to execute the laws of the United States can view those in rebellion against them in no other light than traitors to their country, and those who assume by their authority a right to plunder the property of our citizens on the high seas, as pirates and robbers."[101] In his opinion, neither the jury's feelings nor the feelings of the accused had legal force. Rather, the jury represented "our citizens" unified against traitorous and piratical threats. In contrast, the judges in *Savannah* personally rejected Confederate sovereignty on similar judicial grounds but did not prevent the jury from considering whether the individual sailors were pirates. As Weitz notes, this treatment of sovereignty as a "factual question" open to interpretation allowed issues of emotional orientation to remain legally viable.[102]

The self-serving appeal to a "law of nations" against pirates, which lay at the heart of these and other antebellum piracy trials, become even more evident in what were known as the *Prize Cases* (1863). In them, the U.S. Supreme Court addressed the southern blockade's legality relative to the capture of neutral foreign ships and considered Lincoln's right to initiate an act of war without congressional approval. Justice Robert Grier, who had served on the bench in the *Jefferson Davis* civil case, wrote the majority opinion in the *Prize Cases*. In it, he legalized the Union's blockade of southern ports. He also implicitly recognized the legal status of belligerents as opposed to pirates. The decision made both the Union blockade and any subsequent prize taking constitutional, even without a formal war declaration. It also legally acknowledged secessionist acts at sea, demonstrating that Grier's legal theory of piracy had shifted according to political need. His opinion in the *Prize Cases*, as legal historian Stephen Neff writes, was "incompatible, certainly in spirit, if not in letter, with the jury instructions given in the earlier privateers' cases." Put simply, Grier had denied the existence of a civil war in 1861 but admitted its existence in 1863. This new frame did not lead him to expressly grant the Confederacy the rights of a sovereign nation, but it did make the secessionist government a belligerent with a strong claim to independence. This judicial shift reflected new political realities. A language of threatened but unbroken union in 1861 could negate nascent Confederate sovereignty. By 1863, the ongoing burden of southern legal and martial threats necessitated an uneasy and incomplete recognition of the Union's dissolution.[103]

While Justice Grier foreclosed debate in the *Jefferson Davis* piracy case, he did not prevent ongoing narrative battles. In a December 1861 editorial in *The New York Times*, a New York City judge named Charles Daly largely negated Grier's view. An expanded version of the editorial, published in early 1862, presented a legal argument steeped in sympathy and practicality. Daly rejected the idea that the Constitution or related antebellum piracy statutes should apply to this remarkable "state of things." He wrote, "The civil war now prevailing is, in its magnitude, beyond anything previously known in history." Even so, Daly's legal argument shared features with Lincoln's inauguration speech. He continued, "We are not to forget that we are carrying on this war for the restoration of the Union." National union dictated that legal ties must be protected above all else, and prior ordering narrations on piracy could not apply.[104] Another editorial writer stated in the *London Herald*, "It will never do to sanction the judicial murder of Southerners captured on the ocean." His opinion, reprinted in *The New York Times*, appeared to carry the day: no Confederate sailors were hung as pirates.[105] Instead, the defendants in both the *Jefferson Davis* and *Savannah* cases were moved to military prisons in February 1862 and were later released. Nonetheless, this treatment did not resolve persistent questions of secessionist sovereignty, indissoluble union, and postbellum abolition.

"HOMES FOR WHITE MEN": WHITE SUPREMACY AND WARTIME APPEASEMENT

Abraham Lincoln had rejected the prospect of legal abolition in both his 1854 speech in Peoria and his March 1861 inaugural address. But by the time the president presented his first State of the Union speech in December of that year, secessionist privateers had successfully floated secessionist sovereignty. In response, he called upon Congress to aid those who sought to "defend themselves against and to capture pirates." One path to this martial support, he said, was "maintaining a chargé d'affaires" with the "new states" of Haiti and Liberia. These free Black republics, founded in 1804 and 1847, now merited a long-denied home in the family of nations. Haiti's long legal limbo, I have shown, reflected the antebellum government's customary alignment of Black-led radical abolition with piracy. Liberia had declared its independence from the American Colonization Society in a revolution that had been without bloodshed but lacked federal legal recognition. Befitting the war's shifting moral and political calculus, the threat of secessionist maritime action now outweighed fears of these Black sovereigns. As "diplomatic" outposts with clear martial purpose, each could materially aid the fight against Confederate maritime policy. In other words, these nations could gain partial and belated shares of the sovereignty that each had, in fact, already legally secured by revolutionary action.[106]

According to Lincoln, this belated recognition of Black sovereignty would not threaten white middle-class citizens' primacy in postbellum legal culture. In fact, Haiti and Liberia could make failed colonization strategies viable once more. Lincoln admitted that, for some, the "only legitimate object of acquiring territory [was] to furnish homes for white men." He mused that the prospective "emigration of colored men" to Liberia and Haiti would also make "additional room for white men remaining or coming here." Black Americans were not pirates, but that did not make them desirable citizens. Notably, Lincoln did not mention the fact that descendants of those enslaved aboard the pirate vessel *Antelope*, including the family members of those who had been reenslaved to appease Spain, likely remained in Liberia (see chapter 1). In a further retread of antebellum postal policy, the president also noted that Postmaster General Montgomery Blair had reintroduced the potential use of subsidized mail ships in service of colonization, thus removing the "only obstacle to a perpetual union of the States." Such appeals to colonization as a political panacea was met with "open skepticism" in *The New York Times* and other northern papers, which recognized the need for Black labor and concentrated efforts against southern armies.[107] Northern popular and political writers' relative investments in "homes for white men" informed their representations of secession. Some aligned secessionists with prior alleged pirates, including those with ties to Haiti. To them, the fact that Haitian sovereignty had broken from slavery and that Confederate sovereignty had secured enslavement mattered less than the would-be nations' piratical deviation from state policy. Others, however, believed that resentment that could lead to revolutionary and perhaps piratical Black violence was a fitting response to an enslaving nation.

A look back at the 1861 Confederate privateer trials confirms policymakers' pervasive tendency to align piracy with both enslaving violence and unruly

Blackness. According to the prosecution in *Jefferson Davis*, the Confederates had intended to sell Jacob Garrick, the Black cook on the captured Union ship the *Enchantress*, in Charleston for $1,500. The prosecution called this act "an offense without feeling," thus proving piracy. The attorney continued, "To tear a man from his home and enslave him forever, against the usages of warfare, stamps this transaction just in the light I wish you to look at it, . . . [as] a piratical, outrageous aggression, without any of the colors or forms of law."[108] The Confederate government that made Black people "contraband of war" also enslaved entire families. Though such enslavement had been continually appeased in antebellum law, the prosecution framed secessionist actions as without "colors or forms of law." In abolitionist sentimental jurisprudence, to "tear a man from his home" proved the need to remove the piratical enslaver. Only pirates, all knew, were capable of offenses without feeling.

Notably, neither the prosecution nor the defense in the *Jefferson Davis* case mentioned William Tillman, the steward of the Union vessel *Waring*, also captured by the *Jefferson Davis*. On being told of his imminent enslavement and sale in a secessionist prize court, Tillman killed three Confederate privateers. His actions were immediately recounted in newspapers such as *The New York Herald*, which noted Tillman's "care and affability" upon landing in New York City even as it quoted his claim that secessionists' desecration of the flag had "made [his] blood boil." Tillman became a "Black hero" in an abolitionist press that included *The Liberator* and *Douglass' Monthly*. On August 3, 1861, *Harper's Weekly* published extensive engravings of the attack on the *Waring*, as did *Frank Leslie's Illustrated Newspaper*.[109] A popular account titled *The Rebel Pirate's Fatal Prize: The Bloody Tragedy of the Prize Schooner Waring* (1862) fictionalized the events using sentimental tropes of Black familial love as proof of enslavers' piratical crimes against feeling. The story's main message may be drawn from an evocative broadside advertisement headlined "Undercurrents of the Southern Conspiracy!" The sheet promises the "stirring Life Story" of the "brave and daring negro" as he "murdered the Pirate Prize Master" of the ship *Jefferson Davis*. With a hatchet raised to protect a cowering woman, Tillman announces, "Back, sirs! She is my wife, she is not slave! Seize her at your peril!" The broadside advertisesd the narrative's publication alongside accounts of the *Jefferson Davis* and other ships' capture as well as their sailors' subsequent trials. Throughout, the display celebrates secessionist pirates' justified deaths at sea and in the courts. Black lives over enslavers' feelings: this abolitionist appeal, though not the celebration of Black violence, was embedded in the *Jefferson*

Davis trial. Meanwhile, the historical Tillman became a wartime celebrity, which included a stint as an attraction in P. T. Barnum's Museum in New York City, and would remain visible in postbellum Black print culture.[110]

This refusal to restage Black violence was, perhaps, informed by ongoing fears of Black resistance to white supremacist state power. As Lincoln was calling for foreign relations with Haiti, the prosecutors in *Jefferson Davis* were mobilizing antebellum rejections of Haitian sovereignty. Rather than juxtapose Black sovereignty with secessionist piracy, they rendered both equally piratical. Legal precedents that made Haitian independence a matter of colonial permission applied equally to the Confederate case. Specifically, the prosecution appealed to the Supreme Court's decision in *Rose v. Himeley* (1808), quoting verbatim in court: "It is for governments to decide whether they will consider St. Domingo as an independent nation, and until such decision shall be made, or France shall relinquish her claim, courts of justice must consider the ancient state of things as remaining unaltered, and the sovereign power of France over that colony as still subsisting."[111] When deciding a proper response to revolutionary action, the prosecution implied, one must default to a political status quo. In keeping with precedent, sovereignty was a right given by the imperial sovereign and protected by "the ancient state of things." In this case, the "ancient state" in question was the existence of union and the primacy of the U.S. federal government at the nation's head.

Yet that claim demonstrates the mutability of laws imagined to be passed down as if by blood. Enslavement had been respected as an "ancient state of things" throughout the antebellum era. It remained the Confederacy's legal lifeblood. Prior judicial appeasement for enslavement could become precedence amid shifting politics. All that mattered to the prosecutors in *Jefferson Davis* was that both Haiti and the Confederacy were, in their moment, pirates against a colonial state. This precedent "applies with ten-fold force," they concluded, because the U.S. government retained a measure of power in the region. The link has a legal logic, though a perverse one. For their cases to be joined, Haiti had to be stripped of its historical specificity and ideological threat. The terms that made Haitian independence a matter of colonial permission could be applied equally to an opposite Confederate case. Nonetheless, this claim did not require abolition or Haitian sovereignty. After all, neither were federal policy in 1861.

Haitian legal and cultural precedent could also inform a reassessment of antebellum legal culture. Lasting foreign relations with Haiti could prove the need for normalized domestic relations with Black Americans. One example was *The War Powers of the President*, an immensely popular book series by William Whiting, a Harvard-educated lawyer who eventually became solicitor of the War Department. Part of a ten-volume set, this work was published in two editions prior to 1863. In response to the question of wartime federal authority, including power over those "captured as spies, as pirates, as guerillas or bush-whackers," Whiting refuted the belief that union necessitated treating Confederates as pirates.[112] He joined the *Jefferson Davis* prosecution in aligning the United States with colonial France and the Confederacy with revolutionary Haiti. But he did so to affirm both federal union and domestic abolition. Notably, he claimed that the "civil war between St. Domingo and France" led the Supreme Court in *Rose vs. Himley* to recognize the "right of a country to treat its rebellious citizens both as *belligerents and as subjects*."[113] Appealing to international law's power as a national inheritance, Whiting forcefully validated emancipation. Specifically, he wrote, French commissioners' 1793 "Proclamation of Emancipation" showed that "France recognize[d] the right, under martial law, to emancipate the slaves of an enemy." Thus, in his view, the federal government could likewise abolish slavery. In a tacit response to fears of abolition, Whiting asserted that "commerce, industry, and general prosperity was rapid and satisfactory" following the Haitian Revolution. Formerly enslaved Haitians "retained their liberty" and had now "entered into diplomatic relations with the United States."[114] He thereby reimagined Lincoln's strategic pivot toward Haiti as proof of Black Americans' legal rights. In the process, he presaged the Emancipation Proclamation, a policy that he directly influenced.[115]

Sumner, along with other abolitionist figures such as Wendell Phillips and Lydia Maria Child, echoed Whiting's turn to Haiti. They also added a warning: Haiti was proof that just resentment followed slavery's protraction. Deeply divided public responses to such speeches, as Matthew J. Clavin notes, reflected the Haitian Revolution's status as "a nightmare to dread or a singular triumph worthy of admiration." These speeches also indicated ongoing investments in just resentment as a natural response to piratical crimes against feeling. Each rejected the white supremacist sympathies that defined notions of abolitionist piracy. "It is according to an old law, that bloody inventions return to plague the inventor," Sumner asserted, alluding to William Shakespeare's play *Macbeth*. He presented revolution as precedent: "The story of St. Domingo, so often quoted against [the African Slave], testifies to his humanity." Only the threat of reenslavement would lead to bloodshed, he believed. Black Americans' legal protection would preserve fellow feeling and political stability. Child likewise proclaimed in 1862, "It was never the *granting* of rights to the colored people that produced bloodshed" but "*withholding* those rights" and a "forcible attempt to *take them away*." Phillips, the champion of John Brown, asked an audience in March 1862 to prevent "a war of races and a war of nations" like that had occurred in a sovereign Haiti. With Haiti as model, a national family could "avert that necessity from our land" and instead "raise into peaceful liberty the four million committed to our care." Like Sumner and Child, Phillips balanced the potential for just Black violence with a paternal appeal to white "care."[116]

Federal policy was to treat secession as a form of piracy. Even so, the legal status of the enslaved remained fraught. Two wartime postal covers highlight the patent white supremacy at the heart of wartime legal culture. The first, titled "Secession Calvary," portrays four Confederates hoisting the pirate flag and sitting astride the enslaved (fig. 6). The evocative image pairs secession's legal status with slaveholding practice: secessionists are piratical, it implies, because their legal claims are made on the backs of the enslaved. The suggestion is that proslavery forms of bond were null on land and at sea: the Piracy Act of 1820 hadn't gone far enough. The second cover, titled "The Union 34 Pounder," illustrates the possible fate of piratical secessionists and, indirectly, Black Americans

FIGURE 6. Illustrated postal cover, "Secession Calvary" (c. 1861–1865). Courtesy of the American Antiquarian Society.

(fig. 7). On it, a serpent-tongued figure hangs from the gallows. His bulging eye and blue-black skin show that he is choking. Only his uniform, emblazoned with "Secession," shows that he is a Confederate sailor. Union martial power on land and at sea have overcome secessionist piracy.[117] The sailor's hat, emblazoned with the Jolly Roger and topped with a Confederate flag, confirms this narrative. The pirate's blackened face signals white supremacist death. It also draws attention, perhaps unintentionally, to the white supremacist state's historical complicity in Black deaths. The lynch mob had long been a feature of Black American life. The extrajudicial act's increase during the Civil War "mark[ed] a distinct and crucial phase in the history of lynching in America," according to historian Manfred Burg.[118] This striking figure on the gallows was featured on one of the few postal covers that represented blackness, if not Black people, beyond enslavement. Perhaps covers that suggested the benefits

FIGURE 7. Illustrated postal cover, "The Union 34 Pounder" (c. 1861–1865). Courtesy of the American Antiquarian Society.

of Black citizenship in a remade Union were less commercially viable. Whatever the case, popular and political narrators privileged homes for white men as alternatives to both secessionist piracy and Black citizenship.

Although white supremacy maintained unmistakable sway during the war, the prosecution of oceanic enslavers as pirates indicated political shifts had occurred. Take, for example, the fate of an enslaver whose piracy trials preceded the war and ended during it. On February 21, 1862, Captain Nathaniel Gordon of the enslaving vessel *Eerie* was executed for the crime of piracy under the Piracy Act of 1820. Gordon was the first and only American to be convicted and executed for enslaving piracy. His life belied claims of northern moral purity. A native of Maine and the son of an illegal deep-sea enslaver, Gordon had allegedly begun his own career as a pirate in 1848. His miserable ships, it seems, crossed the same ocean as the newly subsidized postal letters did. In August 1860, the *Eerie* was captured off Africa's South Atlantic coast. It was carrying 897 enslaved humans as cargo. Gordon's June 1861 piracy trial in a New York City circuit court had resulted in a mistrial, but the jury in a second trial, which took place in November, found him guilty. The Supreme Court declined to hear the case, and President Lincoln refused to stay the execution despite political and private pressure. In an appeal to sympathy with clear legal precedent, Rhoda E. White, the wife of a New York judge, wrote to Lincoln in February 1862 requesting clemency "for the sake of an afflicted mother and wife who are bowed down with sorrow." She suggested a private audience between the president and Gordon's family. The family members instead met with First Lady Mary Todd Lincoln, who allegedly pleaded on their behalf. Nonetheless, the convicted pirate's claim to familial feeling no longer held legal merit against those of the enslaved. Nathaniel Gordon's death in 1862 signaled that a legal culture of appeasement would not, in this instance, protect an enslaving pirate.[119]

Indeed, Gordon's death marked a shift in antebellum legal culture's proslavery appeasements, if not its undergirding sympathies. "The hanging of Gordon is an event in the history of our country," asserted an editor for *Harper's Weekly* in March 1862. Until that moment, as the editor noted, "the sympathy of the Government and its officials" had remained with enslaving pirates. Or, as John Quincy Adams had asserted during the *Amistad* trial, sympathy was wrong before. Until 1861, federal courts had followed the legal and moral bifurcation that defined the Piracy Act of 1820. The editor asserted, "It seemed so absurd to hang a man for doing at sea that which, in half the Union, is done daily without censure on land, that no one has ever been punished under the Act." Abolition had ebbed and flowed. Only after secession had proven that enslavement was incompatible with union could the antebellum state finally remove the enslaving pirate from its protection. *Harper's* printed an engraving of Gordon's hanging to commemorate this historical shift. In the image, genteel men in formal dress intermingle with armed guards to view Gordon on the gallows, indicating the violent act's apparent legal and social propriety. Perhaps the postal prints that showed Jefferson Davis hanging for piracy were signs of what would come to pass.[120] In keeping with antebellum visions, hope remained that American imperial supremacy would follow piratical secession's removal.

"STRETCHING FROM OCEAN TO OCEAN": POSTING POSTWAR SUPREMACY

At the war's outset, Charles Magnus's printed postal cover had identified a "WORLD IN COMMOTION." A later postal cover, printed during the war, called on the imperial hopes that many imagined as the conflict's desired outcome. The cover is undated, but its display of optimism suggests that it was issued in 1864 or 1865. Titled "Our Country," it shows a world that is decidedly not in commotion (fig. 8). Instead, the nation is doubly housed in oceanic space. The globe itself floats in a watery expanse, its lower half submerged, as if to render southern spaces both secondary to and undeniably linked with global oceanic systems. After all, southern ports and routes would have to be reconstructed in the new national order. As if to reinforce this domestic power, "Our Country" is cast across the globe's landed and oceanic contours. The united country is not confined to the continent but conquers the entire globe. An American flag is planted at the North Pole. The subtitle indicates that the nation is "Ours to preserve—Ours to enjoy—Ours to transmit." Internal preservation, fellow feeling, and imperial supremacy, it suggests, are part of a shared national identity. Postbellum empire is thing to be preserved, enjoyed, and transmitted. Global war must give way to imperial peace.[121]

While Charles Sumner began with domestic discord and broken foreign relations in his 1863 speech, he, too, imagined an imperial future in keeping with antebellum visions. In a closing section, titled "Our Duty," he asserted, "Stretching from ocean to ocean . . . [the United States] will be more than conqueror. Nothing too vast for its power; nothing too minute for its care." His parallelism is telling. If expansion were to be a moral rather than imperial act, exercises of "power" must be inseparable from acts of "care." The harmony

FIGURE 8. Illustrated postal cover, "Our Country" (c. 1861–1865). Courtesy of the American Antiquarian Society.

of "vast" oceanic space and "minute" domestic space would be state-backed. State power would reach "where any member of the Human Family is the succored" and thus would be as boundless as humanity's capacity for feeling. Here, Sumner marked a return to prior imperial politics: if a "family of nations" were a collection of separate sovereign nations, then a single imperial sovereign could head the "human family." This vision required material infrastructure that included the transoceanic postal empire he had so championed. Sumner closed by lauding the United States as the "upstart among the nations, . . . as the steam-engine, the telegraph, and chloroform are upstart." Emergent technology confirmed the nation's imperial scope and moral power. "With Comforter and Helper like these," he concluded, "[the Republic] can know no bounds to its empire over a willing world." Colonization of the "willing" would be an exercise in sympathy. Of course, Sumner's imagined empire of fellow feeling could only occur after secession's defeat.[122] This defeat had not yet occurred and, perhaps, never would.

This mix of uncertainty and hope permeated the late-career writings of Maria Susanna Cummins. In 1854, she had repeated Sumner's call for American supremacy via the transoceanic post and, to a lesser degree, his demonization of enslavement as piratical. By 1864, however, Cummins's legal thinking more closely paralleled that of Daniel Webster, a man with political ties to her father and whose abolitionist legal advocacy gave way to proslavery compromise.[123] *Haunted Hearts* (1864), her final domestic fiction (and the subject of chapter 5), epitomized wartime attempts to preserve antebellum legal culture. The historical pirate novel is set in New England during the War of 1812 but is narrated in a Civil War present. Befitting its current obscurity, the most sustained analysis on *Haunted Hearts* appears in Nina Baym's brief nod to its "wartime setting" and "fraternal conflict" as "key to its contemporary purpose" in her scholarly introduction to *The Lamplighter*. An extended reading complicates the idea that "either the national family was shattered or the attempt to think of the nation in the image of the family was ludicrous in the first place." True, the piety of women such as Gertrude Flint would not win the Civil War. Even so, Cummins lay national failures squarely on the deck of secessionist pirates and their mistaken sympathizers. Rather than champion Black citizenship in response, however, she staged a postbellum future defined by homes for white women.[124] In other words, *Haunted Hearts* affirms the durability of antebellum legal culture despite unmistakable rupture.

CHAPTER FIVE

PRESERVATION

Maria Susanna Cummins, Haunted Hearts *(1864), and* Texas v. White *(1869)*

Just as Abraham Lincoln appealed to antebellum "bonds of affection" prior to the Civil War's outset, Maria Susanna Cummins attempted to preserve antebellum sympathy in a postbellum nation. In the process, she fashioned the period's most historically layered and ideologically tangled pirate. This chapter is anchored by a recovery of her final novel, the domestic pirate fiction *Haunted Hearts* (1864), as well as an ongoing account of her underappreciated place in antebellum legal culture. In the years after *The Lamplighter* (1854), her parable of postal empires, Cummins continued to engage with shifting political exigencies. Her next two novels, *Mabel Vaughn* (1857) and *El Fureidîs* (1860), maintained her global approach to domestic life. Both were less commercially successful than *The Lamplighter* and have since garnered considerably less scholarly attention. In them, Cummins introduced families who could weather ongoing fracture. While neither novel relies on an uncomplicated North-South union, both model ways to endure, if not prevent, domestic discord and strained foreign relations. Pirates remain active, though unseen. The era's explicit violence is largely unrepresented. Yet even after the war began, the depth of Cummins's faith in fellow feeling as a way to combat piracy made her a paradigmatic figure. Throughout her career, she provided no clear alternatives to the state violence and white supremacy that defined the antebellum era. This, too, made her emblematic. After all, the era did not end with a full accounting of prior enslavement or ongoing domestic violence. Instead, it saw incomplete and contentious attempts at narratives of unbroken familial union. In all cases, piracy's narrative and legal marks could still be felt.

Cummins's broader literary career reminds one that narratives of domestic interiority engaged ocean politics. *Mabel Vaughn*, for example, was less a domestic fiction than an oceanic epic of landed national feeling amid familial death. It focuses on a widowed heiress who sails the "boundless waves of the rolling prairie" in the American West after losing her family and fortune in New York City. Unlike Catharine Maria Sedgwick, Cummins could not locate national moral union in the North. Other antebellum works such as Caroline Kirkland's *A New Home, Who'll Follow? Or, Glimpses of Western Life* (1839) invoked "maritime plots and images to emphasize that the promise of western settlement is unstable," as Melissa Gniadek has shown. While Cummins, too, displayed this instability, she also aligned the West with the ocean's regenerative power of sympathy. The competing forces she faced in *Mabel Vaughn* were akin to those in *The Lamplighter*.[1] Like the prior novel, *Mabel Vaughn* takes place during violent conflicts about enslavement's spread on land and at sea. Cummins presented the West as oceanic and therefore necessarily divorced from piratical enslavement.

Cummins did not wield the Piracy Act of 1820 against enslaving pirates in *Mabel Vaughn* as Harriet Beecher Stowe had in *Uncle Tom's Cabin*. Notably, however, she embedded the fictional politician Bayard Percival's sentimental speech against the Compromise of 1850. Percival's words against enslavement spread "in the heart of our free and enlightened state." Enslavement, he suggests, is a bodily violence against the entire nation: "Shall that fatal institution be suffered to settle down upon the land, which dooms one race to slavery and dishonor and another to stagnation and decay?" The politician seeks in his speech "not merely to rouse . . . generous patriotism" but to translate feeling into political action. Deeply moved, Mabel aligns this orator of "manly virtues" with the man who protected her after her husband's death.[2] In other words, the oceanic prairie affords familial and political regeneration via an abolitionist politics that nonetheless privileges homes for white men and women. The novel's "near-egalitarian western community is implicitly all white," Mary Templin notes in her extensive account of Cummins's "domesticated West." As she concludes, Mabel and Percival's eventual marriage after his election to Congress—which leads them to split time between Washington and Illinois—confirms that "the problem of slavery requires a political solution rather than a social one."[3] American policymakers' moral compass, the narrator suggests, must be oriented toward the "greatness and beauty of that vast inland ocean, in which the giant nature of the West mirrors its face." Enslavement or abolition's spread, either westward or oceanward, remains an open question. Pirates lie dormant. Even so, remaking the nation as an "inland ocean" of moral feeling may yet restore political union.[4]

By 1860, Cummins had expanded a latent theme from *The Lamplighter*—sentimental union across the globe and victory over transcolonial Bedouin rogues—into her orientalist novel, *El Fureidîs*, which translates as "The Paradise." Set in Lebanon, it "eliminates all traces of domestic political turmoil and crisis," as Steven Hamelman writes. An imperial tale of the Ottoman Mediterranean, the novel stages American domestic interiority as deeply mobile and perhaps not solely tied to the terrestrial nation. As Etsuko Taketani shows, *El Fureidîs* is a parable of "diasporic whiteness" that helps confirm that "colonialism functions even without establishing formal colonies."[5] Meredith, a wealthy English explorer, wins the heart of Havilah, a Christian Syrian girl with a New England–born father, foiling the courtship of Abdul, a weak and vaguely piratical Muslim rival. Like Thomas Jefferson in the Declaration of Independence, Cummins created a fictional Ottoman empire whose potentially unbridgeable cultural differences—described as "the disturbing current, . . . the fountain whence our [Muslim] race began, down to the eternal ocean at its close, the cold stream, the dark gulf"—breed antagonist transcolonial collaborators whose alleged crimes against feeling may or may not merit the charge of piracy found in Jefferson's 1776 rebuke.

Unlike numerous other treatments of the Ottoman Mediterranean as piratical, however, Cummins presented clearly legal, though largely unsympathetic, familial order in her novel.[6] Colonization of a weak-hearted foe, rather than ongoing struggle with a pirate-nation, seems to be the most likely outcome to foreign relations in the region. When the heroes are violently disturbed by a "volley of threats, exclamations, and epithets," they are not beset by a "crew of mutineers," as one may expect. Instead, they witness the early-morning work of "camel-drivers and attendants" in their "familiar style of oratory."[7] An image of the spurned Abdul with "a savage face, a sharpened dagger, and a soul thirsty for blood" evokes Barbary iconography. Yet Abdul's pretended status as the "heir of a boundless realm" that he peoples with an intimately described Bedouin family renders him more pitiful than piratical.[8] Abdul remains jealous of his imperial and romantic victor. "What could he *need*!" he asks of his British rival. "Why need he come hither to buy up the hearts of my tribe, and sit in my green oasis, and drink from the fountain of my hopes, and pluck the solitary flower that grew thereby."[9] Cummins valorized English and American empire even as she attempted, somewhat weakly, to extend familial feeling across ethnic, racial, and national bounds. Above all, white supremacist foreign relations reign supreme in the novel. Meredith's tales of the Crimean War unlock the initially skeptical Havilah's heart, for they "appealed to her woman's sympathies in behalf of the desolate homes and broken hearts of England." Whether such appeals apply to the domestic United States remains unsaid. The novel's primary themes—that unbridgeable difference can be pacified, if not overcome, and that a war's "desolate home and broken hearts" may lead to familial reunion—undeniably shaped Cummins's approach to the internecine Civil War that began a year later. The pirate was soon inside the house, trying to make it home.[10]

Haunted Hearts was Cummins's final attempt to preserve a legal culture that had only become more fractured. As I made clear in chapter 4, wartime legal debates rested on secessionist sailors' relative connection to national families or historical piracies. Fittingly, then, Cummins's final novel is a historical pirate fiction with an obtrusive present-day Unionist narrator. Set in New Jersey during the War of 1812, it centers on a young French-American woman, Angie Cousin, and her American lover, George Rawle. Read in light of its wartime release, the first volume becomes a parable of mistaken feeling for secession. Black Bullet, who pretends to be a British prisoner but is actually a transcolonial pirate, sells George Rawle into slavery while framing him for murder. Bullet has ties to Spain, England, New England, the Caribbean, and the Ottoman Mediterranean; and the narrator suggests that the identities he inhabits—that of a seductive British naval officer, a mercenary corsair, and a violent Black revolutionary—are the Confederates' true antecedents. The narrator, speaking from a wartime present, explicitly compares Bullet's piracy to "the recent revival of the crime which makes it now a familiar outrage."[11] The temporarily defeated heroine's body, the narrator notes, is the symbolic site of "our decimated battalions . . . the face of our bloody battle-fields."[12] The novel's resolution—Bullet is captured by George at sea and found guilty of piracy in court—models something like postbellum union. By the end, George and Angie's income from an unnamed trade in (slaveholding) Surinam fortifies an idyllic home in New Jersey. During a final appeal to the Civil War present, the narrator declares that Angie's family, as generations pass, remains secure in "the serene and joyful hopes which gild their sunset."[13] In practice, however,

Haunted Hearts secures homes for white men. The piracy of both enslavement and Black sovereignty justifies the supreme legal status of white middle-class subjects. Cummins thus aligned herself with wartime northern women writers who, in the words of Lyde Cullen Sizer, mobilized "republican rhetoric to call for a strengthened sense of purpose that largely avoided issues of racial or economic strife."[14] Via the pirate's removal, she preserved an antebellum home built on white supremacy. An old home: who'll follow?

Today *Haunted Hearts* is a relatively obscure example of domestic pirate fiction. Nonetheless, it is *the* emblematic Civil War legal fiction. Its study also models future scholarly recoveries. In it, Cummins staked a final antebellum vision that met her contemporary moment and held sway long afterward. I begin my examination of the work by turning first to *Low v. Routledge* (1865), a copyright piracy trial spurred by the novel's international publication. I then place the novel in its wartime context before considering the Supreme Court's comparable return to antebellum precedents in the war's legal aftermath. Antebellum legal culture ended where it began, caught in an infinite loop. It was pirates all the way down.

"THE LITERARY WORLD" OF *HAUNTED HEARTS*

Befitting domestic fiction's role in international copyright and foreign relations, the publication history of *Haunted Hearts* echoes the novel's primary themes. The novel was embroiled in a historic piracy trial with wide-reaching legal implications, one that took place before many readers ever watched Black Bullet take the fictional stand. In May 1864, Cummins's property was taken from her by an entity who claimed that a domestic and global union was invalid. Prior legal precedent on piracy did not apply, it argued, because she had not demonstrated true attachment to a sovereign. The ocean had broken that attachment, and thus her property was a loose fish. Cummins and her camp subsequently had that entity tried as a pirate in hopes of destroying an alternative legal order that would use her as precedent.

The pirate in question was not a Confederate but a London-based publisher. The property was not ships at sea but a novel written in the United States and copyrighted in London via letters from Canada. The sovereignty at issue was not the Confederacy's but Britain's and Canada's. The question of domestic attachment was not whether a privateer could be bound to the Confederate government by a letter of marque but whether an "alien author" could be bound to the

British government by a letter of copyright.[15] Though each dealt with distinct types of pirates, both *Low v. Routledge* (1865) and the Civil War piracy cases hinged on questions of jurisdiction, national attachment, and sovereignty's oceanic extensions. England and other so-called neutral nations had not proven themselves willing to pass judgment on secessionist challenges to American sovereignty (see chapter 4). Just as the content of *Haunted Hearts* evinces a deep investment in negating secessionist sympathy as piratical, the novel's publication history reveals the ocean politics that such competitions involved.

As I have shown, literary production was not incidental to wartime legal claims to oceanic space. The international literary field, like the ocean, was a global venue in which domestic nations floated their membership in a family of nations. Notions of the free sea ostensibly established it as a space of statist union against piracy. Secessionist literary nationalism powered claims to the free sea as a symbolic gesture and a legal fact. In the months prior to the war, for example, Representative T. R. R. Cobb of Georgia asserted that a new international copyright resolution passed by the Confederacy's provisional congress would "operate strongly to bring the literary world, especially of Great Britain, to sympathize with us against the Yankee literary pirates."[16] Where the literary world went, the political world would follow, or so was his thinking. Both would join the South, Cobb believed, once they recognized that Yankees, not southerners, were pirates who did not respect property rights. His outcry against "Yankee literary pirates" referred to northern control over southern literary properties but also hinted at abolitionist threats against southern claims to human property. For Cobb, secessionist sovereignty would secure southern sympathy across the terraqueous globe. British reliance on southern cotton bolstered his optimistic belief in the power of secessionist literary nationalism. Melissa Homestead, for example, treats Cobb's legislation for international copyright as part of the Confederates' "three-pronged plan" for garnering European support. The other prongs were "a scheme for regulating the cotton trade, and a prohibition of Sunday mail delivery." Affixed to a central secessionist maritime policy, these prongs formed a trident of Confederate legal culture.[17] Secessionist founding documents made legal claim to domestic union and global sovereignty. Each required that secessionists beat the charge of piracy. The very existence of *Haunted Hearts* confirmed the stakes that Cobb was emphasizing in his account of secessionist literary production. Power in the global literary marketplace could fundamentally shape international responses to secessionist forms of bond.

Haunted Hearts entered a global literary marketplace that was swimming with real and fictional pirates. An August 1864 "Literary Notice" in *Godey's Lady's Book* stated that "the main incident in the story will be recognized as a veritable occurrence."[18] Cummins herself affirmed that the "principal crime" in *Haunted Hearts* was "the basis and groundwork of more than one popular feast which fiction has served to the public."[19] Of the novel's generic tropes, piracy serves as the most visible and widespread. *Haunted Hearts* had a global release befitting its global genre. While its spread was not as extensive as *The Lamplighter*'s, the novel was printed in American, German, French, and multiple British editions in 1864 and later years. Over the course of her career, Cummins's royalties had risen steadily: she received 10 percent of sales for her first two novels, 15 percent for her third, and thirty cents a copy for her last, even as she failed to replicate her debut novel's success.[20] An advertisement in *Coleman's Rural World* set the U.S. price of *Haunted Hearts* at $2. In the New York City–based magazine *The Independent*, a publisher's notice for "Ten New Books" gave it top billing, describing it as "the great novel by the author of 'The Lamplighter.' Published in England and the United States simultaneously May 23."[21] Such appeals to simultaneous publication demonstrated an imagined connection between literary worth and global reach. Yet transoceanic wandering led to trouble during Civil War battles on land, at sea, and in the courts.

Cummins displayed her global literary imagination in her legal approach to international copyright. Her fight against pirates reveals the wartime challenges of navigating legal culture on both land and water. Cummins had traveled to London to secure copyright for *Mabel Vaughn* on the advice of her British publisher, Sampson Low and following the pattern of other American authors. In an 1860 letter regarding her third novel, *El Fureidîs*, Low wrote, "The Copyright by your residence amongst us, we see no reason to doubt the soundness of the legal position and hold that any foreign writer if in England during the publication of his or her works has a copyright for that work under the provisions of her Copyright Law." Legal attachment to a foreign sovereign, he believed, could be proven by a temporary homestead, and "Mrs. Stowe, Mr. Hawthorn[e] Mrs. Southworth and others are deriving the benefit of it."[22] Nathaniel Hawthorne, it seems, was once again sailing in the same proverbial boat as a crew of scribbling women. Indeed, Harriet Beecher Stowe was one of the first American authors to use this law: *Dred* (1856) and *The Minister's Wooing* (1859) received British copyrights after she traveled to England for their publication.[23] However, in 1864, the raging Civil War (and its own pirates) made such travel impossible. In

May, Cummins therefore went to the British colony of Montreal, Canada. From there, she wrote a letter to Low, who then released the novel in two volumes at a cost of sixteen shillings. The publisher delivered a copy to the British Museum, placing the fiction in an imperial home. Cummins was convinced that she had received British copyright in accordance with the law.

In keeping with the ideas in her prior fiction, Cummins had supposed that domestic attachment extended across the ocean, especially if aided by letters. However, the publisher Routledge did not agree and made plans to sell copies of the work for two shillings. Ultimately, the Court of the British Lord Justices was forced to consider whether it could assert domestic bonds to a noncitizen who had strategically invoked British imperial sovereignty. The case that followed, *Low v. Routledge* (1865), confirmed the expansion of imperial power that led to maritime piracy's downfall in the period. According to the decision, literary property rights in Britain were transferrable to a foreign agent if they produced a domestic attachment. Like the 1861 secessionist piracy trials in America, *Low v. Routledge* forced the British courts to consider whether a sovereign could control exchanges taking place at and across the sea. According to *Jeffreys v. Boosey* (1854), an author had to be present in "British dominion" during publication to receive copyright.[24] This ruling suggested that only bodies made domestic could create the sympathetic bond needed to claim legal attachment with Britain. Routledge's defense was that the prior statute "could not refer to colonies with legislatures of their own." British law did not apply to "an alien coming into Canada for the purpose of publishing a work."[25] The argument was that Canada's sovereignty and Cummins's inability to claim national sympathy produced an invalid legal bond. In the process, Routledge posited a theory of sovereignty via confederated but distinct bodies with independent relations to piracy. The American Articles of Confederation similarly limited a central sovereign's power to define and punish piracy globally. The Confederate government went further, stating that alternative secessionist sympathies powered a valid legislature.

In a decision reminiscent of the 1863 *Prize Cases*, the British court reasserted a central government's global reach. The U.S. Supreme Court had affirmed the federal government's right against secessionist piracy wherever it threatened national union. In *Low v. Routledge* (1865), the British court affirmed the Crown's rights over all "British dominions" across the globe: "Every alien coming into a British colony is temporarily a subject of the Crown, bound by, subject and entitled to the benefits which affect all British subjects."[26] In other words, the nation's oceanic reach and binding power validated Cummins's copyright. Anyone, citizenship notwithstanding, could be domesticated as a "British subject" and sympathetically "bound" to the nation. Britain's claim to sovereign power was akin to the arguments of northern figures who treated secessionists as if they were still under the Union's domestic dominion. The British court also denied Routledge's attempts to invalidate copyright due to delays in certain registrations. The court forgave the delay, attributing them to "the necessities of communicating with Miss Cummins, who was then in America." The maritime forces that had made Cummins's oceanic travels impossible could not prevent sympathy's global spread. Letters had a binding power of attachment between national subjects, a claim similar to those argued in the 1848 Anglo-American Postal Treaty. The mail could also overcome fellow feeling's temporal or spatial delays. Cummins, "an alien friend," was legally entitled to "gift, trade, or other lawful means, any treasure or goods personal whatsoever as an Englishman." Cummins, like Gertrude Flint in *The Lamplighter*, had legally enacted global ties via gifts. She was bound, in both feeling and law, "as an Englishmen," for as long as she was in the British dominion. Routledge was deemed piratical, despite its objections, and ordered to cease publication of *Haunted Hearts*. Beyond validating Cummins's legal claim, this literary infrastructure affirmed an imperial sovereign's role as the guardian of property rights and the distributor of fellow feeling. Future cases hinged on whether authors had correctly registered their work in the British Empire.[27]

Reactions to the decision followed sovereign allegiances amid ongoing global competitions over literary spoils. The opinion was met with some scrutiny in both England and Canada due to its tilting of British imperial protection toward Americans. Editors at *The Atheneum*, a London-based arts journal, admitted the decision's "unquestionable" legal accuracy but concluded that *Low v. Routledge* "should be objected to" as a model for foreign relations. "It will enable those authors who are subjects of the United States to evade the policy of *reciprocity*," they asserted in an appeal to legalized fellow feeling. Legal flows now traveled only in one direction: Americans had "secure[d] their rights in the British dominions" while British authors remained "debarred from protecting their works against piracy in the United States."[28] In other words, the British decision had the secondary effect of giving a temporarily domesticated subject a degree of global sovereignty not afforded to a British citizen in the United States.[29] The decision's positive reception in the U.S. publishing system was also defined by self-interested sympathy. *The American Literary Gazette and Publishers' Circular* devoted multiple pages to outlining the decision, which editors considered to be "in perfect accord, not only with the opinion of the [publishing] profession, but also with the feeling of the public in favor of authors of works of literature."[30] The copyright decision was therefore part of a larger global infrastructure of fellow feeling that had legal force. The logic of state-sanctioned fellow feeling that protected a domestic novelist also protected a merchant vessel: both forwarded forms of sympathy and capital exchange that must be regulated by a sovereign. Cummins herself must have been pleased. A congratulatory letter from Sampson Low playfully affirmed, "Messrs Routledge will doubtless ponder what it is to have 'Haunted Hearts.'"[31] Of course, such victories over literary pirates paled in comparison to the ongoing war. As her prior letter to Low had made clear, Cummins had already been pondering "what it was to have 'Haunted Hearts.'" The author's wartime answers powered her final preservation of antebellum legal culture.

"BREAKING HEARTS ALL OVER": LEGAL CULTURE IN PALIMPSEST

While *Haunted Hearts* is set during the War of 1812, it does not describe battles on land or at sea. Perhaps the ongoing Civil War's violence, which the obtrusive narrator often recalls, made such accounts unnecessary. By setting the novel in an earlier era, Cummins mobilized a literary and legal precedent for her current domestic fracture. Historical fiction could model a path toward preserving antebellum legal culture, as had been the case with Catharine Maria Sedgwick in *Hope Leslie* (1827). *Haunted Hearts* holds both past and present maritime conflicts in shared suspension. The narrator takes part in what Susan Gilman calls the "strategic anachronisms" of palimpsestuous nineteenth-century sentimental fictions. A *palimpsest* is a text shaped by continued etchings, erasings, and reinscribings that never fully wipe clean. In relation to fiction, Gilman defines *palimpsest* as the "disjunctive presence either of time past or future in the work's present."[32] In *Haunted Hearts*, the familial fractures of 1812 are the real-world fractures of 1861. The national union of 1820 will be the national union of 1864. Pirates sail in both times and spaces simultaneously. The ocean is deep. Time is a flat circle. The first section's domestic fracture—in which Angie's love interest, George, is thought to be dead but proven to be alive—is an allegory for Civil War deaths and hoped-for family reunions. The narrator says, "In these days of terrible uncertainty, long suspense, premature despair, which are breaking Hearts all over this our land, such instances of earthly resurrection may not be rare." Separated families may still be reunited. In a nod to inescapable violence, however, she prays that "the lives of the lost" will be "pure from every stain."[33] If titular "haunted hearts" are not to be fully mended in the wartime present, a turn to past "haunted hearts" will remind one of the stakes: victory over pirates and the rebirth of national fellow feeling. This abiding preservation of familial feeling promotes a postwar union predicated on antebellum models. Prior to this resolution, however, the novel must show hearts being broken.

Though Cummins eventually did invoke her belief in the Union and obliquely ended her novel in a Civil War present, her preface alternatively reveals and obscures the novel's contemporary connections. It names her preoccupation with shared violence and, in a careful teleology, makes wartime misery proof that national fellow feeling is still at work. In this way, it addresses the national family's fracture. In a shrewd sentimental turn, however, the preface brands "haunted hearts" as *proof* of sympathy. Specifically, it shows how probing "false lights, such hidden ghosts, such stalking spectres" can "awaken a respect and sympathy for truths buried in life's unfathomed wells." Such an awareness reveals a "debt of love, compassion, forgiveness, sympathy, which each owes to all." The period's inescapable violence, as well as the shared break in domestic ties, creates attachment. All must repay the current "debt" of fellow feeling. Cummins's sentimental vision necessitated a return to what Peter Coviello refers to as early national "agonizing affect." She, like Jefferson, presented a "vision of the new nation as, precisely, a collectivity of the mutually wounded and bereaved, held together by nothing so much as citizens' shared feelings of 'agonizing' loss."[34] In a Civil War present, shared agony and collectivity resulted from ubiquitous violence. The preface concludes by asking, "Who is there who does not, may not, must not, carry in his breast that pitiful thing—A HAUNTED HEART?"[35] Shared pain makes all national subjects capable of attachment. All can be seen on the rack. Such tortured optimism informed Cummins's approach to antebellum legal culture. It also evinced her lingering fear of unruly agents who were seemingly incapable of fellow feeling. Pirates, or those without haunted hearts, remained an existential and political threat. The narrator does not plainly state whether American southerners were pained kin or vindictive pirates, an elision she shares with Abraham Lincoln and other policymakers.

In the novel, wartime crisis is made evident by the pirate's relative ease in entering the central characters' social world. In *The Lamplighter*, a rakish man from New Orleans fails to enact sexual and social violence against a northern family. In *Haunted Hearts*, however, a rakish pirate succeeds. The novel opens on December 23, 1812 and its first half establishes a historical distance that does not preclude its contemporary power. The narrator begins, "Every circle has its centre. To describe a circle, one must choose a given point, and radiate thence at equal distances. The north-eastern corner of New Jersey is that part of the earth's surface on which I propose to describe a circle, and the centre of that circle is Stein's Tavern."[36] The opening language of the "circle," "its centre," and its radiance from a single point echoes the arguments of the 1861 defense in the *Jefferson Davis* case. But while those attorneys presented the sailor William Smith as part of this web—and therefore legally not a pirate—Cummins denied secessionist mariners that legal or moral claim. In *Haunted Hearts*, they are pirates with clear precedent. The parallel between the novel and this specific defense is likely a coincidence, but it affirms that sympathy was central to the period's legal culture. The New Jersey tavern, which "in some degrees shared the fortunes of the new republic," houses a domestic community beset by piratical forces from without and within. The disguised pirate Black Bullet first arrives in New Jersey as a British lieutenant and "gintleman prisoner" named Captain Josselyn. In a testament to American sympathy, he is treated more hospitably than a typical prisoner of war would be.[37] The pirate's ability to foster fellow feeling speaks to his political power. Even so, the attention bestowed to a foreign military gallant may be read as itself an act of sedition.

Despite the pirate's clear villainy, the narrator tells us how the heroine and her community unknowingly harbor, forward, and protect such destructive agents. Via the explicit theme of "haunted hearts," the narrative demonstrates that wartime violence and haunting are not perpetrated by the pirate alone. False sympathy and familial discord empower piracy's spread. In addition to coddling Captain Josselyn, unscrupulous townspersons knowingly and unknowingly provide the false officer with monetary support and legal cover. Tellingly, the tavern, thought to be center of a domestic circle, is in fact the location of "the secret rendezvous of [Bullet's] fellow-conspirators," headed by George's cousin Pete. In a side plot, Pete fakes George's suicide to receive an inheritance, helps to rig a horserace that leads to George's disownment, and assists Bullet without knowing his true identity. Pete's flaws can be traced to a lingering foreignness: "All the phlegm of his Dutch ancestry had in him degenerated into downright stupidity."[38] In this way, the novel suggests that acts of sedition begin in the home and may be tied to foreign relations. Moreover,

Bullet has a claim to Angie that is not present between Gertrude and Bruce in *The Lamplighter*. His arrival at Angie's home gives her "a little flutter of pleasurable excitement" and sets the stage for the novel's fundamental crisis.[39] Angie's lapses in character—namely, her seeming preference for this libertine—can be traced to her patrilineal Frenchness and the absence of a matrilineal American example. Angie is not a plain-looking American orphan like Gertrude Flint is; instead, she is "an exotic, and a rare one" whose deceased mother was "of strict Puritan birth and training" and whose father was "a Frenchman" who had "maintained . . . something of the wit and deportment of a true Parisian."[40] As a French-American woman, Angie embodies the inherent unruliness of foreign relations. Her full name, Angevine, also makes reference to the English royal house that ruled all of France and much of Western Europe in the late Middle Ages. In other words, the novel hints that American transcolonial bloodlines are suspect because they have an affinity with other transcolonial agents. Angie is not a pirate, but she remains susceptible to their charms.

The first chapters of *Haunted Hearts* contain little explicit discussion of the Civil War. The novel's entry into that wartime conflict begins, much like the war itself, with violence in Baltimore. As a seaport and railroad center, Baltimore had social and commercial ties to both domestic and transoceanic infrastructures. It was also home to the nation's largest free Black population. The Baltimore riot, which took place in April 1861 before the state of Maryland had declared its sympathies, was the site of the war's first casualties and a signal that internecine violence was at hand.[41] Cummins's novel offers a similar signal, but its crisis originates in mistaken responses to domestic discord and misappropriation of a transcolonial inheritance. During Bullet's visit, George arrives at Angie's home greatly distressed. His cantankerous uncle and closest paternal relative, Baltimore Rawle, has disinherited him due to the machinations of Bullet and George's cousins. The source of George's inheritance, a cache of "old guineas or Spanish dollars," suggests that the transfer of British and Spanish imperial spoils will fund American domestic lines. Gold also stands for other global commodities, including enslaved humans as cargo.[42] After Angie unsuccessfully tries to hide Bullet's presence in the house, George departs suddenly and in great despair. The next morning, Baltimore Rawle is dead, George has disappeared, and Rawle's golden guineas are gone. Bullet has secretly escaped after paying a poor farmer "two Spanish dollars" for the use of a horse.[43] A seditious murder, a patricide of sorts, has cut the Rawle paternal line and has prevented its continuation through George's marriage with Angie. The fear that had been endemic to domestic pirate fictions like Sedgwick's *Hope Leslie* had come true: an American family's transcolonial inheritance is now bankrolling transoceanic piracy of unclear racial character.

As the narrator makes clear, the New Jersey community's actions are an allegory for mistaken sympathy across the antebellum era. She clearly links the Revolutionary War, the War of 1812, and an ongoing Civil War. She explicitly judges Bullet's success in terms of readers' proper feelings toward their Civil War present. In the process, she presents a genealogy of American martial power and indissoluble union. If the novel's characters cannot trace this line, its readers must. The New Jersey community members are aware of the War of 1812, but it is being "fought at a distance . . . on an element to which they [are] strangers," and it will lead to the "insurance of rights of which they had never dreamed of being dispossessed." Bullet's actions prove that perhaps they should have recognized that ocean politics shape domestic space. After all, the War of 1812 was protecting the inheritances they had won in the Revolutionary War, that "hand-to-hand struggle in which their grandfathers had achieved freedom." Independence had been won by a national family that was unified in feeling against piracy. To what degree contemporary readers will live up to this revolutionary standard will determine the Civil War, the present-day "life-and-death grapple to which their grandchildren have lately sprung in her defence."[44] The narrator assumes that the "grandchildren" of the America Revolution serve solely on the side of the Union. Secessionist sympathies, though unnamed, are not given a form of bond.

Haunted Hearts focuses on the painful struggle of an individual body to elicit national fellow feeling in a union preserved by haunted hearts. The novel's fallen heroine not only models mistaken sympathy's violent effects but also shows how Civil War agony may become the basis for positive domestic bonds. The circumstances surrounding Baltimore Rawle's murder and George's supposed suicide remain a mystery to Angie. She is left to struggle with the seeming fact of a union that will be forever delayed. Her moral and embodied capacity to withstand deep violence makes her an incarnation of the Civil War landscape. George's "death" is followed by a five-year gap in the narrative, during which the War of 1812 ends. While Angie sits "musing on the ruins of those [castles] demolished five years ago," the narrator highlights her marked body: her "first flush of youth is passed," her frame shows "languor and debility," and her form is no longer beautiful but "patient and peaceful." She is undeniably scarred. In keeping with the novel's preface, however, this negative account primes an affirmation: "And this, then, is victory! Certainly; why not?" The narrator asks, "Tell me, is victory beautiful? Is it not wounded, stained, scarred, just in proportion as it is hard-won and glorious? Does it not come with tattered banners, and broken ranks, and weary steps, as tokens of its triumph? Who sees in our decimated battalions, or on the face of our bloody battle-fields, the cheering signs of conquest? It is known only by its fruits. It is felt, not seen."[45] The lessons of the ongoing Civil War, unnamed but unmistakably invoked, provide a key to understanding how positive beauty does not guarantee moral victories. Angie's body maps ongoing scenes of carnage, which, in turn, validate both her silent suffering and the current war effort. The Civil War's presence in the scene builds in power and specificity. The narrator evokes the "wounded, stained, scarred," then grimly introduces "tattered," "broken," and "weary" wartime figures. Finally, she recalls "our decimated battalions" and "our bloody battlefields" in a Civil War present. Facile "cheering signs of conquest" are not evident, but this doubly "victorious" account marks a shift from easy feeling. For both Angie and the novel's readers, the "fruits" of conquest are "felt, not seen." Even so, the narrator indicates a lingering doubt by framing these appeals as questions. Such troubled optimism befits a seemingly endless war.

The fact that *Haunted Hearts* deeply harms its heroes rather than simply raising the threat of harm shows that their world is not *The Lamplighter*'s. In the earlier novel, Willie's seeming lapse in sympathy forces Gertrude's domestic crisis. In the latter text, Angie's true lapse in sympathy forces a crisis deeper than those that might have been triggered by her individual faults. Though Angie does not have Gertrude's piety, she embodies the current Civil War landscape. Yet both heroines must demonstrate proper piety and a capacity for selflessness in the face of an external threat. In light of undeniable domestic breaks, union can occur only after the piratical source of disruption is subdued both at sea and in the courts.

"THE TRIAL OF A GANG OF NOTORIOUS PIRATES": SECESSION ON TRIAL

Due to an extraordinary set of circumstances, Angie comes to face Bullet in a New York City courtroom. As the narrator makes clear, however, it is the Confederacy that is actually on trial. The novel's second half thus presents an appraisal of wartime legal culture: piratical violence, once sanctioned, is overcome by rebuilding a fractured union, and that union is guaranteed by the removal of secessionist threats at sea, at home, and in the courts. Angie's mistaken sympathy shows how such removals may be thwarted. George's privateering heroics model how to remove pirates on both land and water.

The climactic chapter of *Haunted Hearts* begins with a knowing sentence: "The trial of a gang of notorious pirates would prove an eventful circumstance, in any seaport city of the Old or New World."[46] This would include, one may assume, 1860s New York City. Cummins's oblique references to Civil War pirate trials, though easily missed by modern readers, are clear once read alongside the history I analyzed in chapter 4. Like many New Yorkers during the 1861 *Savannah* trial, Angie Cousins finds herself in a courtroom filled with a notorious gang. Through a remarkable coincidence, she witnesses Black Bullet's highly publicized trial without knowing his former identity or his connection to George. As I have shown, in the months leading up to the 1860s trials, national papers debated the secessionist mariners' legal status and transcribed each trial's daily arguments. But in a seeming slight to Civil War contemporaries, the narrator rejects journalists' ability to truly convey the law's emotional depths, dismissing "the reporter for the Chronicle . . . [as] but a superficial observer of the minor features of the trial" such as journalistic facts and transcribed arguments.[47] The pirate's lawyer, she tells the reader, has a "magnetic power over audiences and juries" that indicates the possibility that mistaken sympathy will carry from the courthouse into print.[48] The implication is that only a novelist can reveal emotional interiority and the trials' true sentimental political import. For the narrator, the trial of Black Bullet confirms that mistaken sympathy has been applied to Confederate sailors.

As in the novel's first section, the trial scenes open with a series of deliberate connections between this historical fiction and the Civil War present. The narrator presents Black Bullet's lawyer, "Trump, the oily-tongued, Trump, the thunderer," as a man whose oratory skill is matched only by his mercenary unfeeling. In a nod to prior historical defenses of enslaving pirates, Trump attempts to show that George is not fit to bear witness against Bullet due to failures of familial attachment. As the defense notes, "when men run away, disappear, seek to be forgotten, it is generally for some good reason—or some *bad* reason rather."[49] This assertion, made with "insolence and menace," attempts to mistake the jury's sympathy. Perhaps George is in fact the pirate. To ensure that readers recognize Bullet's relation to secessionist legal culture, the narrator explicitly places the defense's opening statement in a Civil War context. She summarizes the lawyer's defense of the five "buccaneers" on trial thusly:

> It was the old story of deception, robbery, and cruelty, all summed up in the dark word, Piracy,—a story so old, a deed so dark, as almost to be forgotten and lost in oblivion, but for the recent revival of the crime which makes it now a familiar outrage. But lawless freebooters may yet claim legal sanction for their deeds, and indifference to others' rights may be fostered by sophistry or imaginary wrongs.[50]

Cummins was responding, perhaps unintentionally, to legal defenses by alleged secessionist pirates. After all, their defense had been founded on the possibility that even the "meanest wretch" could be part of a domestic circle. For Cummins, "piracy" was a form of unruliness whose universal evil overshadowed any historical specificity. Piracy was not merely an act of "robbery," she affirmed, but an improper relation to feeling itself. It was "deception" and "cruelty" incarnate. The "recent revival of the crime" and its "familiar outrage" in a Civil War present referred to secessionist piracy trials as well to ongoing maritime action. Confederate privateering and its "lawless freebooters," the novel's narrator implies, are no better than common pirates. Their outrage is "familiar" in the multiple meanings of the word: piracy is known across vast spaces. It also contains a sexual threat inherent to familial and intimate contact. In other words, pirates are the seducers that Jefferson Davis claimed they were not. The narrator does not directly name the supposed "legal sanction" for Bullet's deeds, nor does she recount the "sophistry or imaginary wrongs" that make them possible. Public trials and ongoing debates make further explanation unnecessary. No matter the Confederate claim, one may cast it aside as an "old story" of piratical offenses without feeling.

Cummins blamed this domestic crisis on foreign relations, much as Sumner had done in his 1863 speech against secession. Mistaken sympathy had led to pirates' false protection. Her novel's narrator declares, still speaking in the Civil War present, that "in some instances . . . life may be held sacred while property is sacrificed, and the eyes of neutrals may be blinded to the outrage by a certain pretence of justice and discrimination. No such affectation of mercy, no such partial distinctions softened the crimes of these men, or qualified their deeds.[51] In other words, not hanging Confederate pirates was a too-soft judgment that favored life over property. This frame was somewhat in tension with Union policies. After all, secessionism rested on valuing enslaved property more than Black lives. Moreover, a fully recovered Union would appear to include secessionist agents. In this case, however, the narrator believes that a fundamental rejection of unnamed wartime pirates aligns with proper feeling. As she implies, pirates' lives are less "sacred" and thereby fit for removal. She makes clear, however, that the pirate's legal status is not merely a domestic one: the phrase "the eyes of neutrals" stands for the nations that Sumner decried. The "neutral" status of such nations, the narrator affirms, is based on a "pretence of justice and discrimination" rather than proper feeling. Those "blinded to the outrage" of piracy draw "partial distinctions" whose legal grounds are in fact the false "affectation of mercy." Black Bullet and the men on trial are not "softened" or "qualified" by this mistaken sympathy because their actions are self-evidently evil. Moreover, they have no access to Confederate legal arguments. Even so, Bullet and the secessionist sailors share a practical lineage. Hanging both will restore proper domestic relations.

In the novel, the threat of the Confederacy and the power to defeat it can be traced to maritime battles against the British and the freedom from bondage at the hands of African corsairs. In other words, Cummins placed the War of 1812 in a historical trajectory whose Civil War connections run directly counter to secessionist legal culture. The hero George Rawle is a member of the generation that "chained the dastardly tyrant of the Mediterranean" and is the patriarch of her readers' Civil War present. Those early national wars had "given our infant navy her earliest title to a nation's praise,—a foretaste of the future triumphs which now fill her sails, as she sweeps on in the march of freedom; praise which has swelled into a hymn of thanksgiving as we feel how, in this our day of trial, she girds us with her strength." Cummins's panegyric applied to the nation as a whole, but she focused on the navy as the guarantor of union and a counter to secession. The state's power over oceanic space reaffirms its domestic validity in the novel. Yet the appeal's temporal tangle shows that the author was attempting to launch a historical ship of state in uncertain waters. The nation's "earliest title" to maritime power foretold "future triumphs which now fill her sails," but the Civil War remained an ongoing "day of trial." The narrator cannot say for certain that this ongoing battle is won. Therefore, the "hymn of thanksgiving" is not a song that heralds present victory. It instead affirms that "we feel" the connection between past victory and the strength to fight. Who constitutes "us" and "we" is stated primarily by their opposite: we are neither pirates nor tyrants but part of a "march of freedom." In other words, unionism remains a moral and martial check to piratical crimes against feeling. Even so, the "African slavery" that represents the novel's "crime of the darkest dye" does not take place on southern plantations. It is the enslavement of a white merchant in slaveholding Surinam by African corsairs and a "Black Bullet."[52] In other words, the novel pits secessionist transcolonial piracy against a transcolonial unionism defined by ongoing white supremacy.

"UNDER AN AFRICAN SUN": BLACK BULLETS AND WHITE SUPREMACY

More than any other wartime fiction, *Haunted Hearts* exposes ongoing political fears about both slavery and emancipation as threats to domestic order. This tension powered many Civil War representations of secessionist piracy as well as antebellum pirates more broadly. The pirate Black Bullet is a transcolonial terror with links to the Haitian Caribbean and the Ottoman Mediterranean. These ties bind him to the Confederacy. He ensnares white women and enslaves white men. Notably, he also shares historical waters with Emmanuel Appadocca, for both are products of the revolutionary 1790s Caribbean. Though there is no indication that Cummins knew anything about Michel Maxwell Philip's novel, both works of fiction depict the same legal culture. Each consider whether the manumission and enfranchisement of formerly enslaved subjects and their heirs could restore American moral sense and foster domestic relations. Yet while the character Appadocca embodies a just resentment of white hegemony and global slavery, the retrograde Black Bullet is a "deepest dyed villain" whose removal portends the national removal of genocidal secessionists and the restoration of white racial hegemony. In the process, Cummins's novel presents a narrative akin to Jefferson's appeal to "piratical warfare" in his drafted Declaration of Independence. The removal of piratical unruliness by white heroes will lead to indissoluble union despite an unprecedented domestic break. In *Haunted Hearts*, the white middle-class home is therefore a model of comfort for all. In short, Cummins provides homes for white men. Her legal theory, though a powerful counter to a genocidal Confederate form of bond, denies nonwhite figures their rightful share in a postwar domestic union.

Cummins did reject secessionist claims about the happily enslaved among moral southern families. But rather than make such subjects the center of new national models, her novel's sole nonwhite character who isn't a pirate enters domestic space only to leave it. "Old Happy Boose," the sole formerly enslaved Black subject, is a minor character with no narrated interiority. She is happily bound to a free North and serves as the site for Angie's development. In a repudiation of secessionist legal culture, Happy presents the only direct account of Southern slavery. After the British officer's absence brings another character to tears, she says, "Ole Hap thought mebbe Miss Angie was a beatin' yer; same as ole missus down South used to beat dis yer nigger-wench."[53] The matter-of-fact account of domestic violence perpetrated by "ole missus down South" signals that southern homes are violently ordered. This fact creates a comparison with Happy's uncomplicated contentment as a northern domestic worker. If a happy nonwhite domestic line must be invoked to counter secessionist ideology, it cannot proliferate in the union that Cummins was imagining. Angie alone models proper citizenship by proving her capacity for virtue and household labor. After George's disappearance, Angie spends the months prior to Happy's death "nursing the faithful servant and performing the household drudgery besides."[54] The image of domestic labor performed by northern white women in the absence of Black support stands in contrast with an unnamed southern domestic order that cannot sustain without enslavement. Happy may be both sanctified and removed from a familial lineage that extends to the narrative's Civil War present.

While the novel's stock Black character quickly leaves the white national family, the paradigmatic pirate evinces a more complicated racial politics. Ultimately, Bullet's ability to perform across a spectrum of racial, ethnic, and national identity makes him antebellum legal culture's most complete (and convoluted) transcolonial pirate. He is "Bullet, or the Black Bull of the Indies." He "learned his trade among the African corsairs" in the 1790s and had earned his "reputation as the king of pirates" in the Mediterranean shortly thereafter. Above all, Bullet is a transcolonial threat set in stark contrast to white domestic purity. A witness hopes Bullet will "answer fur some o' the black deeds he's fathered, under one name or another."[55] "The "black deed's he's fathered" explicitly refer to his piracy but also introduce the specter of miscegenation. The Caribbean-based pirate is part of a familial lineage set apart from national fellow feeling. Readers do learn that Bullet sires and abandons a son, as if to affirm his virility as well as his utter rejection of domesticity. Indeed, a witness "don't care what high soundin' title he's borrowed or stolen, it's all the same whether you call him Hebrew Bullet, the Black Bull o' the Indies, Cap'n Josselyn of his Majesty's Roy'l Navy, or the very Evil One himself."[56] The pirate's "borrowed or stolen" transnational identity informs the extent of his evil and reflects his false claims to multiple sovereigns. The pirate's alignment with Africanness, Jewishness, and West Indian Blackness code his threat as a racial and multinational subject. His capacity to pass as an Englishman shows that such unruliness may hide under the cover of whiteness. Bullet's "apt use of French phrases," also a characteristic of the pirate Henrique Pedrillo in Catharine Maria Sedgwick's *Clarence*, powers his influence over individuals and nations.[57]

This alleged pirate, the like English pirate king George and the reputed Confederate president Jefferson Davis, controls a powerful oceanic force with claims to sovereignty. The narrator makes it clear that piracy implicates an entire community whose appeals to fellow feeling do not remove their guilt. In the *Jefferson Davis* and *Savannah* trials, the defense attempted to argue that the defendants' earnest attachment to secession and its sympathetic power distinguished them from pirates. Cummins rejected this line of thinking. Bullet's capacity to bind men to his cause, or his dark and enslaving power of sympathy, aligns him with both Confederate officials and revolutionaries who are capable of fomenting revolution across racial lines. His "mastery over his men" and the "despotism of his iron will" are so "tyrannic," "fierce," and "cruel" that at first these men seem to "[serve] simply as his tools" or be "his slaves." Bullet has an absolute power of sympathy and, it seems, an enslaver's lack of feeling. Even so, the narrator notes that "all shared the guilt."[58] One pities men under the control of stronger natures, she implies, but those feelings do not remove piratical agents' responsibility to the law. Moreover, Bullet "evidently had some early opportunities, and [he] at least affects education and refinement."[59] As in prior narratives, a pirate who has been exposed to moral sentiments is the most dangerous of all. He reveals that not all freely give themselves to the state or its families.

As the novel's privateering hero, George not only has the material means to reject piracy but also models a march to freedom that may or may not include Black subjects. George and his companion, who have been captured by Algerian corsairs, demonstrate the domestic nation's martial powers against pirates when they are, "by the prowess of our infant navy, released from their hopeless bondage."[60] Sumner had mobilized the Algerian captivity narrative to frame abolitionist sympathies. *Haunted Hearts*, however, does not explicitly connect white slaves to Black ones. Instead, it establishes a seemingly clear anti-Confederate paradigm that nonetheless maps an unclear and ambivalent racial politics. In a reversal of the middle passage, George is shipped from the Americas and forced to toil "under an African sun." Such charged language both connects to and abstracts from the novel's contemporary moment. George's place in a Surinam merchant house makes plantation spoils a fit reward for moral action. After his escape from enslavement, he accepts the "countenance, aid, and advancement of his interests which grew naturally out of his friendly and sympathetic relations with the family of the Surinam merchant." During this "natural" economic advancement, George's investment in a slave economy is neither addressed nor commented upon. The Dutch had abolished slavery in Surinam in 1863, a year before the novel's publication, but a ten-year so-called transitional period ensured its practical sanction. The slave trade was certainly still in effect in 1817, the year the novel recounts. In other words, latent threats to white middle-class domesticity are overcome by an environment of white colonial control.[61]

In an exercise of transcolonial power, George captains the vessel of a Surinam merchant to capture Bullet in a daring privateering raid. George's ship is named the *Antelope*, just like the enslaving vessel at the center of the 1825 Supreme Court case. As I discussed in chapter 1, in an uncharacteristic deferral to foreign sovereigns, the Court sent the majority of the enslaved aboard the *Antelope* to their Spanish and Portuguese enslavers. Enslavement was not piracy when done in the service of an enslaving foreign relation, the Piracy Act of 1820 notwithstanding. The *Antelope* case made piratical oceanic enslavement legally compatible with the trade's domestic protections. Whether intentional or not, this echo speaks to Cummins's shared investment in a sentimental jurisprudence of appeasement and proslavery foreign relations. Only a racially pure Dutch-American hero whose name aligns him with George Washington can overcome the racially ambiguous villain. The narrator affirms, "Nature meant [George] to be, the best specimen of the best stock" according to the standards of "birth and blood."[62] The fetishization of his lineage, this naming of his distinction from men such as Bullet, relies on racially charged discourses of "blood" and "stock" that aim to naturalize his whiteness and class standing. White supremacy remains entrenched in appeals to natural law. As the novel's white privateering hero, George binds himself to both nation and global economic interests. In the process, he acts as a symbol for those held under enslaving pirates such as Black Bullet and, it seems, the Confederacy. George explains that his zeal in attacking Bullet via a Surinam merchant ship can be attributed "to five years of bondage and cruelty, and hard labour imposed on me by men of their stamp; to my knowing what it is to be my own master, and what it is to be a slave; to the chains that have eaten my flesh to the bone."[63] This speech shares the language of abolitionism: enslavement's "bondage and cruelty" is a crime against familial feeling, which George defines as "homesickness . . . eaten into my heart." Echoes of Judge Joseph Story remain. In the novel, Black figures have no share of sympathy despite their centrality in systems of piratical enslavement. Racial otherness, when invoked, is attributable to the "barbarities" of pirates whose very subjectivity is attached to "crimes of the darkest dye."[64] Likewise, George's familial characterization of Surinam and its leading merchants belies the port's centrality in the South American slave trade.

The novel's paradigmatic marriage, made domestically but linked to Surinam, echoes Lincoln's "prioritization of Latin America over Liberia" as a site for Black postwar colonization and domestic homes for white men. After Bullet's guilty verdict, George and Angie consecrate their reunion by traveling to Surinam. The trip reaffirms white land ownership and benevolent colonization as a form of fellow feeling. The days following their reunion find George showing Angie "an account of travels in South America" that are corroborated by his own experience. He recalls, "O, the sail up that river is delightful! . . . I was thinking of you all the time I was there!" The narrator does not state why George sailed into Surinam's interior, though the image is as incongruous as a delightful sail down the river in the American South. Nor do readers learn of the work he performed there. Instead, George simply declares that "breathing the delicious climate" will rejuvenate Angie after her period of trouble.[65] The pestilential Brazil dramatized in *The Lamplighter* is part of a violent southern circuit. This South American nation can be made amenable with white domesticity. As in *The Lamplighter*, the foreign mail is a tool for and a symbol of sympathy's extension in an American global empire. The couple's success in Surinam, as well as in "future and more extended voyages," is "evidenced by scraps of foreign correspondence" and "by a reciprocal friendship . . . between her and George's friends at the South American port."[66] The black mark of piracy has given way to a model domestic marriage predicated on white supremacy. Indian muslin may replace U.S. southern cotton as a material and symbolic support of American empire. Seeing Angie handle "a certain piece of India muslin (one of his gifts)," George boasts, "You must wear it the day we send for the dominie; and in Surinam half a dozen such dresses wont be too many; they all wear white in Surinam." The fine white wedding dress worn on "the day we send for the dominie" (the term for a pastor in the Dutch Reformed Church) will multiply into many such dresses when she enters the Surinam merchants' social circle. Indeed, a predominantly non-abolitionist church performs this sanctification of northern domesticity. As historian of religion Evan Haefeli notes, the Dutch Reformed Church "did not play a role in the ending of slavery. In fact,

Dutch Americans in New York and New Jersey proved to be some of the fiercest opponents of abolition."[67]

Her novel's elisions on abolition notwithstanding, Cummins's political vision in *Haunted Hearts* is more explicitly ambivalent than it had been in previous fiction. As in *The Lamplighter*, the novel's final reunion of would-be lovers necessitates the removal of miscommunications that had prevented true feeling's expression. The miscommunication in the 1854 novel is banal: Gertrude believes, with reason, that Willie has romantic feelings for his boss's daughter. In contrast, the final hurdle in *Haunted Hearts* reflects persistent wartime obstacles. First, Angie must convince George she does not still love the pirate Bullet, for he believes "if she ha[s] pined for anyone, it ha[s] been for this deceitful gallant." George must also forgive Angie for thinking he was, in his words, "an unnatural, cruel, bloodthirsty villain" who murdered his uncle. In this period of wartime fratricide, such mistaken sympathy for pirates may be both unspeakably wicked and politically plausible.[68] While the would-be lovers' internal resolution is hard won, the pirate Bullet is not made compatible with fellow feeling. Nor is this fundamental source of domestic disruption explained. As the Civil War itself had shown, not all subjects could be redeemed. In a late chapter, titled "The Dark Side of the Picture," readers learn that no charges have been filed against the murderers of George's uncle or against the cousin responsible for faking George's suicide. Justice against evil is therefore incomplete, and the seeds of familial and national discord remain. Moreover, Bullet's utter depravity undermines sympathy's material power as a form of natural law. As he awaits his execution, the jail chaplain notes that the pirate has "revealed to me more of the possible degradation of our human nature than I ever saw before or expect to see again." Bullet's execution brings no great joy to the murdered man's wife or community, who "could derive [no] satisfaction from such horrors."[69] Such death, though framed as necessary, does not prevent the violence that preceded it. One's best hope is to remove the pirate from domestic and transoceanic space.

As in *The Lamplighter* and other domestic fictions, the economically secure domestic space stands in for a national ideal. Cummins's conclusion, published as the Civil War entered its fourth year, reveals a desire to maintain a prior union despite an unprecedented domestic break. It ostensibly resolves the novel's lingering unrest and, in the process, preserves antebellum legal culture for a postbellum future. The model for repaying the "debt of love, compassion, forgiveness, sympathy, which each owes to all," as promised in the preface, appears to be the restoration of white middle-class hegemony that shaped many antebellum visions of national union. Indeed, George and Angie's home is indistinguishable from Gertrude and Willie's. After some time at sea, George becomes a "landlord, farmer, citizen, and benefactor."[70] Through a domestication of privateering (and potentially slaveholding) spoils, he models the agrarian citizen-subject who may replace the slaveholder and the enslaved, while Angie stands as "the centre and light of a domestic circle." Although the *Jefferson Davis* defense had argued that "the meanest wretch . . . is still the centre of a circle," the narrator of *Haunted Hearts* affirms a "centre and light" defined by a model white middle-class subject. Cummins extended this familial model to her contemporary moment: the tavern that initially serves as Black Bullet's lair is, by novel's end, "the centre to which old hearts cling, haunted only now by grateful memories of the blessings which have crowned their days, and by the serene and joyful hopes which gild their sunset."[71] The space invaded by pirates may be restored, even if the pirates cannot. "Haunted hearts" may turn "grateful." Reference to the now-aged Angie and George's "serene and joyful hopes" during the "sunset" of their lives ties them to contemporaneous readers in a shared Civil War present. In this moment of temporal union, Cummins chose to cling to antebellum models of removing piratical sources of discord. She retained racial hierarchies while also rejecting enslavement. In other words, she called for the protection of white supremacy even after the granting of Black legal rights, an approach that Catharine Maria Sedgwick and her political contemporaries had previously championed (see chapter 1). Continued reliance on these antebellum models of appeasement left both Cummins and other legal thinkers without a clear response to postbellum realities.

"AN INDISSOLUBLE RELATION": UNIONIST PALIMPSEST IN *TEXAS V. WHITE* (1869)

Cummins's preservation of union, which necessitated the healing of haunted hearts and the rejection of domestic breaks, would find its most complete legal backing in the postbellum Supreme Court. By 1869, the Court would legally negate secession as piratical. Like Cummins, the postbellum Court was attempting to preserve the sovereign nation's legal coherence amid political conflict. Drawing from the Constitution as a shared memory, the ostensibly neutral justices treated antebellum legal precedence as both palimpsest and fixed point. Then and now, past legal precedent exists in a continual present and must be projected onto an uncertain future. Judicial opinions accrete like geological strata in an ever-growing legal record. Any such "textual trope of law as palimpsest," notes theorist Frans-Willem Korsten, "emphasizes a temporality that involves the law's textual and archival history." In this case, the legal theories embedded in palimpsestuous pirate fictions such as *Haunted Hearts* are mirrored in judicial decisions whose plots verge on historical fiction. Like Cummins, the postbellum Supreme Court promoted temporally layered narratives to preserve national familial union as a thing of the past, present, and future. Justices' reliance on palimpsest also led, somewhat counterintuitively, to declarations of legal fixity across time. Their legal declarations attempted to define the present, redefine the past, and predefine the future in a Unionist image. Where to fix the law remained up for debate by the war's close, as did the federal judiciary's ability to erase past wrongs, particularly in regards to enslavement. As the Court confirmed in *Texas v. White*, appeasements of white supremacist policy and denials of Black enfranchisement would define postbellum legal culture.[72]

The postbellum Court faced these questions of Union and palimpsest when adjudicating the secessionist government's legal legacy. Though the Confederacy surrendered on May 9, 1865, its legal status was not securely decided until April 12, 1869. As historian Stephen Neff notes, surrender gave the Confederacy the legal status of "subjugation," a defeated side "utterly vanquished and occupied" and "wholly disappeared as a legal and political entity." Even so, questions remained as to "whether that would-be nation [had] left any legal residues" in the new postbellum United States.[73] Could the legal slate be wiped clean? Would Confederate foes, conquered on the battlefield, be tried as treasonous pirates? Would proslavery laws have legal power? The war may have been over by 1865, but the question of Black enfranchisement and domestic reparations loomed large. Reconstruction was a legal, political, and martial program for occupying former secessionist states. Its goal, ostensibly, was to install something like Black enfranchisement and postbellum legal order. The Constitution's Fourteenth Amendment, ratified in 1868, protected the citizenship of all persons "born or naturalized in the United States," giving them "equal protection of the laws" and "due process of law." The amendment also stripped the representational power of former secessionist states, allegedly limiting voting rights following "participation in rebellion, or other crime" and denying rights to federal office to those who had "engaged in insurrection or rebellion."[74] Postbellum legal culture was, constitutionally speaking, abolitionist. As before, however, the power of white familial supremacy would remain strong. Despite ongoing domestic breaks, Cummins's sentimental vision—one of temporary threat giving way to domestic security and imperial expansion—aligned with federal projections of postwar global order. The postbellum Supreme Court, like Cummins, treated secessionists as pirates whose feelings were criminal and thus had no legal power. The Court's appeal to a loving familial state did not resolve the era's pervasive political fractures.

An unresolved question in both *Haunted Hearts* and federal law was secessionist legal culture's postbellum definition and punishment. Notably, Jefferson Davis's fitness to stand trial for treason was set be heard by the Supreme Court in 1868, following years of legal debate, but President Andrew Johnson's December 1868 declaration of amnesty for all Confederates allowed that question to be deferred. As Cynthia Nicoletti writes, shortly after Johnson decriminalized secessionist forms of bond in the name of political reconciliation, bureaucratic questions about federal bonds provided "a far less volatile context" to legally negate secession. *Texas v. White* hinged on whether Texas-owned U.S. federal bonds had been illegally sold by the Confederate government and therefore could be reclaimed by postbellum Texas. The Court invalidated the sale and decided five to three in favor of Texas. Although the decision represented a "halfhearted attempt to settle the secession question," it also preserved antebellum legal culture's claim to sympathy.[75] At heart, the Court argued that the Confederacy had never possessed sovereignty according to the Constitution. In other words, it appealed to the power to "define and punish piracy" that had been key in antebellum legal culture. Befitting ongoing legal and political tangles, however, the dissent presented an alternative vision: that postbellum legal culture required necessary checks against Reconstruction policy. This dissent was written by Justice Robert C. Grier, who had directed the jury against secessionist sailors in the 1861 *Jefferson Davis* piracy case and argued against secessionist maritime policy in the 1863 *Prize Cases*. With the war won, Grier was now presenting a more sympathetic vision of secessionist fellow feeling that ran contrary to his wartime thinking. As *Texas v. White* made clear, legal narrations of fellow feeling would not solve persistent questions about Black political enfranchisement and white piratical terror. Even so, the decision shared many narrative and ideological features with *Haunted Hearts*: the Court framed the sovereignty of the United States as unbroken, characterized the sympathy among its citizens as one of voluntary moral virtue, and named the shared domesticity that resulted as perfect. In short, it made the preservation of union the final legal act against antebellum piracy.

As in prior legal decisions, popular narrations, and Cummins's *Haunted Hearts*, the Supreme Court tied colonial fellow feeling to postbellum union. "The Union of States never was a purely artificial and arbitrary relation," wrote Chief Justice Salmon Chase. "It began among the Colonies, and grew out of common origin, mutual sympathies, kindred principles, similar interests, and geographical relations." In short, the nation was based on subjects' attachment to each other via willful fellow feeling: "mutual sympathies" and "kindred principles" created domestic legal bonds whose only limits were "geographic relations." Sympathy—and, by extension, federal union—could not be "artificial" or "arbitrary." This legal claim, which echoes Charles Sumner's appeal to an American postal empire, sympathetically aligns the federal state's growth with its subjects' fellow feeling. Incorporated states such as Texas were made domestic because of later enactments of sympathy, or "the incorporation of a new member into the political body." This later union "was final, . . . as complete, as perpetual, and as indissoluble as the union between the original States." Confederate sovereignty was denied due to a supposedly axiomatic premise: federal union was "perfect and unimpaired" because, once entered, it created "an indissoluble relation." Chase thus framed the war as a "suppression of rebellion" rather than an act of secessionist sovereignty.

For Chase, any proposed alternative to total union was an unacceptable deviation from antebellum legal culture because such proposals required the recognition of feelings beyond the federal state. Indeed, the judge claimed that any other decision would render the prior events a "war for conquest and subjugation" in which "the State must have become foreign, and her citizens foreigners." Because Confederate sovereignty was based on this very premise, neither Texas nor any seceding state could be said to have broken domestic union. National sympathy once again held legal sway. Chase, however, maintained that the states were like so many individual bodies freely giving themselves to sentimental union: "The perpetuity and indissolubility of the Union by no means implies the loss of distinct and individual existence, or the rights of self-government by the states." Each state and national subject's "distinct and individual existence" necessarily fed into the national whole. Self-interest led to a national family, as had been the case in antebellum domestic fictions. The pirate lacked legal or moral stake in this union.[76]

Though Grier would come to dissent against this 1869 opinion, he had previously relied on a similar language of threatened but unbroken sympathy to reject Confederate sovereignty. National union could not be adjudicated, or so he directed jurors in the 1861 *Jefferson Davis* piracy trial. Indeed, he had expressly forbidden that jury from considering the Confederacy as sovereign because this was a *political* rather than strictly *judicial* question. He had used the premise that the court could only "execute the laws of the United States" and therefore must define piracy as action against that state and punish accordingly. "The right to secede is not to be found in the Constitution," he had told the jury and had prevented them from claiming secessionist sovereignty as a legal defense to the charges of piracy. Instead, he had told the jury they must consider the defendants' crimes against a "Government and Constitution ordained by the people of the Whole United States for all time." In a deviation from prior legal thinking, he had defined piracy as an act that could not be qualified by sympathetic attachment to a sovereign. Had the defendants done what was alleged? If so, they were pirates whose claims to secessionist forms of bond had no legal standing. This new directive foreclosed any legal alternative to temporal, geographic, and affective union. To consider otherwise was to falsely treat the Constitution as "a mere temporary compact of independence and sovereign confederates." In other words, constitutionalism required feelings of union.[77] This directive may explain why the *Jefferson Davis* jury had seen guilty pirates whereas the *Savannah* jury had not.

The Court's dissenting opinion in *Texas v. White* revealed that such sentimental union remained elusive. Grier had rejected any claim of Confederate sovereignty in the *Jefferson Davis* case. He had validated federal power over secessionists in the *Prize Cases*. Now, however, he challenged both opinions after the war had been won. National feeling was fit for adjudication amid the Reconstruction-era policies that Grier abhorred. Unlike Chase, he favored what he called the "political fact" of secessionist sovereignty over a "legal fiction" of postbellum union: "*Politically*, Texas is not a State in this Union." In a domestic fiction of his own, Grier presented Texas as a sovereign matriarch whose poor family management did not give an equally suspect postbellum patriarch the right to ravage her body. A "very ill-advised" secession was, in his opinion, "the sovereign act of a sovereign State" because it had been "submitted to a vote of the people." Texas had, in selling "her" government bonds, performed home economics in a time of war: "She . . . set aside all her contracts . . . with her own citizens, for food, clothing, or medicines." This decision must be judged "in her own courts" rather than the federal court, Grier argued, because secessionist Texas had not been political or culturally reincorporated into the national family. The Court lacked standing, despite "her" request that it hold "the contradictory positions that she is a State in the Union and was never out of it, and yet not a State at all for four years." If "she acted and claims to be 'an organized political body'" during the war, then "she is estopped from denying her identity" when recovering the bonds would be politically expedient. Eschewing federal law for feelings of domestic aggrievement presumed to have legal force, he judged that reconstruction policy was not that of a benevolent patriarch. The federal government "govern her as a conquered province, to subject her to military domination, and keep her in pupilage." Setting aside federal law in favor of something like popular sovereignty, he thus argued that statehood relied on a mutual exchange of fellow feeling between national subjects. Without it, Texas had not been freely incorporated as a free state. It was akin to "Indian tribes, who are governed by military force." In practice, the systematic breaking of legal treaties proved that the state had ignored legal sovereignty in the name of white supremacist "union." In a careful reversal, Grier focused on the violence felt by secessionist states. Despite the majority appeal to restored union, this secessionist fellow feeling shaped a postwar period defined by both Black political gains and persistent disenfranchisement.[78]

As was the case in antebellum legal culture, modern invocations of *White v. Texas* rely on competing visions of national familial union amid racial disunion. The decision is, according to Mark R. Killenbeck, one of "three seismic events" in the repudiation of secessionist legal approaches. The other two are the Confederacy's legal surrender at Appomattox Courthouse in 1865 and the Supreme Court's repudiation of the Arkansas governor's attempt to nullify federal desegregation in *Cooper v. Aaron* (1958).[79] Although the court rejected secession's legality in *White v. Texas*, Christopher Heath Wellman notes that they distinguished between "unilateral secession and secession by mutual agreement." A national divorce could theoretically happen if all parties desired, although neither the Court nor the Constitution provided ready mechanisms. After all, the state's legal power was predicated on mutual sympathies and national union. Yet alternative legal visions abound. Wellman, for example, argues for a "moral right to secede" so long as the "political divorce" leaves both political bodies functional. In a modern spin of a secessionist legal culture, he asserts that one must respect the "rationality of feeling connected to conationals" as akin to a form of "fellow feeling among teammates."[80] New secessionist sovereignties have not come to pass. Yet they continue to hold legal sway. Indeed, *Texas v. White* continues to be cited in Supreme Court decisions that uphold states' rights as a feeling stronger than legal federalism. One example includes the gutting of civil rights–era voting protections in *Shelby County v. Holder* (2013) due to their alleged anachronism. The 1965 Voting Rights Act was itself a response to postbellum failures at Black enfranchisement. As in *Texas v. White*, the decision in *Shelby County* contained majority and dissenting opinions with competing sentimental narrations. Each hinged on whether racial animosity persisted and if such feeling would translate into legal inequality. In a testament to fellow feeling's pernicious potential, conservative justices successfully claimed that modern racial harmony as well as states' rights under *Texas v. White* justified a rollback of prior legal protections. This decision, we have seen, opened the door for racist policies of voter disenfranchisement in the present day.[81]

Antebellum legal culture was preserved if not perfected in *Texas v. White*. The antebellum era remained in narrative suspension, just as it had in Cummins's final novel. The circularity of Justice Chase's 1869 argument—union remained legally undissolved because it was an "indissoluble relation"—did not prevent its legal power. Nor did the circularity of Cummins's 1864 literary assertion—union will overcome haunted hearts because haunted hearts are proof of union—preclude its narrative potency. Both legal thinkers preserved antebellum fellow feeling to project a postbellum union. Neither took full account of the white supremacist backlash that followed abolition and Black citizenship. To name the fictionality of these unionist legal and literary narratives is not to wish for secessionist alternatives. There is no single pirate foe to be slain, although white supremacy seems to be the closest candidate. American legal culture's white supremacist sympathies goes back to Jefferson and beyond. Legal thinkers' resulting representations of piracy have not been ideologically coherent, geographically fixed, or historically accurate. The pirate's legal potency derived from the nation's political instability. Figures such Cummins and the Supreme Court justices invoked sympathy to recall the past, define the present, and project the future. As they made clear, 1869 was a flashpoint. And so it remains.

EPILOGUE

MARRIAGE

Walt Whitman, "Passage to India" (1869), and A. S. R. v. Trump *(2025)*

> Year at whose open'd, wide-flung door I sing!
> Year of the purpose accomplish'd!
> Year of the marriage of continents, climates and oceans!
>
> —Walt Whitman, "Passage to India" (1869)

Though Walt Whitman first published "Passage to India" in the second edition of *Leaves of Grass* (1872), he began drafting the poem during the Civil War.[1] In 1889, three years before his death, the poet gave his biographer Horace Traubel an outline for "one of the war-time manuscripts—written in Washington." The outline's prefatory page reads: "? quite a long piece—/ The spinal Idea That the divine efforts of heroes, and their ideas, faithfully lived up to, will finally prevail, and be accomplished however long deferred."[2] Like Maria Susanna Cummins and other wartime writers, Whitman had tried to imagine how moral union could follow global unrest. In 1869, the year of *Texas v. White*, Whitman was still working on "Passage to India," a poem that shares the Supreme Court's logic in the case. Antebellum "divine efforts" had sanctified union and prevailed over temporary fracture. For Whitman, antebellum victory—and, with it, the postbellum empire—could be proven by the opening of the Suez Canal. "Every great problem," according to his manuscript outline, "is The Passage to India." Whitman had drawn two hands pointing to this line, as if inserting his body into the sentence to make its power felt.[3] Writings in the popular press largely matched this jubilant vision. In a May 1869 cover story, a reporter for *The New York Times* declared, "The link which binds the civilization of the most ancient time to the most modern—which unites the age of Solomon . . . to this living and breathing century—is trade with the Indies."[4] Both poet and reporter announced an imminent spatial, temporal, and imperial union. "The whole earth," the poet sang of the canal's completion, "shall be completely justified." This justification would be narrative, moral, and martial. Once technology was in place, all bodies would be sympathetically attached. And all would be *compelled* to enjoy American imperial supremacy. Without crimes against feeling, the tensions that had plagued antebellum legal culture would cease to be. The pirate could finally marry a family of nations in a networked globe.[5]

In one sense, Whitman was correct. The year 1869 marked a shift to a postbellum imperialist legal culture. Historicizing this moment is key to combatting destructive forms of state violence performed in the name of moral feeling, an issue that persists to the present day. The Suez Canal's completion that year was the product of complex foreign relations and ongoing political competition.[6] The canal was, as the Egyptologist Valeska Huber explains, "a nodal point and lynchpin of various forms of mobility during an earlier wave of global interconnection." It "increasingly regulated and stigmatized" certain forms of movement and ushered in new forms of political violence.[7] Whitman, however, imagined the canal as transcending ocean politics. Scholars have likewise celebrated his poem's grand political and metaphysical scope. As David S. Reynolds writes, the poem was a "quintessential statement of Whitman's relationship to the new America." This postbellum nation remained deeply tied to antebellum legal culture around piracy.[8] Whitman announced 1869 as the "year of the marriage of continents, climates and oceans!" With the completion of the Suez Canal and the American transcontinental railroad, also finished that year, the world had ostensibly transcended national boundaries in favor of global infrastructure. Whitman wrote:

> In the Old World, the east, the Suez canal,
> The New by its mighty railroad spann'd,
> The seas inlaid with eloquent, gentle wires.[9]

Antebellum figures had presented such infrastructures as key to defeating piracy. Now the transcontinental "mighty railroad" linked the "the east" to the terrestrial United States. The transoceanic French-Atlantic cable, yet another project completed in 1869, created "seas inlaid with eloquent gentle wires." As

Charles Sumner had done, Whitman imbued these wires with deep feeling that portended an ever greater global union. In this modern world, Gertrude Flint's letters would move faster than ever.

No pirates invade Whitman's poem. In antebellum legal culture, pirates had embodied a host of anxieties about enslavement, white supremacy, and imperial hierarchies. Antebellum figures had invoked piracy in part to acknowledge their families' morally complicated ocean politics. Most had staged pirates' defeat to justify dominant imperial subjects' legal sanction and moral supremacy. For Whitman, however, the events of 1869 had negated all possible crimes against feeling. This lack of anxiety, and the accompanying absence of piracy, powered his seemingly more politically inclusive yet unmistakably violent domestic fiction. "The races, neighbors, to marry," the poet announced, "Europe to Asia, Africa join'd, and they to the New / World." In his vision, the racial tension typically introduced by the pirate has been replaced with a triumphant ease. All sovereign subjects shall be "brides and bridegrooms hand in hand." The world will share domestic interiority. In "lands to be welded together," spaces with no contested oceans, piracy is materially impossible.[10] The promise of the feeling state has been realized.

Such a vision, shared by the era's imperialist vanguard, promoted bounding progress and binding violence. Take, for example, the 1869 Suez dispatches of the Civil War veteran Henry Morton Stanley (who notably had served on both the Confederate and Union sides). Stanley wrote for the *New York Herald*, which had covered many of the period's piracy trials. Echoing Sumner's hoped-for "empire over a willing world," Stanley now asserted that "the world, moved by steam and girded by telegraphs, [would] be made one in community of interest." This new world empire, he concluded, would arise thanks to "the enlightened bond which unites, and the powerful leverage which moves, it may be said almost thinks for, the whole." In reality, many subjects objected to a forced marriage with empire. Yet Whitman's poetry and Stanley's journalism denied the legal force and very existence of such feelings. In practice, Stanley's imperial explorations aided King Leopold II of Belgium as he instituted his 1885 genocidal policies in the Congo Free State. The ensuing European pillage of Africa was, to quote Whitman with some of my own added resentment, "along all history, down the slopes."[11]

Whitman, like many of this book's figures, was nothing if not sincere. His note to Traubel that the poem was "more of me, the essential ultimate me, . . . than [is] in any of the [other] poems" suggests as much.[12] "Passage to India," like antebellum sentimental culture itself, was an earnest attempt to imagine global connection. Scholars such as Marianne Noble have deftly pushed against assumptions of sympathy's "dubious value" to show a "passionate yearning for genuine human contact."[13] One may appreciate such sincerity's cultural history without apologizing for its politics. "Sincerity triumphs by forgetting alternatives," cautions Ana Schwartz in her biopoetical study of colonial American sincerity's deep violence. Sincere belief by God's self-styled chosen people brought many anguishes to its colonial believers and led to much political violence against Indigenous communities.[14] Antebellum sincerity about piracy often functioned similarly. The desire for a national family was, it seems, often sincerely felt. While I do not fully share this sincerity, I do, as Schwartz models, take such feelings seriously. This book has foregrounded sentimental fictions whose historical specificity and deep sincerity have perhaps diminished their current cultural purchase. Vitally, I also take seriously the forgotten alternatives that such writers appeared to sincerely reject. Proponents of white upper-class heterosexual supremacy feel little for political alterity, even as sympathy's political complexity is often overlooked. Antebellum legal culture is historically valuable because of these moral complexities, not in spite of them. So, too, are sentiments whose supposed basis in piratical unfeeling—including resentment, anger, and disgust toward the American state—often derives from an equally sincere rejection of antebellum white supremacy as a legal and moral model.

MAKE AMERICA ANTEBELLUM AGAIN: LEGAL CULTURE UNDER TRUMP

Whitman's appeal to "The Past! the Past! the Past!" recalls us to piracy's enduring power across modern legal culture. The "piracy analogy"—that is, presentations of piracy as a legal precedent and a moral antecedent—remains a powerful tool in domestic courts' claims to universal jurisdiction over international human rights violations, as Mark Chadwick has shown. In particular, as Joel H. Samuels writes, the piracy case *United States v. Smith* (1820) "continues to spawn core arguments in modern-day civil cases" on global issues "ranging from environmental degradation in Latin America to apartheid-era investment in South Africa, as well as criminal trials of foreign terrorists."[15] The United States' own international human rights violations during an early twentieth-century "war on terror" relied, as Rebecca Sanders has shown, on "plausible legality." Both Democrats and Republicans defined and punished piratical terrorism via laws whose speculative merits need not rise to the standard of sound legal proof in a politically complicit legal culture.[16] More recently, antebellum piracy law has served white supremacy in a retrograde legal culture dedicated to "Make America Great Again." White supremacy under the guise of fellow feeling retains legal force. State violence persists in the name of national union against piracy. President Donald Trump has indicated that no court will prevent his policies of mass deportation, extrajudicial murder, and civil rights violations. Whether a modern Supreme Court led by Chief Justice John Roberts and defined by rightwing political capture will check executive power remains to be seen. History suggests some doubts. After all, the antebellum court did not end enslavement. It did not stop Andrew Jackson's illegal policies of removal. Fittingly, then, one of Trump's first acts during his first and second terms was to redisplay Jackson's portrait in the Oval Office. Gazing backward, the Trump administration aims to make American legal culture antebellum again.

In Whitman's survey of ocean politics, the antebellum pirate could finally be married to a transcendent postbellum order. Contemporary rightwing political figures are demanding we renew more explicitly white supremacist vows they attribute to Jefferson's Declaration. Such legal demands hit home for teachers at Florida public schools, the state where I currently teach. For example, according to current state standards for public K–12 instructors, U.S. history "shall be defined as the creation of a new nation based largely on universal principles stated in the Declaration of Independence."[17] University faculty teaching in the core curriculum have a near-identical charge. A survey course containing this book's piracy texts is, arguably, illegal in Florida. It is unclear if the drafted version of the Declaration—and, with it, Jefferson's removed pirates—would add to this alleged crime. The existence of "something other" and the caveat "largely" represent a fissure in American history that is not fully closed by appeals to "universal principles." Left unstated is which version of the many-contested state we should feel toward, to say nothing of the alternative collectivities that figures such as the pirate provoked.

The primary demand, it seems, is that white supremacist feeling retains legal force. Related bans of critical race theory—accurately defined but demonized by the Florida legislature as "the theory that racism is not merely the product of prejudice, but that racism is embedded in American society and its legal systems in order to uphold the supremacy of white persons"—present political alternatives to white nationalism as piratical attacks. Included in this ban are accounts of piratical enslavement that began in 1619. After all, K–12 public teachers "may not utilize material from the 1619 Project." Piracy, when present, is aligned with racial and religious alterity whose defeat serves white supremacy. Public guidelines on "African American History," for example, promote a pernicious comparative history "on the condition of slavery as it existed in Africa, Asia, the Americas, and Europe prior to 1619." Teacher must stress "how trading in slaves developed in African lands." They are to highlight "the practice of Barbary pirates in kidnapping Europeans and selling them to slavery in Muslim countries."[18] As in many domestic pirate fictions, enslavement is staged as an African-derived institution directed against white people. Then and now, white supremacy may be justified as preferable to piratical Blackness. To feel otherwise is to become, perhaps, a pirate with no moral sense and therefore be removed as an agent of the state. Our teaching conditions—and, by extension, students' learning conditions—are thus defined by demands to foster a weak imitation of antebellum legal culture. Crosscurrents of history and identity flow into a single channel. The legalized impoverishing of interpretive possibility is a true crisis in our communities. The ship has sailed. Its ultimate destination is unknown.

Faced with white supremacist nostalgia for an antebellum past, at least one federal judge has invoked domestic pirate fiction to justify Trump's deportation policies. In *A. S. R. v. TRUMP* (2025), for example, the American Civil Liberties Union sued the Trump administration for its removal of ten Venezuelan migrants without due process. Each were alleged, without evidence, to be members of the supposed Tren de Aragua (TdA) gang. The administration justified its acts as both constitutional and supported by early American law such as the 1798 Alien Enemies Act. Detained migrants, it asserted, represent a "cohesive group of individuals united by a common goal," which goal, they infer, is unfeeling piratical unruliness against blameless American families. The result is an attempted removal of those nonwhite subjects who are deemed to be incompatible with the white supremacist state. Contrary to prior rulings, U.S. District Judge Stephanie Haines agreed in *A. S. R. v. Trump* that TdA represented a piratical "predatory incursion" and a "significant disruption to public safety." She did not consider "terrorist" to be the case's defining legal category, a word that, as she noted, was "not in significant use in 1798." Instead, she turned to piracy. "The Court calls the reader's attention to the fact that 'incursions' was used here in reference to both pirates and robbers," Haines wrote in reference to Secretary of State Marco Rubio's invocation of antebellum and modern law. "In reading this quotation, the Court cannot help but ask: Is a Foreign

Terrorist Organization like TdA not the modern equivalent of a pirate or robber?" Via an informal fallacy of begging the question, the Trump-appointed judge presumed the pirate analogy's legal application to migrants. Admittedly, she denied that foreign migration alone represented a "predatory incursion." Even so, she defined piracy as a way to punish migrants whom the state had deemed to be racially undesirable. She cited the piratical language of *Samuel Johnson's Dictionary* (1798) and Noah Webster's *American Dictionary* (1828) and legally outlined *predatory* as "plundering; practicing rapine" or "plunderng (*sic*); pillaging." As in the antebellum era, the power to define is linked to the power to punish.

Antebellum legal culture around piracy remains powerful due to its status as precedent. Judicial ignorance or obtuseness over an antebellum piracy case's context does not preclude its application, as cases such as *Rose v. Himley* (1808) have made clear. Notably, Haines also cited federal legal jurisdiction against "savages" as well as "enemies, pirates, and robbers" as established in *Worcester v. Georgia* (1832) to justify the administration's actions. In practice, that landmark Supreme Court case, heard by Justices John Marshall and Joseph Story, checked unmitigated federal power by affirming tribal sovereignty. Of course, President Jackson famously ignored the decision. Like Jackson's, Trump's feeling toward the law has been given legal force. The president's ability to define and punish piracies appears to be both universal and superior to the legislature's constitutionally granted power. The migrant, when proclaimed to be akin to the pirate and terrorist, has no legal right or state protection. Even as Haines presented the plaintiffs as united in piratical crimes against feeling, she later disbanded their claims as co-plaintiffs. The only relief she provided was a "continued temporary restraining order" on deportation so the plaintiffs could have time to understand the charges against them.[19] One recognizes traces of the judicial sleights of hand found in *Antelope*, *Amistad*, and other piracy cases. Jurists' faint checks to state violence on procedural grounds allow them to evade political reality. Legally dubious agents of the state capture and carry humans. They separate families. They murder activists. In short, they commit crimes against feeling.

No matter what follows, one thing is apparent: antebellum legal culture was not transcended in 1869. Both Whitman's marriage of pirates and modern political reality rest on intricate antebellum precedents. As Whitman himself declared, "The past! the infinite greatness of the past! / For what is the present, after all, but a growth out of the past?" The law! For what is the present law, after all, but a growth out of the past? Antebellum infrastructure, the poet claimed, was a "passage to more than India." It paralleled spiritual expansion. He applauded the "reckless" soul that voyaged "where mariner has not yet dared to go." We voyage to places that Whitman did not imagine. In a way, however, the poet named our present moment. He beckoned the sailor: "O farther, farther, farther sail!" He is still singing our days, singing the great achievements of the present legal culture. From this vantage, Whitman's eulogy sounds an alarm: "And we will risk the ship, ourselves and all."[20] We risk the ship. We risk ourselves. We risk all.

The appeasement of white supremacists in the name of an imagined political stability only increases these risks, as antebellum history makes clear. Antebellum legal culture's role in our present crisis, in addition to domestic pirate fiction's enduring descriptive power, is best concluded by a trial scene from *Haunted Hearts*. "Trump had wrought himself up to quite a pitch of excitement already; he had made some impression, too, on the jury and the audience; this he always did,—he had a magnificent power over audiences and juries."[21] Past impressions speak to our present beyond their historical bounds, as the law tends to do. The magnificent power to define and punish grows more capricious under a veneer of legality. International law, legal activism, and, indeed, civil disobedience have important roles to play in our collective response. Crimes against feeling—and, with them, the demands of legal, literary, and historical interpretation—will outlive the presidency of Donald J. Trump. A renewed dedication to legal reform, economic reparations, and social justice for those violated by the American state, rather than fictions of national moral union against piratical foes, must power the trials to come. All rise.

NOTES

INTRODUCTION

1. Pauline Maier, *American Scripture: Making the Declaration of Independence* (New York: Vintage, 1998), 120; David Armitage, *The Declaration of Independence: A Global History* (Cambridge, MA: Harvard University Press, 2008), 58; Thomas Jefferson, "'original Rough draught' of the Declaration of Independence," in *The Papers of Thomas Jefferson, Digital Edition*, eds. James P. McClure and J. Jefferson Looney (Charlottesville: University of Virginia Press, 2008).
2. William B. Warner, *Protocols of Liberty: Communication, Innovation, and the American Revolution* (Chicago: University of Chicago Press, 2013).
3. David Armitage, *The Declaration of Independence: A Global History* (Cambridge, MA: Harvard University Press, 2008), 58.
4. Paul M. Baepler, *White Slaves, African Masters: An Anthology of American Barbary Captivity Narratives* (Chicago: University of Chicago Press, 1999); Jacob Crane, *Blood and Ink: The Barbary Archive in Early American Literary History* (Amherst: University of Massachusetts Press, 2023).
5. Jefferson, "original Rough draught." See also Annette Gordon-Reed, *The Hemingses of Monticello: An American Family* (New York: Norton, 2009).
6. Richard A. Posner, *Law and Literature*, 3rd ed. (Cambridge, MA: Harvard University Press, 2009). For debates on law as literature, see Guyora Binder and Robert Weisberg, *Literary Criticisms of Law* (Princeton, NJ: Princeton University Press, 2000). For an overview of the field in an international context, see Alexandra Juster, *Law, Literature and Legal Counterfactuals: A Method of Contrastive Discourse Analysis Using the Example of Contemporary Literature* (New York: Springer, 2025). I cite numerous other examples throughout.
7. Lawrence M. Friedman, "Legal Culture and Social Development," *Law and Society Review* 4, no. 1 (1969): 34. See also José Juan Toharia, "Exploring Legal Culture: A Few Cautionary Remarks from Comparative Research," in *Law, Society, and History: Themes in the Legal Sociology and Legal History of Lawrence M. Friedman*, eds. Robert W. Gordon and Morton J. Horwitz (Cambridge, UK: Cambridge University Press, 2011), 90–100.
8. Rebecca Sanders, *Plausible Legality: Legal Culture and Political Imperative in the Global War on Terror* (Oxford, UK: Oxford University Press, 2018), 6. Saunders provides a compelling overview of legal culture's development as a scholarly keyword.
9. For a comprehensive breakdown of law in relation to speech acts, see Janet Ainsworth,

Lawrence Solan, and Roger W. Shuy, eds., *Speaking of Language and Law: Conversations on the Work of Peter Tiersma* (Oxford, UK: Oxford University Press, 2015).

10. M. H. Hoeflich, *Legal Publishing in Antebellum America* (Cambridge, UK: Cambridge University Press, 2010); Richard H. Brodhead, *Cultures of Letters: Scenes of Reading and Writing in Nineteenth-Century America* (Chicago: University of Chicago Press, 1993).
11. Cathy N. Davidson and Jessamyn Hatcher, eds., *No More Separate Spheres! A Next Wave American Studies Reader* (Durham, NC: Duke University Press, 2002).
12. Amy Kaplan, "Manifest Domesticity," *American Literature* 70, no. 3 (1998): 582.
13. "The Haitian Declaration of Independence," in *The Haitian Declaration of Independence: Creation, Context, and Legacy*, ed. Julia Gaffield (Charlottesville: University of Virginia Press, 2016), 239–40. Gaffield provides a translation and extensive context on the founding document's production and reception.
14. "Allegorical figure of America," Civil War Ephemera Collection, CW env. 2760, American Antiquarian Society, Worcester, MA.
15. Gary Peller, Kendall Thomas, Kimberlé Crenshaw, and Neil Gotanda, eds., *Critical Race Theory: The Key Writings That Formed the Movement* (New York: New Press, 1995); Richard Delgado and Jean Stefancic, eds., *Critical Race Theory: An Introduction*, 3rd ed. (New York: New York University Press, 2017).
16. Faith Barter, *Black Pro Se: Authorship and the Limits of Law in Nineteenth-Century African American Literature* (Chapel Hill: University of North Carolina Press, 2025), 1. See also Martha S. Jones, *Birthright Citizens: A History of Race and Rights in Antebellum America* (Cambridge, UK: Cambridge University Press, 2018); and Eric Cheyfitz, *The Colonial Construction of Indian Country: Native American Literatures and Federal Indian Law* (Minneapolis: University of Minnesota Press, 2023).
17. Sara E. Johnson, *Encyclopédie noire: The Making of Moreau de Saint-Méry's Intellectual World* (Chapel Hill: University of North Carolina Press, 2023); Sowande M. Mustakeem, *Slavery at Sea: Terror, Sex, and Sickness in the Middle Passage* (Champaign: University of Illinois Press, 2016).
18. Hazel Carby, *Reconstructing Womanhood: The Emergence of the Afro-American Novelist* (Oxford, UK: Oxford University Press, 1987), 31; Emily A. Owens, *Consent in the Presence of Force: Sexual Violence and Black Women's Survival in Antebellum New Orleans* (Chapel Hill: University of North Carolina Press, 2023), 14; Saidiya V. Hartman, "Venus in Two Acts." *Small Axe*, 26 (June 2008): 1.
19. Jefferson, "original Rough draught."
20. Peter Onuf, *Jefferson's Empire: The Language of American Nationhood* (Charlottesville: University of Virginia Press, 2000), 14.
21. Elizabeth Barnes, *States of Sympathy: Seduction and Democracy in the American Novel* (New York: Columbia University Press, 1997), 1–2.
22. Hans Turley, *Rum, Sodomy, and the Lash: Piracy, Sexuality, and Masculine Identity* (New York: New York University Press, 1999); Christopher Chitty, *Sexual Hegemony: Statecraft, Sodomy, and Capital in the Rise of the World System* (Durham, NC: Duke University Press, 2020).

23. Eric Schliesser, "Introduction: On Sympathy," in *Sympathy: A History*, ed. Eric Schliesser (Oxford, UK: Oxford University Press, 2015), 3; Adam Smith, *The Theory of Moral Sentiments* (1859), ed. Ryan Patrick Hanley (New York: Penguin, 2010), 13–14; Caleb Crain, *American Sympathy: Men, Friendship, and Literature in the New Nation* (New Haven, CT: Yale University Press, 2001), 4.
24. Ian Ward, "The Echo of a Sentimental Jurisprudence," *Law and Critique* 13, no. 1 (2002): 107–25.
25. Marianne Noble, "Introduction," in *Rethinking Sympathy and Human Contact in Nineteenth-Century American Literature: Hawthorne, Douglass, Stowe, Dickinson*, ed. Marianne Noble (Cambridge, UK: Cambridge University Press, 2019), 4. Scholarship by Shirley Samuels, Lora Romero, Karen Sanchez-Eppler, Dana Nelson, and Peter Coviello appears in Shirley Samuels, ed., *The Culture of Sentiment: Race, Gender, and Sentimentality in Nineteenth-Century America* (Oxford, UK: Oxford University Press, 1992).
26. Saidiya V. Hartman, *Scenes of Subjection: Terror, Slavery, and Self-making in Nineteenth-Century America* (Oxford, UK: Oxford University Press, 1997), 4; Lauren Berlant, *The Female Complaint: The Unfinished Business of Sentimentality in American Culture* (Durham, NC: Duke University Press, 2008), 35. See also Kyla Schuller, *Biopolitics of Feeling: Race, Sex, and Science in the Nineteenth-Century* (Durham, NC: Duke University Press, 2018); Erica Fretwell, *Sensory Experiments: Psychophysics, Race, and the Aesthetics of Feeling* (Durham, NC: Duke University Press, 2020); and Xine Yao, *Disaffected: The Cultural Politics of Unfeeling in Nineteenth-Century America* (Durham, NC: Duke University Press, 2021).
27. Sianne Ngai, *Ugly Feelings* (Cambridge, MA: Harvard University Press, 2005); Sara Ahmed, *Complaint!* (Durham, NC: Duke University Press, 2021); Kyla Wazana Tompkins, *Deviant Matter: Ferment, Intoxicants, Jelly, Rot* (New York: New York University Press, 2024).
28. Duncan Faherty, *The Haitian Revolution in the Early Republic of Letters* (Oxford, UK: Oxford University Press, 2023), 207; Davis Luis-Brown, *Waves of Decolonization: Discourses of Race and Hemispheric Citizenship in Cuva, Mexico, and the United States* (Durham, NC: Duke University Press, 2008), 47.
29. David Hume, "Essays Moral, Political, and Literary," in *David Hume on Morals, Politics, and Society*, eds. Andrew Valls and Angela Coventry (New Haven, CT: Yale University Press, 2018), 166. See also Geoffrey Sayre-McCord, "Hume and Smith on Sympathy, Approbation, and Moral Judgment," in Schliesser, *Sympathy*, 208–46.
30. Smith, *Moral Sentiments*, 13–14.
31. Smith, *Moral Sentiments*, 49.
32. Smith, *Moral Sentiments*, 51.
33. Ann Laura Stoler, *Along the Archival Grain: Thinking Through Colonial Ontologies* (Princeton, NJ: Princeton University Press, 2008), 58.
34. Suzanne Keen, "Affect and Empathy Studies," in *The Oxford Handbook of Law and Humanities*, eds. Bernadette Meyler, Maksymilian Del Mar, and Simon Stern (Oxford, UK: Oxford University Press, 2020), 191.

35. Joshua M. White, *Piracy and Law in the Ottoman Mediterranean* (Stanford, CA: Stanford University Press, 2017), 3.
36. Alexandra Ganser, *Crisis and Legitimacy in Atlantic American Narratives of Piracy: 1678–1865* (New York: Palgrave Macmillan, 2020), 175.
37. Frederick Schauer, “Why the Declaration of Independence Is Not Law—and Why It Could Be,” *South Carolina Law Review* 89, no. 1 (2016): 619–36.
38. Greta Olson, *From Law and Literature to Legality and Affect* (Oxford, UK: Oxford University Press, 2022), 6.
39. Jeannine Marie DeLombard, *Slavery on Trial: Law, Abolitionism, and Print Culture* (Chapel Hill: University of North Carolina Press, 2007); Joyce W. Warren, *Women, Money, and the Law: Nineteenth-Century Fiction, Gender, and the Courts* (Iowa City: University of Iowa Press, 2005); Karla F. C. Holloway, *Legal Fictions: Constituting Race, Composing Literature* (Durham, NC: Duke University Press, 2014).
40. Hans J. Lind, ed., *Fictional Discourse and the Law* (London: Routledge, 2020).
41. Ravit Reichman, “Law’s Affective Thickets,” in *New Directions in Law and Literature*, eds. Bernadette Meyler and Elizabeth S. Anker (Oxford, UK: Oxford University Press, 2017), 110.
42. Smith, *Moral Sentiments*, 257.
43. Stuart Banner, *The Decline of Natural Law: How American Lawyers Once Used Natural Law and Why They Stopped* (Oxford, UK: Oxford University Press, 2021), 2–3. See also Fabrizio Simon, “Adam Smith and the Law,” in *The Oxford Handbook of Adam Smith*, eds. Christopher J. Berry, Maria Pia Paganelli, and Craig Smith (Oxford, UK: Oxford University Press, 2013), 393–416; and Andrew Forsyth, *Common Law and Natural Law in America: From the Puritans to the Legal Realists* (Cambridge, UK: Cambridge University Press, 2019).
44. Smith, *Moral Sentiments*, 283–84.
45. Smith, *Moral Sentiments*, 14.
46. Smith, *Moral Sentiments*, 281.
47. Barnes, *States of Sympathy*, 85; Ken MacMillan, “Imperial Constitutions: Sovereignty and Law in the British Atlantic,” in *Britain’s Oceanic Empire: Atlantic and Indian Ocean Worlds, c. 1550–1850*, eds. H. V. Bowen, Elizabeth Mancke, and John G. Reid (Cambridge, UK: Cambridge University Press, 2012), 70.
48. For a legal overview of sovereign recognition within this system, see Sean D. Murphy and Edward T. Swaine eds., *The Law of U.S. Foreign Relations* (Oxford, UK: Oxford University Press, 2023). For a literary history of antebellum popular sovereignty, see Jennifer Greiman, *Democracy’s Spectacle: Sovereignty and Public Life in Antebellum American Writing* (New York: Fordham University Press, 2011).
49. Brian Russell Roberts and Michelle Stephens, “Introduction: Archipelagic American Studies: Decontinentalizing the Study of American Culture,” in *Archipelagic American Studies*, eds. Brian Russell Roberts and Michelle Stephens (Durham, NC: Duke University Press, 2017), iv. See also Brian Russell Roberts, *Borderwaters: Amid the Archipelagic States of America* (Durham, NC: Duke University Press, 2021).

50. Markus Rediker, *Villains of All Nations: Atlantic Pirates in the Golden Age* (New York: Verso, 2004), 29–30.
51. Lauren Benton, *A Search for Sovereignty: Law and Geography in European Empires, 1400–1900* (Cambridge, UK: Cambridge University Press 2010), 119–21.
52. Guy Chet, *The Ocean Is a Wilderness: Atlantic Piracy and the Limits of State Authority, 1688–1856* (Amherst: University of Massachusetts Press, 2014), 3–4.
53. Smith, *Moral Sentiments*, 178; Mark Chadwick, *Piracy and the Origins of Universal Jurisdiction: On Stranger Tides?* (Leiden: Brill Nijhoff, 2018), 6.
54. Lauren Benton and Lisa Ford, *Rage for Order: The British Empire and the Origins of International Law, 1800–1850* (Cambridge, MA: Harvard University Press, 2016), 119.
55. Benton, *Search for Sovereignty*, 134.
56. Smith, *Moral Sentiments*, 178, 270. For a comparative study of Smith and Grotius, see Fonna Forman, "Smith on 'connexion,' Culture, and Judgment," in *New Voices on Adam Smith*, eds. Leonidas Montes and Eric Schliesser (Routledge, 2006), 89–114.
57. Stephen D. Krasner, *Sovereignty: Organized Hypocrisy* (Princeton, NJ: Princeton University Press, 2001), 6. See also Anthony Giddens, *A Contemporary Critique of Historical Materialism: The Nation-State and Violence* (Berkeley: University of California Press, 1987).
58. Peter Linebaugh and Marcus Rediker, *The Many-Headed Hydra: Sailors, Slaves, Commoners, and the Hidden History of the Revolutionary Atlantic* (Boston: Beacon, 2000).
59. Mark G. Hanna, *Pirate Nests and the Rise of the British Empire, 1570–1740* (Chapel Hill: University of North Carolina Press, 2015), 16.
60. Charles Johnson, *A General History of the Robberies and Murders of the Most Notorious Pirates* (1724), ed. Arthur Hayward (London: Routledge, 1955), x–xi.
61. Douglas R. Burgess, *The Politics of Piracy: Crime and Civil Disobedience in Colonial America* (Lebanon, NH: University Press of New England, 2014), 3.
62. Hanna, *Pirate Nests*, 16.
63. U.S. Articles of Confederation, art. 6, para. 5, National Archives, Washington, DC, https://www.archives.gov.
64. Beth Stephens, "Federalism and Foreign Affairs: Congress's Power to 'Define and Punish . . . Offenses Against the Law of Nations,'" *William and Mary Law Review* 42, no. 447 (2000): 449–552; Eugene Kontorovich, "The 'Define and Punish' Clause and the Limits of Universal Jurisdiction," *Northwestern University Law Review* 103, no. 1 (2009): 150–204; Neil S. Siegel, *The Collective-Action Constitution* (Oxford, UK: Oxford University Press, 2024), 230–42.
65. Mary Sarah Bilder, *Madison's Hand: Revising the Constitutional Convention* (Cambridge, MA: Harvard University Press, 2015), 104; James Madison, "Madison Debates: Tuesday, September 14, 1787," in "Notes on the Debates in the Federal Convention," Avalon Project at the Yale Law School, http://avalon.law.yale.edu.
66. U.S. Constitution, art. 1, sec. 8, clause 10. National Archives, Washington, DC, https://www.archives.gov.

67. Madison, "Madison Debates: Tuesday, September 14, 1787."
68. U.S. Constitution, art. 1, sec. 8, clause 11.
69. Chet, *The Ocean Is a Wilderness*, 28.
70. Kylie A. Hulbert, *The Untold War at Sea: America's Revolutionary Privateers* (Athens: University of Georgia Press, 2022), 5.
71. "Resolutions of the Virginia Convention Calling for Independence. In Convention May the 15th, 1776," in McClure and Looney, *The Papers of Thomas Jefferson, Digital Edition*.
72. Thomas Jefferson, *Notes on the State of Virginia (1785)*, ed. Robert Pierce Forbes (New Haven, CT: Yale University Press, 2001), 213; Yao, *Disaffected*, 17.
73. Kevin P. McDonald, *Pirates, Merchants, Settlers, and Slaves: Colonial America and the Indo-Atlantic World* (Berkeley: University of California Press 2015), 19, 17. See also Nikole Hanna-Jones, ed., *The 1619 Project: A New Origin Story* (New York: Random House, 2021).
74. Jennifer L. Morgan, "Partus sequitur ventrem: Law, Race, and Reproduction in Colonial Slavery," *Small Axe* 22, no. 1 (2018): 3–6. See also Jennifer L. Morgan, *Laboring Women: Reproduction and Gender in New World Slavery* (Philadelphia: University of Pennsylvania Press, 2004).
75. Jack Russell Weinstein, *Adam Smith's Pluralism: Rationality, Education, and the Moral Sentiments* (New Haven, CT: Yale University Press, 2013), 86.
76. Adam Smith, *Lectures on Jurisprudence* (1762), eds. Ronald L. Meek, D. D. Raphael, and Peter Stein (Oxford, UK: Oxford University Press, 1978), 5.
77. Yao, *Disaffected*, 13.
78. Smith, *Moral Sentiments*, 239–40.
79. U.S. Constitution, art.1, sec. 2, clause 3.
80. James Madison, essay 54 (1788), in *The Federalist Papers*, ed. Ian Shapiro (New Haven, CT: Yale University Press, 2009), 278.
81. U.S. Constitution, art.1, sec. 9, clause 1.
82. U.S. Congress, An Act to Prohibit the Carrying on the Slave Trade from the United States to Any Foreign Place or Country, 1 Stat. 347 chap. 11 (1794), Avalon Project at the Yale Law School, http://avalon.law.yale.edu. For a legal history of such statutes, see Paul Finkelman, "The American Suppression of the African Slave Trade: Lessons on Legal Change, Social Policy, and Legislation," *Akron Law Review* 42, no. 2 (2000), 432–67.
83. Robert Mitchell, *Sympathy and the State in the Romantic Era: Systems, State Finance, and the Shadows of Futurity* (London: Routledge, 2014), 28.
84. Joseph Fichtelberg, *Critical Fictions: Sentiment and the American Market, 1780–1870* (Athens: University of Georgia Press, 2003), 7.
85. Margaret Cohen, "Literary Studies on the Terraqueous Globe," *PMLA* 125, no. 3 (2010), 658. See also Margaret Cohen, *The Novel and the Sea* (Princeton, NJ: Princeton University Press, 2021).
86. Melissa Gniadek, *Oceans at Home: Maritime and Domestic Fictions in Nineteenth-Century American Women's Writing* (Amherst: University of Massachusetts Press,

2021), 1. My frame complicates Amy Kaplan's claim that "movement outward into the world threatens to incorporate the foreign and dismantle the domestic" in the period's domestic fictions; see Kaplan's *The Anarchy of Empire in the Making of U.S. Culture* (Cambridge, MA: Harvard University Press, 2002), 12.

87. Michelle Burnham, "Oceanic Turns and American Literary History in Global Context" in *Turns of Event: American Literary Studies in Motion*, ed. Hester Blum (Philadelphia: University of Pennsylvania Press, 2016), 154. Like transoceanic studies, blue humanities treats oceanic environments as the central theoretical node. See Steve Mentz, *An Introduction to the Blue Humanities* (London: Routledge, 2023). These approaches are akin to various maritime area studies across the globe.
88. Margaret Fuller, *Woman in the Nineteenth-Century* (1845), in *The Essential Margaret Fuller*, ed. Jeffrey Steele (New Brunswick, NJ: Rutgers University Press, 1992), 345.
89. Mary Katherine Eyring, *Captains of Charity: The Writing and Wages of Postrevolutionary Atlantic Benevolence* (Durham: University of New Hampshire Press, 2017).
90. Jane Tompkins, *Sensational Designs: The Cultural Work of American Fiction, 1790–1860* (Oxford, UK: Oxford University Press, 1985), 1; Melissa J. Homestead, *American Women Authors and Literary Property, 1822–1869* (Cambridge, UK: Cambridge University Press, 2005), 3. See also Doron S. Ben-Atar, *Trade Secrets: Intellectual Piracy and the Origins of American Industrial Power* (New Haven, CT: Yale University Press, 2004).
91. Robin Miskolcze, *Women and Children First: Nineteenth-Century Sea Narratives and American Identity* (Lincoln: University of Nebraska Press, 2007); Ganser, *Crisis and Legitimacy*; Paul A. Gilje, *To Swear Like a Sailor: Maritime Culture in America, 1750–1850* (Cambridge, UK: Cambridge University Press, 2016); Sharada Balachandran Orihuela, *Fugitives, Smugglers, and Thieves: Piracy and Personhood in American Literature* (Chapel Hill: University of North Carolina Press, 2018).
92. James L. Machor, *Reading Fiction in Antebellum America: Informed Response and Reception Histories, 1820–1865* (Baltimore: Johns Hopkins University Press, 2011), 202.
93. Michelle Burnham, *Transoceanic America: Risk, Writing, and Revolution in the Global Pacific* (Oxford, UK: Oxford University Press, 2019), 2. For other national literary traditions, see Manushag N. Powell, ed., *British Pirates in Print and Performance* (New York: Palgrave Macmillan, 2015); Nina Gerassi-Navarro, *Pirate Novels: Fictions of Nation Building in Spanish America* (Durham, NC: Duke University Press, 1999); Doris L. Garraway, *The Libertine Colony: Creolization in the Early French Caribbean* (Durham, NC: Duke University Press, 2005); and Yuanfei Wang, *Writing Pirates: Vernacular Fiction and Oceans in Late Ming China* (Ann Arbor: University of Michigan Press, 2021).
94. Maria Windell, *Transamerican Sentimentalism and Nineteenth-Century US Literary History* (Oxford, UK: Oxford University Press, 2020), 2. Windell tracks African American, Native American, Latinx, and Anglo-American women writers' responses to the Haitian Revolution, Indigenous removal, the U.S.-Mexican War, Cuba's wars of independence, and other hemispheric American political events.

95. Lora Romero, *Home Fronts: Domesticity and Its Critics in the Antebellum United States* (Durham, NC: Duke University Press, 1997), 7.
96. Nina Baym, *Woman's Fiction: A Guide to Novels by and about Women in America, 1820–1870* (Champaign: University of Illinois Press, 1993).
97. Elizabeth Maddock Dillon and Michael Drexler, "Introduction: Haiti and the Early United States, Entwined," in *The Haitian Revolution and the Early United States: Histories, Textualities, Geographies*, eds. Elizabeth Maddock Dillon and Michael Drexler (Philadelphia: University of Pennsylvania Press, 2016), 2.
98. James Alexander Dun, *Dangerous Neighbors: Making the Haitian Revolution in Early America* (Philadelphia: University of Pennsylvania Press, 2016); Peter Reed, *Staging Haiti in Nineteenth-Century America: Revolution, Race, and Popular Performance* (Cambridge, UK: Cambridge University Press, 2022)
99. Marlene Daut, *Tropics of Haiti: Race and the Literary History of the Haitian Revolution in the Atlantic World, 1789–1865* (Liverpool, UK: Liverpool University Press, 2015), 3. See also Grégory Pierrot, Marion Christina Rohrleitner, and Marlene L. Daut, eds., *Haitian Revolutionary Fictions: An Anthology* (Charlottesville: University of Virginia Press, 2022).
100. Faherty, *Haitian Revolution*, 1.
101. Sara E. Johnson, *The Fear of French Negroes: Transcolonial Collaboration in the Revolutionary Americas* (Berkeley: University of California Press, 2012), 2, 93, 8.
102. Shelley Streeby, *American Sensations: Class, Empire, and the Production of Popular Culture* (Berkeley: University of California Press, 2002), xvii.
103. Burnham, *Transoceanic America*, 71.
104. Thomas Jefferson, "Anecdotes of Benjamin Franklin, 4 Dec. 1818," in McClure and Looney, *The Papers of Thomas Jefferson, Digital Edition*; U.S. Continental Congress, Declaration of Independence, July 4, 1776, National Archives, Washington, DC, https://www.archives.gov.
105. Jefferson, "Anecdotes of Benjamin Franklin."
106. "John Adams to Horatio Gates, 23 March 1776," National Archives, Washington, DC, http://founders.archives.gov. See also U.K. Parliament, Prohibitory Act of 1775 (16 Geo. 3. c. 5) in *American Legal History to the 1860s*, ed. Richard Keyser (Madison: University of Wisconsin Pressbooks, 2020), https://wisc.pb.unizin.org.
107. "John Adams to Timothy Pickering, 6 August 1822," National Archives, Washington, DC, http://founders.archives.gov.
108. Michael E. Woods, *Emotional and Sectional Conflict in the Antebellum United States* (Cambridge, UK: Cambridge University Press, 2014), 2.

CHAPTER ONE

1. James Monroe, "Special Message to the Senate of the United States, May 21, 1824," in *The American Presidency Project*, eds. Gerhard Peters and John Woolley, https://www.presidency.ucsb.edu. Monroe directly embedded the House resolution and the terms of the convention in his address.
2. Treaty of Peace and Amity Between the United States and Great Britain, December

24, 1814, U.S. National Archives, Washington DC, www.archives.gov; James Madison, "Proclamation—Announcement of a State of War Between the United States and the United Kingdom, June 19, 1812," in *The American Presidency Project*. For an emotional history of the war, see Nicole Eustace, *1812: War and the Passions of Patriotism* (Philadelphia: University of Pennsylvania Press, 2012).

3. Monroe, "Special Message." For resolutions, letters, and other materials related to this speech, see *Documents Accompanying the Message of the President of the United States, To Both Houses of Congress, At the Commencement of the Second Session of the Eighteenth Congress* (Washington, DC: Government Printing Office, 1824). On British-American foreign relations in this period, see Sam Walter Haynes, *Unfinished Revolution: The Early American Republic in a British World* (Charlottesville: University of Virginia Press, 2010).
4. Seymour Drescher, *Abolition: A History of Slavery and Antislavery* (Cambridge, UK: Cambridge University Press, 2009).
5. Monroe, "Special Message."
6. Tyson Reeder, *Smugglers, Pirates, and Patriots: Free Trade in the Age of Revolution* (Philadelphia: University of Pennsylvania Press, 2019), 2. See also Matthew McCarthy, *Privateering, Piracy, and British Policy in Spanish America, 1810–1830* (Martlesham, UK: Boydell, 2013).
7. Jenny Martinez, *The Slave Trade and the Origins of International Human Rights Law* (Oxford, UK: Oxford University Press, 2012), 114.
8. "The Slave Trade," *Niles Weekly Register*, June 12, 1824. See also Norval Neil Luxon, "H. Niles, the Man and the Editor," *Mississippi Valley Historical Review* 28, no. 1 (1941): 27–40.
9. "Catharine M. Sedgwick," in *The National Portrait Gallery of Distinguished Americans*, eds. James Herring and James B. Longacre (Philadelphia: Perkins, 1834), 1:364, 372; "Address," in Herring and Longacre, *The National Portrait Gallery*, 1:1.
10. Catharine Maria Sedgwick, "Modern Chivalry," in *The Atlantic Souvenir* (Philadelphia: Carey and Lea, 1827), 30. The narrative and its publication history are available in Deborah Gussman and Lucinda Damon Bach, eds., *Sedgwick Stories: The Shorter Works of Catharine Maria Sedgwick*, https://sedgwickstories.omeka.net.
11. "Miss Sedgwick to Mrs. Channing. New York, February 21, 1822," in *Life and Letters of Catharine M. Sedgwick*, ed. Mary E. Dewey (New York: Harper and Brothers, 1872), 147; Catharine Maria Sedgwick, *Clarence: A Tale of Our Own Times* (1830), ed. Melissa J. Homestead (Guelph, ON: Broadview, 2012), 334.
12. U.S. Congress, An Act to Prohibit the Importation of Slaves, 2 Stat. 426 (1807), chap. 22, Avalon Project at the Yale Law School, http://avalon.law.yale.edu.
13. Thomas Jefferson, *Notes on the State of Virginia (1785)*, in *The Papers of Thomas Jefferson, Digital Edition*, eds. James P. McClure and J. Jefferson Looney (Charlottesville: University of Virginia Press, 2008); "Thomas Jefferson to Joel Yancy, January 17th 1819," in McClure and Looney, *The Papers of Thomas Jefferson*. See also Adam Rothman, *Slave Country: American Expansion and the Origins of the Deep South* (Cambridge, MA: Harvard University Press, 2005).

14. U.S. Congress, An Act to Prohibit the Importation of Slaves; U.S. Congress, An Act in Addition to "An Act to Prohibit the Importation of Slaves," 3 Stat. 450 (1818), chap. 91, Avalon Project at the Yale Law School, http://avalon.law.yale.edu; U.S. Congress, An Act to Protect the Commerce of the United States and Punish the Crime of Piracy, 3 Stat. 510, (1819), chap. 77, Avalon Project at the Yale Law School, http://avalon.law.yale.edu; Paul Finkelman, "The American Suppression of the African Slave Trade: Lessons on Legal Change, Social Policy, and Legislation," *Akron Law Review* 42, no. 2 (2000): 463.
15. U.S. Congress, An Act to Continue in Force "An Act to Protect the Commerce of the United States, and Punish the Crime of Piracy," 3 Stat. 600 (1820), chap. 113, Avalon Project at the Yale Law School, http://avalon.law.yale.edu, hereafter cited as the Piracy Act of 1820.
16. U.S. Congress, Piracy Act of 1820.
17. Kevin Arlyck, *The Nation at Sea: The Federal Courts and American Sovereignty, 1789–1825* (Cambridge, UK: Cambridge University Press, 2025), 3. Arlyck provides extensive legal histories of each of the cases found in this chapter. See also G. Edward White, "The Marshall Court and International Law: The Piracy Cases," *American Journal of International Law* 83, no. 4 (1989): 728.
18. *Rose v. Himeley*, 8 U.S. 241 (1808); *Hudson v. Guestier*, 8 U.S. 293 (1808); Marlene Daut, "The 'Alpha and Omega' of Haitian Literature," in *The Haitian Revolution and the Early United States: Histories, Textualities, Geographies*, eds. Elizabeth Maddock Dillon and Michael Drexler (Philadelphia: University of Pennsylvania Press, 2016), 305.
19. John Quincy Adams, *Memoirs of John Quincy Adams: Comprising Portions of His Diary from 1795 to 1848*, ed. Charles Francis Adams (Philadelphia: Lippincott, 1875), 416. See also David Head, *Privateers of the Americas: Spanish American Privateering from the United States in the Early Republic* (Athens: University of Georgia Press, 2015).
20. *United States v. Palmer*, 16 U.S. 610 (1818).
21. *United States v. Smith*, 18 U.S. 153 (1820).
22. William Smith, "Punishment for Piracy," 16th Cong., 2nd sess. (1821), *Annals of Congress* (Washington, DC: Government Printing Office, 1824), 654–55.
23. Jeffrey R. Young, *Proslavery and Sectional Thought in the Early South, 1740–1829: An Anthology* (Columbia: University of South Carolina Press, 2006), 208.
24. Smith, "Punishment for Piracy," 655.
25. Adams, *Memoirs*, 363.
26. Manisha Sinha, *The Counterrevolution of Slavery: Politics and Ideology in Antebellum South Carolina* (Chapel Hill: University of North Carolina Press, 2000), 33.
27. "Joseph Story," in Herring and Longacre, *The National Portrait Gallery of Distinguished Americans* (1836), 3:335; Joseph Story, "Letter from Joseph Story to Hon. Ezekiel Bacon, 19 November 1843," in *Life and Letters of Joseph Story*, ed. W. W. Story (Boston: Little, Brown, 1851), 2:431

28. William P. Mason, *A Report of the Case of the Jeune Eugenie* (Boston: Wells and Lilly, 1822), 1.
29. Paul Finkelman, *Supreme Injustice: Slavery in the Nation's Highest Court* (Cambridge, MA: Harvard University Press, 2018), 115, 120.
30. William W. Wiecek, "Slavery and Abolition before the United States Supreme Court, 1820–1860," in *Abolitionism and American Law*, ed. John R. McKivigan (New York: Garland, 1999), 135. See also Earl M. Maltz, *Slavery and the Supreme Court, 1825–1861* (Lawrence: University Press of Kansas, 2009).
31. "International Norms and Politics in the Marshall Court's Slave Trade Cases," *Harvard Law Review* 128, no. 4 (2015): 1186.
32. Joseph Story, "A charge delivered to the grand juries of the Circuit court, at October term, 1819, in Boston, and at November term, 1819, in Providence, and published at their unanimous request," in *The African Slave Trade and American Courts: The Pamphlet Literature*, ed. Paul Finkelman (New York: Garland, 1988), 1:5. For an analysis of this charge in the context of Story's other piracy cases, see Leonardo Marques, *The United States and the Transatlantic Slave Trade to the Americas, 1776–1867* (New Haven, CT: Yale University Press, 2016), 56–60.
33. "International Norms," 1205. See also Roxana Banu, *Nineteenth Century Perspectives on Private International Law* (Oxford, UK: Oxford University Press, 2018).
34. Mason, "A Report," 16–17.
35. Maurice Glen Baxter, *Daniel Webster and the Supreme Court* (Amherst: University of Massachusetts Press, 1966), v; "Daniel Webster to Joseph Story, December 1, 1821," in *The Papers of Daniel Webster, Digital Edition*, ed. Charles M. Wiltse (Charlottesville: University of Virginia Press, 2018).
36. Mason, "A Report," 68–70, 73
37. Andrew Forsyth, *Common Law and Natural Law in America: From the Puritans to the Legal Realists* (Cambridge, UK: Cambridge University Press, 2019), 99.
38. Mason, "A Report," 69–70.
39. Mason, "A Report," 69–70.
40. Mason, "A Report," 92.
41. Joseph Story, "Letter from Joseph Story to Hon. Ezekiel Bacon," in Story, *Life and Letters*, 2:431. Story's modern biographer upholds this idea, though I am more circumspect (see R. Kent Newmyer, *Supreme Court Justice Joseph Story: Statesman of the Old Republic* [Chapel Hill: University of North Carolina Press, 1985], 208); *Mima Queen v. Hepburn*, 11 U.S. 290 (1813). For an analysis of this freedom suit, see William G. Thomas, *A Question of Freedom: The Families Who Challenged Slavery, from the Nation's Founding to the Civil War* (New Haven, CT: Yale University Press, 2020).
42. Sharla M. Fett, *Recaptured Africans: Surviving Slave Ships, Detention, and Dislocation in the Final Years of the Slave Trade* (Chapel Hill: University of North Carolina Press, 2016), 26.
43. Forsyth, *Common Law and Natural Law*, 100.

44. *The Antelope*, 23 U.S. (10 Wheat.) 66 (1825), quoted in John T. Noonan Jr., *The Antelope: The Ordeal of the Recaptured Africans in the Administrations of James Monroe and John Quincy Adams* (Berkeley: University of California Press, 1977), 158. For a more extended literary analysis of the decision, see Jeannine Marie DeLombard, *In the Shadow of the Gallows: Race, Crime, and American Civic Identity* (Philadelphia: University of Pennsylvania Press, 2012).
45. "Article III. A Report of the Case of the Jeune Eugenie, Determined in the Circuit Court of the United States for the First Circuit, at Boston, December 1812," *Christian Disciple and Theological Review* 4, no. 19 (1822): 37; "Case of the Jeune Eugenie," *United States Law Journal* 1, no. 2 (1822): 257; Story, *Life and Letters*, 1:356–58.
46. "U.S. Circuit Court," *The Liberator*, October 19, 1838; "Every Slaveholder a Pirate," *The Liberator*, May 04, 1838.
47. Mark B. Kelley, "Pirates, Bloodhounds, and White Heirs: Catharine Maria Sedgwick's Fictions of Haiti," *Legacy* 38, nos. 1–2 (2021): 1–25.
48. Melissa J. Homestead, "Introduction," in Sedgwick, *Clarence*, 27.
49. Catharine Maria Sedgwick, "A Voyage across the Atlantic," in *The United States Magazine and Democratic Review* (September 1841): 23; Robert Sampson, *John L. O'Sullivan and His Times* (Kent, OH: Kent State University Press, 2003), 2–3.
50. Newmyer, *Supreme Court Justice*, 57; David McCullough, *John Adams* (Simon and Shuster, 2001), 506, 524.
51. Gretchen Murphy, *New England Women Writers, Secularity, and the Federalist Politics of Church and State* (Oxford, UK: Oxford University Press, 2021), 2; Catharine Maria Sedgwick, "29 November 1829," in *The Power of Her Sympathy: The Autobiography and Journal of Catharine Maria Sedgwick*, ed. Mary Kelley (Boston: Massachusetts Historical Society, 1993), 124.
52. Melissa J. Homestead, "The Shape of Catharine Sedgwick's Literary Career," in *The Cambridge History of American Women's Literature*, ed. Dale M. Bauer (Cambridge, UK: Cambridge University Press, 2012), 185–203.
53. Melissa J. Homestead, *American Women Authors and Literary Property, 1822–1869* (Cambridge, UK: Cambridge University Press, 2005), 16.
54. Wendy Warren, *New England Bound: Slavery and Colonization in Early America* (New York: Liveright, 2016).
55. Charlene Avallone, "Catharine Sedgwick's White Nation-Making: Historical Fiction and *The Linwoods*," *ESQ* 55, no. 2 (2009): 100.
56. Karen Woods-Weierman, "'A Slave Story I Began and Abandoned': Sedgwick's Antislavery Manuscript," in *Catharine Maria Sedgwick: Critical Perspectives*, eds. Lucinda Damon-Bach and Victoria Clements (Boston: Northeastern University Press, 2003), 122.
57. Christopher C. Apap, *The Genius of Place: The Geographic Imagination in the Early Republic* (Durham: University of New Hampshire Press, 2016), 58.
58. Catharine Maria Sedgwick, *A New-England Tale; or, Sketches of New-England Character and Manners* (1822), ed. Victoria Clements (Oxford, UK: Oxford University

Press, 1995), 153; Catherine Q. Forsa, "A Model Heart: Public Displays of Emotion in Sedgwick's *A New-England Tale*," *ESQ* 61, no. 3 (2015): 412.

59. Catharine Maria Sedgwick, *Redwood; A Tale* (1824), ed. Jenifer B. Elmore (Edinburgh, UK: Edinburgh University Press, 2021), 36; Murphy, *New England Women*, 134, 123.
60. Sedgwick, *Redwood* 313; Homestead, "The Shape," 192; Jenifer Elmore, "Editor's Introduction," in Sedgwick, *Redwood*, xxix.
61. Paul Pasquaretta, *Gambling and Survival in Native North America* (Tucson: Arizona University Press, 2003), 28.
62. Catharine Maria Sedgwick, *Hope Leslie; Or, Early Times in the Massachusetts* (1827), ed. Carolyn L. Karcher (New York: Penguin, 1998), 4, 334.
63. Mark G. Hanna, *Pirate Nests and the Rise of the British Empire, 1570–1740* (Chapel Hill: University of North Carolina Press, 2015), 85.
64. Sarah Sillin, "'Made to Feel Wretched': Royall Tyler and the Trouble with Global Sympathy," *Early American Literature* 51, no. 1 (2016): 121.
65. Sedgwick, *Hope Leslie*, 335–36.
66. Sedgwick, *Hope Leslie*, 334, 167, 342.
67. Laura Doyle, *Freedom's Empire: Race and the Rise of the Novel in Atlantic Modernity, 1640–1940* (Durham, NC: Duke University Press, 2008), 278, 335.
68. Leslie M. Harris, *In the Shadow of Slavery: African Americans in New York City, 1626–1863* (Chicago: University of Chicago Press, 2004).
69. Sedgwick, *Clarence*, 67, 83; Lori Merish, *Sentimental Materialism: Gender, Commodity Culture, and Nineteenth-Century American Literature* (Durham, NC: Duke University Press, 2000), 131.
70. Sedgwick, *Clarence*, 372, 374.
71. Sedgwick, *Clarence*, 214, 370–71.
72. Sedgwick, *Clarence*, 398, 404.
73. Catharine Maria Sedgwick, "Dogs," in *Juvenile Miscellany* 4, no. 1 (1828): 34–36. See also Kelley, "Pirates, Bloodhounds, and White Heirs."
74. Sedgwick, *Clarence*, 181, 171.
75. Sedgwick, *Clarence*, 173; Jerzy Lukowski, *The European Nobility in the Eighteenth Century* (New York: Palgrave Macmillan, 2003), 186.
76. Sedgwick, *Clarence*, 366; Susan K. Harris, "The Limits of Authority: Catharine Maria Sedgwick and the Politics of Resistance," in *Catharine Maria Sedgwick: Critical Perspectives*, eds. Lucinda Damon-Bach and Victoria Clements (Boston: Northeastern University Press, 2003), 279.
77. Merish, *Sentimental Materialism*, 134. See also David Faflik, *The Literary Gift in Early America* (Stanford, CA: Stanford University Press, 2025). Sedgwick, *Clarence*, 410, 415.
78. Sedgwick, *Clarence*, 173, 412, 415.
79. Avallone, "Catharine Sedgwick's White Nation-Making," 99; Catharine Maria Sedgwick, *The Linwoods, or, "Sixty Years Since" in America* (1835), ed. Maria Karafilis (Hanover, NH: University Press of New England, 2002), 118, 119.

80. Sedgwick, *The Linwoods*, 118; Michelle Sizemore, *American Enchantment: Rituals of the People in the Post-Revolutionary World* (Oxford, UK: Oxford University Press, 2018), 15.
81. Homestead, "Introduction," 35.
82. Homestead, "Introduction," 35; Sedgwick, *Clarence*, 172; Catharine Maria Sedgwick, "Slavery in New England," in *Bentley's Miscellany* 34 (1853): 417–24.
83. Catharine Maria Sedgwick, *Married or Single?* (1857), ed. Deborah Gussman (Lincoln: University of Nebraska Press, 2015), 227; Catharine Maria Sedgwick, "Miss Sedgwick to Rev. Dr. Dewey. New York March 1857," in Dewey, *Life and Letters of Catharine M. Sedgwick*, 369.
84. Deborah Gussman, "Editor's Introduction," in Sedgwick, *Married or Single?*, xxxii–xxxiii; Jordan L. Von Cannon, "Leaving Giants Unslain: Idle Activism in Catharine Sedgwick's *The Linwoods* and Other Writings," *Legacy* 42, vol. 1 (2025): 1.
85. Don E. Fehrenbacher, *The Slaveholding Republic: An Account of the United States Government's Relations to Slavery* (Oxford, UK: Oxford University Press, 2002), 155.
86. Ernest Obadele-Starks, *Freebooters and Smugglers: The Foreign Slave Trade in the United States after 1808* (Little Rock: University of Arkansas Press, 2007), 34; Sara E. Johnson, *The Fear of French Negroes: Transcolonial Collaboration in the Revolutionary Americas* (Berkeley: University of California Press, 2012), 96–97.
87. The Webster-Ashburton Treaty. Treaty to Settle and Define the Boundaries between the Territories of the United States and the Possessions of Her Britannic Majesty in North America, for the Final Suppression of the African Slave Trade, November 10, 1842, Avalon Project at the Yale Law School, http://avalon.law.yale.edu.
88. Trans-Atlantic Slave Trade Database, Rice University, https://www.slavevoyages.org.
89. Manisha Sinha, *The Slave's Cause: A History of Abolition* (New Haven, CT: Yale University Press, 2016).
90. "Pirates," *The Liberator*, October 23, 1846.
91. John Howison, "The Florida Pirate," *Blackwoods Edinburgh Magazine* 9 (1821): 522, 531; Gretchen J. Woertendyke, *Hemispheric Regionalism Romance and the Geography of Genre* (Oxford, UK: Oxford University Press, 2016), 53. See also Michele Currie Navakas, *Liquid Landscape: Geography and Settlement at the Edge of Early America* (Philadelphia: University of Pennsylvania Press, 2018), 59–65.
92. Story, *Life and Letters* (1851), 2:573–75; Charles Sumner, "Our Foreign Relations" (1863), in *The Works of Charles Sumner* (Boston: Lee and Shepard, 1873), 7:434; Henry Wadsworth Longfellow, "Letter to George W. Greene, August 6, 1838," in *The Letters of Henry Wadsworth Longfellow, 1814–1843*, ed. Andrew R. Hilen Jr. (Cambridge, MA: Harvard University Press, 1990), 93. See also Zaakir Tameez, *Charles Sumner: Conscience of a Nation* (New York: Holt, 2025).

CHAPTER TWO

1. Abraham Lincoln, "Speech at Peoria, Illinois, October 16, 1854," in *The Collected Works of Abraham Lincoln*, ed. Roy P. Basler (New Brunswick, NJ: Rutgers University Press 1953), 2:263–65.

2. "Abraham Lincoln to Hon. T. J. Henderson, December 15 1854," in Basler, *Collected Works*, 2: 293.
3. John Burt, *Lincoln's Tragic Pragmatism: Lincoln, Douglas, and Moral Conflict* (Cambridge, MA: Harvard University Press, 2013), 28.
4. Burt, *Lincoln's Tragic Pragmatism*, 28. See also Michael P. Zuckert, *A Nation So Conceived: Abraham Lincoln and the Paradox of Democratic Sovereignty* (Lawrence: University of Kansas Press, 2023).
5. Lincoln, "Speech at Peoria," 2:255–56.
6. John C. Calhoun, "Remarks on the Disturbances in the District of Columbia. In the Senate, April 20 1848," in *The Papers of John C. Calhoun*, eds. Clyde N. Wilson and Shirley Bright Cook (Columbia: University of South Carolina Press, 1999), 25:343. See also Josephine F. Pacheco, *The Pearl: A Failed Slave Escape on the Potomac* (Chapel Hill: University of North Carolina Press, 2005), 166–90.
7. John C. Calhoun, "Speech on the Slavery Question, Delivered in the Senate, March 4th, 1850," in *The Works of John C. Calhoun* (New York: Appleton, 1854), 4:572; Daniel Webster, "The Constitution and Union" (1850), in *The Great Speeches and Orations of Daniel Webster*, ed. Edwin P. Whipple (Boston: Little, Brown, 1895), 601. For extended analyses of these speeches in context, see Holman Hamilton, *Prologue to Conflict: The Crisis and Compromise of 1850* (Lexington: University Press of Kentucky, 2014); and Richard J. M. Blackett, *The Captive's Quest for Freedom: Fugitive Slaves, the 1850 Fugitive Slave Law, and the Politics of Slavery* (Cambridge, UK: Cambridge University Press, 2018).
8. Daniel Webster, "First Settlement of New England. A Discourse Delivered at Plymouth, on the 22nd of December 1820," in *The Great Speeches*, 49. See also "Daniel Webster," in *Lives of the Illustrious: The Biographical Magazine* (London: Partridge and Oakley, 1853), 3:76.
9. Webster, "Constitution and Union," 616, 623–24.
10. Ralph Waldo Emerson, "Address to the Citizens of Concord on the Fugitive Slave Law, 3 May 1851," in *The Later Lectures of Ralph Waldo Emerson, 1843–1871*, eds. Ronald A. Boscoe and Joel Myerson (Athens: University of Georgia Press, 2001), 1:265–67. See also Greg Garvey, *Emerson and the Defense of Equality* (Amherst: University of Massachusetts Press, 2025).
11. Michael L. Frazer, *The Enlightenment of Sympathy: Justice and the Moral Sentiments in the Eighteenth Century and Today* (Oxford, UK: Oxford University Press, 2010), 92–93.
12. Adam Smith, *The Theory of Moral Sentiments* (1859), ed. Ryan Patrick Hanley (New York: Penguin, 2010), 97.
13. Smith, *Moral Sentiments*, 85.
14. Smith, *Moral Sentiments*, 99.
15. Adam Smith, *Lectures on Jurisprudence* (1762), eds. Ronald L. Meek, D. D. Raphael, and Peter Stein (Oxford, UK: Oxford University Press, 1978), 7.
16. John Quincy Adams, *Argument of John Quincy Adams, Before the Supreme Court of the United States* (New York: Benedict, 1841), 7. Adams's lengthy testimony was

not published with the initial transcripts. *United States v. Schooner Amistad*, 40 U.S. 518 (1841); Peter Charles Hoffer, *John Quincy Adams and the Gag Rule, 1835–1850* (Baltimore: Johns Hopkins University Press, 2017).

17. Manisha Sinha, *The Slave's Cause: A History of Abolition* (New Haven, CT: Yale University Press, 2016), 407–8.
18. *Amistad.*
19. *Amistad.*
20. *Amistad.*
21. *Amistad.*
22. Adams, *Argument*, 6–7
23. Adams, *Argument*, 8–10.
24. Adams, *Argument*, 124.
25. Adams, *Argument*, 126–27.
26. *Amistad*; Hoffer, *John Quincy Adams*, 47; Paul Finkelman, "Slavery in the United States: Persons or Property?," in *The Legal Understanding of Slavery: From the Historical to the Contemporary*, ed. Jean Allen (Oxford, UK: Oxford University Press, 2012), 124.
27. "*United States v. James Smith: Indictment*," September 30, 1854, Records of District Courts of the United States, Criminal Case Files, NAID 278381, U.S. National Archives, Washington DC, https://www.archives.gov; "Important Trial. The African Slave Trade. Trial of Captain James Smith for Piracy," *The New York Times*, November 7, 1854; Jeannine Marie DeLombard, *In the Shadow of the Gallows: Race, Crime, and American Civic Identity* (Philadelphia: University of Pennsylvania Press, 2012), 253. DeLombard analyzes five related cases as well as fictions such as Melville's *Benito Cereno*.
28. "From the N.Y. *Evangelist*. The Slave Trade in New York," *Frederick Douglass' Paper*, December 22, 1854; "Trial for Slave Trading," *Antislavery Reporter* 3, no. 1 (1855): 8.
29. Sharla M. Fett, *Recaptured Africans: Surviving Slave Ships, Detention, and Dislocation in the Final Years of the Slave Trade* (Chapel Hill: University of North Carolina Press, 2016), 11; *Report of the Trials in the "Echo" Cases, in Federal Court, Charleston, S.C., April, 1859: Together with Arguments of Counsel and Charge of the Court* (Columbia, SC: Gibbes 1859), 67, 94–96.
30. Lenora Warren, *Fire on the Water: Sailors, Slaves, and Insurrection in Early American Literature, 1789–1886* (Lewisburg, PA: Bucknell University Press, 2019), 72, 84.
31. On Webster's legal reasoning about *Creole*, in contrast to Frederick Douglass's, see Carrie Hyde, *Civic Longing: The Speculative Origins of U.S. Citizenship* (Cambridge, MA: Harvard University Press, 2018), 85–115.
32. Frederick Douglass, "The Heroic Slave," in *Autographs for Freedom. By Mrs. Harriet Beecher Stowe and Thirty-Five Other Eminent Writers* (Boston: Jewett, 1853), 225–26.
33. John W. Frick, *"Uncle Tom's Cabin" on the American Stage and Screen* (New York: Palgrave Macmillan, 2016), 91; Sarah Meer, *Uncle Tom Mania: Slavery, Minstrelsy, and Transatlantic Culture in the 1850s* (Athens: University of Georgia Press, 2005), 137.

34. Nathan Wolff, *Not Quite Hope and Other Political Emotions in the Gilded Age* (Oxford, UK: Oxford University Press, 2019), 39; Martha Schoolman, *Abolitionist Geographies* (Minneapolis: University of Minnesota Press, 2014), 127.
35. Melissa J. Homestead, *American Women Authors and Literary Property, 1822–1869* (Cambridge, UK: Cambridge University Press, 2005), 16.
36. Charles Beecher, *The Duty of Disobedience to Wicked Laws. A Sermon on the Fugitive Slave Law* (New York: Gray, 1851), 7, 16.
37. James Baldwin, "Everybody's Protest Novel," in *Notes of a Native Son* (Boston: Beacon, 1984), 14.
38. Lauren Berlant, *The Female Complaint: The Unfinished Business of Sentimentality in American Culture* (Durham, NC: Duke University Press, 2008), 58–59.
39. Harriet Beecher Stowe, *Uncle Tom's Cabin; or, Life among the Lowly (1852)*, ed. Elizabeth Ammons (New York: Norton, 2010), 342, 307; Cynthia Alicia Smith, "Uncle Tom's (Ship) Cabin," *ESQ* 66, no. 1 (2020): 47.
40. Stowe, *Uncle Tom's Cabin, 307*; U.S. Congress, "An Act to Continue in Force 'An Act to Protect the Commerce of the United States, and Punish the Crime of Piracy,'" 3 Stat. 600 (1820), chap. 113, Avalon Project at the Yale Law School, http://avalon.law.yale.edu.
41. Stowe, *Uncle Tom's Cabin*, 311.
42. Stowe, *Uncle Tom's Cabin*, 403.
43. Harriet Beecher Stowe, *A Key to "Uncle Tom's Cabin"* (Boston: Jewett, 1853), 253, 252.
44. Stowe, *A Key*, 123, 39.
45. Stowe, *Uncle Tom's Cabin*, 408, 404.
46. Stowe, *Uncle Tom's Cabin*, 95, 104.
47. Stowe, *Uncle Tom's Cabin*, 85, 96, 84, 83–84.
48. Maria Windell, *Transamerican Sentimentalism and Nineteenth-Century US Literary History* (Oxford, UK: Oxford University Press, 2020), 174–75.
49. Harriet Beecher Stowe, *Dred: A Tale of the Great Dismal Swamp* (1856), ed. Robert S. Levine (Chapel Hill: University of North Carolina Press, 2000), 204.
50. Stowe, *Dred*, 204, 3–4; Laura H. Korobkin, "Appropriating Law in Harriet Beecher Stowe's *Dred*," *Nineteenth-Century Literature* 62, vol. 3 (2007): 381. For other legal readings of Stowe, see Deak Nabers, *Victory of Law: The Fourteenth Amendment, the Civil War, and American Literature, 1852–1867* (Baltimore: Johns Hopkins University Press, 2006); and Jeffory Clymer, *Family Money: Property, Race, and Literature in the Nineteenth Century* (Oxford, UK: Oxford University Press, 2013).
51. Jeannine Marie DeLombard, *Slavery on Trial: Law, Abolitionism, and Print Culture* (Chapel Hill: University of North Carolina Press, 2007), 174.
52. Stowe, *Dred*, 17, 352.
53. Stowe, *Dred*, 355–56, 24.
54. Stowe, *Dred*, 393, 211–12.
55. Stowe, *Dred*, 496.
56. Stowe, *Dred*, 209–10.

57. Kevin Pelletier, *Apocalyptic Sentimentalism: Love and Fear in U.S. Antebellum Literature* (Athens: University of Georgia Press, 2015), 144. See also Christina Zwarg, *The Archive of Fear: White Crisis and Black Freedom in Douglass, Stowe, and Du Bois* (Oxford, UK: Oxford University Press, 2020).
58. Stowe, *Dred*, 499.
59. Hyde, *Civic Longing*, 73.
60. Melissa Gniadek, *Oceans at Home: Maritime and Domestic Fictions in Nineteenth-Century American Women's Writing* (Amherst: University of Massachusetts Press, 2021), 121; Harriet Beecher Stowe, *The Minister's Wooing* (London: Sampson Low, 1859), 358; Harriet Beecher Stowe, *The Pearl of Orr's Island: A Story of the Coast of Maine* (1862; Boston: Houghton Mifflin, 1896), 205.
61. Denise Kohn, Sarah Meer, and Emily B. Todd, "Reading Stowe as a Transatlantic Writer," in *Transatlantic Stowe: Harriet Beecher Stowe and European Culture*, eds. Denise Kohn, Sarah Meer, and Emily B. Todd (Iowa City: University of Iowa Press, 2009), xxvi.
62. Belinda Edmondson, *Caribbean Middlebrow: Leisure Culture and the Middle Class* (Ithaca, NY: Cornell University Press, 2009), 50–51.
63. Christine Levecq, *Slavery and Sentiment: The Politics of Feeling in Black Atlantic Antislavery Writing, 1770–1850* (Durham: University of New Hampshire Press, 2008), 3.
64. William E. Cain, "Introduction: *Emmanuel Appadocca* in Its American Context," in *Emmanuel Appadocca; or, Blighted Life: A Tale of the Boucaneers* (1854), by Michel Maxwell Philip, ed. Selwyn R. Cudjoe (Amherst: University of Massachusetts Press, 1997), xliii, xliii, xxxvii. Belinda Edmondson forwards a valid skepticism of *Uncle Tom's Cabin* as a direct forebear: she questions, "we must ask what, beyond its obvious dramatic and sentimental power, is this American novel's appeal for a free colored population in the Caribbean where slavery has been over for a generation?" (*Caribbean Middlebrow*, 63).
65. Xine Yao, *Disaffected: The Cultural Politics of Unfeeling in Nineteenth-Century America* (Durham, NC: Duke University Press, 2021), 5.
66. Yao, *Disaffected*, 2.
67. Philip, *Emmanuel Appadocca*, 106; Cudjoe, "Afterword," in ibid., 257.
68. Philip, *Emmanuel Appadocca*, 215.
69. Cudjoe, "Afterword," 249. For more recent affirmations of Philip's role in this intellectual tradition, see Candace Ward, *Crossing the Line: Early Creole Novels and Anglophone Caribbean Culture in the Age of Emancipation* (Charlottesville: University of Virginia Press, 2017); and Christopher Taylor, *Empire of Neglect: The West Indies in the Wake of British Liberalism* (Durham, NC: Duke University Press, 2018).
70. Philip, *Emmanuel Appadocca*, 6; Walter Johnson, ed., *The Chattel Principle: Internal Slave Trades in the Americas* (New Haven, CT: Yale University Press, 2004).
71. The Fédon Rebellion of 1795 was an insurrection of enslaved and free Grenadians led by Philip's uncle Julien Fédon. For an account of the Philip family's genealogy alongside this and other revolutions, see Selwyn R. Cudjoe, *Beyond Boundaries: The Intellectual Tradition of Trinidad and Tobago in the Nineteenth Century* (Amherst:

University of Massachusetts Press, 2003); and Kit Candlin, *The Last Caribbean Frontier, 1795–1815* (New York: Palgrave Macmillan, 2012).

72. Selwyn R. Cudjoe and Lauren Zykorie, *Michel Maxwell Philip: A Trinidad Patriot of the 19th Century* (Wellesley, MA: Calaloux, 1999).
73. Edmondson, *Caribbean Middlebrow*, 50.
74. C. L. R. James, "Michel Maxwell Philip: 1829–1888" (1931), in *From Trinidad: An Anthology of Early West Indian Writing*, eds. Reinhard Sander and Peter K. Ayers (London: Africana, 1978), 52; Cain, "Introduction," xlv.
75. Philip, *Emmanuel Appadocca*, 102.
76. Philip, *Emmanuel Appadocca*, 103–5.
77. Philip, *Emmanuel Appadocca*, 105–6. For a related reading that does not discuss Smith, see Gesa Mackenthun, *Fictions of the Black Atlantic in American Foundational Literature* (London: Routledge, 2004).
78. Philip, *Emmanuel Appadocca*, 70.
79. Philip, *Emmanuel Appadocca*, 70.
80. Philip, *Emmanuel Appadocca*, 212, 215.
81. Philip, *Emmanuel Appadocca*, 242, 243, 248; Edmondson, *Caribbean Middlebrow*, 64.
82. Raphael Dalleo, *Caribbean Literature and the Public Sphere: From the Plantation to the Postcolonial* (Charlottesville: University of Virginia Press, 2011), 53.
83. Smith, *Moral Sentiments*, 85–86.
84. Philip, *Emmanuel Appadocca*, 116.
85. Lenora Warren, "Melville's Spectral Mutinies," in *A New Companion to Herman Melville*, eds. Christopher Ohge and Wyn Kelley (Hoboken, NJ: Wiley, 2022), 373–74.
86. Andy Doolen, *Fugitive Empire: Locating Early American Imperialism* (Minneapolis: University of Minnesota Press, 2006), 195; Hester Blum, "Atlantic Trade," in Ohge and Kelley, *A Companion to Herman Melville*, 122. For a compatible comparative reading of *Emmanuel Appadocca* and *Benito Cereno*, see Alexandra Ganser, *Crisis and Legitimacy in Atlantic American Narratives of Piracy: 1678–1865* (New York: Palgrave Macmillan, 2020), 190–218.
87. Herman Melville, *Benito Cereno* (1855), ed. Brian Yothers (Peterborough, ON: Broadview, 2019), 58, 65, 68.
88. Yao, *Disaffected*, 20; Melville, *Benito Cereno*, 108.
89. Yao, *Disaffected*, 30; Melville, *Benito Cereno*, 106–7, 108.
90. Melville, *Benito Cereno*, 127–28.
91. William M. Wiecek, *The Dark Past: The US Supreme Court and African Americans, 1800–2015* (Oxford, UK: Oxford University Press, 2024), 17.
92. *Dred Scott v. Sandford*, 60 U.S. 393 (1857); A. Leon Higginbotham, *Shades of Freedom: Racial Politics and Presumptions of the American Legal Process* (Oxford, UK: Oxford University Press, 1998), 57. See also Alfred L. Brophy, *University, Court, and Slave: Pro-Slavery Thought in Southern Colleges and Courts, and the Coming of Civil War* (Oxford, UK: Oxford University Press, 2016).
93. *Dred Scott*; Don Edward Fehrenbacher, *The Dred Scott Case: Its Significance in American Law and Politics* (Oxford, UK: Oxford University Press, 2001), 337.

94. Pelletier, *Apocalyptic Sentimentalism*, 30, 140. See also John Stauffer and Zoe Trodd, eds., *The Tribunal: Responses to John Brown and the Harpers Ferry Raid* (Cambridge, MA: Harvard University Press, 2012).
95. Ralph Waldo Emerson, "Speech of Ralph Waldo Emerson," in *The John Brown Invasion: Authentic History of the Harper's Ferry Tragedy*, ed. Thomas Drew (Boston: Campbell, 1860), 103–5.
96. Wendell Phillips, *Disunion: Two Discourses at Music Hall, on January 20th, and February 17th, 1861* (Boston: Walcutt, 1861), 18. For a history of the speech's political circumstances, see James M. McPherson, *The Struggle for Equality: Abolitionists and the Negro in the Civil War and Reconstruction* (Princeton, NJ: Princeton University Press, 2014).
97. Phillips, *Disunion*, 89–90.
98. Phillips, *Disunion*, 89–90.
99. Jacob Crane, *Blood and Ink: The Barbary Archive in Early American Literary History* (Amherst: University of Massachusetts Press, 2023), 177; George B. Cheever, "Sermon by George B. Cheever," in *Echoes of Harper's Ferry*, ed. James Redpath (Boston: Thayer and Eldridge, 1860), 155.
100. Wendell Phillips, "An Address by Wendell Phillips, Delivered at Brooklyn, N.Y., Nov. 1 1859," in Drew, *The John Brown Invasion*, 95.
101. Our Special Reporter, "The Harper's Ferry Outbreak," *New York Herald*, October, 21, 1859; Daniel J. Burge, "John Brown, Filibuster: Republicans, Harpers Ferry, and the Use of Violence, 1855–1860," *Journal of the Early Republic* 43, no. 2 (2023): 246. Burge quotes the *Herald* story and other examples.
102. Daniel W. Voorhees, "Defense of John E. Cook" (1860), in *Forty Years of Oratory: Daniel Wolsey Voorhees Lectures, Addresses, and Speeches*, ed. Harriet Cecilia Voorhees (Indianapolis: Bobbs-Merrill, 1897), 381–89.
103. "Frederick Douglass to James Redpath, June 29, 1860," Frederick Douglass Papers Project, eds. John R. McKivigan and Jeffery A. Duvall, https://frederickdouglasspapersproject.com. For shifts in Douglass's thinking, see Kellie Carter Jackson, *Force and Freedom: Black Abolitionists and the Politics of Violence* (Philadelphia: University of Pennsylvania Press, 2020).
104. Charles Sumner, *The Barbarism of Slavery: Speech of Hon. Charles Sumner, on the Bill for The Admission of Kansas as a Free State, In the United States Senate, June 4, 1860* (New York: Young Men's Republican Union, 1863). On the caning of Sumner in context, see William James Hull Hoffer, *The Caning of Charles Sumner: Honor, Idealism, and the Origins of the Civil War* (Baltimore: Johns Hopkins University Press, 2010); and Joanne B. Freeman, *The Field of Blood: Violence in Congress and the Road to Civil War* (New York: Farrar, Straus and Giroux, 2018).

CHAPTER THREE

1. Charles Sumner, "Cheap Ocean Postage: Speech of the Hon. Charles Sumner," *Merchants' Magazine and Commercial Review* 26, no. 5 (1852): 648; Daniel Webster, "The Constitution and Union" (1850), in *The Great Speeches and Orations of Daniel Webster*, ed. Edwin P. Whipple (Boston: Little, Brown, 1895), 601.

2. Freeman Hunt, "The Editor to His Friends and Patrons," *Merchants' Magazine and Commercial Review* 21, no. 1 (1849): 143.
3. "The Post-Office as It Has Been, Is, and Should Be: As a Means of Modern Civilization," *Merchants' Magazine and Commercial Review* 35, no. 6 (1856): 692. For official subsidy levels in 1854, see "Appropriations for Transporting the U.S. Mail by Steamers," *Merchants' Magazine and Commercial Review* 29, no. 1 (1853): 121.
4. Wayne Fuller, *Morality and the Mail in Nineteenth-Century America* (Champaign: University of Illinois Press, 2003), 209.
5. J. D. B. De Bow, "Convention of South and West," *De Bow's Review* 1, no. 1 (1846): 4.
6. John F. Kvach, *De Bow's Review: The Antebellum Vision of a New South* (Lexington: University Press of Kentucky, 2013), 2.
7. De Bow, "Convention of South and West," 7.
8. Mary T. Freeman, *Abolitionists and the Politics of Correspondence* (Philadelphia: University of Pennsylvania Press, 2026). See also Lacy K. Ford, *Deliver Us from Evil: The Slavery Question in the Old South* (Oxford, UK: Oxford University Press, 2009), 482–99.
9. Peter Shulman, *Coal and Empire: The Birth of Energy Security in Industrial America* (Baltimore: Johns Hopkins University Press, 2015), 16.
10. David Henkin, *The Postal Age: The Emergence of Modern Communications in Nineteenth-Century America* (Chicago: University of Chicago Press, 2006), 6. See also Richard John, *Spreading the News: The American Postal System from Franklin to Morse* (Cambridge, MA: Harvard University Press, 1995).
11. Henkin, *The Postal Age*, 173.
12. Henkin, *The Postal Age*, 17.
13. For an overview of U.S. prices between 1858 and 1874 (the period before standardization), see Charles Starnes, *United States Letter Rates to Foreign Destinations, 1847 to GPU-UPU* (Louisville: Philatelic Bibliopole, 1982).
14. Fuller, *Morality and the Mail*, 195.
15. For descriptions of Naval Committee Chair Thomas Butler King's campaign for more ships in response to fears of British imperialism, see Matthew Karp, *This Vast Southern Empire: Slaveholders at the Helm of American Foreign Policy* (Cambridge, MA: Harvard University Press, 2016), 202.
16. "The Post-Office as It Has Been," 692
17. For an expanded account of the 1847 treaty's development, see Shulman, *Coal and Empire*, 23–25.
18. Gesu Mackenthun, "Imperial Archaeology: The American Isthmus as Contested Scientific Zone," in *Surveying the American Tropics: A Literary Geography from New York to Rio*, eds. Lesley Wylie, Maria Cristina Fumagalli, Owen Robinson, and Peter Hulme (Liverpool, UK: Liverpool University Press, 2003), 101.
19. "American Ocean Steam Navigation: Or the First American Steamship to Bremen," *The Merchants' Magazine and Commercial Review* 17, no. 4 (1847): 357.
20. For discussion of the British policy's effects on U.S. mail trade, see Shulman, *Coal and Empire*, 15–23
21. For an account of the challenges facing British maritime and imperial structures in

the period, see Howard Fuller, *Empire, Technology, and Seapower: Royal Navy Crisis in the Age of Palmerston* (London: Routledge, 2013).

22. Postal Convention with Great Britain; December 15, 1848, Avalon Project at the Yale Law School, http://avalon.law.yale.edu.
23. *Report of Naval Committee on Establishing a Line of Mail Steamships to the Western Coast of Africa and Thence via the Mediterranean to London. With an Appendix Added by the American Colonization Society* (Washington, DC: Gideon, 1850), 9.
24. "George Bancroft, United States Minister to Great Britain, to James Buchanan, Secretary of State of the United States," in *Diplomatic Correspondence of the United States: Canadian Relations, 1784–1860*, ed. William Ray Manning (Washington, DC: Carnegie Endowment, 1940), 3:1171; George Bancroft, letter to Cave Johnson, December 8, 1848, George Bancroft Papers, 1823–90, collection 196, box 2, Manuscripts and Archives Division, New York Public Library.
25. R. B. F, "Art. II.—Of the Establishment of a Line of Mail Steamers," *Merchants' Magazine and Commercial Review* 29, no. 5 (1853): 549.
26. R. B. F., "Art. II," 550.
27. Jodi A. Byrd, *The Transit of Empire: Indigenous Critiques of Colonialism* (Minneapolis: University of Minnesota Press, 2011), 6.
28. R. B. F., "Art. II," 550.
29. Konstantin Dierks, *In My Power: Letter Writing and Communications in Early America* (Philadelphia: University of Pennsylvania Press, 2009), 168, 284.
30. "The Post-Office as It Has Been," 697.
31. Susan Williams, *Reclaiming Authorship: Literary Women in America, 1850–1900* (Philadelphia: University of Pennsylvania Press, 2006), 78.
32. Nina Baym, "Again and Again, the Scribbling Women," in *Hawthorne and Women: Engendering and Expanding the Hawthorne Tradition*, eds. John L. Idol and Melinda M. Ponder (Amherst: University of Massachusetts Press, 1999), 20–35.
33. Susan Williams, "'Promoting an Extensive Sale': The Production and Reception of *The Lamplighter*," *New England Quarterly* 69, no. 2 (1996): 180.
34. H. Philip Bolton, *Women Writers Dramatized: A Calendar of Performances from Narrative Works Published in English to 1900* (London: Bloomsbury, 2000), 127.
35. Nina Baym, "Introduction," in Maria Susanna Cummins, *The Lamplighter*, ed. Nina Baym (New Brunswick, NJ: Rutgers University Press, 1988), xix. For an overview of scholarship on the novel, see Cindy Weinstein, *Family, Kinship, and Sympathy in Nineteenth-Century American Literature* (Cambridge, UK: Cambridge University Press, 2004).
36. James Fichte, *So Great a Proffit: How the East Indies Trade Transformed Anglo-American Capitalism* (Cambridge, MA: Harvard University Press, 2010), 4. See also Rajender Kaur and Anupama Arora, eds., *India in the American Imaginary, 1780s–1880s* (New York: Palgrave Macmillan, 2017).
37. Maria Susanna Cummins, *The Lamplighter* (1854), ed. Nina Baym (New Brunswick, NJ: Rutgers University Press, 1988), 106.
38. Amy Kaplan, *The Anarchy of Empire in the Making of U.S. Culture* (Cambridge, MA: Harvard University Press, 2002), 43; Cummins, *The Lamplighter*, 167, 199.

39. Joseph Roach, *Cities of the Dead: Circum-Atlantic Performance* (New York: Columbia University Press, 1996), 131.
40. "Purchasing Power Today of a US Dollar Transaction in the Past" (2026), https://www.measuringworth.com.
41. John Sidebottom, *The Overland Mail: A Postal Historical Study of the Mail Route to India* (London: Allen and Unwin, 1948), 60.
42. "The Mails From India," *The New York Times*, September 5, 1853.
43. On the period's philatelic marks, see Richard Winter, *Understanding Transatlantic Mail* (New York: American Philatelic Society, 2006). For an account of the India mail routes, see Sidebottom, *The Overland Mail.*
44. Cummins, *The Lamplighter*, 147.
45. Nina Baym, "Introduction," in Cummins, *The Lamplighter*, xxiii.
46. Cummins, *The Lamplighter*, 140.
47. Cummins, *The Lamplighter*, 140.
48. Lori Merish, *Sentimental Materialism: Gender, Commodity Culture, and Nineteenth-Century American Literature* (Durham, NC: Duke University Press, 2000), 133.
49. Merish, *Sentimental Materialism*, 133.
50. Carl H. Scheele, *A Short History of the Mail Service* (Washington, DC: Smithsonian Institution Press, 1970), 70.
51. Charles Sumner, *The Crime Against Kansas. The Apologies for the Crime. The True Remedy. Speech of Hon. Charles Sumner, in the Senate of the United States, 19th and 20th May 1856* (Boston: Jewett, 1856), 2. See also Charles Sumner, "No Recognition Where Slavery Is the Corner-Stone" (1861), in *The Works of Charles Sumner* (Boston: Lee and Shepard, 1873), 7:425.
52. Charles Sumner, *White Slavery in the Barbary States: A Lecture before the Boston Mercantile Library Association, Feb. 17, 1847* (Boston: Ticknor, 1847), 11–12, 56, 78, 108.
53. Paul Quigley, *Shifting Grounds: Nationalism and the American South, 1848–1865* (Oxford, UK: Oxford University Press, 2011), 95.
54. "William Gilmore Simms to John Pendleton Kennedy, 12 May 1851," in *The Simms Reader: Selections from the Writings of William Gilmore Simms*, ed. John Caldwell Guilds (Charlottesville: University of Virginia Press, 2001), 65–66.
55. Quigley, *Shifting Grounds*, 95.
56. Shulman, *Coal and Empire*, 30. Schulman provides a compelling environmental history of these postal debates.
57. Robert Stone, *A Caribbean Neptune: The Maritime Postal Communications of the Greater and Lesser Antilles in the 19th Century* (New York: Philatelic Foundation, 1993), 275–76.
58. Scheele, *A Short History of the Mail Service*, 80.
59. Fuller, *Morality and the Mail*, 208.
60. Stone, *A Caribbean Neptune*, 276.
61. "Appropriations for Transporting the U.S. Mail by Steamers," 121.
62. Matthew Pratt Guterl, *American Mediterranean: Southern Slaveholders in the Age of Emancipation* (Cambridge, MA: Harvard University Press, 2008), 100.

63. Rodrigo Lazo, *Writing to Cuba: Filibustering and Cuban Exiles in the United States* (Chapel Hill: University of North Carolina Press, 2005), 4.
64. Kirsten Silva Gruesz, "The Gulf of Mexico System and the 'Latinness' of New Orleans," *American Literary History* 18, no. 3 (2006): 472–73, 485. See also Kirsten Silva Gruesz, *Ambassadors of Culture: The Transamerican Origins of Latino Writing* (Princeton, NJ: Princeton University Press, 2002).
65. "Connections of the Atlantic with the Gulf-Interests of Alabama," *De Bow's Review* 14, no. 6 (1853): 567–72; "Florida—Its Positions, Resources, and Destiny," *De Bow's Review* 14, no. 4 (1853): 312–36; "The Baltimore Southern Commercial Convention," *De Bow's Review* 14, no. 4 (1853): 373–79.
66. Matthew Fontaine Maury, "Harry Bluff, On the Right of Search," *Southern Literary Messenger* 8, no. 3 (1842): 298; Karp, *This Vast Southern Empire*, 42. See also Gerald Horne, *The Deepest South: The United States, Brazil, and the African Slave Trade* (New York: New York University Press, 2007).
67. Walter Johnson, *River of Dark Dreams: Slavery and Empire in the Cotton Kingdom* (Cambridge, MA: Harvard University Press, 2013), 297.
68. Matthew Maury, "The Commercial Prospects of the South," *Southern Literary Messenger* 17, no. 10 (1851): 692, 687, 696, 692.
69. Maury, "The Commercial Prospects," 698.
70. Matthew Maury, "Direct Foreign Trade of the South," *De Bow's Review* 12, no. 2 (1852): 126–48; "On Extending the Commerce of the South and West by Sea," *De Bow's Review* 12, no. 4 (1852): 381–99; "Shall the Valleys of the Amazon and Mississippi Reciprocate Trade?" *De Bow's Review* 14, no. 2 (1853): 136–45; "Valley of the Amazon," *De Bow's Review* 14, no. 5 (1853): 449–60; "Valley of the Amazon, No. II," *De Bow's Review* 14, no. 6 (1853): 556–67.
71. Robert E. May, *Slavery, Race, and Conquest in the Tropics: Lincoln, Douglass, and the Future of Latin America* (Cambridge, UK: Cambridge University Press, 2013), 111.
72. R. B. F., "Art. II," 558.
73. R. B. F., "Art. II," 559.
74. Moon-Ho Jung, *Coolies and Cane: Race, Labor, and Sugar in the Age of Emancipation* (Baltimore: Johns Hopkins University Press, 2006); Lisa Yun, *The Coolie Speaks: Chinese Indentured Laborers and African Slaves in Cuba* (Philadelphia: Temple University Press, 2009).
75. May, *Slavery, Race, and Conquest*, 70.
76. Robert E. May, *Manifest Destiny's Underworld: Filibustering in Antebellum America* (Chapel Hill: University of North Carolina Press, 2003), 174.
77. Cummins, *The Lamplighter*, 155.
78. Robert E. May, "Reconsidering Antebellum U.S. Women's History: Gender, Filibustering, and America's Quest for Empire," *American Quarterly* 57, no. 4 (2005): 1159.
79. "Letter 5," *The New York Times*, March 2, 1854.
80. May, *Slavery, Race, and Conquest*, 115.
81. Cummins, *The Lamplighter*, 321.
82. Cummins, *The Lamplighter*, 400.

83. Kaplan, *The Anarchy of Empire*, 47.
84. Octavia Walton Le Vert, *Souvenirs of Travel* (Mobile, AL: Goetzel, 1857), 97.
85. Guterl, *American Mediterranean*, 98.
86. Le Vert, *Souvenirs of Travel*, 287
87. Cummins, *The Lamplighter*, 287.
88. Guterl, *American Mediterranean*, 100.
89. Le Vert, *Souvenirs of Travel*, 288
90. Cummins, *The Lamplighter*, 167.
91. Guterl, *American Mediterranean*, 100.
92. Le Vert, *Souvenirs of Travel*, 301.
93. Cummins, *The Lamplighter*, 167.
94. Cummins, *The Lamplighter*, 181.
95. Cummins, *The Lamplighter*, 202, 200.
96. Cummins, *The Lamplighter*, 201.
97. "The Post Office as It Has Been," 692.
98. R. E. Fenton, "The Postal System. Speech of Hon. R. E. Fenton, of New York, in the House of Representatives, June 1854," *Congressional Globe* 33, no. 1 (1854): 1017.
99. "The Post Office as It Has Been," 693.
100. "Ocean Mail Service," *The New York Times*, June 18, 1858.
101. Fuller, *Morality and the Mail*, 204.
102. Wayne Fuller, *The American Mail: Enlarger of the Common Life* (Chicago: University of Chicago Press, 1972), 205; Joshua Giddings, "The American Slave Trade, February 13, 1843," in *Speeches in Congress, Joshua R. Giddings* (Boston: Jewett, 1853), 39–40.
103. Fuller, *The American Mail*, 206; Mark Scroggins, *Robert Toombs: The Civil Wars of a United States Senator and Confederate General* (Jefferson, NC: McFarland, 2014), 103–4.
104. Cummins, *The Lamplighter*, 167.
105. Cummins, *The Lamplighter*, 168.
106. Cummins, *The Lamplighter*, 341. See also Muhammad Suwaed, *Historical Dictionary of the Bedouins* (Lanham, MD: Rowman and Littlefield, 2015).
107. Alan Mikhail, *Nature and Empire in Ottoman Egypt: An Environmental History* (Cambridge, UK: Cambridge University Press, 2011), 117.
108. Elizabeth Barnes, *States of Sympathy: Seduction and Democracy in the American Novel* (New York: Columbia University Press, 1997), 90.
109. Ann Stoler, "Intimidations of Empire: Predicaments of the Tactile and Unseen" in *Haunted by Empire: Geographies of Intimacy in North American History*, ed. Ann Stoler (Durham, NC: Duke University Press, 2006), 1, 4.
110. Konstantin Dierks, *In My Power: Letter Writing and Communications in Early America* (Philadelphia: University of Pennsylvania Press, 2009), 11.
111. Amy Kaplan, "'Left Alone with America': The Absence of Empire in the Study of American Culture," in *Cultures of United States Imperialism*, eds. Amy Kaplan and Donald E. Pease (Durham, NC: Duke University Press, 1993), 14.
112. Johnson, *River of Dark Dreams*, 98.

113. Shelley Streeby, *American Sensations: Class, Empire, and the Production of Popular Culture* (Berkeley: University of California Press, 2002), 77.
114. Streeby, *American Sensations*, 8.
115. As part of the same New England elite as Sedgwick, Cummins attended the school run by Sedgwick's sister-in-law and frequently visited by Sedgwick (the Young School in Lenox, Massachusetts). The two likely met, but any specific connection can only be gleaned from their shared literary themes. See Philip F. Gura, *Truth's Ragged Edge: The Rise of the American Novel* (New York: Farr, Straus, and Giroux, 2013), 115–17.
116. For an account of this London trip, see Heidi L. M. Jacobs, "Maria Susanna Cummins's London Letters: April 1860," *Legacy* 19, no. 2 (2002): 241–54.
117. Maria Susanna Cummins, letter to Sampson Low and Company, December 17, 1860, Sampson Low Collection, Open University Digital Archive, Buckinghamshire, UK.
118. Manisha Sinha, *The Counterrevolution of Slavery: Politics and Ideology in Antebellum South Carolina* (Chapel Hill: University of North Carolina Press, 2000), 153. Sinha provides an extensive history of the *Echo* case and its fallout.
119. J. D. B. De Bow, *The Interest in Slavery of the Southern Non-Slave-Holder: The Right of Peaceful Secession* (Charleston: Evans and Cogswell, 1860), 30; "Importation of Africans," *The Times* (Columbus, Ohio), March 17, 1859.
120. Charles Sumner, "The Proclamation of Emancipation" (1863), in *Works*, 7:425.
121. "The Whole World in Commotion," Civil War Ephemera Collection, CW env. 1947, American Antiquarian Society, Worcester, MA. Warren F. Spencer, *The Confederate Navy in Europe* (Tuscaloosa: University of Alabama Press, 1983), 1.
122. Steven R. Boyd, *Patriotic Envelopes of the Civil War: The Iconography of Union and Confederate Covers* (Baton Rouge: Louisiana State University Press, 2010), 2–4. For an extended analysis of pirate-themed covers, see Alexandra Ganser, *Crisis and Legitimacy in Atlantic American Narratives of Piracy: 1678–1865* (New York: Palgrave Macmillan, 2020), 223–38.
123. Shirley Samuels, *Facing America: Iconography and the Civil War* (Oxford, UK: Oxford University Press, 2004); Matthew J. Gallman, *Defining Duty in the Civil War: Personal Choice, Popular Culture, and the Union Home Front* (Chapel Hill: University of North Carolina Press, 2015).

CHAPTER FOUR

1. Abraham Lincoln, "First Inaugural Address (March 4, 1861)," Abraham Lincoln Papers, ser. 1, General Correspondence, 1833–1916, Library of Congress, Washington, DC, https://www.loc.gov.
2. "The Union Is Dissolved," *Charleston Mercury*, December 20, 1860.
3. Jennifer Rae Greeson, *Our South: Geographic Fantasy and the Rise of National Literature* (Cambridge, MA: Harvard University Press, 2010), 229.
4. "Confederate Postage Stamps, 10 Cent Blue, General Issue 1861, type 2," Confederate Collection, P&W 22001, Boston Athenaeum. See also Robert W. Grant, *The Handbook of Civil War Patriotic Envelopes and Postal History* (Hanover, MA: Romano,

1977); and Mark E. Neely, Harold Holzer, and Gabor S. Boritt, *The Confederate Image Prints of the Lost Cause* (Chapel Hill: University of North Carolina Press, 2000).

5. August Dietz, *The Postal Service of the Confederate States of America* (Richmond, VA: Dietz, 1989); James W. Milgram, *Federal Civil War Postal History* (Brookfield, WI: Northbrook, 2007).
6. "The Envelope Mania," Civil War Miscellanies, Ephemera Collection, box 2, folder 56, Library Company of Philadelphia.
7. "Our Position," *Charleston Mercury*, April 1, 1861.
8. Elizabeth Duquette, *Loyal Subjects: Bonds of Nation, Race and Allegiance in Nineteenth-Century America* (New Brunswick, NJ: Rutgers University Press, 2010), 23.
9. John Quincy Adams, *Argument of John Quincy Adams, Before the Supreme Court of the United States* (New York: Benedict, 1841), 7.
10. *Papers Relating to the Foreign Relations of the United States. Transmitted to Congress with the Annual Message of the President, December 2, 1872*, 42nd Cong., 3rd sess. H.R. Doc. 1 (Washington, DC: Government Printing Office, 1873), 215, 216.
11. "British Opinion on Civil War in the United States," *The Independent* (New York), May 23, 1861; "Validity of the Blockade. From the *London Post*," *The New York Times*, May, 17 1861.
12. For 1861 neutrality resolutions by England (May 13) France (June 10), the Netherlands (June 16), Spain (June 17), and Brazil (August 1), see *Papers Relating to the Foreign Relations*, 215–21.
13. Charles Sumner, *Our Foreign Relations* (Boston: Wright and Potter, 1863), 5.
14. Sumner, *Our Foreign Relations*, 5.
15. Sumner, *Our Foreign Relations*, 6.
16. Jan M. Lemnitzer, *Power, Law, and the End of Privateering* (New York: Palgrave Macmillan, 2014).
17. "The Secession Rebellion," *The New York Times*, May 23, 1861.
18. Sumner, *Our Foreign Relations*, 74, 79.
19. Sumner, *Our Foreign Relations*, 74, 70.
20. The bound edition's editors cited this number of spectators and listed prominent New York City men "who preferred to retain seats near the ladies whom they escorted to the meeting" (Sumner, *Our Foreign Relations*, 3). See also "Our Foreign Relations," *The New York Times*, September 11, 1863.
21. Howard Jones, *Blue and Gray Diplomacy: A History of Union and Confederate Foreign Relations* (Chapel Hill: University of North Carolina Press, 2010).
22. "R. M. T. Hunter to James N. Mason," in *The War of Rebellion: A Compilation of the Official Records of the Union and Confederate Armies* (Washington, DC: Government Printing Office, 1897), 2: 1207–9.
23. Constitution of the Confederate States, art. 1, sec. 8, cl. 10–11, Avalon Project at the Yale Law School, http://avalon.law.yale.edu.
24. "An act recognizing the existence of war between the United States and the

Confederate States; and concerning letters of marque., prizes, and prize goods . . . Approved May 6th, 1861," Confederate States of America Laws, Statutes, etc., Library of Congress, Washington DC, https://www.loc.gov.

25. "An act recognizing the existence of war."
26. "An act recognizing the existence of war."
27. "An act recognizing the existence of war."
28. Mark A. Weitz, *The Confederacy on Trial: The Piracy and Sequestration Cases of 1861* (Lawrence: University Press of Kansas, 2005), 20.
29. "An act recognizing the existence of war."
30. Confederate States of America, Department of the Treasury, "Confederate currency, $5 bills, type 37 (April 7, 1862 to September 12, 1862), Confederate Collection, P&W 25036, Boston Atheneum.
31. Pierre Fricke, *Confederate Currency* (London: Bloomsbury, 2012).
32. James Mooney, *Dictionary of American Naval Fighting Ships* (Washington, DC: Department of the Navy, 1959), 2:584–85.
33. Spencer Tucker, *Blue and Gray Navies: The Civil War Afloat* (Annapolis: Naval Institute Press, 2006), 74.
34. J. D. B. De Bow, "Privateers and Privateering," *De Bow's Review* 7, no. 6 (1861): 477, 485; "Policy of European Nations—Recognition," *Charleston Mercury*, November 4, 1862.
35. Robert R. Howison, "History of the War, Chapter VI," *Southern Literary Messenger* 34, no. 12 (1862): 593.
36. Robert R. Howison, "History of the War, Chapter VIII," *Southern Literary Messenger* 37, no. 9 (1863): 513.
37. Coleman Hutchison, *Apples and Ashes: Literature, Nationalism, and the Confederate States of America* (Athens: University of Georgia Press, 2012), 3. See also Michael T. Bernath, *Confederate Minds: The Struggle for Intellectual Independence in the Civil War South* (Chapel Hill: University of North Carolina Press, 2010).
38. Hutchinson, *Apples and Ashes*, 114, 116.
39. Nicholas Greenberry Ridgely, "Our Hope," American Song Sheet Manuscripts, box 5, item 707, David M. Rubenstein Rare Book and Manuscript Library, Digital Collections, Duke University, Durham, NC; "Southern Sentiments," American Song Sheet Manuscripts, box 3, item 1411, David M. Rubenstein Rare Book and Manuscript Library, Digital Collections, Duke University, Durham, NC.
40. Nicholas Greenberry Ridgely, "Song of the Privateer. October 10, 1861," American Song Sheet Manuscripts, box 3, item 1228, David M. Rubenstein Rare Book and Manuscript Library, Digital Collections, Duke University, Durham, NC.
41. Ridgely, "Song of the Privateer."
42. Ridgely, "Song of the Privateer"; "Hail! To the South," American Song Sheet Manuscripts, box 1, item 305, David M. Rubenstein Rare Book and Manuscript Library, Digital Collections, Duke University, Durham, NC.
43. Desmos, *Old Toney and His Master, or, The Abolitionist and the Land-Pirate: Founded on Facts: A Tale of 1824–1827* (Nashville: Southwestern, 1861), viii.

44. Desmos, *Old Toney*, 34, 13.
45. Joy Jordan-Lake, *Whitewashing Uncle Tom's Cabin: Nineteenth-Century Women Novelists Respond to Stowe* (Nashville, TN: Vanderbilt University Press, 2005), 7.
46. Desmos, *Old Toney*, 23.
47. Desmos, *Old Toney*, 23.
48. Desmos, *Old Toney*, 385, 388.
49. Desmos, *Old Toney*, 393.
50. "The Envelope Mania," *Littell's Living Age*, August 10, 1861.
51. Alice Fahs, *Imagined Civil War: Popular Literature of the North and South, 1861–1865* (Chapel Hill: University of North Carolina Press, 2001), 43. Fahs relays a similar history of the "rage for envelopes."
52. Steven R. Boyd, *Patriotic Envelopes of the Civil War: The Iconography of Union and Confederate Covers* (Baton Rouge: Louisiana State University Press, 2010), 34.
53. "Pirate's Chorus. From The Enchantress," American Song Sheet Manuscripts, box 3, item 1358, *David M. Rubenstein Rare Book and Manuscript Library, Digital Collections*, Duke University, Durham, NC.
54. "The Envelope Mania."
55. "Pirate. Jeff Davis's Letters of Mark," Civil War Ephemera Collection, CW env. 1025, American Antiquarian Society, Worcester, MA; "The Savannah. Confederate privateer, Savannah, letter of Marque No. 1 Captured off Charleston, by the U.S. Brig Perry. Lieut. Parrott," Civil War Ephemera Collection, CW env. 6588, American Antiquarian Society, Worcester, MA.
56. Stephen C. Neff, *Justice in Blue and Gray: A Legal History of the Civil War* (Cambridge, MA: Harvard University Press, 2010).
57. Abraham Lincoln, "A Proclamation by the President of the United States of America," *Civil War Prize Case Files Series*, identifier 620244, U.S. National Archives, Washington, DC.
58. "Letters of Marque and Reprisal," *The New York Times*, April 23, 1861.
59. "What Compromise with the Rebels Means," *The New York Times*, February 9, 1863.
60. "From *The Spectator*, 4 May. The Civil War in America," *Littell's Living Age*, June 8, 1861.
61. Charles Hodge, *England and American* (Philadelphia: Martien, 1862), 1, 2.
62. "From *The Spectator*, 4 May."
63. "John Bull on the Fence," Civil War Ephemera Collection, CW env. 0372, American Antiquarian Society, Worcester, MA.
64. "Secession Web," Civil War Ephemera Collection, CW env. 0781, American Antiquarian Society, Worcester, MA; Mary Howitt, "The Spider and the Fly," in *The New Years' Gift and Juvenile Souvenir*, ed. Mrs. Alaric Watts (London: Longman, 1829), 49–53.
65. John Thomas Scharf, *History of the Confederate States Navy from Its Organization to the Surrender of Its Last Vessel* (New York: Rogers and Sherwood, 1887), 75–76; "That Flag of Truce," *The New York Times*, August 1, 1861.
66. "The Charleston Pirates," *Chicago Tribune*, June 26, 1861.
67. "About Prisoners of War, Privateers, &c.," *The New York Times*, August 7, 1861. See

also “Are They Pirates?” *The New York Times*, June 23, 1861; and “How to Clear the Seas of Privateers,” *The New York Times*, June, 30, 1863.

68. “The Disposal of Prisoners,” *The New York Times*, August 19, 1861.
69. “Jefferson Davis and His Pirates,” *The New York Times*, July 21, 1861.
70. “Privateering,” *Charleston Mercury*, May 2, 1861.
71. For a more complete legal history, see Weitz, *The Confederacy on Trial.*
72. D. F. Murphy, ed., *The Jeff Davis Piracy Cases: Full Report of the Trial of William Smith for Piracy* (Philadelphia: King and Baird, 1861), 82–83.
73. *New York Times* trial coverage of the *Savannah* case included “The Trial of the Privateers of the *Savannah*,” October 23, 1861; “The *Savannah* Privateers,” October 24, 1861; “The Privateer *Savannah*,” October 25, 1861; “The *Savannah* Privateers,” October 26, 1861; “Case of the Privateer *Savannah*,” October 29, 1861; “The *Savannah* Privateers,” October 31, 1861; and “The *Savannah* Privateers,” November 3, 1861. The day after the jury’s decision, the paper also published an editorial opposing the decision: “The Privateer Trial Disagreement of the Jury,” November 1, 1861. *The New York Herald* published near-daily accounts of the *Jefferson Davis* trial: “The First Case of the Privateersmen,” October 24, 1861; “The Case of the Privateersmen,” October 25, 1861; “The Case of the Privateersmen,” October 26, 1861; “The Case of the Privateersmen,” October 27, 1861; “The Case of the Privateersmen,” October 29, 1861; “The Case of the Privateersmen,” October 30, 1861; and “The Case of the Privateersmen,” October 31, 1861. See also “The Trial of Pirates at Philadelphia,” *New York Herald*, October 31, 1861.
74. “The Privateer *Savannah*,” October 25, 1861.
75. “First Case,” October 24, 1861.
76. “Case,” October 26, 1861.
77. “Case,” October 29, 1861.
78. “Case,” October 30, 1861.
79. Murphy, *The Jeff Davis Piracy Cases*, 60.
80. Weitz, *The Confederacy on Trial*, 79–83.
81. Murphy, *The Jeff Davis Piracy Cases*, 55.
82. *Trial of the Officers and Crew of the Privateer Savannah. On the Charge of Piracy, in the United States Circuit Court for the Southern District of New York. Hon. Judges Nelson and Shipman, Presiding* (New York: Baker and Godwin, 1862), 232.
83. *Trial of the Officers*, 234.
84. Murphy, *The Jeff Davis Piracy Cases*, 71.
85. Murphy, *The Jeff Davis Piracy Cases*, 94.
86. *Trial of the Officers*, 19, 342.
87. Murphy, *The Jeff Davis Piracy Cases*, 92.
88. *Trial of the Officers*, 210.
89. Murphy, *The Jeff Davis Piracy Cases*, 73.
90. Murphy, *The Jeff Davis Piracy Cases*, 60.
91. *Trial of the Officers*, 227.
92. *Trial of the Officers*, 230.
93. Murphy, *The Jeff Davis Piracy Cases*, 91–92.

94. *Trial of the Officers*, 231–34.
95. "Case," October 29, 1861. The subsequently printed transcript repeated this claim exactly. See *Trial of the Officers*, 282.
96. *Trial of the Officers*, 238.
97. *Trial of the Officers*, 238.
98. Murphy, *The Jeff Davis Piracy Cases*, 70.
99. *Trial of the Officers*, 235.
100. Weitz, *The Confederacy on Trial*, 197.
101. Murphy, *The Jeff Davis Piracy Cases*, 96.
102. Weitz, *The Confederacy on Trial*, 197.
103. Neff, *Justice in Blue and Gray*, 26; Murphy, *The Jeff Davis Piracy Cases*, 66; *Prize Cases*, 67 U.S. (2 Black) 635 (1863).
104. Charles P. Daly, *Are the Southern Privateersmen Pirates? Letter to the Hon. Ira Harris, United States Senator* (New York: Kirker, 1862), 8–9. See also Charles P. Daly, "Are Southern Privateersmen Pirates?" *The New York Times*, December 31, 1861.
105. "Shall Privateersmen Be Treated as Pirates? The British Government to Assert Itself," *The New York Times*, November 25, 1861.
106. Abraham Lincoln, "First Annual Message," December 3, 1861, The American Presidency Project, https://www.presidency.ucsb.edu.
107. Lincoln, "First Annual Message"; Paul D. Escott, *"What Shall We Do with the Negro?" Lincoln, White Racism, and Civil War America* (Charlottesville: University of Virginia Press, 2009), 36. Escott provides an extended history of the speech alongside contemporary print responses.
108. Murphy, *The Jeff Davis Piracy Cases*, 70.
109. "William Tillman, The Colored Steward of the S. J. Waring," *New York Herald*, July 23, 1861. See also "The Schooner S. J. Waring, Recaptured from the Pirates by the Negro Wm Tillman," *Harper's Weekly*, August 3, 1861, 485; "The Negro Steward, Tillman, Killing the Prize Captain of the S. J. Waring," *Frank Leslie's Illustrated Newspaper*, August 3, 1861, 192; "A Black Hero," *Douglass' Monthly*, August 1861, 499; and "Recaptured Prize of a Black Hero," *The Liberator*, August 2, 1861. For a more expansive history, see Brian McGinty, *The Rest I Will Kill: William Tillman and the Unforgettable Story of How a Free Black Man Refused to Become a Slave* (New York: Liveright, 2016).
110. "Undercurrents of the Southern Conspiracy!" (1862), Library Company of Philadelphia, Digital Collections. See also *The Rebel Pirates Fatal Prize; or, The Bloody Tragedy of the Prize Schooner Waring* (Philadelphia: Barclay, 1862).
111. Murphy, *The Jeff Davis Piracy Cases*, 54.
112. William Whiting, *The War Powers of the President, and the Legislative Powers of Congress in Relation to Rebellion, Treason and Slavery* (Boston: Shorey, 1862), 15.
113. Whiting, *The War Powers of the President*, 44.
114. Whiting, *The War Powers of the President*, 73.
115. For Whiting's influence on Lincoln's proclamation, see Louise L. Stevenson, *Lincoln in the Atlantic World* (Cambridge, UK: Cambridge University Press, 2015), 180–85.

116. Matthew J. Clavin, *Toussaint Louverture and the American Civil War: The Promise and Peril of a Second Haitian Revolution* (Philadelphia: University of Pennsylvania Press, 2011), 4; Charles Sumner, "The Proclamation of Emancipation" (1863), in *The Works of Charles Sumner* (Boston: Lee and Shepard, 1873), 7:226; Lydia Maria Child, *The Right Way The Safe Way, Proved by Emancipation in the British West Indies, and Elsewhere* (New York, 1862), 86; Wendell Phillips, "Toussaint L'Ouverture" (1862), in *Speeches, Lectures, and Letters* (Boston: Lee and Shepard, 1884), 475, 492.
117. "Secession Calvary," Civil War Ephemera Collection, CW env. 0765, American Antiquarian Society, Worcester, MA; "The Union 34 Pounder," Civil War Ephemera Collection, CW env. 0792, American Antiquarian Society, Worcester, MA.
118. Manfred Berg, *Popular Justice: A History of Lynching in America* (Chicago: Dee, 2011), 69. See also Daniel Kato, *Liberalizing Lynching: Building a New Racialized State* (Oxford, UK: Oxford University Press, 2016).
119. Rhoda E. White, letter to Abraham Lincoln, February 17, 1862, *Abraham Lincoln Papers, ser. 1, General Correspondence*, Library of Congress, Washington, DC, https://www.loc.gov. Lincoln allegedly admitted his natural capacity to "be moved to pity and to pardon the perpetrator of almost the worst crime," except by those who "can rob Africa of her children to sell into interminable bondage." The words, quoted by Congressman John B. Alley twenty years later, are impossible to confirm (*Reminiscences of Abraham Lincoln by Distinguished Men of His Time*, 6th ed. [New York: North American Publishing, 1888], 583). See also Jonathan W. White, "The Presidential Pardon Records of the Lincoln Administration," *Journal of the Abraham Lincoln Association* 39, no. 2 (2018): 55–65; and Ron Soodalter, *Hanging Captain Gordon: The Life and Trial of an American Slave Trader* (New York: Atria, 2010).
120. Don E. Fehrenbacher, *The Slaveholding Republic: An Account of the United States Government's Relations to Slavery* (Oxford, UK: Oxford University Press, 2001), 199–200; engraving of Nathaniel Gordon's hanging, *Harper's Weekly*, March 8, 1862, 157.
121. "Ours to preserve—Ours to enjoy—Ours to transmit," Civil War Ephemera Collection, CW env. 1510, American Antiquarian Society, Worcester, MA.
122. Sumner, *Our Foreign Relations*, 79–80.
123. Cummins's father had graduated from Dartmouth Law School soon after Webster and was invited to the Whig presidential candidate's 1851 nominating convention. See "Letter to Cummins, re: delegation to speak at Daniel Webster convention, 1851," David Cummins Papers, 1806–55, box 1, folder 2, Phillips Library, Peabody Essex Museum, Rowley, MA.
124. Nina Baym, "Introduction," in Maria Susanna Cummins, *The Lamplighter* (1854; New Brunswick, NJ: Rutgers University Press, 1988), xxiii.

CHAPTER FIVE

1. Maria Susanna Cummins, *Mabel Vaughn* (Boston: Jewett, 1857), 452; Melissa Gniadek, *Oceans at Home: Maritime and Domestic Fictions in Nineteenth-Century American Women's Writing* (Amherst: University of Massachusetts Press, 2021), 1.

2. Cummins, *Mabel Vaughn*, 426, 428.
3. Mary Templin, *Panic Fiction: Women and Antebellum Economic Crisis* (Tuscaloosa: University of Alabama Press, 2014), 205.
4. Cummins, *Mabel Vaughn*, 453.
5. Steven Hamelman, "Orientalism and Sympathy in Maria Susanna Cummins's *El Fureidîs*," *Legacy* 25, no. 1 (2008): 64; Etsuko Taketani, *U.S. Women Writers and the Discourses of Colonialism, 1825–1861* (Knoxville: University of Tennessee Press, 2003), 186. See also Bruce A. Harvey, *American Geographics: U.S. National Narratives and the Representation of the Non-European World, 1830–1865* (Stanford, CA: Stanford University Press, 2001).
6. Maria Susanna Cummins, *El Fureidîs* (Boston: Ticknor and Fields, 1860), 126.
7. Cummins, *El Fureidîs*, 326.
8. Cummins, *El Fureidîs*, 319.
9. Cummins, *El Fureidîs*, 302.
10. Cummins, *El Fureidîs*, 343.
11. Maria Susanna Cummins, *Haunted Hearts* (Boston: Tilton, 1864), 400.
12. Cummins, *Haunted Hearts*, 312.
13. Cummins, *Haunted Hearts*, 554.
14. Lyde Cullen Sizer, *The Political Work of Northern Women Writers and the Civil War, 1850–1872* (Chapel Hill: University of North Carolina Press, 2000), 120.
15. *Low v. Routledge*, 10 LTR 838 (1865).
16. "T. R. R. Cobb to Marion Cobb, 26 Feb. 1861," *Publications of the Southern History Association* 11, no. 4 (1907): 242. See also Howard Jones, *Blue and Gray Diplomacy: A History of Union and Confederate Foreign Relations* (Chapel Hill: University of North Carolina Press, 2010).
17. Melissa J. Homestead, *American Women Authors and Literary Property, 1822–1869* (Cambridge, UK: Cambridge University Press, 2005), 199.
18. "Literary Notices," *Godey's Lady's Book* (August 1864): 176.
19. Cummins, *Haunted Hearts*, 4.
20. The third British edition did not appear until 1868, and the French edition—*Les Fantômes du Coeur*—was published in 1878. See Michael Davitt Bell, "Women's Fiction and the Literary Marketplace in the 1850s," in *The Cambridge History of American Literature, vol. 2., Prose Writing, 1820–1865*, ed. Sacvan Bercovitch (Cambridge, UK: Cambridge University Press, 2008), 89–90.
21. "Advertisement, *Haunted Hearts*," *Coleman's Rural World*, May 1, 1865, 70; "Ten New Books," *The Independent*, June 9, 1864. See also "Ten New Books," *American Literary Gazette and Publishers' Circular*, June 15, 1864, 129.
22. Sampson Low, letter to Maria Susanna Cummins, February 8, 1860, Maria Susanna Cummins Papers, 1851–68, box 1, folder 1, Phillips Library, Peabody Essex Museum, Rowley, MA.
23. Catherine Seville, *The Internationalisation of Copyright Law: Books, Buccaneers, and the Black Flag in the Nineteenth Century* (Cambridge, UK: Cambridge University Press, 2006).

24. *Jeffreys v. Boosey*, 4 HLC 816 (1854).
25. *Low v. Routledge.*
26. *Low v. Routledge.*
27. Ronan Deazley, *Rethinking Copyright: History, Theory, Language* (Cheltenham, UK: Elger, 2006).
28. "Literary and Musical Copyright," *The Athenaeum* (London), October 29, 1864.
29. *Low v. Routledge.*
30. "An Important English Copyright Case," *American Literary Gazette and Publishers' Circular*, January 15, 1866, 174.
31. Sampson Low, letter to Maria Susanna Cummins, November 25, 1865, Maria Susanna Cummins Papers, 1851–68, box 1, folder 1. Phillips Library, Peabody Essex Museum, Rowley, MA.
32. Susan Gillman, "Whose Protest Novel? *Ramona*, the *Uncle Tom's Cabin* of the Indian," in *The Oxford Handbook of Nineteenth-Century American Literature*, ed. Russ Castronovo (Oxford, UK: Oxford University Press, 2014), 387. See also Gérard Genette, *Palimpsests: Literature in the Second Degree* (Lincoln: University of Nebraska Press, 1997).
33. Cummins, *Haunted Hearts*, 409, 410.
34. Peter Coviello, "Agonizing Affection: Affect and Nation in Early America." *Early American Literature* 37, vol. 3 (2002): 443.
35. Cummins, *Haunted Hearts*, 5.
36. Cummins, *Haunted Hearts*, 9.
37. Cummins, *Haunted Hearts*, 11, 39.
38. Cummins, *Haunted Hearts*, 521, 520.
39. Cummins, *Haunted Hearts*, 124.
40. Cummins, *Haunted Hearts*, 49.
41. Harry A. Ezratty, *Baltimore in the Civil War: The Pratt Street Riot and a City Occupied* (Charleston, SC: History Press, 2010).
42. Cummins, *Haunted Hearts*, 499.
43. Cummins, *Haunted Hearts*, 86, 184.
44. Cummins, *Haunted Hearts*, 308.
45. Cummins, *Haunted Hearts*, 311–12.
46. Cummins, *Haunted Hearts*, 374.
47. Cummins, *Haunted Hearts*, 437.
48. Cummins, *Haunted Hearts*, 394.
49. Cummins, *Haunted Hearts*, 404, 414.
50. Cummins, *Haunted Hearts*, 400–401.
51. Cummins, *Haunted Hearts*, 401.
52. Cummins, *Haunted Hearts*, 374–75.
53. Cummins, *Haunted Hearts*, 212.
54. Cummins, *Haunted Hearts*, 257.
55. Cummins, *Haunted Hearts*, 317, 417, 429.
56. Cummins, *Haunted Hearts*, 429.

57. Cummins, *Haunted Hearts*, 125.
58. Cummins, *Haunted Hearts*, 401.
59. Cummins, *Haunted Hearts*, 529.
60. Cummins, *Haunted Hearts*, 477.
61. Cummins, *Haunted Hearts*, 510, 479; Johannes M. Postma, *The Dutch in the Atlantic Slave Trade, 1600–1815* (Cambridge, UK: Cambridge University Press, 1990).
62. Cummins, *Haunted Hearts*, 55.
63. Cummins, *Haunted Hearts*, 415–16.
64. Cummins, *Haunted Hearts*, 374.
65. Robert E. May, *Slavery, Race, and Conquest in the Tropics: Lincoln, Douglass, and the Future of Latin America* (Cambridge, UK: Cambridge University Press, 2013), 250; Cummins, *Haunted Hearts*, 535.
66. Cummins, *Haunted Hearts*, 550.
67. Cummins, *Haunted Hearts*, 537, 434; Evan Haefeli, "Dutch Reformed Church and African Americans," in *Encyclopedia of African American History, 1619–1895*, ed. Paul Finkelman (New York: Oxford University Press, 2006), 2:434. See also Gerald Francis De Jong, "The Dutch Reformed Church and Negro Slavery in Colonial America," *Church History* 40, no. 4 (1971): 423–36.
68. Cummins, *Haunted Hearts*, 492.
69. Cummins, *Haunted Hearts*, 528, 529, 530.
70. Cummins, *Haunted Hearts*, 553.
71. Cummins, *Haunted Hearts*, 551, 554.
72. Frans-Willem Korsten, *Art as an Interface of Law and Justice: Affirmation, Disturbance, Disruption* (London: Bloomsbury, 2021), 60.
73. Neff, *Justice in Blue and Gray*, 207–8.
74. U.S. Constitution, 14th amendment, secs. 1–3, U.S. National Archives, Washington, DC, https://www.archives.gov. For a legal history, see William E. Nelson, *The Fourteenth Amendment: From Political Principle to Judicial Doctrine* (Cambridge, MA: Harvard University Press, 2009). For literary responses, see Brook Thomas, *The Literature of Reconstruction: Not in Plain Black and White* (Baltimore: Johns Hopkins University Press, 2017).
75. Cynthia Nicoletti, *Secession on Trial: The Treason Prosecution of Jefferson Davis* (Cambridge, UK: Cambridge University Press, 2017), 7, 13.
76. *Texas v. White*, 74 U.S. 700 (1869).
77. D. F. Murphy, ed., *The Jeff Davis Piracy Cases: Full Report of the Trial of William Smith for Piracy* (Philadelphia: King and Baird, 1861), 93, 96.
78. *Texas v. White*, 74 U.S. 700 (1869), (Grier, J., dissenting).
79. Mark R. Killenbeck, "Political Facts, Legal Fictions," in *Nullification and Secession in Modern Constitutional Thought*, ed. Sanford Levinson (Lawrence: University of Kansas Press, 2016), 223.
80. Christopher Heath Wellman, *A Theory of Secession* (Cambridge, UK: Cambridge University Press, 2005), 171, 102.
81. Killenbeck, "Political Facts, Legal Fictions," 244; *Shelby County v. Holder*, 570 U.S. 529

(2013). For an analysis of the decision's legal and political fallout, see Jesse Hessler Rhodes, *Ballot Blocked: The Political Erosion of the Voting Rights Act* (Stanford, CA: Stanford University Press, 2017).

EPILOGUE

1. I focus on the 1869 manuscript version of the poem in order to highlight its historical moment. See Walt Whitman, "Passage to India: 13 leaves, handwritten," Oscar Lion Papers, MssCol 1767, Digital Collections, New York Public Library. See also Walt Whitman, "Passage to India," in *Leaves of Grass* (New York: Redfield, 1871), 5–15.
2. Horace Traubel, *With Walt Whitman in Camden*, ed. Sculley Bradley (Philadelphia: University of Pennsylvania Press, 1953), 4:398. See also B. R. McElderry Jr., "The Inception of 'Passage to India,'" *PMLA* 71, no. 4 (1956): 837–39.
3. Walt Whitman, "Notebook for 'Passage to India'; 1869," Oscar Lion Papers, MssCol 1767, Digital Collections, New York Public Library.
4. "Eastward to the Indies," *The New York Times*, May 15, 1869.
5. Whitman, "Passage to India."
6. Zachary Karabell, *Parting the Desert: The Creation of the Suez Canal* (New York: Knopf, 2003).
7. Valeska Huber, *Channelling Mobilities: Migration and Globalisation in the Suez Canal Region and Beyond, 1869–1914* (Cambridge, UK: Cambridge University Press, 2013), 1, 3.
8. David S. Reynolds, *Walt Whitman's America: A Cultural Biography* (New York: Knopf, 1995), 499. See also Martin T. Buinicki, *Walt Whitman's Reconstruction: Poetry and Publishing Between Memory and History* (Iowa City: University of Iowa Press, 2011)
9. Whitman, "Passage to India."
10. Whitman, "Notebook for 'Passage to India."
11. Henry Morgan Stanley, "Suez Canal. Complete Success of the Great Work," *New York Herald*, November 21, 1869. See also Clare Pettit, *Dr. Livingstone, I Presume? Missionaries, Journalists, Explorers, and Empire* (Cambridge, MA: Harvard University Press, 2007).
12. Gary Schmidgall, ed., *Intimate with Walt: Whitman's Conversations with Horace Traubel* (Iowa City: University of Iowa Press, 2021), 17.
13. Marianne Noble, "Introduction," in *Rethinking Sympathy and Human Contact in Nineteenth-Century American Literature: Hawthorne, Douglass, Stowe, Dickinson*, ed. Marianne Noble (Cambridge, UK: Cambridge University Press, 2019), 4, 1.
14. Ana Schwartz, *Unmoored: The Search for Sincerity in Colonial America* (Chapel Hill: University of North Carolina Press, 2023), 40.
15. Mark Chadwick, *Piracy and the Origins of Universal Jurisdiction: On Stranger Tides?* (Leiden: Brill Nijhoff, 2018), 6; Joel H. Samuels, "The Full Story of *United States v. Smith*, America's Most Important Piracy Case," *Penn State Journal of Law and International Affairs* 1, no. 2 (2012): 320.
16. Rebecca Sanders, *Plausible Legality: Legal Culture and Political Imperative in the Global War on Terror* (Oxford, UK: Oxford University Press, 2018), 1.

17. "Public K–12 Educational Instruction—Required Instruction," SS.1003.42 (2025), https://www.flsenate.gov.
18. "Florida's State Academic Standards—Social Studies," SS.912.AA.1.1 (2025), https://www.flsenate.gov.
19. *A. S. R. v. Trump* (2025) 3:25-cv-00113 (W.D. Pa.).
20. Whitman, "Passage to India."
21. Maria Susanna Cummins, *Haunted Hearts* (Boston: Tilton, 1864), 404.

INDEX

Page numbers in italics indicate a figure.

MARK B. KELLEY is assistant professor of English at Florida International University. He received his MA from Marquette University and his PhD from the University of California, San Diego under the direction of Nicole Tonkovich and Sara Johnson. Mark has received fellowships from the American Antiquarian Society, the Library Company of Philadelphia, the National Endowment for the Humanities, the University of Virginia, Mystic Seaport Museum, and the John Carter Brown Library, among others. His work has been published in forums such as *Legacy: A Journal of American Women Writers*, *American Literary Realism*, and the *Journal of the Midwest Modern Language Association*. Mark lives with his wife, Nicole, and their son, Remy.